BRIEF LIVES

John Aubrey's *Brief Lives*, those racy portraits of the great figures of 17th-century England, stand alongside Pepys's diary as a vivid evocation of the period; in recent years they have been brought memorably to life on television and in the theatre by Roy Dotrice. Yet Aubrey never actually completed his project, nor did he ever manage to put even a single life into logical order. All we have are the raw materials, his jumbled, confused notebooks. Added to this, his language and spelling are often obscure for the reader of today, and it is therefore surprising that there has never been a 'complete' edition in modern spelling. Richard Barber provides just this, reproducing as closely as possible what Aubrey wrote, modernising the spelling and paraphrasing obsolete words, in a version that will allow many new readers to enjoy this vivid and eccentric masterpiece.

John Aubrey was born in 1626, the son of a Wiltshire squire. He never completed his education at Oxford or at the Middle Temple, and when he inherited the family estate at the age of 26 he fought a losing struggle with his father's debts. He finally went bankrupt in the 1670s, and led a sociable, rootless existence at the houses of friends, pursuing the antiquarian studies which had always obsessed him. He published only one book in his lifetime, suitably entitled *Miscellanies*, and died in 1697, leaving a mass of notes and manuscripts, among them the material for *Brief Lives*.

BRIEF LIVES

John Aubrey

*A modern English version
edited by Richard Barber*

THE BOYDELL PRESS

© 1975, 1982 Richard Barber

First published in this series 1982
by The Boydell Press
an imprint of Boydell and Brewer Ltd
PO Box 9, Woodbridge, Suffolk, IP12 3DF

British Library Cataloguing in Publication Data

Aubrey, John
Brief Lives.—Rev. ed.
1 Great Britain—Biography
I. Title   II. Barber, Richard
920′.041   DA304

ISBN 0-85115-206-6

Printed in Great Britain by
Nene Litho, Wellingborough, Northants

Introduction

John Aubrey's *Brief Lives* is one of the strangest books—if indeed this collection of notes, excerpts, gossip and dry facts can be called a book—to have achieved literary fame. Their author was equally strange, in his way: a gentleman with a learned turn of mind, yet little formal education, a lover of books and manuscripts, yet almost penniless, a would-be scholar who loved worldly company as much as that of serious men, who spent the last twenty years of his life living in other people's houses, on the run from his creditors.

Aubrey's own life is best told in his own words, and the various jottings about himself which occur in his manuscripts are given as the first entry in the text. But a short outline of his career will help to set the scene. He was born in 1626, eldest son of a Wiltshire squire whose estates were fairly heavily encumbered with debt. He was given a good 'grammar education', but his university studies were interrupted by the outbreak of the Civil War in 1642, and although he returned to Oxford in 1646, and also tried to study at the Middle Temple at the same time, he never took a degree or was called to the bar. Instead, at the end of 1648, he had to return home to help his father manage his estates during his illness. His father died four years later, and Aubrey was faced with fairly considerable debts. Handicapped by these and a subsequent series of lawsuits, over property in Wales and over an action brought by a lady whom he had once hoped to marry, his affairs went from bad to worse, ending in bankruptcy in the early 1670s. Aubrey put it all down to a bad horoscope at birth, evaded his creditors, and settled down to enjoy 'a happy delitescency' or concealment, with the aid of his friends. This sociable, rootless existence suited him well, though it did not help him to complete any of the various antiquarian projects to which he now turned his hand.

Aubrey's chief interest was in the antiquarian tradition of Leland and Camden, the collection of items which we should now classify as archaeology, topography and local history. His most ambitious scheme was to have been called *Monumenta Britannica*, and the parts that he completed include a fine study of Avebury and Stonehenge, while he came nearest to finishing his *Natural History of Wiltshire*, which covered much the same range of subjects. His only published work was the *Miscellanies* of 1696, a book of superstitions and strange happenings, which are really a kind of scholar's gossip, the fruits of a lifetime's interest in mere curiosities as well as more serious matters: it did his reputation no good at all.

He worked at these topics as well as various other ingenious and equally incomplete projects, until his death in 1697. He lived mostly in

1

London, with occasional visits to the country and to Oxford, which was still his favourite haunt. In London, he frequented the coffee-houses, and went to the meetings of the newly formed Royal Society, of which he had been a member since 1664. Here he met the most distinguished men of science of his day, and indulged his interest in mathematics, which had always been one of his favourite studies. Like Evelyn and Pepys, he was one of the onlookers rather than contributors when it came to serious debates, but he had his own distinctive knowledge to draw on for the more general topics which were equally part of the Society's discussions. His general interest in science and mathematics comes out in the *Lives*, which include a very large number of the leading men in both fields. By contrast, he has little to say about members of Charles II's court, but harks back frequently to the time he spent in London under the Commonwealth.

At Oxford, one particular friend was all-important to him. This was Anthony Wood (or Anthony à Wood, as he liked to style himself). Wood, although a cantankerous and difficult character, had made a reputation for himself through his researches into Oxford history. Wood's account of their first meeting (although retouched after they had quarrelled twenty-five years later) sets the general tone of their friendship as Wood saw it.

31 August 1667. John Aubrey of Easton Piers in the parish of Kington St Michael in Wiltshire was in Oxford with Edward Forest, a bookseller living against All Souls' College, to buy books. He then saw lying on the stall Notitia Academiae Oxoniensis, *and asking who the author of that book was, he [the bookseller] answered, the report was that one Mr Anthony Wood of Merton College was author, but was not. Whereupon Mr Aubrey, a pretender to antiquities, having been contemporary to A. Wood's elder brother in Trinity College and well acquainted with him, he thought he might as well be acquainted with A.W. himself. Whereupon repairing to his lodgings and telling him who he was, he got his acquaintance, talked to him about his studies, and offered him what assistance he could make, in order to the completion of the work that he was in hand with. Mr Aubrey was then in a sparkish garb, came to town with his men and two horses, spent high, and flung out A.W. in all his reckonings [cheated him]. But his estate of £700 per annum being afterwards sold and he reserving nothing of it to himself, lived afterwards in a very sorry condition, and at length made shift to rub out by hanging on Edmund Wyld esquire, living in Bloomsbury near London, on James, Earl of Abingdon, whose first wife was related to him, and on Sir John Aubrey his kinsman, living sometimes in Glamorganshire and sometimes at Boarstall near Brill in Bucks. He was a shiftless person, roving and maggotty-headed,* and*

* Before dismissing this as mere spite, it is worth noting that Ralph Sheldon wrote in 1679 of 'honest Mr John Aubrey, whose head is so full that it will not give his tongue leave to utter one word after another. I assure you he is (to my appearance) as mad as anyone almost in the university of Bedlam.'

sometimes little better than crazed. And being exceedingly credulous would stuff his many letters sent to A.W. with fooleries and misinformations, which sometimes would guide him into the paths of error.

In the early days of their friendship, Wood seems to have been glad enough of Aubrey's company and help. He was engaged on his collection of biographies of famous members of Oxford university, which was to form an appendix to his work on the history of the city and university and their buildings. Wood's main task was therefore antiquarian, just as Aubrey's real interest was in this field. But, as with Aubrey, the collection of biographical material soon took precedence. Wood had begun this project at the suggestion of Dr Fell, the patron of the University Press, and it was a novelty for the period. There were very few models on which to base the work. Classical writers (such as Plutarch and Suetonius) and medieval saints' lives were hardly relevant to the task in hand. The preface to Thomas Fuller's *History of the Worthies of England*, which appeared in 1662 gives some idea of how Wood and Aubrey might have regarded their task:

England may not unfitly be compared to a house, not very great, but convenient; and the several shires may properly be resembled to the rooms thereof. Now, as learned Mr Camden and painful Master Speed, with others, having described the rooms themselves, so it is our intention, God willing, to describe the furniture of these rooms; such eminent commodities which every county doth produce, with the persons of quality bred therein, and some other observables coincident with the same subject.

Wood's work, the *Athenae Oxonienses* printed in two volumes in 1691–2, is certainly in the formal and learned antiquarian vein; despite suggestions that it would be more widely read in English, it appeared in Latin, and is a far cry from the material which Aubrey provided for it. Even so, it provoked quite enough criticism, and when the second volume was published, Wood was arraigned on a charge of *scandalum magnatum* for suggesting that the first Earl of Clarendon had accepted bribes. As Clarendon had died some eighteen years earlier, and the same accusation had been included in the bill of impeachment drawn up against him before his exile, it seems as though some influential person had decided to pick a quarrel with Wood. At all events, Wood was found guilty, fined, and expelled from the University, and parts of the *Athenae* were publicly burnt. Privately, Wood blamed Aubrey for his misfortune, and indeed let it be known that he had the information from Aubrey. Aubrey learnt of this, and wrote to protest:

The libel was printed and not uncommon: could not you have said that you bought it? or had it of George Ent, or someone that is dead? To be short, my Lord is resolved to undo me: pray let me know by the next post, what 'tis you have done against me, that I may be better enabled to make my defence.

In fact, Aubrey escaped untroubled, and the report was a joke on Lord Abingdon's part which annoyed Wood still further. At all events, when Aubrey tried to make up the quarrel, Wood replied with a furious letter, accusing Aubrey of deserting him as soon as he was in trouble—which was not entirely unjustified. Aubrey continued to send letters to Wood until his death in 1695, and on receiving news of his friend's decease, wrote to a mutual acquaintance:

I am extremely sorrowful for the death of my dear friend and old correspondent Mr Anthony Wood: who (though his spleen used to make him chagrin and to chide me) yet we could not be asunder, and he would always see me at my lodging, with his dark lanthorn, which should be a relic.

The bulk of the *Lives* were written in 1679–80, and Wood kept the manuscript by him as a source of reference—supplemented by Aubrey's frequent correspondence—until the publication of the *Athenae* twelve years later. Before he returned it, however, he removed the first 44 pages of the second volume, perhaps because it contained dangerous material and he feared that his papers would be searched in the aftermath of the *débâcle* over Clarendon. When he discovered this Aubrey wrote furiously on the flyleaf:

INGRATITUDE! *this part the second, Mr Wood has gelded from page 1 to page 44 and other pages too are wanting wherein are contained truths, but such as I entrusted nobody with the sight of but himself (whom I thought I might have entrusted with my life). There are several papers that may cut my throat. I find too late* remember to distrust *was a saying worthy of one of the sages. He has also embezzled the index of it—which N.B. It was stitched up when I sent it to him. 29 November 1692.*

When Aubrey deposited the manuscrips in the Ashmolean Museum the next year, he not unnaturally asked that Wood should not learn that they had been placed there. It was a sad ending to a fruitful collaboration.

The *Lives* pose a formidable problem to any editor. Aubrey never proposed at any time to publish more than part of them, the *Life of Thomas Hobbes* and the *Lives of the English Mathematicians*. These usually represent his most finished work: but even here his constitutional incapability to finish anything shows through very clearly. There is a great deal of material on Hobbes, but it is only loosely classified and sorted, and there are endless scraps and notes added later. Other *Lives* are simply notes for Anthony Wood's information, and it would really do Aubrey more justice to give his work the title 'Notes on the Lives of Eminent Men, as a contribution to Mr Wood's *Athenae Oxonienses*'. For this is what we have, and it is useless to pretend that Aubrey would ever have written a coherent version of them for publication which even faintly resembled what is printed here. The more probable result can be

4

seen at the beginning of the *Life of Hobbes*, a weighty, measured prose in the best seventeenth century style, which would be as little read today as Thomas Fuller's *Worthies of England*. It is precisely because Aubrey is writing freely, privately and informally to Wood that the material comes across so vividly. Aubrey himself makes this point in the covering letter to Anthony Wood, sent with the manuscript in 1680 (see p. 6 below). Everything that comes to his curious mind tumbles out higgledy-piggledy: some of the pages bear witness to his mood as he wrote—the notes on his own life are scrawled as though his pen could barely keep up with his thoughts, other notes are written after a hard night's drinking in a spidery scribble, and then there will come a page of neat Italianate calligraphy when he decides to put on his best style.

So the reader may like to know how far Aubrey has been 'tidied up' in the present edition. The general principles have been these:

The material for each life is presented in the following order: first, material found in the main manuscript of the *Lives*, then additional material from elsewhere in the Aubrey manuscripts or from his letters to Anthony Wood. Breaks in sequence or changes of source are indicated by the sign ¶, to show that paragraphs were written at different times.

Marginal notes in the manuscript have usually been incorporated into the main text, except for material which is obviously a footnote or qualification. Footnotes are Aubrey's own, except where indicated.

A certain amount of material of minor interest has been omitted, chiefly horoscopes, heraldry, and genealogy: a life may often start with an astrological diagram of a horoscope, the coat of arms in trick, and a rough family tree. Lists of publications by an author, and notices of burials and monuments have also been excluded. 'Lives' which consist wholly of such material have been omitted. Excerpts from an author's books, or from standard historical works have been left out; but any remaining quotations have been identified as such.

The text itself has been modernised in spelling, and abbreviations have been expanded. Single Latin words have been translated, as have Aubrey's occasional Latin phrases. Obscure words have been para-phrased, and words added to fill obvious gaps or obscurities. Latin abbreviations—Sarum, Winton, Oxon—have been Englished. Words in square brackets are editorial additions or explanations.

What follows is not a 'complete' text in the sense that it includes every piece of biographical information Aubrey ever recorded; but it does give, as completely and with as little alteration as possible, a modern version of everything of substance in his scattered manuscript notes.

RICHARD BARBER

5

To my worthy friend Mr Anthony à Wood, Antiquary of Oxford

Sir!
I have according to your desire, put in writing these minutes and lives, tumultuously as they occurred to my thoughts; or as occasionally I had information of them: they may easily be reduced into order at your leisure by numbering them with red figures, according to time and place etc. 'Tis a task that I never thought to have undertaken, till you imposed it upon me, saying that I was fit for it by reason of my general acquaintance, having now not only lived above half a century of years in the court, but have also been much tumbled up and down in it; which has made me well known: besides, the modern advantage of coffee-houses in this great city; before which, men knew not how to be acquainted, but with their own relations, or societies: I might add, that I come of a long-lived race, by which means I have filched some feathers of the wings of time, for several generations; which does reach high. When I first began, I did not think I could have drawn it out to so long a thread. I here lay down to you (out of the conjunct friendship between us) the truth, the naked and plain truth: which is here exposed so bare, that the very pudenda are not covered, and afford many passages that would raise a blush in a young virgin's cheek. So that after your perusal, I must desire you to make castration (as Raderus to Martial), and to sew some fig-leaves, i.e. to be my *Index Expurgatorius*. What uncertainty do we find in printed histories; they either treading too near on the heels of truth, that they dare not speak plain; or else for want of intelligence (things being antiquated) become too obscure and dark! I do not here repeat anything already published (to the best of my remembrance) and I fancy myself all along discoursing with you; alleging those of my relations and acquaintances (whom either you knew or have heard of) to vouch for the truth. So that you make me to renew my acquaintance with my old and deceased friends, and to rejuvenesce (as it were) which is the pleasure of old men. 'Tis pity that such minutes had not been taken 100 years since or more; for want whereof many worthy men's names and inventions are swallowed up in oblivion; as much of these also would have been, had it not been through your instigation: and perhaps this is some of the usefullest pieces that I have scribbled. I remember one saying of General Lambert's, *'That the best men are but men at the best'*, of this you will meet with divers examples in this rude and hasty collection. Now these Arcana are not fit to let lie abroad, till about thirty years hence; for the author and the persons (like medlars) ought to be rotten first. But in whose hands must they be deposited in the mean time? Advise me, who am, Sir, your very affectionate friend to serve you.
[1680]   John Aubrey.

6

John Aubrey
1626–97

To be interponed as a sheet of waste paper only in the binding of a book.

> *I press not to the choir . . .*
> *Thus devout penitents of old were wont,*
> *Some without dore, and some beneath the font.*

His* life is more remarkable in an astrological respect than for any advancement of learning, having from his birth (till of late years) been labouring under a crowd of ill directions: for his escapes of many dangers, in journeys both by land and water, forty years. He was born (long-lived, healthy kindred) at Easton Piers, a hamlet in the parish of Kington Saint Michael in the hundred of Malmesbury in the county of Wilts, his mother's (daughter and heir of Mr Isaac Lyte) inheritance, 12 March (St Gregory's day) A.D. 1625, about sun-rising, being very weak and like to die, so that he was christened before morning prayer.

I got not strength till I was 11 or 12 years old; but had sickness of vomiting, for 12 hours every fortnight for some years, then about monthly, then quarterly, and at last once in half a year. About 12 it ceased.

When a boy, bred at Easton, an eremitical solitude, was very curious; his greatest delight to be continually with the artificers that came there (e.g. joiners, carpenters, coopers, masons), and understood their trades.

1634, was entered in his Latin Grammar by Mr R. Latimer, rector of Leigh Delamere, a mile's fine walk, who had an easy way of teaching: and every time we asked leave to go forth, we had a Latin word from him which at our return we were to tell him again: which in a little while amounted to a good number of words. 'Twas my unhappiness in half a year to lose this good informer by his death, and afterwards was under several dull† rest-in-house teachers till 1638 (aged 12), at which time I was sent to Blandford School in Dorset. (William Sutton, BD, who was ill-natured). Here I recovered my health, and got my Latin and Greek, best of any of my contemporaries. The usher had (by chance) a Cowper's Dictionary, which I had never seen before. I was then in Terence: perceiving his method, I read all in the book where Terence was, and then Cicero—which was the way by which I got my Latin. 'Twas a wonderful help to my fancy, my reading of Ovid's *Metamorphoses* in

---

* Aubrey uses the first and third person to refer to himself indiscriminately in these notes. *Ed.*

† My grandfather Aubrey died young, leaving my father, who was not educated to learning but to hawking.

7

English by Sandys, which made me understand the Latin better. Also, I met accidentally a book of my mother's Lord Bacon's *Essays*, which first opened my understanding as to morals (for Tully's *Offices* were too crabbed for my young years) and the excellence of the style, or hints and transitions.

I was always enquiring of my grandfather of the old time, the rood-loft etc, ceremonies, of the priory, etc. At 8, I was a kind of engineer; and I fell then to drawing, beginning first with plain outlines, e.g. in draughts of curtains. Then at 9 (crossed herein by father and schoolmaster), to colours, having nobody to instruct me; copied pictures in the parlour in a table book—they were like the originals.

At Blandford, in idle hours, I drew and painted Bates's book—ask its name.

I was wont (I remember) much to lament with myself that I lived not in a city, e.g. Bristol, where I might have access to watchmakers, locksmiths, etc. I did not very much care for grammar—apprehension enough, but my memory not tenacious. So that then was a promising morn enough of an inventive and philosophical head. I had a musical head, inventive, wrote blank verse, a strong and early impulse to antiquity (strong impulse to Saturn*). My wit was always working, but not adroit for verse. Exceeding mild of spirit; mighty susceptible of fascination. My idea very clear; fancy like a mirror, pure crystal water which the least wind does disorder and unsmooth—so noise etc would.

2 May 1642 I went to Oxford.

Peace.

Looked through logic and some ethics. 1642, *Religio Medici* printed, which first opened my understanding, which I carried to Easton, with Sir Kenelm Digby's *Observations* on it.

But now Bellona thundered, and as a clear sky is sometimes suddenly overstretched with a dismal cloud and thunder, so was this serene peace by the Civil Wars through the factions of these times; see Homer's Odyssey.

In August following my father sent for me home, for fear.

In February following, with much ado I got my father to let me to beloved Oxford again, then a garrison for the king.

I got Mr Hesketh, Mr Dobson's man, a priest, to draw the ruins of Osney two or three ways before 'twas pulled down. Now the very foundation is digged up.

In April I fell sick of the smallpox at Trinity College; and when I recovered, after Trinity week, my father sent for me into the country again; where I conversed with none but servants and rustics and soldiers quartered, to my great grief (I hate the ignorant crowd, and keep away†)

---

* Patron of antiquities in astrology.*Ed.*   † Horace, *Carmina*, 3, 1, 1. *Ed.*

for in these days fathers were not acquainted with their children. It was a most sad life to me, then in the prime of my youth, not to have the benefit of an ingenious conversation and scarcely any good books—almost a consumption. This sad life I did lead in the country till 1646, at which time I got (with much ado) leave of my father to let me go to the Middle Temple, 6 April 1646; admitted.

24 June following, Oxford was surrendered, and then came to London many of the king's party, with whom I grew acquainted (many of them I knew before). I loved not debauches, but their martial conversation was not so fit for the muses.

6 November, I returned to Trinity College in Oxford again to my great joy; was much made of by the fellows; had their learned conversation, looked on books, music. Here and at Middle Temple (off and on) I (for the most part) enjoyed the greatest felicity of my life (ingenious youths, as rosebuds, imbibe the morning dew) till December 1648 (Christmas Eve's eve) I was sent for from Oxford home again to my sick father, who never recovered: where I was engaged to look after his country business and solicit a law-suit.

In 1652, October, my father died, leaving me £1800 of debts and brothers' portions £1000.*

What did I do that was worthy, leading this kind of life? Truly nothing; only shadows, that is, Osney abbey ruins, etc, antiquities. A whetstone, itself incapable of cutting,† e.g. my universal character. That which was neglected and quite forgotten and had sunk had not I engaged in the work, to carry on the work, name them.

He began to enter into pocket memorandum books philosophical and antiquarian remarks, 1654, at Llantrithid.

In 1656 I began my law-suit on the entail in Brecon, which lasted till . . . . and it cost me £1200.

In 1657 I was to have married Mistress K. Ryves, who died when to be married, £2000 or more, besides counting guardianship of her brother, £1000 per annum.

In . . . . I made my will and settled my estate on trustees, intending to have seen the antiquities of Rome and Italy for . . . , and then to have returned and married, but (The gods above thought otherwise). My mother, to my inexpressible grief and ruin, hindered this design, which was my ruin.

My estate *hardly* £100; plus Brecon.

Then debts and lawsuits, work and profit, borrowing of money and perpetual riding. To my praise, wonderful credit in the country for money. In [1661?] sold manor of Bushelton in Herefordshire to Dr T. Willis. In 1663 sold the manor of Stratford in the same county to

* Money owing to his brothers under his father's will. *Ed.*

† Horace, *Ars Poetica*, 305. *Ed.*

Herbert, lord bishop of Hereford.

Then in 1664, 11 June, went into France. October, returned. Joan Sumner.‡ Then law-suit with her. Then sold Easton-Piers and the farm at Broad Chalk. Lost £500 and £200 and goods and timber. Absconded as a banished man.

Then in the mount of the Lord it shall be seen§ I was in as much affliction as a mortal could be, and never quiet till all was gone, and I wholly cast myself on God's providence. Monastery. I wished monasteries had not been put down, that the reformers would have been more moderate as to that point. Nay, the Turks have monasteries. Why should our reformers be so severe? Convenience of religious houses—Sir Christopher Wren—fit there should be receptacles and provision for contemplative men; if of 500, but one or two. There are compensations. What a pleasure 'twould have been to have travelled from monastery to monastery. The reformers in the Lutheran countries were more prudent than to destroy them (e.g. in Alsace, etc); they only altered the religion.

But notwithstanding all these embarrassments I did gradually (as they occurred) take notes of antiquity; and having a quick draught, have drawn landscapes on horseback symbolically e.g. journey to Ireland in July 1660.

Earl of Thanet gave me ease at Heathfield.

Never quiet, nor anything of happiness till divested of all, 1670, 1671: at what time providence raised me (unexpectedly) good friends—the right honourable Nicholas, Earl of Thanet, with whom I was delitescent, lying hidden at Heathfield in Kent near a year; Sir Christopher Wren; Mr Ogilby; then Edmund Wyld esquire FRS of Glasely Hall, Salop, took me into his arms, with whom I most commonly take my diet and sweet cases.

In 1671, having sold all and disappointed as aforesaid of moneys I received, I had so strong an impulse to (in good part) finish my *Description of Wilts*, two volumes in folio, that I could not be quiet till I had done it, and that with danger enough, like a dog in the Nile for fear of the crocodiles, i.e. bailiffs.—And indeed all I have done and that little that I have studied have been just after that fashion, so that had I not lived long my want of leisure would have afforded but a slender harvest . . .

A man's spirit rises and falls with his fortune: makes me lethargic.

Stomach so tender that I could not drink claret without sugar, nor with wine, but would disgorge. Not well ordered till 1670.

A strange fate that I have laboured under never in my life to enjoy one entire month* or six weeks case.

---

‡ See *Accidents*, below, p. 25. *Ed.*   § *Genesis* xxii, 14. *Ed.*
* Once at Chalke in my absconding, October . . .; at Weston in . . .

10

My studies (geometry) were on horseback† and in the house of office: (my father discouraged me). My head was always working; never idle, and even travelling (which from 1649 till 1670 was never off my horse's back) did glean some observations, of which I have a collection in folio of two quires of paper or more, a dust basket, some whereof are to be valued.

His chief virtue, gratitude.

Never riotous or prodigal; but (as Sir E. Leech said) sloth and carelessness are equivalent to all other vices.

My fancy lay most to geometry. If ever I had been good for anything, 'twould have been a painter, I could fancy a thing so strongly and had so clear an idea of it.

When a boy, he did ever love to converse with old men, as living histories. He cared not for play, but on play-days, he gave himself to drawing and painting. At 9, a portraiter.

Real character, that lay dead, antiquities, I caused to revive by engaging six or seven? to record them. I busied myself as a whetstone etc.

Whereas very sickly in youth; *Deo gratias*, healthy from 16. *Friends:* A. Ettrick, Trinity College; Middle Temple, John Lydall; Francis Potter— a hundred letters from him; Sir J. Hoskyns, baronet; Edmund Wyld esquire of Glasley Hall, whom I name out of the highest gratitude; Mr Robert Hooke, Gresham College; Mr Hobbes, 165–; A. Wood, 1665; Sir William Petty, my special friend; Sir James Long, baronet, of Draycot, Mr Ch. Seymour, father of the Duke of Somerset; Sir John Stawell, Middle Temple; Bishop of Salisbury [Seth Ward]; Dr W. Holder. He wrote: 'The Natural History of Wiltshire'; these 'Lives' (for Anthony Wood 1679–80) 'Idea of education of the noblesse' in Mr Ashmole's hands; *Item*, 'Remainders of gentilism', being observations on Ovid's *Fastorum; memorandum, 'Villare Anglicanum* interpreted'; *item*, *Faber Fortunae* (for his own private use).

J.A. lived most at Broad Chalk; sometimes at Easton Piers; at London every term. Much of his time spent in journeying to south Wales (entail) and Herefordshire. I now indulge my genius with my friends and pray for the young angels. Rest at Mrs More's near Gresham College (Mrs More's in Hammond Alley in Bishopsgate farthest house opposite to old Jairer tavern). I expect preferment through Sir Llewellyn Jenkins.

It was J.A. that did put Mr Hobbes upon writing his treatise *De legibus* [*On Laws*], which is bound up with his Rhetoric so that one cannot find it but by chance; no mention of it in the first title.

Memorandum. J. Aubrey in the year 1666, waiting then upon Joan Sumner to her brother at Seend in Wilts, there made a discovery of a chalybeate waters and those more impregnated than any waters yet heard

---

† So I got my algebra, Oughtred in my pocket, with some information [teaching] from Edward Davenant DD of Gillingham, Dorset.

of in England. I sent some bottles to the Royal Society in June 1667, which were tried with galls before a great assembly there. It turns so black that you may write legibly with it, and did there, after so long a carriage, turn as deep as a deep claret. The physicians were wonderfully surprised at it, and spoke to me to recommend it to the doctors of Bath (from whence it is but about ten miles) for that in some cases 'tis best to begin with such waters and end with the Bath, and in some *vice versa*. I wrote several times but to no purpose, for at last I found that, though they were satisfied of the excellency of the waters and what the London doctors said was true, they did not care to have company go from the Bath. So I inserted it in Mr Lilly's almanac, and towards the later end of summer there came so much company that the village could not contain them, and they are now preparing for the building of houses against next summer. John Sumner says (whose well is the best) that it will be worth to him £200 per annum. Dr Grew in his History of the Repository of the Royal Society mentions this discovery, as also of the iron ore there not taken notice of before.

I have written '*an Idea of the education of the Noblesse* from the age of 10 (or 11) till 18'; left with Elias Ashmole, esquire.

¶ *9.15 pm Thursday* 5 *March* 1673, J.A. arrested . . . Gardiner, serjeant, a lusty fair haired solar* fellow, proud, insolent, and everything of that kind.

¶ 25 March 1675, my nose bled at the left nostril about 4 p.m. I do not remember any event which followed this bad omen.

¶ 31 July 1677, I sold my books to Mr Littlebury, that is when my imposthume in my head did break. About 50, imposthume in the head.

¶ Captain Poyntz (for service that I did him to the Earl of Pembroke and the Earl of Abingdon) did very kindly make me a grant of a thousand acres of land in the Island of Tobago, 2 February 1686. He advised me to send over people to plant and to get subscribers to come in for a share of these 1000 acres, for 200 acres he says would be enough for me. In this delicate island is the mother of silver.

William Penn, Lord Proprietor in Pennsylvania, did, of his own accord and especial grace, give me, (16– –) a grant under his seal, of six hundred acres in Pennsylvania: without my seeking or dreaming of it. He advises me to plant it with French protestants for seven years *gratis* and afterwards get them to pay such a rent. Also he tells me, for 200 acres ten pounds per annum rent for ever, after three years.

¶ Now if I would be rich, I could be a prince. I could go into Maryland, which is one of the finest countries of the world; same climate with France; between Virginia and New England. I can have all the favour of my lord Baltimore I could wish. His brother is his

* i.e. the Sun astrologically in the ascendant in his horoscope. *Ed.*

lieutenant there; and a very good-natured gentleman. Plenty of all things; there is land 2000 miles westwards. I could be able I believe to carry a colony of rogues; another, of ingenious artificers; and I doubt not one might make shift [manage] to have five or six ingenious companions, which is enough.

¶ John Aubrey, 20 March 1693, about 11 at night robbed and 15 wounds in my head. 5 January 1694, an apoplectic fit, about 4 p.m.

My uncle Anthony Browne's nag threw me dangerously the Monday after Easter, 1639. Just before it I had an impulse of the briar under which I rode, which tickled him, at the upper end of Berylane. Thanks be to God!

¶ *Accidents of John Aubrey*

Born at Easton Piers, 12 March 1626, about sun-rising: very weak and like to die, and therefore christened that morning before prayer. I think I have heard my mother say I had an ague shortly after I was born.

1629: about 3 or 4 years old, I had a grievous ague. I can remember it. I got not health till 11, or 12: but had sickness of vomiting for 12 hours every fortnight for . . . years; then, it came monthly for . . . years; then, quarterly; and then, half-yearly; the last was in June 1642. This sickness nipped my strength in the bud.

1633: 8 years old, I had an issue (natural) in the coronal suture of my head, which continued running till 21.

1634. October: I had a violent fever that was like to have carried me off. 'Twas the most dangerous sickness that ever I had.

About 1639 (or 1640) I had the measles, but that was nothing: I was hardly sick.

1639: Monday after Easter week my uncle's nag ran away with me, and gave me a very dangerous fall.

1642: 3 May, entered at Trinity College, Oxford.

1643: April and May, the small-pox at Oxford; and shortly after, left that ingenious place; and for three years led a sad life in the country.

1646: April, admitted of the Middle Temple. But my father's sickness, and business, never permitted me to make any settlement to my study.

1651: about 16 or 18 April, I saw that incomparable good conditioned gentlewoman Mistress M. Wiseman, with whom I was at first sight in love—the deadly reed fast in the flesh★.

1652: 21 October: my father died.

1655: (I think) 14 June, I had a fall at Epsom, and broke one of my ribs and was afraid it might cause an aposthumation.

1656: September 1655, or rather (I think) 1656, I began my expensive and tedious law-suit about the entail in Brecknockshire and Monmouthshire.

★ Virgil, *Aeneid* IV. 73. *Ed.*

This year, and the last, was a strange year to me, and contradictions; that is love for M.W. and law-suits.

1656: December: the disease of love.

1657: 27 November, the lady Katherine Ryves died, with whom I was to marry, to my great loss.

1659: March or April, like to break my neck in Ely minster, and the next day, riding a gallop there, my horse tumbled over and over, and yet (I thank God) no hurt.

1660: July, August, I accompanied A. Ettrick into Ireland for a month; and returning were like to be shipwrecked at Holyhead, but no hurt done.

1661, 1662, 1663: about these years I sold my estate in Herefordshire.

[1664?]: January, had the honour to be elected fellow of the Royal Society.

1664: 11 June, landed at Calais. In August following, had a terrible fit of the spleen, and piles, at Orleans. I returned in October.

1664, or 1665: Monday after Christmas, was in danger to be spoiled by my horse, and the same day received a wound in the testicles which was like to have been fatal. Ask R. Wiseman when—I believe 1664.

1665: 1 November; I made my first address (in an ill hour) to Joan Sumner.

1666: this year all my business and affairs ran kim kam. Nothing took effect, as if I had been under an ill tongue. Treacheries and enmities in abundance against me.

1667: December: arrested in Chancery Lane, at Mrs Sumner's suit.

[1668]: 24 February, about 8 or 9 a.m., trial with her at Salisbury. Victory and £600 damage, though devilish opposition against me.

1668: 6 July, was arrested by Peter Gale's malicious contrivance, the day before I was to go to Winchester for my second trial, but it did not retain me above two hours; but did not then go to trial.

1670: 5 March, was my trial at Winchester from 8 to 9, the judge being exceedingly made against me, by my Lady Hungerford. But four of the venue appearing, and with much ado, got the moiety of the Salisbury verdict, viz £300.

1669 and 1670: I sold all my estate in Wilts.

From 1670, to this very day (I thank God), I have enjoyed a happy concealment.

1671: danger of arrests.

1677: later end of June, an imposthume broke in my head.

¶ Memorandum: St John's night, 1673, in danger of being run through with a sword by a young gallant at Mr Burges' chamber in the Middle Temple.

Ask the year that I lay at Mrs Neve's; for that time I was in great danger of being killed by a drunkard in the street opposite Gray's Inn gate—a gentleman whom I never saw before, but (*thanks be to God*) one of his companions hindered his thrust. (Memorandum: horoscope thus.)

Danger of being killed by William Earl of Pembroke, then Lord Herbert, at the election of Sir William Salkeld for Salisbury.

I see Mars in [blank] threatens danger to me from falls.

I have been twice in danger of drowning.

¶ In 1633, I entered into my grammar at the Latin school at Yatton Keynell, in the church, where the curate, Mr Hart, taught the eldest boys Virgil, Ovid, Cicero, etc. The fashion then was to preserve the binding of their books with a false cover of parchment, that is, old manuscript, which I was too young to understand; but I was pleased with the elegancy of the writing and the coloured initial letters. I remember the rector here, Mr Wm. Stump, great grandson of Stump the clothier of Malmesbury, had several manuscripts of the Abbey. He was a proper man and a good fellow; and, when he brewed a barrel of special ale, his use was to stop the bunghole, under the clay, with a sheet of manuscript; he said nothing did it so well: which methought did grieve me then to see. Afterwards I went to school to Mr Latimer at Leigh Delamere, the next parish, where was the like use of covering of books. In my grandfather's days the manuscripts flew about like butterflies. All music books, account books, copy books, etc, were covered with old manuscripts, as we cover them now with blue paper or marbled paper; and the glovers at Malmesbury made great havoc of them; and gloves were wrapped up no doubt in many good pieces of antiquity. Before the late wars a world of rare manuscripts perished hereabout; for within half a dozen miles of this place were the abbey of Malmesbury, where it may be presumed the library was as well furnished with choice copies as most libraries of England; and perhaps in the library we might have found a correct Pliny's Natural History, which Camitus, a monk here, did abridge for King Henry the Second. Within the aforesaid compass was Broadstock Priory, Stanleigh Abbey, Farleigh Abbey, Bath Abbey, eight miles, and Cirencester Abbey, twelve miles. In 1638, I was transplanted to Blandford School, in Dorset, to Mr Wm. Sutton. (In Mr Wm. Gardner's time it was the most eminent school for the education of gentlemen in the west of England.) Here also was the use of covering of books with old parchments, that is, leases etc, but I never saw anything of a manuscript there. Hereabouts were no abbeys or convents for men. One may also perceive by the binding of old books how the old manuscripts went to wrack in those days. In 1647 I went to Parson Stump out of curiosity, to see his manuscripts, whereof I had seen some in my childhood; but by that time they were lost and dispersed. His sons were gunners and soldiers, and scoured their guns with them; but he showed me several old deeds granted by the Lords Abbots, with their seals annexed, which I suppose his son Capt. Tho. Stump of Malmesbury hath still.

George Abbot

1562–1633

Born into a humble but able family (another brother became Bishop of Salisbury), he earned a reputation at Oxford as an eloquent preacher. He was strongly puritan in his views, and as vice-chancellor of Oxford in the 1600s had religious pictures burnt in the marketplace. He helped to restore the bishops in the Scottish church in 1608 and 1610, and largely as a result of this was chosen Archbishop of Canterbury in 1610. However, his influence at court quickly declined, and he was not helped by a hunting accident in 1621 in which he killed a gamekeeper with a crossbow. After Charles I's accession, he was entirely out of sympathy with the mood at court, and was temporarily deprived of office in 1628. He died in 1633, and was buried at Guildford.

Old Nightingale was his servant, and weeps when he talks of him. Everyone that knew, loved him. He was sometimes choleric.

¶ He was born in the house (of old Flemish building, timber and brick) now an alehouse, the sign 'Three Mariners', by the river's side by the bridge on the north side of the street in St Nicholas parish on the right hand as you go out of the town [Guildford] northwards.

¶ He was the son of a clothcutter. His mother, with child of him, longed for a pike, and dreamed that if she could eat a jack, her son should be a great man. The next morning, going to the river, which runs by the house (which is by the bridge), with her pail, to take up some water, a good jack came into her pail; which she ate up, all, herself. This is generally received for a truth.

His godfather and godmothers sent him to the university, his father not being able.

Thomas Allen

1542–1632

Famous as a mathematician and collector of manuscripts on astronomy and antiquities, Thomas Fuller said of him that he had 'succeeded to the skill and scandal of Friar Bacon'. His correspondence was extensive, with many famous men of the period; but he wrote nothing for publication.

Mr Theodore Haak, a German, Fellow of the Royal Society, was of Gloucester Hall, Oxford, 1626, and knew this learned worthy old gentleman, whom he takes to have been about ninety-six years old when he died, which was about 1630. He says that Mr Allen was a very cheerful, facetious man, and that everybody loved his company, and every house on their feast days were wont to invite him.

His picture was drawn at the request of Dr Ralph Kettell and hangs in the dining room of the President of Trinity College, Oxford (of which college he first was, and had his education there); by which it appears he was a handsome sanguine man, of an excellent habit of body.

There is mention of him in *Leicester's Commonwealth* that the great Dudley, Earl of Leicester, made use of him for casting nativities; for he was the best astrologer of his time. In those dark times, astrologer, mathematician and conjurer were accounted the same things, and the vulgar did verily believe him to be a conjurer. He had a great many mathematical instruments and glasses in his chamber, which did also confirm the ignorant in their opinion, and his servitor (to impose on freshmen and simple people) would tell them that sometimes he should meet the spirits coming up his stairs like bees. R. Power, one of our parish was of Gloucester Hall about seventy years and more since, and told me this from his servitor. Now there is to some men a great lechery in lying, and imposing on the understandings of believing people, and he thought it for his credit to serve such a master.

He was generally well known, and every long vacation he rode into the country to visit his old acquaintance and patrons, to whom his great learning, mixed with much sweetness of humour, rendered him very welcome. One time, being at Holm Lacy in Herefordshire, at Mr John Scudamore's (grandfather to the Lord Scudamore), he happened to leave his watch in the chamber window (watches were then rarities): the maids came in to make the bed, and hearing a thing in a case cry *Tick, tick, tick*, at once concluded that that was his devil, and took by the string with the tongs, and threw it out of the window into the moat (to drown the devil). It so happened that the string hung on a sprig of an elder that grew out of the moat, and this confirmed to them that it was the devil. So the good old gentleman got his watch again.

Sir Kenelm Digby loved him much, and bought his excellent library of him, which he gave to the University.

¶ Queen Elizabeth sent for him to have his advice about the new star which appeared in the Swan or Cassiopeia (but I think the Swan), to which he gave his judgement very learnedly.

Edward Alleyn
1566–1626

Actor and partner in the Fortune Theatre, built in 1600. He specialised in tragic parts.

. . . Mr Alleyn, being a tragedian, and one of the original actors in many of the celebrated Shakespeare plays, in one of which he played a demon, with six others, and was in the midst of the play, surprised by an apparition of the devil, which so worked on his fancy, that he made a vow, which he performed at this place (Dulwich College). . . . Notwithstanding all the solemnity of this deed of gift, the founder lived to change his mind upon a second marriage, when he was very desirous of revoking his charity, but was not allowed to.

Lancelot Andrewes
1555–1626

Son of a London merchant, he was intended for a business career, but his masters persuaded his parents that he should become a scholar. He was master of Pembroke Hall at Cambridge from 1590 to 1605, when he became Bishop of Chichester. He later became Bishop of Ely, and then Bishop of Winchester in 1619. His greatest work was the preparation of the Authorised Version of the Bible, in which he played a leading part. He was renowned as a preacher, and his theological works, mostly published after his death, further increased his reputation: he had been widely expected to become Archbishop of Canterbury in 1610, but George Abbot was chosen instead. Aubrey criticises his preaching, but fashions had changed by the 1670s, and the old learned style, full of quotations and play on words, was no longer admired.

Lancelot Andrewes, Lord Bishop of Winchester, was born in London; went to school at Merchant Tailors school. Mr Mulcaster was his schoolmaster, whose picture he hung in his study. Old Mr Sutton, a very learned man of those days, of Blandford in Dorset was his schoolfellow, and said that Lancelot Andrewes was a great long boy of 18 years old at least before he went to the university.

He was a fellow of Pembroke Hall in Cambridge (called the *College of*

Bishops, for that, at one time, in those days, there were of that house so many bishops). The Puritan faction did begin to increase in those days, and especially at Emmanuel College: that party had a great mind to draw in this learned young man, whom (if they could make theirs) they knew would be a great honour to them. They carried themselves outwardly with great sanctity and strictness so that 'twas a very hard matter to [cavil] as to their lives. They preached up very strict keeping and observing the Lord's day; made, upon the matter, damnation to break it, and that it was less sin to kill a man than break the Sabbath. Yet these hypocrites did bowl in a private green at their college every Sunday after sermon; and one of the college (a loving friend to Mr L. Andrewes) to satisfy him one time lent him the key of a private back door to the bowling green, on a Sunday evening, which opening, discovered these zealous preachers, with their gowns off, earnest at play. But they were strangely surprised to see the entry of one that was not of the brotherhood.

There was then at Cambridge a good fat alderman that was wont to sleep at church, which the alderman endeavoured to prevent, but could not. Well! this was preached against as a sign of *wickedness*. The good man was exceedingly troubled at it, and went to Andrewes' chamber to be satisfied in point of conscience. Mr Andrewes told him, that was an ill habit of body, not of mind, and that it was against his will; advised him on Sundays to make a more sparing meal and to mend it at supper. The alderman did so, but sleep comes on him again for all that, and he was preached at. He comes again to be resolved for advice, with tears in his eyes. Andrewes then told him he would have him make a good hearty meal as he was wont to do, and immediately take out his full sleep. He did so; came to St Mary's church, where the preacher was prepared with a sermon to damn all who slept at sermon, a certain sign of *wickedness*. The good alderman having taken his full nap beforehand, looks on the preacher all sermon time, and spoiled the plan. But I should have said that Andrewes was most extremely spoken against and preached against for offering to assoil or excuse a sleeper in sermon time. But he had learning and wit enough to defend himself.

His great learning quickly made him known in the university, and also to King James, who much valued him for it, and advanced him, and at last made him Bishop of Winchester; which bishopric he ordered with great prudence as to government of the parsons, preferring of ingenious persons that were staked to poor livings and did waste away. He made it his enquiry to find out such men. Amongst several others (whose names have escaped my memory) Nicholas Fuller (he wrote *Critica Sacra*) minister of Allington near Amesbury in Wiltshire, was one. The bishop sent for him, and the poor man was afraid and knew not what hurt he had done. He makes him sit down to dinner; and after

19

the dessert, was brought in in a dish his institution and introduction, or the donation of a prebend [a cathedral appointment]: which was his way. He chose out always able men to be his chaplains, whom he advanced.

He did not have that smooth way of oratory as now. It was a shrewd and severe criticism of a Scottish lord, who, when King James asked him how he liked Bishop Andrewes's sermon, said that he was learned, but he did play with his text, as a monkey does, who takes up a thing and tosses and plays with it, and then he takes up another, and plays a little with it—'here's a pretty thing, and there's a pretty thing!'

Thomas Archer
1554–?1630

Mr Archer, rector of Houghton Conquest, was a good scholar in King James I's days, and one of his majesty's chaplains. He had two thick quarto manuscripts of his own collection; one, jests and tales etc, and discourses at dinners; the other, of the weather. I have desired parson Poynter, his successor, to enquire after them, but I find him slow in it. No doubt there are delicate things to be found there.

William Aubrey
1529–95

John Aubrey's great-grandfather, and the most celebrated of his ancestors.

William Aubrey; Doctor of Laws: extracted from a manuscript of funerals, and other good notes, in the hands of Sir Henry St George, Clarenceux King at Arms. I guess it to be the handwriting of Sir Daniel Dun, LlD, who married Joan, third daughter of Dr William Aubrey:

> . . . This gentleman in his tender years learned the first grounds of grammar in the college of Brecon, in Brecknock town, and from thence about his age of fourteen years he was sent by his parents to the University of Oxford, where, under the tuition and instruction of one Mr Morgan, a greatly learned man, in a few years he so

much profited in the humanities and other recommendable knowledge, especially in rhetoric and history, that he was found to be fit for the study of civil law, and thereupon was also elected into the fellowship of All Souls College in Oxford (where the same law has always much flourished). In which college he earnestly studied and diligently applied himself to the lectures and exercise of the house, so that he there attained the degree of a doctor of civil law at his age of 25 years, and immediately afterwards he had bestowed on him the queen's public lectureship in law in the university; he read his lectures with such success that his fame for learning and knowledge was spread far abroad and he was esteemed worthy to be called to public office. Wherefore, shortly afterwards, he was made judge marshal of the queen's armies at St Quentin in France. Which wars finished, he returned into England, and he decided, in more peaceable manner and according to his former education, to pass on the course of his life in the exercise of law; he became an advocate in the Court of Arches, and remained so for many years, but with such fame and credit both for his rare skill and knowledge of law, and for his sound judgement and good experience therein, that, among men best qualified to judge, he was generally accounted without equal in that branch of learning. For this reason, when there was occasion to employ a civil lawyer, his service was often used both within the realm and in foreign countries. In which employments he always used such care and diligence and balanced judgement that, as his valour and virtues became more evident each day, so they provided the means to his further advancement, insomuch that he was preferred to be one of the council of the Marches of Wales, and shortly after took his place as Master of the Chancery, and the appointed judge of the Audience, and was made Vicar General to the Lord Archbishop of Canterbury throughout the whole province, and last, by the especial grace of the queen's most excellent majesty, Queen Elizabeth, he was taken into her highness' close service and made one of the Masters of Request in Ordinary. All which titles and offices (except the mastership of Chancery which did not seem compatible with the office of Master of the Rolls) he, by her princely favour, possessed and enjoyed until the time of his death. Besides the great learning and wisdom with which this gentleman was plentifully endowed, Nature had also framed him so courteous of disposition and affable of speech, so sweet of conversation and amiable in behaviour, that there was never anyone in his position better beloved all his life; nor was he himself more especially favoured of her majesty and the greatest personages in the realm in any part of his life than he was when he drew nearest his death. He was not tall in stature, nor yet over-low;

21

not gross in body, and yet of good habit; somewhat inclining to fatness of face in his youth; round, well favoured, well coloured and handsome; and although in his later years sickness had much impaired his strength and the freshness of his complexion, yet there remained there still to the last in his countenance such comely and decent gravity, that the change added to rather than diminished in any way his former dignity. He left behind him when he died by a virtuous gentlewoman Wilgiford his wife (the first daughter of Mr John Williams of Tainton in the county of Oxford; whom he married very young, as a maiden, and enjoyed to his death, the two of them living together in great love and kindness for the space of forty years) three sons and six daughters, all of them married and having issue. . . . His third son John*, being then of the age of 18 years (or thereabouts) was married to Rachel, one of the daughters of Richard Danvers of Tockenham in the County of Wilts, esquire.

Memorandum: he was one of the delegates (together with Dr Dale etc) for the trial of Mary Queen of Scots, and was a great stickler for the saving of her life, which kindness was remembered by King James at his coming-in to England, who asked after him, and probably would have made him Lord Keeper, but he died, as we have seen, a little before that good opportunity happened. His majesty sent for his sons, and knighted the two eldest, and invited them to court, which they modestly and perhaps prudently declined. They preferred a country life.

Memorandum: old Judge Atkins (the father) told me that the Portuguese ambassador was tried for his life for killing Mr Greenway in the New Exchange under the commonwealth, on the precedent of the Scottish bishop of Ross, a trial undertaken on Dr W. Aubrey's advice.

He was a good statesman and queen Elizabeth loved him and used to call him 'her little Doctor'. Sir Joseph Williamson, principal secretary of State, has told me that in the Letter Office are a great many letters of his to the queen and council.

He sat many times as Lord Keeper, at the queen's pleasure, and made many decrees, which Mr Shuter, etc told me they had seen.

Memorandum: the *Penkenol*, i.e. chief of the family, is my cousin Aubrey of Llannelly in Brecknockshire, who inherited estates worth about £60 or £80 a year; and the doctor should have used a distinguishing mark on his arms†; for want of which in a badge on one of his servants'

---

* (Aubrey's grandfather. *Ed.*) John Whitgift, Archbishop of Canterbury was his guardian, and the doctor's great friend. I have heard my grandmother say that her husband told her that his grace kept a noble house, and did so with admirable order and economy; and that there was not one woman in the household.

† In heraldry, only the eldest son has the right to use arms without 'difference'. *Ed.*

blue coats, his cousin William Aubrey, also LlD, who was the chief, plucked it off.

The learned John Dee was his great friend and kinsman, as I find by letters between them in the custody of Elias Ashmole, esq., viz, John Dee wrote a book *The Sovereignty of the Sea*, dedicated to queen Elizabeth, which was published in folio. Mr Ashmole has it, and also the original copy in John Dee's handwriting, and annexed to it is a letter from his cousin to William Aubrey, whose advice he desired in writing on that subject.

He purchased Abercunwrig (the ancient seat of the family) from his cousin Aubrey. He built the great house at Brecknock: his study looks on the river Usk. He could ride nine miles together on his own land in Breconshire. In Wales and England he left £2500 per annum, of which there is now none left in the family. He made one Hugh George (his chief clerk) his executor, who ran away into Ireland and cheated all the legatees, and among other my grandfather (his youngest son), for the addition of whose estate he had contracted for Pembridge castle in Herefordshire, and for which his executor was to have paid. He made a deed of entail in 1594 which is also mentioned in his will, whereby he entails the Brecon estate on the issue male of his eldest son, and in defailer, to skip the second son (for whom he had well provided, and who had married a great fortune) and to come to the third. Edward, the eldest, had seven sons; and his eldest son, Sir William, had also seven sons; and so I am heir, being the eighteenth man in remainder† which puts me in mind of Dr Donne:

> For what doeth it availe
> To be the twentieth man in an entaile?

Old Judge Sir Edward Atkins remembered Dr Aubrey when he was a boy; he lay at his father's house in Gloucestershire; he kept his coach, which was rare in those days. The judge told me that they then (vulgarly) called it a *Quitch*. I have his original picture. He had a delicate, quick, lively and piercing black eye, fresh complexion and a secure eyebrow. The figure in his monument at St Paul's is not like him; it is too big.

The curse of heroes' sons: he used up all the wit of the family, so that none descended from him can pretend to have any. It was a pity that Dr Fuller did not mention him amongst his worthies in that county‡.

When he lay dying, he desired them to send for a goodman; they thought he meant Dr Goodman, dean of St Paul's, but he meant a priest*, as I have heard my cousin John Madock say. Captain Pugh used

---

† i.e. if seventeen other heirs died in turn without issue, Aubrey would inherit. *Ed.*
‡ See introduction p. 3, for Fuller's *Worthies of England*. *Ed.*
* i.e. a Roman Catholic priest. *Ed.*

to say that civil lawyers (like most learned gentlemen) inclined naturally to the Church of Rome; and common lawyers, as more ignorant and clownish, to the Church of Geneva.

This Dr William Aubrey was related to the first William, Earl of Pembroke in two ways (as appears by comparing the old pedigree at Wilton with that of the Aubreys); by Melin and Philip ap Elider (the Welshmen are all kin); and it is exceeding probable that the earl was instrumental in his rise. When the earl of Pembroke was General at St Quentin in France, Dr Aubrey was his judge advocate. In the doctor's will is mention of a great piece of silver plate, the bequest of the right honourable the earl of Pembroke.

Sir Robert Ayton
1570–1638

A courtier and diplomat under James I and Charles I, whose contemporary reputation as a poet has not stood the test of time.

He is buried in the south aisle of the choir of Westminster Abbey, where there is erected to his memory an elegant marble and copper monument and inscription. His bust is of copper, curiously cast, with a laurel held over it by two figures of white marble.

That Sir Robert was one of the best poets of his time—Mr John Dryden says he has seen verses of his, some of the best of that age, printed with some other verses—enquire for them.

He was acquainted with all the wits of his time in England. He was a great acquaintance of Mr Thomas Hobbes of Malmesbury, whom Mr Hobbes told me he had made use of (together with Ben Jonson) for an Aristarchus [critic and editor] when he made his epistle dedicatory to his translation of Thucydides. I have been told (I think by Sir John himself) that he was eldest brother to Sir John Ayton, Master of the Black Rod, who was also an excellent scholar.

Francis Bacon
Lord St Albans, 1561–1626

Francis Bacon was born into the highest rank of the Tudor Civil service: his father was Lord Keeper, and Burghley, Elizabeth's chief minister, was his uncle. He soon made a parliamentary career for himself, but never actively sought favour at court. His opposition to taxation in 1593 earned him Elizabeth's displeasure, and his friendship with Essex made him suspect in 1600, when Essex led an armed rebellion in London. However, despite Essex's past gifts to him, Bacon played a leading part in Essex's prosecution, which he justified on the grounds that his first loyalty was to the queen. It was not until late in James's reign that Bacon's opportunity came, and early in 1618 he had risen to the lord chancellorship, a title which James reintroduced. But he had made many enemies; and in 1621 he was tried for having accepted money from people involved in lawsuits, even though it was acknowledged that he had in all cases given judgement against them. He was found guilty, and spent the rest of his life in retirement. His philosophical works, written both during his political career and in his retirement, were largely uncompleted, and it is as the writer of the Essays *that he is best remembered; but he was one of the pioneers of modern scientific thinking, rejecting 'ancient authority' in favour of observation and logical thought.*

In his lordship's prosperity Sir Fulke Greville, Lord Brooke, was his great friend and acquaintance; but when he was in disgrace and want, he was so unworthy as to forbid his butler to let him have any small beer, which he had often sent for, his stomach being delicate, and the small beer of Gray's Inn not to his taste. This has done his memory more dishonour than Sir Philip Sidney's friendship engraved on his monument has done him honour.

Richard, Earl of Dorset, was a great admirer and friend of the Lord Chancellor Bacon, and was wont to have Sir Thomas Billingsley along with him, to remember, and to put down in writing my lord's sayings at table.

Mr Ben Jonson was one of his friends and acquaintance, as appears by his excellent verses on his lordship's birthday in his second volume, and in his *Underwoods*, where he gives him a character and concludes that 'about his time, and within his view were all born the clever men that could honour a nation or help study'.

He came often to Sir John Danvers at Chelsea. Sir John told me that when his lordship had written the *History of Henry VII*, he sent the manuscript copy to him to desire his opinion of it before it was printed. Said Sir John, 'Your lordship knows I am no scholar.' 'Tis no matter,' said my lord, 'I know what a scholar can say; I would know what *you*

25

can say.' Sir John read it, and gave his opinion what he misliked (which I am sorry I have forgot) which my lord acknowledged to be true, and mended it: 'Why,' said he, 'a scholar would never have told me this.'

Mr Thomas Hobbes of Malmesbury was beloved by his lordship, who was wont to have him walk with him, in his delicate groves, where he did meditate; and when a notion darted into his mind, Mr Hobbes was at once to write it down, and his lordship was wont to say that he did it better than anyone else about him; for that, many times, when he read their notes, he scarcely understood what they had written, because they understood it not themselves. In short, all that were great and good loved and honoured him.

Sir Edward Coke, Lord Chief Justice, always envied him, and would be criticising his knowledge of law, as you may find in my lord's letters, and I knew old lawyers that remembered it.

He was Lord Protector during King's James's progress into Scotland, and gave audience in great state to ambassadors in the banqueting-house at Whitehall.

His lordship would many times have music in the next room to where he meditated. The aviary at York House* was built by his Lordship; it did cost £300. At every meal, according to the season of the year, he had his table strewed with sweet herbs and flowers, which he said did refresh his spirits and memory.

When his lordship was at his country house at Gorhambury, St Albans seemed as if the court were there, so nobly did he live. His servants had liveries with his crest (a boar); his watermen† were more employed by gentlemen than any other, even the king's.

King James sent a buck to him, and he gave the keeper fifty pounds.

He was wont to say to his servant Hunt, (who was a notably thrifty man, and loved this world, and the only servant he had that he could never get to stand surety for him) 'The world was made for man (Hunt!) and not man for the world.' Hunt left an estate of £1,000 per annum in Somerset.

None of his servants dared appear before him without Spanish leather boots; otherwise he would smell the calf's leather which offended him.

The East India merchants presented his lordship with a cabinet of jewels, which his page, Mr Cockaine, received and deceived his lord.

His lordship was a good poet, but concealed, as appears by his letters. See excellent verses of his lordship's which Mr Farnaby translated into Greek and printed both in his anthology, that is:

---

* On the site of the Adelphi. *Ed.*

† On the Thames small boats rowed by watermen were one of the chief means of transport in London. *Ed.*

The world's a bubble, and the life of man
    Less than a span;
In his conception wretched, from the womb
    So to the tomb;
Cursed from his cradle, and brought up to years
    With cares and fears.
Who then to frail mortality shall trust
But limns in water or but writes in dust.

Yet since with sorrow here we live oppressed,
    What life is best?
Courts are but only superficial schools
    To dandle fools;
The rural parts are turned into a den
    Of savage men;
And where's a city from vice so free,
But may be termed the worst of all the three?

Domestic cares afflict the husband's bed
    Or pains his head;
Those that live single take it for a curse,
    Or do things worse;
Some would have children; those that have them moan,
    Or wish them gone.
What is it then to have, or have no wife,
But single thralldom or a double strife?

Our own affections still at home to please
    Is a disease;
To cross the sea to any foreign soil,
    Perils and toil;
Wars with their noise affright us; when they cease
    We're worse in peace.
What then remains? but that we still should cry
Not to be born, or being born, to die.

At the end of his *Novum Organum* [Bacon's great work on philosophy]
Hugh Holland wrote these verses:

> *This book is such that no fool could have written it,*
> *nor would a wise man have wished to: that is Hugh's opinion.*

¶ *Sayings* His lordship being in York House garden looking on fishers
as they were throwing their net [in the Thames], asked them what they

would take for their catch; they answered, so much: his lordship would offer them no more but so much. They drew up their net, and in it were only two or three little fishes: his lordship told them it had been better for them to have taken his offer. They replied, they hoped to have had a better draught: 'but,' said his lordship, 'Hope is a good breakfast, but an ill supper.'

When his lordship was in disfavour, his neighbours, hearing how much he was in debt, came to him with a motion to buy Oak Wood* off him. His lordship told them that 'he would not sell his feathers'.

The Earl of Manchester being removed from his place of Lord Chief Justice of the Common Pleas to be Lord President of the Council, told my lord (upon his fall) that he was sorry to see him made such an example. Lord Bacon replied that 'it did not trouble him since *he* was made a president'.†

The Bishop of London did cut down a noble cloud of trees at Fulham. The lord chancellor told him that he was 'a good expounder of dark places'.

Upon his being in disfavour his servants suddenly went away; he compared them to the flying of the vermin when the house was falling.

Someone told his lordship that it was now time to look about him. He replied, 'I do not look *about* me, I look *above* me'.

Sir Julius Caesar (Master of the Rolls) sent to his lordship in his necessity a hundred pounds for a present.

His lordship would often drink a good draught of strong beer (March beer) at bedtime, to lay his working fancy asleep: which otherwise would keep him from sleeping a great part of the night.

I remember Sir John Danvers told me that his lordship much delighted in his curious garden at Chelsea, and as he was walking there one time, he fell down in a dead swoon. My Lady Danvers rubbed his face, temples etc and gave him cordial water: as soon as he came to himself, said he: 'Madam, I am no good footman'.

Three of his lordship's servants (Sir Thomas Meautys, Mr Bushell and Mr Idney) kept their coaches, and some kept race-horses.

He was a homosexual. His Ganymedes and favourites took bribes; but his lordship always gave judgement according to justice and honesty. His decrees in Chancery stand firm, i.e. there are fewer of his decrees reversed than of any other chancellor.

His widow married her gentleman usher, Sir (Thomas, I think) Underhill, whom she made deaf and blind with too much of Venus. She

---

* Part of his estate at Gorhambury: see below. *Ed.*

† Referring to the Earl of Manchester's promotion to Bacon's old position; but with the double meaning that 'a precedent was made for him'. *Ed.*

was living since the beheading of the late king [Charles I].—Query where and when she died.

He had a delicate, lively hazel eye; Dr Harvey told me it was like the eye of a viper.

I have now forgotten what Mr Bushell said, whether his lordship enjoyed his Muse best at night, or in the morning.

Mr Hobbes told me that the cause of his lordship's death was trying of an experiment: viz, as he was taking the air in a coach with Dr Witherborne (a Scotchman, physician to the king) towards Highgate, snow lay on the ground, and it came into my lord's thoughts, why flesh might not be preserved in snow, as in salt. They were resolved they would try the experiment at once. They alighted out of the coach, and went into a poor woman's house at the bottom of Highgate Hill, and bought a hen, and made the woman gut it, and then stuffed the body with snow, and my lord did help to do it himself. The snow so chilled him, that he immediately fell so extremely ill, that he could not return to his lodgings (I suppose at Gray's Inn), but went to the Earl of Arundel's house at Highgate, where they put him into a good bed warmed with a pan, but it was a damp bed that had not been lain-in about a year before, which gave him such a cold that in two or three days, as I remember he [Mr Hobbes] told me, he died of suffocation.

I will write something of St Albans, and his house at Gorhambury. At St Albans is to be seen, in some few places, some remains of the wall of this city. This magnanimous Lord Chancellor had a great mind to have made it a city again: and he had designed it to be built with great uniformity: but Fortune denied it him, though she proved kinder to the great Cardinal Richelieu, who lived both to design and finish that handsome town of Richelieu, where he was born; before, an obscure and small village. (The plan of this town and palace is nobly engraved.)

Within the bounds of the walls of this old city of St Albans (his lordship's barony) was Verulam House, about half a mile from St Albans, which his lordship built, the most ingeniously contrived little pile, that ever I saw. (I am sorry I measured not the front and breadth; but I little suspected it would be pulled down for the sale of the materials). No question but his lordship was the chiefest architect; but he had for his assistant a favourite of his (a St Albans man), a Mr Dobson (who was his lordship's right hand) a very ingenious person (Master of the Alienation office); but he spending his estate luxuriously upon women, necessity forced his son William Dobson to be the most excellent painter that England has yet bred.

The view of this house from the entrance into the gate by the highway is thus. The respective sides answer one another. I do not well remember if on the east side were bay windows, which his lordship much affected, as may be seen in his essay *Of Building*. Query whether

29

the number of windows on the east side were five or seven: to my best remembrance, but five.

Verulam House

This house did cost nine or ten thousand the building and was sold about 1665 or 1666 by Sir Harbottle Grimston, baronet, (now Master of the Rolls), to two carpenters for four hundred pounds; of which they made eight hundred pounds. Memorandum: there were good chimney-pieces; the rooms very lofty, and all were very well panelled. Memorandum: there were two bathing rooms or stuffs, whither his lordship retired in the afternoons, as he saw cause. All the tunnels of the chimneys were carried into the middle of the house, and round about them were seats. The top of the house was well leaded. From the leads was a lovely prospect to the ponds, which were opposite to the east side of the house, and were on the other side of the stately walk of trees that leads to Gorhambury House: and also over that long walk of trees, whose tops afford a most pleasant variegated verdure, resembling the workers in Irish stitch [embroidery varying shades of the same colour]. The kitchen, larder, cellars etc are underground. In the middle of this house was a delicate staircase of wood, which was curiously carved, and on the posts of every interstice was some pretty figure, as of a grave divine with his book and spectacles, a mendicant friar etc (not one thing twice). Memorandum: on the doors of the upper storey on the outside (which were painted dark umber) were the figures of the gods of the Gentiles (viz on the south door, second storey, was Apollo; on another, Jupiter with his thunderbolt, etc) bigger than the life, and done by an excellent hand; the heightenings were of hatchings of gold, which when the sun shone on them made a most glorious show.

Memorandum: the upper part of the uppermost door on the east side had inserted into it a large looking glass, with which the stranger was very gratefully deceived, for (after he had been entertained a pretty while with the prospects of the ponds, walks and country which this door faced) when you were about to return into the room, one would have sworn at first glance that he had beheld another prospect through the house; for as soon as the stranger was landed on the balcony, the *concierge* that showed the house would shut the door to put this fallacy on him with the looking-glass. This was his lordship's summer house: for he says (in his essay) one should have seats for summer and winter, as well as clothes.

From hence to Gorhambury is about a little mile, the way easily ascending, hardly so sloping as a desk.

From hence to Gorhambury in a straight line lead three parallel walks; in the middlemost three coaches may pass abreast; in the wing walks two may. They consist of several stately trees of the like growth and height, viz elm, chestnut, beech, hornbeam, Spanish ash, cervice-tree etc, whose tops (as aforesaid) do afford from the walk on the house the finest show that I have seen, and I saw it about Michaelmas, at which time the colour of the leaves are most varied.

The figures of the ponds were thus: they were pitched at the bottoms with pebbles of several colours, which were worked into several figures, as of fishes etc, which in his lordship's time were plainly to be seen through the clear water, now overgrown with flags and rushes.

If a poor body had brought his lordship half a dozen pebbles of a curious colour, he would give them a shilling, so curious was he in perfecting his fish-ponds, which I guess do contain four acres. In the middle of the middlemost pond in the island is a curious banqueting-house of Roman architecture, paved with black and white marble; covered with Cornish slate, and neatly wainscotted.

Memorandum: about midway from Verulam House to Gorhambury, on the right hand, on the side of a hill which faces the passer-by, are set in artificial manner the afore-named trees, whose diversity of greens on the side of the hill are exceeding pleasant. These delicate walks and prospects entertain the eye to Gorhambury House, which is a large well-built Gothic house, built (I think) by Sir Nicholas Bacon, Lord Keeper, father to this lord chancellor, to whom it descended by the death of Anthony Bacon, his middle brother, who died sans issue. The lord chancellor made an addition of a noble portico, which fronts the garden to the south: opposite to every arch of this portico, and as big as the arch, are drawn, by an excellent hand (but the mischief of it is, in watercolours) curious pictures, all emblematical, with mottos under each; for example, one I remember is a ship tossed in a storm, the motto, *There will be another Tiphys*.* Enquire for the rest.

Over this portico is a stately gallery, whose glass windows are all painted; and every pane with several figures of beast, bird and flower: perhaps his lordship might use them as topics for local memory. The windows look into the garden, the side opposite them no window, but that side is hung all with pictures at length, as of King James, his lordship, and several illustrious persons of his time. At the end you enter is no window, but there is a very large picture, thus:—in the middle on a rock in the sea stands King James in armour, with his regal ornaments; on his right hand stands (but whether or no on a rock I have forgot) King Henry IV of France, in armour; and on his left hand, the King of Spain in like manner. These figures are (at least) as big as the life, they are done only with umber and shell gold: all the heightening and illuminated part being burnished gold, and the shadowed umber, as in the pictures of the gods on the doors of Verulam House. The roof

* The superhuman pilot of the Argo in Greek myth. *Ed.*

31

of this gallery is semi-cylindric, and painted by the same hand and same manner, with heads and busts of Greek and Roman emperors and heroes.

In the hall (which is of the ancient building) is a large story very well painted of the feasts of the gods, where Mars is caught in a net by Vulcan. On the wall, over the chimney, is painted an oak with acorns falling from it: the word, *Failing better things*. And on the wall, over the table, is painted Ceres teaching the sowing of corn; the word, *We have better counsels*.

The garden is large, which was (no doubt) excellently planted and kept in his lordship's time. Here is a handsome door, which opens into Oak Wood. The oaks of this wood are very great and shady. His lordship much delighted himself here: under every tree he planted some fine flower, or flowers, some whereof are there still (1656), viz peonies, tulips.

From this wood a door opens into a place as big as an ordinary park, the west part whereof is coppice-wood: where are walks cut out straight as a line, and broad enough for a coach, a quarter of a mile long or better. Here his lordship much meditated, his servant Mr Bushell attending him with his pen and ink to set down his present notions.

The east of this parquet (which extends to Verulam House) was heretofore, in his lordship's prosperity, a paradise; now it is a large ploughed field. This eastern division consisted of several parts; some thickets of plum trees with delicate walks; some of raspberries. Here was all manner of fruit trees that would grow in England; and a great number of choice forest trees; as the wild ash; sorb, cervice, etc; yew. The walks both in the coppices, and other wooded parts were most ingeniously designed: at several belvederes were erected elegant sum-merhouses well built of Roman architecture: well panelled and ceilinged; yet standing, but defaced, so that one would have thought the barbarians had made conquest here. This place in his lordship's time was a sanctuary for pheasants, partridges, etc, birds of several kinds and countries, as white, speckled and other partridges. In April, and the springtime, his lordship would, when it rains, take his coach (open) to receive the benefit of irrigation, which he was wont to say was very wholesome because of the nitre in the air and the *universal spirit of the world*.

His lordship was wont to say, *I will lay my manor of Gorhambury on't*, to which judge —— made a spiteful reply, saying he would not hold a wager against that, but against any other manor of his lordship's he liked. Now this illustrious lord chancellor had only this manor of Gorhambury.

Sir Thomas Badd

Created a baronet in 1642.

The happiness a shoemaker has in drawing on a fair lady's shoe; I know a man the height of whose ambition was to be apprenticed to his mistress's shoemaker on condition he could do so. Sir Thomas Badd's father, a shoemaker, married the brewer's widow of Portsmouth, worth £20,000.

John Barclay
1582–1621

Barclay wrote elegant satires in Latin verse, of which Argenis *is the most famous. Aubrey is wrong about his relationship with Robert Barclay; they were certainly not father and son.*

John Barclay, the Scotsman (from Samuel Butler), was in England some time in the time of King James. He was then an old man, white beard; and wore a hat and a feather, which gave some severe people offence. Dr John Dell tells me that his last employment was library-keeper of the Vatican, and that he was there poisoned.

Memorandum: this John Barclay has a son, now (1688) an old man, and a learned quaker, who wrote a system of the quakers' doctrine in Latin, dedicated to King Charles II, now to King James II. The Quakers mightily value him.

Isaac Barrow
1630–77

Isaac Barrow came of a royalist family, but managed to retain a fellowship at Cambridge from 1649 to 1655, at a time when Commonwealth men dominated the university. He travelled in Europe and the Near East from 1655 to 1659, and it was only at the Restoration that his academic career was resumed. He published two distinguished mathematical books, on optics and geometry, but finding that these aroused little interest, devoted himself to theology. He became Master of Trinity in 1673.

His father, Thomas Barrow, was the second son of Isaac Barrow of Spinney Abbey in the county of Cambridge, esquire, who was a Justice of the Peace there above forty years. The father of Thomas never designed him for a tradesman, but he was so severe to him he could not endure to live with him, and so came to London and was apprentice to a linen-draper. He kept shop at the sign of the White Horse in Forster Lane near St Forster's Church in St Leonard's parish; and his son, Isaac Barrow was christened at St John Zachery's in Forster Lane, for at that time St Leonard's church was pulled down to be re-edified. He was born anno Domini 1630 in October after King Charles II.

Dr Isaac Barrow had the exact day and hour from his father, which may be found among his papers. His father set it down in his English bible, a fair one, which they used at the king's chapel when he was in France and he could not get it again. His father travelled with the King, Charles II, whenever he went; he was sealer to the lord chancellor beyond sea [during the king's exile], and also when he came into England.

He went to school, first to Mr Brookes at Charterhouse two years. His father gave to Mr Brookes £4 per annum, whereas his pay was but £2, to be careful of him; but Mr Brookes was negligent of him, which the captain of the school acquainted his father (his kinsman) and said that he would not have him stay there any longer than he himself did, for the captain instructed him: afterwards to one Mr Holbitch, about four years, at Felsted in Essex: from whence he was admitted of Peterhouse College in Cambridge first, and went to school a year after. Then he was admitted of Trinity College in Cambridge at thirteen years old.

His humour when a boy and after: merry and cheerful and beloved whenever he came. His grandfather kept him till he was seven years old: his father was fain to force him away, for he would have been good for nothing there.

A good poet, English and Latin. He spoke eight several languages.

His father dealt in his trade to Ireland, where he had a great loss, near £1000; upon which he wrote to Mr Holbitch, a Puritan, to be pleased to take a little pains more than ordinary with him, because the times growing so bad, and such a loss then received, he did not know how he might be able to provide for him, and so Mr Holbitch took him away from the house where he was boarded to his own house, and made him tutor to my lord Viscount Fairfax, ward of the lord Viscount Say and Sele, where he continued so long as my lord continued.

(This Viscount Fairfax died a young man.) This Viscount Fairfax, being a schoolboy, married a gentleman's daughter in the town there, who had but a thousand pounds. So leaving the school, would needs have Mr Isaac Barrow with him, and told him he would maintain him.

But the Lord Say was so cruel to Fairfax that he would not allow anything, that 'tis thought he died for want. (The thousand pounds could not serve him long.)

During this time Mr Thomas Barrow was shut up at Oxford and could not hear of his son. But young Isaac's master, Holbitch, found him out in London and courted him to come to his school and that he would make him his heir. But he did not care to go to the school again. When my Lord Fairfax ran into debt and that he grew heavy upon him, he went to see one of his schoolfellows, one Mr Walpole (a Norfolk gent.) who asked him 'What would he do?' He replied that 'he knew not what to do; he could not go to his father at Oxford'. Mr Walpole then told him 'I am going to Cambridge to Trinity College and I will maintain you there'; and so he did for half a year till the surrender of Oxford: and then his father enquired after him and found him at Cambridge. And the very next day after old Mr Barrow came to Cambridge, Mr Walpole was leaving the University, and (hearing nothing of Isaac's father) resolved to take Isaac along with him to his house. His father then asked him what profession he would be of, a merchant or etc? He begged of his father to let him continue in the University. His father then asked what would maintain him. He told him £20 per annum: 'I warrant you,' said he, 'I will maintain myself with it.' His father replied, 'I'll make a shift to allow you that.' So his father then went to his tutor and acquainted him of all this. His tutor, Dr Duport, told him that he would take nothing for his lectures, for that he was likely to make a brave scholar, and he would help him to half a chamber for nothing. And the next news his father heard of him was that he was made a fellow of the college. Dr Hill was then master of the college. He met Isaac one day and laid his hand upon his head and said: 'Thou art a good boy; 'tis pity that thou art a cavalier.'

He was a strong and a stout man, and feared not any man. He would fight with the butchers' boys in St Nicholas' shambles, and be hard enough for any of them.

He went to travel three or four years after the king was beheaded, upon the college account [because the college threatened to expel him as a royalist?]. He was a candidate for the Greek professor's place, but Oliver Cromwell put in Dr Widrington; and then he travelled.

He was abroad five years, viz in Italy, France, Germany, Constantinople. As he went to Constantinople, two men-of-war (Turkish ships) attacked the vessel wherein he was. In which engagement he showed much valour in defending the vessel; which the men that were in that engagement often testify, for he never told his father of it himself. Upon his return, he came in a ship to Venice, which was stowed with cotton wool, and as soon as ever they came on shore the ship fell on fire and was utterly consumed, and not a man lost, but not any goods saved—a wonderful preservation.

His personal valour: at Constantinople, being in company with the English merchants there was a boaster that would fight with any man and bragged of his valour, and dared any man there to try him. So no man accepting his challenge, said Isaac (not then a divine) 'Why, if none else will try you, I will'; and fell upon him and chastised him handsomely, so that he vaunted no more amongst them.

After he had been three years beyond sea, his correspondent died, so that he had no more supply of money; yet he was so well beloved that he never wanted. At Constantinople, he waited on the consul, Sir Thomas Bendish, who kept him there a year and a half whether he would or no.

At Constantinople, Mr Dawes (afterwards Sir Jonathan Dawes, who died Sheriff of London), a Turkey merchant, desired Mr Barrow to stay but such a time and he would return to England with him, but when that time came he could not go; some business detained him. Mr Barrow could stay no longer; so Mr Dawes would have had Mr Barrow have a hundred gold coins. 'No,' said Mr Barrow, 'I know not whether I shall be able to pay you.' ''Tis no matter,' said Mr Dawes. To be short, he forced him to take fifty pistols, which at his return he paid him again.

Memorandum, his pill (an opiate, possibly Matthews his pill), which he was wont to take in Turkey, which was wont to do him good; but he took it excessively at Mr Wilson's, the saddler's (near Suffolk House) where he was wont to lie and where he died, and 'twas the cause of his death. As he lay expiring in the agony of death, the standers-by could hear him say softly 'I have seen the glories of the world.'

I have heard Mr Wilson say that when he was at study, he was so intent at it that when the bed was made, or so, he heeded it not nor perceived it, was so completely absorbed; and would sometimes be going out without his hat on. He was by no means a spruce man, but most negligent in his dress. As he was walking one day in St James's Park, his hat up, his cloak half on and half off, a gent. came behind him and clapped him on the shoulder and said, 'Well, go thy ways for the veriest scholar that ever I met with.'

He was a strong man, but pale as the candle he studied by.

Thomas Batchcroft
?–1670

Master of Gonville and Caius College, Cambridge, 1625–70: ejected under the Commonwealth (1649–60)

Memorandum: in Sir Charles Scarborough's time (he was of Caius College) Dr Batchcroft (the head of that house) would visit the boys' chambers and see what they were studying; and Charles Scarborough's genius led him to mathematics, and he was wont to be reading Clavius on Euclid. The old Doctor had found on the title page '. . . *e Societate Jesu*'* and was much scandalised at it. Said he, 'By all means leave off this author and read Protestant mathematical books.' Someone sent this doctor a pigeon pie from Newmarket or thereabouts, and he asked the bearer whether it was hot or cold. He did outdo Dr Kettell.

Francis Beaumont
1584–1616

Francis Beaumont and John Fletcher began their partnership as playwrights in 1605, and during the next ten years wrote many pieces together, of which The Knight of the Burning Pestle, *a satire on heroic plays, is perhaps the best remembered.*

Mr Francis Beaumont was the son of Judge Beaumont. There was a wonderful sameness of fancy between him and Mr John Fletcher, which caused that dearness of friendship between them. I think they were both of Queen's College in Cambridge. I have heard Dr John Earles (since Bishop of Salisbury), who knew them, say that his main business was to correct the overflowings of Mr Fletcher's wit. They lived together on the Bankside, not far from the playhouse, both bachelors; lay together (from Sir James Hales) etc; had one wench in the house between them, which they did so admire; the same clothes and cloak, etc, between them. He wrote (among many others) an admirable elegy on the countess of Rutland, which is printed with verses before Sir Thomas Overbury's *Characters*. John Earles, in his verses on him, speaking of them.

> 'A monument that will then lasting be,
> When all her marble is more dust than she.'

¶ Mr John Fletcher, poet: in the great plague, 1625, a knight of Norfolk (or Suffolk) invited him into the country. He stayed but to make himself a suit of clothes, and while it was making, fell sick of the plague and died. This I had (1669) from his tailor, who is now a very old man and clerk of St Mary Overy's.

* i.e. Clavius was a Jesuit. *Ed.*

Sir Henry Billingsley
?–1606

This is one of Aubrey's projected Lives of English Mathematicians. *Billingsley studied at Cambridge and went on to make a successful career in the City: he was Lord Mayor in 1596, and M.P. in 1603–4.*

This Sir Henry Billingsley was one of the learnedest citizens that London has bred. This was he that put forth all Euclid's *Elements of Geometry* in English with learned notes and a preface by Mr John Dee, and learned men say it is the best Euclid. He had been Sheriff and Lord Mayor of the City of London. His house was the fair house in Fenchurch Street, where now Jacob Luce lives, a merchant.

Memorandum: P. Ramus in his *Scholia* says that the reason why mathematics did most flourish in Germany was that the best authors were rendered into their mother tongue, and that public lectures of it were also read in their own tongue.

Memorandum: when I was a boy Sir . . . Billingsley had a very pleasant seat with an oak wood adjoining it, about one and a half miles east of Bristol; enquire if he was Sir Henry's descendant.

See on Sir Thomas Billingsley; enquire if descended from Sir Henry.

¶ (Sir Thomas Billingsley was the best horseman in England, and out of England no man exceeded him. He taught the earl of Dorset and his thirty gentlemen to ride the great horse. He taught the Elector Palatine of the Rhine and his brothers*. He ended his days at the Countess of Thanet's, the earl's daughter; died praying on his knees.)

¶ In those days merchants travelled much abroad into Italy and Spain. Ask Mr Abraham Hill of what Company he was. Probably good memorials may be there found of his generous and public spirit. He answers: he was of the Goldsmith's Company, where there is a good picture of him.

¶ Many years since, Mr Abraham Hill, FRS, citizen, told me that Sir Henry Billingsley was of the Goldsmith's Company, and that his picture was in Goldsmith's Hall, which I went lately to see. No picture of him, and besides the clerk of the Company told me he is sure he was never of that company. But Mr Hill tells me since that in Stowe's Survey you may see of what company all the Lord Mayors were.

¶ Friar Whitehead, of Austin Friars (now Wadham College) did instruct him. He (i.e. Billingsley) kept him at his house, and there I think he died.

---

* Charles-Louis and his brothers Prince Rupert and Prince Maurice. *Ed.*

Sir John Birkenhead

1615-79

As founder of Mercurius Aulicus, *Birkenhead ranks as one of the first journalists of distinction. He went with Charles II into exile, but moved between France and England under the Commonwealth.*

Sir John Birkenhead, knight, was born at Northwich in Cheshire. His father was a saddler there, and he had a brother, a saddler, who was a trooper in Sir Thomas Ashton's regiment, who was quartered at my father's, who told me so.

He went to Oxford University at fifteen years old, and was first a servitor at Oriel College. Mr Gwyn, minister of Wilton, was his contemporary there, who told me he wrote an excellent hand, and in 1637 or 8, when William Laud, Archbishop of Canterbury was last there, he had occasion to have some things well transcribed, and this Birkenhead was recommended to him, who performed his business so well, that the archbishop recommended him to All Soul's College to be a fellow, and he was accordingly elected.

After Edgehill fight, when King Charles I first had his court at Oxford, he was chosen as someone fit to write the news; the Oxford newspaper was called *Mercurius Aulicus** which he wrote wittily enough till the surrender of the town (which was on June 24th, 1646). He left a collection of all his *Mercurius Aulicus*'s and all his other pamphlets, which his executors (Sir Richard Mason and Sir Muddiford Bramston) were ordered by the king to give to the Archbishop of Canterbury's library.

After the surrender of Oxford, he was put out of his fellowship by the Visitors, and had to shift for himself as well as he could. The most part of his time he spent at London, where he met with several persons of quality who loved his company, and made much of him.

He went over into France, where he stayed some time, not long, I think. He received grace there from the duchess of Newcastle, I remember he told me.

He got many forty shillings (I believe) by writing pamphlets such as that of 'Col. Pride' and 'The Last Will and Testament of Philip earl of Pembroke' etc.

At the restoration of his majesty, he was made Master of the Faculties, and afterwards one of the Masters of Requests. He was exceedingly confident, witty, not grateful to his benefactors, would lie damnably. He was of middling stature, great goggly eyes, not of a sweet aspect.

He was chosen a burgess of parliament at Wilton in Wiltshire in 1661, i.e. of the King's long parliament. In 1679, on the choosing of

* Roughly, *The Court Messenger. Ed.*

39

this present parliament, he went down to be elected and at Salisbury heard how he was scorned and mocked at Wilton (where he was going), and called *Pensioner* etc; he went not to the borough where he intended to stand, but returned to London and took it so to heart that he gradually decayed and pined away; and so died at his lodgings in Whitehall in December 1679, and was buried on Saturday December 6 in St Martin's Churchyard in the Fields.†

He had the art of remembering places; and his surroundings were the chambers in All Souls College (about 100), so that for a hundred errands he would easily remember. He was created DCL because he had been with the king. His library was sold to Sir Robert Atkins for £200, his manuscripts, (chiefly copies of records) for £900.

Henry Birkhead
1617–96

Remembered as a writer of Latin verse, and founder of the professorship of poetry at Oxford, which was established in 1708 from funds bequeathed by him.

From a letter to Thomas Tanner, November 21, 1696: My old acquaintance, Dr Henry Birkhead, formerly fellow of your college (but first was commoner of Trinity College, Oxford), was an universally beloved man. He had his school education under Mr Farnaby, and was his beloved disciple. He died at the Bird-Cage (at his sister's, Mrs Knight, the famous singer) in St James's Park on Michaelmas eve 1696, aged almost 80.

He was born in London at the Paul's head tavern (which his father kept) in Paul's chain in St Paul's churchyard in 1617; he was baptised on the 25th September. John Gadbury has [astrological details of] his nativity from him.

I will ask his sister (Mrs Knight) for a very ingenious diatribe that he wrote on Martial's epigram *'Jura verpe, per Anchialum'* which he has made clear beyond his master Farnaby, Scaliger or any other. 'Scaliger,' he said, 'speaks the truth, but not the whole truth.' 'Tis pity it should be lost, and I would deposit it in the Ashmolean Museum.

I gave my Holyoke's Dictionary to the Museum. Pray look on the blank leaves at the end of it, and you will find a thundering copy of verses that he gave me, in the praise of this king (Louis XIV) of France. Now he is dead, it may be looked upon.

† His reason (for not being buried in the church as a man of rank—*Ed.*) was because he said they removed the bodies out of the church.

Robert Blake
1599–1657

Admiral under the Commonwealth. He made his reputation as a commander on land in 1642–4, culminating in his defence of Lyme in Dorset and capture of Taunton in 1644, which he held during a year's siege in 1644–5. He was commander of the fleet from 1649 onwards, and fought the Dutch under van Tromp; he campaigned in the Mediterranean from 1655 until 1657, culminating in a great victory over the Spanish at Santa Cruz in the three months before his death on the voyage home.

Robert Blake, admiral, was born in Somerset; he was at St Alban Hall in Oxford. He was there a young man of strong body, and good parts. He was an early riser, and studied well, but also took his robust pleasures of fishing, fowling etc. He would steal swans—from H. Norborne, BD, his contemporary there.

He served in the House of Commons for Bridgewater in 1640. In 1649, he was made admiral. He did the greatest actions at sea that were ever done.

Blake died in 1657, and was buried in King Henry VII's chapel; but upon the return of the king, his body was taken up again and removed; Mr Wells had this done, and where it is now, I know not. Ask Mr Wells of Bridgewater.

Sir Henry Blount
1602–82

Though Aubrey hardly mentions his adventures abroad, Blount was one of the most-travelled men of his age; he had explored the Balkans and Egypt in 1634, and wrote Voyage to the Levant *on his return, which was an immediate success, and went through eight editions in his lifetime.*

Sir Henry Blount, knight: he was born (I presume) at Tittenhanger in the county of Hertford. It was heretofore the summer seat of the Lord Abbot of St Albans.

He was of Trinity College in Oxford, where was a great acquaintance between him and Mr Francis Potter. He stayed there about four years. From thence he went to Gray's Inn, where he stayed, and then sold his chamber there to Mr Thomas Bonham (the poet) and travelled—voyage into the Levant. 7 May 1634 he embarked at Venice for Constantinople:

vide his *Voyage into the Levant*.

He was pretty wild when young, especially addicted to common wenches. He was a second brother: he was a gentleman pensioner to King Charles I, on whom he waited (as it was his turn) to York (when the king deserted the parliament); was with him at Edgehill fight; came with him to Oxford; and so returned to London; walked into Westminster Hall with his sword by his side; the parliamentarians all stared upon him as a *Cavalier*, knowing that he had been with the king; was called before the House of Commons, where he remonstrated to them that he only did his duty, and so they acquitted him.

In those days he dined most commonly at the Haycocks inn, near the Palsgrave Head tavern in the Strand, which was much frequented by parliament men and gallants. One time Colonel Bettridge being there (one of the handsomest men about the town) and bragged how much the women loved him; Sir H. Blount did lay a wager with him that 'let them two go together to a bordello; he only (without money) with his handsome person, and Sir Henry with a twenty-shilling piece on his bald crown, that the wenches should choose Sir Henry before Bettridge'; and Sir H. won the wager. Edmund Wyld esquire was one of the witnesses.

Memorandum: there was about 164 . . . a pamphlet (written by Henry Nevill esquire, *anonymously*) called *The Parliament of Ladies*, three or four sheets in quarto, wherein Sir Henry Blount was first to be called to the bar for spreading abroad that abominable and dangerous doctrine that it was far cheaper and safer to be with common wenches than with ladies of quality.

Anno Domini 1652 he was made one of the committee for regulating the laws. He was severe against tithes, and for the abolishing of them, and that every minister should have £100 per annum and no more.

Since he was . . . years old, he drank nothing but water and coffee. 1647 or thereabouts he married Mrs Hester Wase, who died 1679; by whom he has two sons, ingenious young gentlemen. Charles Blount (his second son) has written *Anima Mundi* (burnt by order of the Bishop of London) and of *Sacrifices*.

I remember twenty years since he inveighed much against sending youths to the universities—query if his sons were there—because they learnt there to be debauched; and that the learning that they learned there they were to unlearn again, as a man that is buttoned or laced too hard must unbutton before he can be at his ease. Drunkenness he much exclaimed against, but he allowed wenching. When coffee first came in he was a great upholder of it, and has ever since been a constant frequenter of coffee houses, especially Mr Farr at the Rainbow by Inner Temple Gate and lately John's coffee house in Fuller's Rents.

The first coffee house in London was in St Michael's Alley in

Cornhill, opposite to the church; which was set up by one Bowman (coachman to Mr Hodges, a Turkey merchant, who suggested it) in or about the year 1652. 'Twas about four years before any other was set up, and that was by Mr Farr. Jonathan Paynter, opposite to St Michael's Church, was the first apprentice to the trade, viz to Bowman. Memorandum: the Bagnio in Newgate Street, was built and first opened in December 1679: built by Turkish merchants.

He is a gentleman of a very clear judgement, and great experience, much contemplation, not of very much reading, of great foresight into government; his conversation is admirable. When he was young, he was a great collector of books, as his son is now.

He was heretofore a great *shammer*, i.e. one that tells falsities not to do anybody any injury, but to impose on their understanding: e.g. at Mr Farr's: he said that at an inn (naming the sign) in St Albans, the innkeeper had made a hog's trough of a free-stone coffin; but the pigs, after that, grew lean, dancing and skipping, and would run up on the tops of the houses like goats. Two young gentlemen that heard Sir H. tell this *sham* so gravely, rode next day to St Albans to enquire; coming there, nobody had heard of any such thing, 'twas altogether false. The next night, as soon as they alighted, they came to the Rainbow, found Sir H., looked threateningly on him, and told him they wondered he was not ashamed to tell such stories. 'Why, gentlemen,' said Sir H. 'have you been there to make enquiry?' 'Yea,' said they. 'Why truly, gentlemen,' said Sir H. 'I heard you tell strange things that I knew to be false. I would not have gone over the threshold to have caught you out lying:' at which all the company laughed at the two young gentlemen.

He was wont to say that he did not care to have his servants go to church, for there servants infected one another to go to the alehouse and learn debauchery; but he did bid them go to see the executions at Tyburn, which work more upon them than all the oratory in the sermons.

His motto over his printed picture is that which I have many years ago heard him speak of, viz: *Speaking is for the mob, perceiving for the wise.*

He is now (1680) near of altogether eighty years, his intellectuals good still, and body pretty strong.

This last week of September 1682, he was taken very ill at London, and his feet swelled; and removed to Tittenhanger.

¶ Sir Henry Blount died 9 October (1682) last in the morning.

43

Edmund Bonner
1495–1569

Bishop of London under Henry VIII, Bonner was imprisoned under Edward VI for refusing to acknowledge fully the royal supremacy over the Church. He led the Counter-Reformation movement under Mary, and was responsible for the burning of a number of Protestants. On Elizabeth's accession, he was imprisoned again, and died in Marshalsea prison.

Mr Stephens, whom I met lately accidentally, informed me thus: that Bishop Bonner was of Pembroke College; that he came thither a poor boy, and was at first a scullion boy in the kitchen, afterwards became a servitor, and so by his industry raised to what he was.

When he came to his greatness, in acknowledgement from whence he had his rise, he gave to the kitchen there a great brass pot, called Bonner's pot.* He has showed the pot to me, I remember. It was the biggest pot, perhaps, in Oxford: ask the old cook how much it contained.

James Bovey

James Bovey esq. was the youngest son of Andrew Bovey, merchant, cash-keeper to Sir Peter Vanore in London. He was born in the middle of Mincing Lane, in the parish of St Dunstan's in the East, London in 1622, on May 7th, at six o'clock in the morning. Went to school at Mercers' Chapel under Mr Augur. At 9 he was sent into the Low Countries; then returned, and perfected himself in the Latin and Greek. At 14, travelled into France and Italy, Switzerland, Germany and the Low Countries. Returned into England at 19; then lived with one Hoste, a banker, 8 years, was his cashier for 8 or 9 years. Then he traded for himself, aged 27, till he was 31; then married the only daughter of William de Vischer, a merchant; lived 18 years with her, then continued single. Left off trade at 32, and retired to a country life, by reason of his indisposition, the air of the city not agreeing with him. Then, in this retirement, he wrote *Negotiative Philosophy* [i.e. a manual on business practice] (a thing not done before) wherein are enumerated all the arts and tricks practised in negotiation, and how they were to be balanced by precautionary rules.

While he lived with Mr Hoste, he kept the cash of the ambassadors of

---

* Anthony Wood notes against this 'false', presumably because he had made his own enquiries and could not find any evidence for the story. *Ed.*

Spain that were here; and the agents called by them *Assentists*, who supplied the Spanish and Imperial armies in the Low Countries and Germany; and also many other large sums of cash, such as that of Sir Theodore Mayerer, etc; his dealing being altogether in money matters; by which means he became acquainted with the ministers of state both here and abroad.

When he was abroad, his chief employment was to observe the affairs of the state and their judicature and to survey the politics in the countries he travelled through, more especially in relation to trade. He speaks Dutch, German, French, Italian, Spanish, dialects and Latin, besides his own language.

When he retired from business he studied merchant law and admitted himself to the Inner Temple, London, about 1660. His judgement has been taken in most of the great causes of his time in points concerning the merchant law. As to his person, he is about 4 foot tall, slender, straight, hair exceeding black and curling at the end, a dark hazel eye, of a middling size, but the most sprightly that I have beheld. Brows and beard of the same colour as his hair. A person of great temperance and deep thoughts, and a working head, never idle. From 14 he had a candle burning by him all night, with pen, ink and paper, to write down thoughts as they came into his head; that in this way he might not lose a thought. He was ever a great lover of natural philosophy. His whole life has been perplexed by law-suits (which has made him expert in human affairs), in which he always overcame. He had many lawsuits with powerful adversaries; one lasted 18 years. Red-haired men never had any kindness for him. He used to say 'Beneath a red head there is never a mind without malice'. In all his travels he was never robbed.

He has one son, and one daughter who resembles him. From 14 he began to take notice of all the rules for prudent conduct that came his way, and wrote them down, and so continued to this day, September 28, 1680, being now in his 59th year. As to his health, he never had it very well, but indifferently, always a weak stomach, which proceeded from the agitation of the brain. His diet was always fine diet; much chicken.

He made it his business to advance the trade of England, and many men have printed his conceptions.

Richard Boyle

first Earl of Cork, 1566–1643

Landing as an almost penniless lawyer in Dublin in 1588, Richard Boyle built up a great estate in County Cork, which he managed with skill and efficiency: Cromwell commented that if every province in Ireland had had a Boyle to look after it, the Irish would never have rebelled. His success in this direction led to a political career, in which he rose to be Lord High Treasurer of Ireland. However, when Strafford became Lord Deputy in 1633, Boyle found himself in conflict with him, and effectively withdrew from politics.

Thomas, Earl of Strafford, made him disgorge £1500 per annum, which he restored to the church.

The Earl of Cork bought of Captain Horsey *forty ploughlands** in Ireland for forty pounds. (A. Ettrick assures me, 'I say again forty ploughlands')

¶ *Aubrey elsewhere quotes at length from the funeral sermon of his daughter Mary, preached, and later published, by Anthony Walker:*

Richard, the first Earl of Cork . . . being born a private gentleman, and younger brother of a younger brother, to no other heritage then is expressed in the device and motto, which his humble gratitude inscribed in all the palaces he built,

God's Providence, mine Inheritance.

By that Providence, and his diligent and wise industry, raised such an honour and estate, and left such a family, as never any subject of these three kingdoms did, and that with so unspotted a reputation of integrity that the most invidious scrutiny could find no blot, though it winnowed all the methods of his rising most severely, which our good lady (his daughter) hath often told me with great content and satisfaction.

This noble lord, by his prudent and pious consort, no less an ornament and honour to their descendants than himself, was blessed with five sons, of which he lived to see four lords and peers of the Kingdom of Ireland.

And a fifth, more than these titles speak, a sovereign and peerless in a larger province—that of universal nature, subdued and made obsequious to his inquisitive mind.

And eight daughters.

And that you may remark how all things were extraordinary in this great personage, it will, I hope, be neither unpleasant nor impertinent, to add a short story I had from our lady's own mouth.

Master Boyle, after Earl of Cork (who was then a widower) came one morning to wait on Sir Jeffrey Fenton, at that time a great officer of state in that Kingdom of Ireland, who being engaged in business, and not knowing who it was desired to speak with him, a while delayed him access; which time he spent pleasantly with his young daughter in her nurse's arms. But when Sir Jeffrey came, and saw whom he had made

* About 4800 acres. *Ed.*

stay somewhat too long, he civilly excused it. But Master Boyle replied, he had been very well entertained, and spent his time much to his satisfaction, in courting his daughter, if he might obtain the honour to be accepted for his son-in-law. At which Sir Jeffrey, smiling (to hear one who had been formerly married, move for a wife carried in arms, and under two years old) asked him if he would stay for her? To which he frankly answered him he would, and Sir Jeffrey as generously promised him he should then have his consent. And they both kept their words honourably.

¶ My lady Petty says he had a wife or two before, and that he married Mistress Fenton without her father's consent.

Robert Boyle
1627–91

One of the pioneers of English scientific research, and a member of the council of the Royal Society from its foundation in 1663. His most famous work was the statement of Boyle's law (that the volume of a gas varies inversely as the pressure), one of the basic theorems of modern physics. His main interest was, however, chemistry, where he transformed the old concepts of the alchemists into the foundations of modern chemical knowledge. Yet he still pursued the alchemists' traditional quest for a means of transmuting base metals into gold. His other great enthusiasm was for theology, on which he wrote a number of books.

The honourable Robert Boyle esq., the son of Richard Boyle, the first Earl of Cork, was born at Lismore in the county of Cork. He was nursed by an Irish nurse, after the Irish manner, where they put the child in a pendulous satchel instead of a cradle, with a slit for the child's head to peep out.

¶ When a boy at Eton, he was very sickly and pale—from Dr Wood, who was his school-fellow.

¶ He went to the University of Leyden. Travelled France, Italy, Switzerland. I have oftentimes heard him say that after he had seen the antiquities and architecture of Rome he cared not for nor esteemed none anywhere else. He speaks Latin very well, and very readily, as most men I have met with. I have heard him say that when he was young, he read over Cowper's dictionary: wherein I think he did very well, and I believe he is much beholding to him for his mastership of that language. His father in his will, when he comes to the settlement and provision for his son Robert, thus—'*Item, to my son Robert, whom I*

47

beseech God to bless with a particular blessing, I bequeath, etc.' Mr R. H.,
who has seen the rental, says it was £3000 per annum: the greatest part
is in Ireland. His father left him the manor of Stallbridge in Dorset,
where is a great freestone house; it was forfeited by the Earl of
Castlehaven.

He is very tall (about six foot high) and straight, very temperate, and
virtuous and frugal: a bachelor; keeps a coach; sojourns with his sister,
the Lady Ranelagh. His greatest delight is chemistry. He has at his
sister's a noble laboratory and several servants (apprentices to him) to
look after it. He is charitable to ingenious men that are in want, and
foreign chemists have had large proof of his bounty, for he will not
spare for cost to get any rare secret. At his own cost and charges he got
translated and printed the New Testament in Arabic, to send into the
Mahometan countries. He was not only a high renown in England, but
abroad; and when foreigners come hither, 'tis one of their curiosities to
make him a visit.

William, Lord Brereton
1631–80

William, Lord Brereton of Leighton: This virtuous and learned lord
(who was my most honoured and obliging friend) was educated at
Breda, by John Pell, DD, then mathematics professor there of the
Prince of Orange's 'illustrious school'. Sir George Goring, earl of
Norwich, (who was my lord's grandfather) did send for him to go over
there, where the Doctor (then Mr John Pell) took great care of him and
made him a very good algebrist.

He was an excellent musician and also a good composer.

Edward Brerewood
?1565–1613

Antiquary and mathematician.

He was of Brasenose College in Oxford. My old cousin Whitney, a
fellow there long since, told me, as I remember, that his father was a
citizen of West Chester; that (I have now forgotten on what occasion,
whether he had run through his allowance from his father, or what) but

he was for some time in straits in the College: that he went not out of the College gates in a good while, nor (I think) out of his chamber, but was in slippers, and wore out his gown and clothes on the board and benches of his chamber, but profited in knowledge wonderfully. He was astronomy professor at Gresham College, London.

'Tis pity I can pick up no more of him.

Henry Briggs
1561–1630

Mathematician.

He was first of St John's College in Cambridge. Sir Henry Savile sent for him and made him his geometry professor. He lived at Merton College in Oxford, where he made the sundials at the buttresses of the east end of the chapel with a bullet for the axis.

He travelled into Scotland to commune with the honourable John Napier of Merchiston about making the logarithmical tables.

Looking once on the map of England, he observes that the two rivers, the Thames and that Avon which runs to Bath and so to Bristol, were not far distant, i.e. about 3 miles—see the map. He sees 'twas but about 25 miles from Oxford; gets a horse and views it and finds it to be a level ground and easy to be digged. Then he considers the charge of cutting between them and the convenience of making a marriage between those rivers which would be of great consequence for cheap and safe carrying of goods between London and Bristol, and though the boats go slowly and with meanders, yet considering they go day and night, they would be at their journey's end almost as soon as the waggons, which are often overthrown and liquors spilt and other goods broken. Not long after this he died and the civil wars broke out. It happened by good luck that one Mr Matthews of Dorset had some acquaintance with this Mr Briggs and had heard him discourse on it. He was an honest simple man, and had spent all his inheritance, and this project did much run in his head. He wanted to revive it (or else it had been lost and forgotten) and went into the country to make an ill survey of it (which he printed) but with no great encouragement from the people of the country or others. Upon the restoration of King Charles II, he renewed his design, and applied himself to the king and council. His majesty espoused it more (he told me) than anyone else. In short, for want of management and his non-ability, it came to nothing and he is now dead of old age. But Sir Jonas Moore (an expert mathematician and a practical man) being sent to survey the manor of Dauntsey in Wilts (which was forfeited to the crown by Sir John Danvers's foolery), went to see these streams and distances. He told me the streams were too small except in winter; but if some prince or the parliament would raise money to cut through the hill by Wooton Bassett, then there would be water enough and streams big enough. He worked out the cost, which I have forgotten, but I think it was about £200,000.

Elizabeth Broughton

Mrs Elizabeth Broughton was daughter of an ancient family in Herefordshire. Her father lived at the manor house at Canon Pyon. Whether she was born there or not, I know not; but there she lost her maidenhead to a poor young fellow, then, I believe, handsome, but, in 1660, a pitiful poor old weaver, clerk of the parish. He had fine curled hair, but grey. Her father at length discovered her inclinations, and locked her up in a turret of the house; but she gets down by a rope; and away she got to London, and did set up for herself.

She was a most exquisite beauty, as finely shaped as nature could frame; and had a delicate wit. She was soon taken notice of at London, and her price was very dear—a second Thais.* Richard, earl of Dorset, kept her (whether before or after Venetia,† I know not, but I guess before). At last she grew commoner and infamous, and got the pox, of which she died.

I remember this much of an old song of those days which I have seen in a collection—'twas by way of litany:

> From the watch at twelve o'clock
> And from Bess Broughton's buttoned smock‡
> Good Lord, deliver us.

In Ben Jonson's execrations against Vulcan, he concludes thus:

> Pox take thee, Vulcan! May Pandora's pox
> And all the ills that flew out of her box
> Light on thee. And if those plagues will not do
> Thy wife's pox take thee, and *Bess Broughton's* too

In the first octavo edition her name is thus at length [given in full]. I see there have been famous women before our times.

> *Many strong men lived before Agamemnon*
>
> (Horace, Odes iv, 9)

---

* The famous courtesan of Alexandra. *Ed.*   † Venetia Stanley (*later* Digby). *Ed.*
‡ Barbara (countess of Castlemaine) had such a one; my sempstress helped to work it.

I do remember her father (1646), nearly 80, the handsomest shaped man that ever my eyes beheld, a very wise man and of an admirable elecution. He was a committee man in Herefordshire and Gloucestershire. He was commissary to colonel Massey. He was of the Puritan party heretofore; had a great gift in praying, etc. His wife (I have heard my grandmother say, who was her neighbour) was as talented as him. He was the first that used to improve his land by spreading soap-ashes, when he lived at Bristol, where they threw them away at that time.

William Brouncker
1620–84

Mathematician and founder-member of the Royal Society in 1662 of which he was President from the beginning. He was a friend of Evelyn, and worked with Pepys at the Navy Office from 1664–1679.

William Brouncker, lord viscount of Castle Lyons in Ireland: he lived in Oxford when 'twas a garrison for the king; but he was of no university, he told me. He addicted himself only to the study of the mathematics, and was a very great artist in that learning.

His mother was an extraordinary great gamester, and played all games, gold play [for stakes in gold]; she kept the box [bank?] herself. Mr Arundel (brother of the lord Wardour) made a song of the characters of the nobility. Among others, I remember this:

> Here's a health to my Lady Brouncker, and the best card in her
> hand,
> And a health to my lord her husband, with ne'er a foot of land.

He was president of the Royal Society about fifteen years. He was of the Navy Office.

He died April 5th 1684; buried on the 14th following in the middle of the choir of St Katherine's near the Tower, of which he was a governor. He gave a fine organ to this church a little before his death; and whereas it was a noble and large choir, he divided it in the middle with a good screen (at his own charge) which has spoiled it.

Sir Richard Bulkeley
1644–1710

Fellow of the Royal Society.

He was a gentleman of large estate in Ireland; but unhappily plunged into debt, by supporting a set of enthusiastic pretenders to prophecy, whose first spawn appeared amonst the seditious and rebellious French Camisards and Huguenots, with whom he engaged so deeply, that not only his estate partly supplied their extravagances, but he prostituted his excellent pen in defence of their frenzy, and misapplied a great capacity and good sense, by submitting them to their groundless delusions.

Robert Burton
1577–1640

The author of The Anatomy of Melancholy, *a brilliant if eccentric book which defies classification.*

Mr Robert Hooke of Gresham College told me that he lay in the chamber in Christ Church that was Mr Burton's, of whom 'tis whispered that notwithstanding all his astrology and his book of melancholy, he ended his days in that chamber by hanging himself.

Thomas Bushell
1594–1674

Thomas Bushell was a protégé of Francis Bacon, and learnt from him a great deal about the science of mining and metals, which after Bacon's fall from power in 1621, he tried to put to practical use, with varying success: his operations in Wales were the most important, and resulted in a revival of the Welsh silver mines.

He was one of the gentlemen that waited on the Lord Chancellor Bacon. 'Twas the fashion in those days for gentlemen to have their suits of clothes garnished with buttons. My lord Bacon was then in disgrace, and his man Bushell having more buttons than usual on his cloak, they said that his lord's breech made buttons and Bushell wore them—from whence he was called 'buttoned Bushell'. He was only an English scholar [i.e. knew no Latin], but had a good wit and a working and contemplative head. His lordship much loved him. His genius lay most towards natural philosophy, and particularly towards the discovery, draining and improvement of the silver mines in Cardiganshire.

He had the strangest bewitching way to draw in people (yea, discreet and wary men) into his projects that ever I heard of. His tongue was a chain and drew in so many to be bound for him and to be engaged in his designs that he ruined a number.

Mr Bushell was the greatest arts-master to run in debt (perhaps) in the world. He died one hundred and twenty thousand pounds in debt; and lived so long that his debts were forgotten, so that they were the great-grandchildren of the creditors.

He wrote a stitched treatise of mines and improving of the ventilation to them and bellows to drive in wind, which Sir John Danvers, his acquaintance, had, and nailed it* to his parlour wall at Chelsea, with some scheme, and I believe is there yet: I saw it there about ten years since.

During the time of the Civil Wars, he lived in Lundy island. In 1647 or 8, he came over into England; and when he landed at Chester, and had but one Spanish threepence (this I had from a gentleman of Great Tew, to whom he told it), said he, 'I could have been contented to have begged a penny, like a poor man.' At that time he said he owed I forget whether it was fifty or sixty thousand pounds; but he was like Sir Kenelm Digby, if he had not fourpence, wherever he came he would find respect and credit.

Memorandum, after his master the lord chancellor died, he married and lived at Easton in Oxfordshire; where having some land lying on the hanging of a hill facing the south, at the foot whereof runs a fine clear stream which petrifies,† and where is a pleasant solitude, he spoke to his servant Jack Sydenham to get a labourer to clear some boscage which grew on the side of the hill and also to dig a cavity in the hill to sit, and read or contemplate. The workman had not worked an hour before he discovered not only a rock, but a rock of an unusual figure with pendants like icicles as at Wookey Hole (Somerset) which was the occasion of making that delicate grotto and those fine walks: here in fine weather he would walk all night. Jack Sydenham‡ sang rarely: so did

---

* Perhaps as counterfeit coins used to be nailed to shop counters, because Danvers had lost money in the scheme? *Ed.*

† Leaves a hard deposit on anything left in the water. *Ed.*

‡ Lived before with Sir Charles Snell at Kington St Michael. He was wont to carry me in his arms: a graceful servant. He gave me this account.

his other servant, Mr Batty. They were very gentlemanly in clothes, and he loved them as his children. He did not encumber himself with his wife, but here enjoyed himself thus in this paradise till the war broke out, and then retired to Lundy isle.

He had done something (I have forgotten what) that made him obnoxious to the parliament or Oliver Cromwell, about 1650; would have been hanged if taken; printed several letters to the Parliament etc dated from beyond sea, and all that time lay privately in his house in Lambeth marsh where the pointed pyramid is. In the garret there, is a long gallery, which he hung all with black, and had some death's heads and bones painted. At the end where his couch was, was in an old Gothic niche (like an old monument) painted a skeleton incumbent on a mat. At the other end, where was his pallet-bed, was an emaciated dead man stretched out. Here he had several mortifying and divine mottoes (he imitated his lord [Bacon] as much as he could) and out of his windows a very pleasant prospect. At night he walked in the garden and orchard. Only Mr Sydenham, and an old trusty woman, was privy to his being in England.

He died about 1676 or 1677, in Scotland Yard near Whitehall; Mr Beach the Quaker can tell me exactly. He was 80 years of age.

His entertainment to Queen Henrietta Maria [wife of Charles I] at Euston was in anno 1636. Insert, i.e. sew in my book (which Jack Sydenham gave my grandfather Isaac Lyte) in this place. Goodall of Christ Church, Oxford composed the music; I remember the student of Christ Church which sang the songs (I now forget his name).

Mr Bushell had a daughter married to a merchant in Bristol.

He was a handsome proper gentleman when I saw him at his house aforesaid at Lambeth. He was about 70, but I should not have guessed him hardly 60. He had a perfect healthy constitution; fresh, ruddy face; hawk-nosed, and was temperate.

As he had the art of running in debt, so sometimes he was attacked and thrown into prison; but he would extricate himself again strangely.

Memorandum: in the time of the civil wars, his hermitage over the rocks at Euston was hung with black baize; his bed had black curtains, etc, but it had no bedposts but hung by four cords (covered with black baize) instead of bedposts. When the queen mother came to Oxford to the king, she either brought (as I think) or somebody gave her an entire mummy from Egypt, a great rarity, which her majesty gave to Mr Bushell, but I believe long before this time the dampness of the place has spoiled it with mouldiness.

Memorandum: the grotto below looks just south; so that when it artificially rains upon the turning of a tap, you are entertained with a rainbow. In a very little pond (no bigger than a basin) opposite to the rock, and hard by, stood (1643, August 8) a Neptune, neatly cut in wood, holding his trident in his hand, and aiming with it at a duck which perpetually turned round him, and a spaniel swimming after her—which was very pretty, but long since spoiled. I hear that the Earl of Rochester, in whose possession it now is, keeps it very well in order.

¶ He had so delicate a way of making his projects alluring and feasible, profitable, that he drew to his baits not only rich men of no design, but also the craftiest knaves in the country, such who had cheated and undone others: e.g. Mr Goodyeere, who undid Mr Nicholas Mees' father.

¶ Mr E. W. says that he tapped the mountain of Snowdon in Wales, which was likely to have drowned all the country; and they were likely to knock him and his men on the head.

Query Dr Plott (author of *Antiquities of Oxfordshire*) of the book I gave him some years since of the songs and entertainment of Mr Bushell to Queen Henrietta Maria at his rocks. If he had not it, perhaps Anthony Wood had it.

Samuel Butler
1612–80

Trained as a painter by Samuel Cooper, Samuel Butler never settled to any particular career, acting as secretary to various country gentlemen. His fame came suddenly, in 1663, with the publication of the anti-puritan satire Hudibras, *which was an immediate success; the second and third parts appeared in 1664 and 1678. The poem was a great favourite with Charles II, who, however, did nothing to reward the author.*

Mr Samuel Butler was born in Worcestershire, hard by Bartonbridge, half a mile from Worcester, in the parish of St John, Mr Hill thinks, who went to school with him. His father was a man but of slender fortune, and to breed him at school was as much education as he was able to reach to. When but a boy he would make observations and reflections on everything one said or did, and censure it to be either well or ill. He never was at the University, for the reason alleged. He came when a young man to be a servant to the Countess of Kent, with whom he served several years. Here, besides his study, he employed his time much in painting and drawing, and also in music. He was thinking once to have made painting his profession—from Dr Duke. His love to and skill in painting made a great friendship between him and Mr Samuel Cooper (the prince of portrait painters of this age). He then studied the common laws of England, but did not practice. He married a well-endowed widow, the relict of one Morgan, by which means he lives comfortably.

After the restoration of his majesty when the court at Ludlow was again set up, he was then the king's steward at the castle there.

He printed a witty poem called *Hudibras*, the first part anno 1663, which took extremely; so that the king and Lord Chancellor Hyde would have him sent for, and accordingly he was sent for (the Lord Chancellor Hyde has his picture in his library over his chimney). They both promised him great matters, but to this day he has got *no* employment, only the king gave him some money.

He is of a middle stature, thickset, high coloured, a head of reddish hair, a severe and sound judgement. He has often said that way (e.g. Mr Edmund Waller's) of quibbling with sense will hereafter grow as much out of fashion and be as ridiculous as quibbling with words: which N.B.

He has been much troubled with the gout, and particularly 1679, he stirred not out of his chamber from October till Easter.

He died of a consumption 25 September 1680, and was buried on the 27th, according to his choice in the churchyard of Covent Garden. About twenty-five of his old acquaintance were at his funeral. I myself being one of the eldest helped to carry the pall. His coffin was covered with black baize.

Mr Saunders (the Countess of Kent's kinsman) said that Mr John Selden much esteemed him for his parts, and would sometimes employ him to write letters for him beyond sea, and to translate for him. He was secretary to the Duke of Buckingham, when he was Chancellor of Cambridge. He might have had preferments at first; but he would not accept any but very good ones, so at last he had none at all, and died in want.

¶ Memorandum: satirical wits disoblige whom they converse with, etc; and consequently make to themselves many enemies and few friends; and this was his manner and case. He was of a leonine-coloured hair, sanguino-choleric, middle-sized, strong.

William Butler

1535–1618

One of the most renowned doctors of his time, William Butler never took the MD degree, and his methods were often fairly eccentric, as Aubrey reports, though there was usually some interesting empirical idea at the bottom of his apparent madness. He had a high reputation for his medicinal receipts, which were still in vogue many years after his death.

William Butler, physician; he was of Clare Hall in Cambridge, never took the degree of Doctor, though he was the greatest physician of his time.

The occasion of his being taken notice of was thus: about the coming-in of King James, there was a minister of a village a few miles from Cambridge, that was to preach before his majesty at Newmarket. The parson heard that the king was a great scholar, and studied so excessively that he could not sleep, so somebody gave him some opium, which would have made him sleep his last, had not Dr Butler used this following remedy. He was sent for by the parson's wife. When he came and saw the parson, and asked what they had done, he told her that she was in danger to be hanged for killing her husband, and so in great choler left her. It was at that time when the cows came into the back side to be milked. He turns back, and asked whose cows those were. She said, her husband's. Said he: 'Will you give one of these cows to fetch your husband to life again?' She said that she would, with all her heart. He then causes one at once to be killed and opened, and the parson to be taken out of his bed and put into the cow's warm belly, which after some time brought him to life, or else he had infallibly died.

Memorandum: there is a parallel story to this in Machiavelli's History of Florence, where 'tis said that one of the Medici, being poisoned, was put into a mule's belly, sewed up, with a place only for his head to come out.

He was a man of great moods. One time King James sent for him to Newmarket, and when he was gone halfway, he left the messenger and turned back; so then the messenger made him ride before him.

I think he was never married. He lived in Crane's, an apothecary's, shop in Cambridge, to whom he left his estate; and he in gratitude erected the monument for him at his own charge, in the fashion he used. He was not greedy of money, except choice pieces of gold or rarities.

He would many times (I have heard say) sit among the boys at St Mary's church in Cambridge (and just so would the famous attorney-general Noy, in Lincoln's Inn, who had many such frolics and humours).

I remember Mr Wodenoth, of King's College, told me that being sent for to a certain gentleman he told him that his disease was not to be found in Galen or Hippocrates*, but in Tully's *Epistles, When you are elsewhere, it will not be because you wanted to live.*

I think he left his estate to the apothecary. He gave to the chapel of Clare Hall, a bowl, for the communion, of gold (cost, I think £2 or 300), on which is engraved a pelican feeding her young with the blood from her breast (an emblem of the passion of Christ) no motto, for the

---

* Famous Greek writers on medicine, regarded as the founders of the science. *Ed.*

emblem explained itself.

He was much addicted to his humours, and would suffer persons of quality to wait sometimes some hours at his door, with coaches, before he would receive them. Once, on the road from Cambridge to London, he took a fancy to a chamberlain or tapster in his inn, and took him with him, and made him his favourite, by whom only accession was to be had to him, and thus enriched him. Dr Gale, of St Paul's school assures me that a Frenchman came one time from London to Cambridge, purposely to see him, whom he made stay two hours for him in his gallery, and then he came out to him in an old blue gown; the French gentleman makes him two or three very low bows down to the ground; Dr Butler whips his legs over his head, and away goes into his chamber, and did not speak with him.

He kept an old maid whose name was Nell. Dr Butler would many times go to the tavern but drink by himself. About 9 or 10 at night old Nell comes for him with a candle and lanthorn and says: 'Come you home, you drunken beast.' By and by Nell would stumble; then her master calls her 'drunken beast'; and so they did *drunken beast* one another all the way till they came home.

¶ A servingman brought his master's water to Doctor Butler, he being then in his study (with the doors barred) but would not be spoken with. After much fruitless importunity, the man told the doctor he was resolved he should see his master's water; he would not be turned away—threw it on the doctor's head. This humour pleased the doctor, and he went to the gentleman and cured him. From Mr R. Hooke.

A gentleman lying a-dying, sent his servant with a horse for the doctor. The horse being exceedingly dry, ducks down his head strongly into the water, and plucks down the doctor over his head, who was plunged in the water over head and ears. The doctor was maddened, and would return home. The man swore he should not; drew his sword, and gave him ever and anon (when he would return) a little prick, and so drove him before him. From Mr Godfrey.

¶ From Mr James Bovey, some instances of Dr Butler's cures. The doctor lying at the Savoy in London, where was a balcony looked into the Thames, a patient came to him that was grievously tormented with the ague. The doctor orders a boat to be in readiness under his window, and discoursed with the patient (a gentleman) in the balcony, when on a signal given, two or three lusty fellows came behind the gentleman and threw him a matter of 20 feet into the Thames. This surprise absolutely cured him.

A gentleman with a red ugly spotted face came to him for a cure. Said the doctor 'I must hang you.' So presently he had a device made ready to hang him from a beam in the roof; and when he was even almost dead, he cuts the veins that fed these pumples, and let out the black ugly blood, and cured him.

Another time one came to him for the cure of a cancer (or ulcer) in the bowels. Said the doctor: 'Can ye shit?' 'Yes' said the patient. So the doctor ordered a bason for him to shit, and when he had so done, the doctor commanded him to eat it up. This did the cure.

From Dr More. More's father was a very strong-bodied man. 'Twas forty purges Dr Butler gave his father; he had almost killed him. Told him he would be the better for it as long as he lived.

That he was interested in chemistry I know by this token that his maid came running in to him one time, like a slut and a fury, with her hair about her ears, and cries 'Butler! come and look to your devils yourself, if you will; the stills are all blown up!' She tended them, and it seems gave too great a heat. Old Dr Ridgeley knew him and I think was at that time with him.

Sir Edward Bysshe
?1615–79

Garter King at Arms under the Commonwealth. He was forced to resign at the Restoration, but became Clarenceux King at Arms instead.

Smallfield is a fair, well built house of freestone, situated by the common and (1672) belonging to Sir Edward Bysshe, Clarenceux King at Arms, by whose father, Edward Byshe, a councillor at law, and bencher of Lincoln's Inn, it was built. This gentleman was a great practiser in the court of wards, where he got his estate, and was wont to say jestingly 'That he built that fine house with woodcocks' heads'. His son Sir Edward complied, and was active in the iniquity of the times, ate the bread of loyalists and accepted of a pension of £600 per annum from sequestrators. In the windows of the house are abundance of late escutcheons of Bysshe, and some matches [quarterings by marriage]; these I have neglected to insert, because it appears from the Heralds' books that they are all false and forged. His true coat is *Ermine on a chief embattled*. During the usurpation, he assumed the coat of de la Bishe, with which he quartered some of the most ancient and noble quarterings of England, to which he had no pretence, to the great scandal of the College of Heralds, who speak hardly of him. I cannot also but term this silly as well as base, because, (notwithstanding all his vaunting, pompous escutcheons in his hall) the descent and arms of his family are well known by the inhabitants here, who call it a new raised, upstart family, of yesterday's growth, and that the bencher's father or grandfather, was a miller; and that there are several Goodman Bysshes in this parish of Tilburstow.

William Camden
1551–1623

The greatest antiquary of the sixteenth and seventeenth century, Camden is chiefly remembered for his Britannia, *first published in 1586. He taught himself Anglo-Saxon and Welsh in order to pursue his researches, and travelled extensively in search of antiquities. Six editions of the* Britannia *appeared in his lifetime; and he also published an account of Elizabeth's reign from 1558 to 1588.*

Mr William Camden, Clarenceux Herald: Mr Edward Bagshawe (who had been second schoolmaster of Westminster school) has told me that Mr Camden had first his place and his lodgings (which is the gatehouse by the Queen's Scholars' Chambers in Dean's Yard) and was after made the head schoolmaster of the school where he wrote and taught *Institutio Graecae Grammatices Compendiaria: in usum Regiae Scholae Westmonasteriensis* which is now the common Greek grammar of England, but his name is not set to it. Before, they learned the prolix Greek grammar of Cleonard.

'Tis reported, that he had bad eyes (I guess short-sightedness) which was a great inconvenience to an antiquary.

Mr Nicholas Mercator has Stadius's *Ephemerides*, which had been one of Mr Camden's, his name is there (I know his hand) and there are some notes by which I find he was astrologically inclined.

In his *Britannia* he has a remarkable astrological observation, that when Saturn is in Capricorn a great plague is certainly in London. He had observed it all his time, and sets down the like made by others before him. Saturn was so positioned in the great plague 1625, and also in the last great plague 1665.

He was basted by a courtier of the queen's in the cloisters at Westminster for libelling Queen Elizabeth in his history—from Dr John Earle, Dean of Westminster.

My honoured and learned friend, Thomas Fludd esquire, a Kentish gentleman, was neighbour and an acquaintance to Sir Robert Filmore, in Kent, who was very intimately acquainted with Mr Camden, who told Sir Robert that he was not suffered to print many things in his *Elizabetha*, which he sent over to his acquaintance and correspondent Thuanus, who printed it all faithfully in his *Annals* without altering a word: which N.B.

Mr Camden much studied the Welsh language, and kept a Welsh servant to improve him that language, for the better understanding of our antiquities.—From Mr Samuel Butler.

Sir William Dugdale tells me that he has minutes of King James's life to a month and a day, written by Mr William Camden: as also his own life, according to years and day, which is very brief, but only two sheets, Mr Camden's own hand writing. Sir William Dugdale had it from Hacket, Bishop of Coventry and Lichfield, who did filch it from Mr Camden as he lay a-dying.

William Canynges
?1399–1474

Five times mayor of Bristol. Most of his trade seems in fact to have been with northern Europe.

The antiquities of the city of Bristol do very well deserve some antiquary's pains (and the like for Gloucester). There were a great many religious houses. The collegiate church (Augustinian priory) is very good building, especially the gate-house. The best built churches of any city in England, before these new ones at London since the conflagration.

St Mary Radcliffe church (which was intended as a chapel) is an admirable piece of architecture of about Henry VII's time. It was built by alderman Canynges, who had fifteen or sixteen ships of his own. He got his estate chiefly by carrying pilgrims to Santiago de Compostela. He had a fair house in Radcliffe Street that looks towards the water side, ancient Gothic building, a large house that, 1656, was converted to glass-factory. See the annotations on Norton's Ordinal in *Theatrum Chemicum*, where 'tis said that Thomas Norton of Bristol got the secret of the philosopher's stone from alderman Canynges' widow.

This alderman Canynges did also build and well endow the religious house at Westbury or Henbury (see Speed's map and chronicle); 'tis about two or three miles from Bristol on the road to Aust ferry. In his old age he retired to this house and entered into that order.

61

William Cartwright
1611–43

Cartwright's plays appeared in the late 1630s, and were much esteemed by the royal court; however, they have not been performed since the seventeenth century, despite the praise of men such as Dr Fell and Ben Jonson.

Gloucestershire is famous for the birth of William Cartwright at a place called Northway near Tewkesbury. Were he alive now he would be sixty-one. He wrote a treatise of metaphysic—query Dr Barlow about this: as also of his sermons, particularly the sermon that by the king's command he preached at his return from Edgehill fight. 'Tis not to be forgotten that King Charles I dropped a tear at the news of his death.

William Cartwright was buried in the south aisle of Christ Church, Oxon. Pity 'tis so famous a bard should lie without an inscription.

¶ His father was a gentleman of £300 per annum. He kept his inn at Cirencester but only a year or thereabouts, where he declined and lost by it too. He had by his wife £100 per annum in Wiltshire, a revenue from church estates, which his son has now (but having many children, lives not handsomely and has lost his learning: he was by the second wife, whose estate this was). Old Mr Cartwright lived sometime at Leekhampton, Gloucestershire, where his daughters now live.

Lucius Cary
Second Viscount Falkland, ?1610–43

Lord Falkland's real interests were poetry and theology, and for many years he lived in semi-retirement in Oxfordshire. He returned to London in 1639, and played a moderate part in politics. In 1642, Charles I offered him the secretaryship of state, which he accepted with hesitation; and he did his best to prevent the outbreak of war in that year.

Lucius Cary, second Lord Falkland, was the eldest son of Sir Henry Cary, Lord Lieutenant of Ireland, the first Viscount Falkland; his mother was daughter and heir of Sir Laurence Tanfield, Lord Chief Baron of the Exchequer, by whom he had Great Tew in Oxfordshire (formerly the Rainesfords') and the Priory of Burford in Oxfordshire, which he sold to Lenthall, the Speaker of the Long Parliament.

He had his university education at the University of Dublin, in Ireland. He travelled, and had a very discreet gentleman to be his governor, whom he respected to his dying day.

He married Letice, the daughter of Sir Richard Morison, by whom he had two sons: the eldest lived to be a man, died without children; the second was father to this Lord Falkland now living.

This Lady Letice was a good and pious lady, as you may see by her life, written about 1649 or 50 by John Duncomb, DD. But I will tell you a pretty story from William Hawes, of Trinity College, who was well acquainted with the governor aforesaid, who told him that my lady was (after the manner of women) much governed by, and indulgent to, the nursery; when she had a mind to beg anything of my lord for one of her women (nurses, or &c.) she would not do it by herself (if she could help it), but put this gentleman upon it, to move it to my lord. My lord had but a small estate for his title; and the old gentleman would say, 'Madam, this is so unreasonable a motion to propose to my lord, that I am certain he will never grant it;' e.g. at one time to let a farm twenty pounds per annum under value. At length, when she could not prevail on him, she would say that, 'I warrant you, for all this, I will obtain it of my lord; 'twill cost me but the expense of a few tears.' Now she would make her words good; and this great wit, the greatest master of reason and judgement of his time, at the long run, being stormed by her tears (I presume there were kisses and secret embraces that were also ingredients), would this pious lady obtain her unreasonable desires of her poor lord.

N.B. My lord in his youth was very wild, and also mischievous, as being apt to stab and do bloody mischiefs; but it was not long before he took up to be serious, and then grew to be an extraordinary hard student. I have heard Dr Ralph Bathurst say that, when he was a boy, my lord lived at Coventry (where he then had a house) and that he would sit up very late at nights at his study, and many times came to the library at the school there.

The studies in fashion in those days (in England) were poetry, and controversy with the church of Rome. My lord's mother was *a zealous papist*, who being very earnest to have her son of her religion, and her son upon that occasion, labouring hard to find the truth, was so far at last from settling on the Romish church, that he settled and rested in the Polish (I mean Socinianism*). He was the first Socinian in England; and Dr Crescy of Merton College (Dean of Leighlin in Ireland, afterwards a Benedictine monk), a great acquaintance of my lord's in those days, told me, at Samuel Cooper's (1669), that he himself was the first that brought Socinus's books; shortly after, my lord coming to him and

---

* So called from Fausto Paolo Sozzini, an Italian theologian, whose personality and particular views on the nature of Christ and of his worship came to dominate the Polish Protestant Church in the late sixteenth century. *Ed.*

casting his eye on them, would needs at once borrow them, to peruse; and was so extremely taken and satisfied with them, that from that time was his conversion.

My lord much lived at Tew, which is a pleasant seat, and about 12 miles from Oxford; his lordship was acquainted with the best wits of that university, and his house was like a college, full of learned men. Mr William Chillingworth, of Trinity College in Oxford, afterwards DD, was his most intimate and beloved favourite, and was most commonly with my lord; next I may reckon (if not equal) Mr John Earles, of Merton College (who wrote the *Characters*); Dr Eglionby, of Christ Church, was also much in esteem with his lordship. His chaplain, Charles Gataker, (son of Gataker of Redriff, a writer) was an ingenious young gentleman, but no writer. For learned gentlemen of the country, his acquaintance was Sir H. Rainesford; Sir Francis Wenman, of Caswell in Witney parish; Mr Sandys, the traveller and translator (that was uncle to my lady Wenman), Ben Jonson, Edmund Waller, Mr Thomas Hobbes and all the excellent wits of that peaceable time.

In the civil wars, he adhered to King Charles I, who after Edgehill fight made him Principal Secretary of State (with Sir Edward Nicholas), which he discharged with a great deal of wit and prudence, only his advice was very unlucky to his majesty, in persuading him (after the victory at Roundway Down and the taking of Bristol) to sit down before Gloucester, which was so bravely defended by that incomparably vigilant governor Colonel Massey, and the diligent and careful soldiers and citizens (men and women) that it so broke and weakened the king's army that 'twas the primary cause of his ruin: *vide* Mr Hobbes. After this, all the king's matters went worse and worse. Anno domini 1643 at the fight at Newbury, my Lord Falkland being there, and having nothing to do decided to charge; as the two armies were engaging, rode in like a madman (as he was) between them, and was (as he needs must be) shot. Some that were your superfine discoursing politicians and fine gentlemen, would needs have the reason of this mad action of throwing away his life so, to be his discontent for the unfortunate advice given to his master as aforesaid; but, I have been well informed, by those that best knew him, and knew the intrigues behind the curtain (as they say) that it was the grief of the death of Mrs Moray, a handsome lady at Court, who was his mistress, and whom he loved above all creatures, was the true cause of his being so madly guilty of his own death, as aforementioned: *there is no great wit without an admixture of madness.**

The next day, when they went to bury the dead, they could not find his lordship's body, it was stripped, trod upon and mangled; so there was one that had waited on him in his chamber would undertake to

---

* Seneca, *De Tranquillitate Animi*, 17, 10. *Ed.*

know it from all other bodies, by a certain mole his lordship had on his neck, and by that mark did find it. He lies interred at Great Tew aforesaid, but, I think, yet without any monument.

In the dining room there is a full length portrait and like him ('twas done by Jacob de Valke, who taught me to paint). He was but a little man, and of no great strength of body; he had blackish hair, rather lank, and I think his eyes black. Dr Earles would not allow him to be a good poet, though a great wit; he wrote, not a smooth verse, but a great deal of sense.

He had an estate in Hertfordshire, which came by his wife's family (as I take it); sold not long before the late civil wars.

Charles Cavendish
1620–43

Charles Cavendish rose rapidly from being a volunteer guards officer to commander of the Duke of York's troop and then to colonel-general for Nottinghamshire and Lincolnshire, in which command he was killed at Gainsborough in 1643.

Charles Cavendish, colonel, was second son to the right honourable Earl of Devonshire, brother to this present earl, William.

He was well educated, and then travelled into France, Italy etc; but was so extremely delighted in travelling, that he went into Greece; all over; and that would not serve his turn, but he would go to Babylon, and then his governor would not adventure to go any further with him; but to see Babylon he was to march in the Turks' army. This account I had many years since, that is, in 1642, from my cousin Edward Lyte, who was then gentleman usher to his mother the countess dowager.

Mr Thomas Hobbes told me, that this Mr Cavendish told him that the Greeks do sing their Greek. In Herefordshire they have a touch of this singing; our old divines had. Our old vicar of Kington St Michael, Mr Hynd, did sing his sermons rather than read them. You may find in Erasmus that the monks used this fashion, who [Erasmus] mocks them, that sometimes they would be very low, and by and by would be mighty high when it had nothing to do with the sense. In 1660 coming to Mr Hobbes, his Greek Xenophon lay open on the board: said he, 'Had you come a little sooner you had found a Greek here that came to see me, who understands the old Greek; I spoke to him to read here in this book, which put me in mind of what Mr Charles Cavendish told me.'

Upon his return into England, the civil wars broke out, and he took a commission as a colonel in his majesty's cause, wherein he did his majesty great service, and gave signal proofs of his valour, e.g. out of *Mercurius Aulicus**:

Grantham in Lincolnshire taken by Colonel Cavendish for the king, 23 March 1643, and afterwards demolished. Young Hotham routed at Ancaster by Col. Cavendish, 11 April 1643. Parliament forces routed or defeated at Dunnington by Col. Cavendish 13 June 1643.

Mercurius Aulicus, Tuesday, 1 August 1643: 'It was advertised from Newark that his majesty's forces having planted themselves at the siege of Gainsborough in the county of Lincoln, were set upon by the united powers of Cromwell, Nottingham and Lincoln, the garrisons of these towns being almost totally drawn out to make up this army, which consisted of 24 troops of horse and dragoons. Against this force, Col. Cavendish having the command of 30 troops of horse and dragoons, draws out 16 only, and leaving all the rest for a reserve, advanced towards them, and engaged himself with this small party against all their strength. Which being observed by the rebels, they got between him and his reserve, routed his 16 troops, being wearied with frequent watches, killed Lieutenant Colonel Markham, most valiantly fighting in defence of his king and country. The most noble and gallant colonel himself, whilst he omitted no part of a brave commander, being cut most dangerously in the head, was struck off his horse, and so unfortunately shot with a brace of bullets after he was on the ground, whose life was most precious to all noble and valiant gentlemen. Whereupon the reserve coming, routed and cut down the party.'

This was done either the twenty-eight or twenty-ninth of July 1643, for upon this terrible rout, the Lord Willoughby of Parham forthwith yielded Gainsborough to the king's party, 30 July; the Earl of Newcastle being then general of that party.

Funeral sermon by William Naylor, Chaplain to the Countess of Devonshire, preached at Derby, 18 February 1674:

He was the soldiers' favourite and his majesty's darling, designed by him general of the northern horse (and his commission was given him), a great mark of honour for one of about five and twenty: 'thus shall it be done to the man whom the king delights to honour.'

Col. Cavendish was a princely person, and all his actions were agreeable to that character: he had in an eminent degree the semblance and appearance of a man made to govern. Methinks he

---

* A Royalist newspaper of the Civil War period. See John Birkenhead. *Ed.*

66

gave clear this indication, the king's cause lived with him, the king's cause died with him—when Cromwell heard that he was slain, he cried upon it, 'We have done our business'.

And yet two things (I must confess) this commander knew not, pardon his ignorance,—he knew not to fly away—he knew not how to ask quarter—though an older did, I mean Henderson; for when this bold person entered Grantham on the one side, that wary gentleman, who should have attacked it, fled away on the other. If Cato thought it usurpation in Caesar to give him his life, Cavendish thought it a greater for traitors and rebels of the common sort to give him his. This brave hero might be oppressed (as he was at last by numbers), but he could not be conquered; the dying words of Epaminondas will fit him, *I have lived enough, and also die unconquered.*

What wonders might have been expected from a commander so vigilant, so loyal, so constant, had he not dropped down in his blooming age? But though he fell in his green years, he fell a prince, and a great one too, in this respect greater than Abner; for Abner that son of Mars deserved his father's epithet, *one of both sides*; first he sets up Isbosheth, and then deserts him. Whereas Cavendish merited such a statue as the Roman senate decreed L. Vitellius, and the same inscription, *one whose loyalty to his great master nothing could shake.*

Secondly, consider the noble Charles Cavendish in his extraction, and so he is a branch of that family, of which some descended that are Kings of Scotland: this the word *Fuimus* joined to his maternal* coat of arms does plainly point at—not to urge at this time his descent by his father's side from one of the noblest families in England. A high extraction to some persons is like the dropsy, the greatness of the man is his disease and renders him unwieldy; but here is a person of great extract free from the swelling of greatness, as brisk and active as the lightest horseman that fought under him. In some parts of India, they tell us, that a nobleman accounts himself polluted if a plebeian touch him; but here is a person of that rank who used the same familiarity† and frankness amongst the meanest of his soldiers, the poorest miner, and amongst his equals; and by stooping so low, he rose the higher in the common account,

---

* His mother was daughter to the Lord Bruce, whose ancestors had been Kings of Scotland.

† Sir Robert Harley (son), an ingenious gentleman and expert soldier has often said that (generally) the commanders of the King's army would never be acquainted with their soldiers, which was an extraordinary prejudice to the King's cause. A captain's good look or good word (sometimes) does infinitely win them, and oblige them; and he would say 'twas to admiration how soldiers will venture their lives for an obliging officer—quod N.B. [Aubrey's note]

and was valued accordingly as a prince, and a great one; thus Abner and Cavendish run parallel in their titles and appellations.

Consider Abner in the manner of his fall, that was by a treacherous hand, and so fell Cavendish. II. Sam. iii. 27, 'And when Abner was returned to Hebron, Joab took him aside in the gate to speak with him quietly, and smote him under the fifth rib, that he died, for the blood of Asahel his brother.' Thus fell Abner; and thus Cavendish; the colonel's horse being mired in a bog at the fight before Gainsborough, 1643, the rebels surround him, and take him prisoner; and after he was so, a base rascal comes behind him, and runs him through. Thus fell two great men by treacherous hands.

Thirdly and lastly, the place of his fall, that was in Israel . . . Here Abner fell in his, and Cavendish fell in our Israel—the Church of England . . . In this Church brave Cavendish fell, and what is more than that, in this Church's quarrel . . .

Thus I have compared Colonel Cavendish with Abner, a fighting and a famous man in Israel; you see how he does equal, how he does exceed him.

Sir Charles Cavendish
d. 1652

(From Mr John Collins, mathematician). Sir Charles Cavendish was the younger brother to William, duke of Newcastle. He was a little, weak, crooked man, and nature not having adapted him for the court nor the camp, he betook himself to the study of the mathematics, wherein he became a great master. His father left him a good estate, the revenue whereof he expended on books and on learned men.

He had collected in Italy, France, etc with no small charge, as many manuscript mathematical books as fill a hogshead [barrel], which he intended to have printed; which if he had lived to have done, the growth of mathematical learning had been thirty years or more forwarder than it is. But he died of the scurvy, contracted by hard study, about 1652, and left an attorney of Clifford's Inn as his executor, who shortly after died, and left his wife as executrix, who sold this incomparable collection aforesaid by weight to the paste-board makers for waste paper. A good caution for those that have good manuscripts to take care to see them printed in their lifetimes.

William Cecil, Lord Burghley
1520–98

Secretary of State to Elizabeth I from her accession in 1558 until 1572, and then lord high treasurer until his death. When she appointed him, Elizabeth said: 'This judgement I have of you, that you will not be corrupted by any gifts, and that you will be faithful to the state.' His career amply bore out her prediction: his greatest success, though won through dubious means, was to secure Elizabeth's protestant kingdom against Roman Catholic subversion.

The first lord Burley (who was Secretary of State) was at first but a country schoolmaster, and (I think Dr Thomas Fuller says, vide *Holy State*) born in Wales.

I remember (when I was a schoolboy at Blandford) Mr Basket, a reverend divine, who was wont to beg us play-days, would always be uncovered [keep his hat off, as a mark of respect] and said that it was the lord Burleigh's custom, *for* (said he) *here is my Lord Chancellor, my Lord Treasurer, my Lord Chief Justice etc, predestinated* [of the future].

'He made Cicero's Epistles his glass, his oracle and his ordinary pocket-book.' (Dr J. Web in preface of his translation of Cicero's *Familiar Epistles*).

¶ I have often admired, that so wise men as the Lord Burghley and his sons were, should so vainly change their name, that is from that of Sitsilt, of Monmouthshire, a family of great antiquity; there are yet of that name there, but the estate is much decayed, and become small. I was in Monmouth church in 1656; and there was in a sash window of the church a very old escutcheon, as old as the church, belonging to the aforesaid family: it did hang a little dangerously, and I fear 'tis now spoiled. They are vulgarly called Seysil. And Mr Verstegan (otherwise an exceeding ingenious gentleman) to flatter this family, would have them to be derived from the Roman *Caecilii*; whereas they might as well have been contented with the real antiquity of this and Monmouthshire, and needed not to have gone as far as Italy for it. In like manner, and about the same time, Skydmore of Herefordshire changed his name to Scudamore; and took his motto, *Scutum Amoris* [Love's shield] when Spenser's Fairy Queen came out, wherein he has a very fine character of (called) Sir Scudamore.

Thomas Chaloner
1595–1661

Thomas Chaloner's anti-monarchist ideas seem to have been the result of foreign travel, combined with the injustice done to his father over the Yorkshire mines. He became a member of Parliament in 1645, and quickly became a leading anti-Royalist. He failed to make his peace at the Restoration, and died in Holland, an exile, in 1661.

Thomas Chaloner esq. was the son of Dr Chaloner, who was tutor (i.e. *informator* [*instructor*] to prince Henry (or prince Charles—vide bishop Hall's Letters about this).

He was a well-bred gentleman, and of very good natural parts, and of an agreeable humour. He had the accomplishments of studies at home, and travels in France, Italy and Germany.

About the year [1600] (ask John Collins) riding a-hunting in Yorkshire (where the alum works now are), on a common, he took notice of the soil and herbage, and tasted the water, and found it to be like that where he had seen the alum works in Germany. Whereupon he got a patent of the King (Charles I) for an alum work (which was the first that ever was in England) which was worth to him two thousand pounds per annum or better: but in the time of Charles I some courtiers did think the profit too much for him, and prevailed so with the King, that notwithstanding the patent aforesaid, he granted a half share, or more, to another (a courtier) which was the reason that made Mr Chaloner so interest himself for the Parliament cause, and, in revenge, to be one of the King's judges.*

He was as far from a puritan as the East from the West. He was of the natural religion, and one of Henry Martyn's gang, and one who loved to enjoy the pleasures of this life. He was (they say) a good scholar, but he wrote nothing that I hear of, only an anonymous pamphlet, octavo, *An account of the Discovery of Moyses's Tombe*; which was written very wittily. It was about 1652. It did set the wits of all the Rabbis of the Assembly then to work, and 'twas a pretty while before the sham was detected.

He had a trick sometimes to go into Westminster Hall in a morning in the law term, when courts were sitting and tell some strange story (sham), and would come thither again about 11 or 12 to have the pleasure to hear how it spread; and sometimes it would be altered, with

---

* Aubrey has confused Sir Thomas Chaloner, Thomas Chaloner's father, and Thomas Chaloner himself. It was the father who discovered the mines, the son who was one of Charles I's judges. *Ed.*

additions, he could scarce know it to be his own. He was neither proud nor covetous, nor a hypocrite: not apt to do injustice, but apt to revenge.

After the restoration of King Charles the Second, he kept the castle at the Isle of Man,* where he had a pretty wench that was his concubine. Where, when news was brought him that there were some come to the castle to demand it for his majesty, he spake to his girl to make him a posset, into which he put, out of a paper he had, some poison, which did, in a very short time, make him fall a-vomiting exceedingly; and after some time vomited nothing but blood. His retchings were so violent that the standers by were much grieved to behold it. Within three hours he died. The men who had demanded the castle came and saw him dead; he was swollen so extremely that they could not see any eye he had, and no more than of his nose than the tip of it, which showed like a wart, and his cods were swollen as big as one's head. This account I had from George Escourt DD, whose brother-in-law, Hotham, was one of those that saw him.

Geoffrey Chaucer
1328–1400

Sir Hamond L'Estrange had his works in MS, a most curious piece, most rarely written and illuminated, which he valued at £100. His grandson and heir still has it from Mr Roger L'Estrange. He taught his son the use of the astrolabe at 10; see his treatise on the astrolabe. Dunnington Castle, near Newbury, was his; a noble seat and strong castle, which was held by the king, Charles I, (who was governor?) but since dismantled.

Near this castle was an oak, under which Sir Geoffrey was wont to sit, called Chaucer's Oak, which was cut down under Charles I; and so it was, that the culprit was called into the star chamber, and was fined it. Judge Richardson harangued against him for a long time, and like an orator, had topics from the Druids etc. This information I had from an able attorney that was at the hearing.

One Mr Goresuch of Woodstock dined with us at Romney Marsh, who told me that at the old Gothic-built house near the park gate at Woodstock, which was the house of Sir Geoffrey Chaucer, that there is his picture which goes with the house from one owner to another—which see.

* This is a mistake. E.W. esq. assures me that 'twas James Chaloner that died in the Isle of Man; and that Thomas Chaloner died or went beyond the sea; but which of them was the elder brother he knows not, but he guesses James to be the elder because he had £1500 per annum (about) which Thomas had not.

William Chillingworth
1602–44

An Oxford theologian who became a Roman Catholic convert from 1630–34.
His defence of the Church of England, published in 1638, was attacked by
both Roman Catholics and Puritans alike. He joined the royalist party early
in the Civil War, and probably served as a chaplain with the royal army.

William Chillingworth, DD, was born in Oxford. His father was a
brewer.

About the year . . . he was acquainted with a man who drew him and
some other scholars over to Douai* where he was not so well entertained
as he thought he merited for his great disputative wit. They made him the
porter (which was to try his temper, and exercise his obedience): so he
stole over and came to Trinity College again, where he was fellow.

William Laud, Archbishop of Canterbury, was his godfather and great
friend. He sent his grace weekly intelligence of what passed in the
university. Sir William Davenant (poet laureate) told me that notwithstanding this doctor's great reason, he was guilty of the detestable crime
of treachery. Dr Gill, son of Dr Gill schoolmaster of St Paul's school, and
Chillingworth conferred each week one with another for some years,
wherein they used to nibble at state matters. Dr Gill in one of his letters
calls King James and his son 'the old fool and the young one', which
letter Chillingworth communicates to W. Laud, Archbishop of Canterbury. The poor young Dr Gill was seized and a terrible storm pointed
towards him, which by the eloquent intercession and advocation of
Edward Earl of Dorset, together with the tears of the poor old doctor his
father, and supplication on his knees to his majesty, was blown over. I am
sorry so great a wit [Chillingworth] should have such a blemish.

'The man who backbites an absent friend; who fails to defend him when
another finds fault; the man who courts the loud laughter of others, and the
reputation of a wit; who can invent what he never saw; who cannot keep a
secret—that man is black at heart; of him beware, good Roman.'

Horace *Satires*, I, iv

He was a little man, blackish hair, of a saturnine countenance.

The Lord Falkland and he had such extraordinary clear reasons, that
they were wont to say at Oxford that if the great Turk were to be
converted by natural reason, these two were the persons to convert him.

He lies buried in the south side of the cloisters at Chichester, where he
died of the camp fever after the taking of Arundel castle by the

* The English Roman Catholic school in France. *Ed.*

72

parliament: wherein he was very much blamed by the king's soldiers for his advice in military affairs there, and they cursed that little priest and imputed the loss of the castle to his advice. In his sickness, he was inhumanely treated by Dr Cheynell [a puritan], who, when he was to be buried, threw his book into the grave with him, saying, 'Rot with the rotten, let the dead bury the dead'. Vide a pamphlet of about six sheets written by Dr Cheynell (maliciously enough) where he gives an account of his life.

My tutor, William Browne, has told me that Dr Chillingworth studied not much, but when he did, he did much in a little time. He much delighted in Sextus Empiricus*. He did walk in the College grove, and there contemplate, and meet with some blockhead or other, and dispute with him and baffle him. He thus prepared himself beforehand. He would always be disputing; so would my tutor. I think it was an epidemic evil of that time, which I think is now grown out of fashion, as unmannerly and boyish.

He was the readiest and nimblest disputant of his time in the university; perhaps none has equalled him since.

I have heard Mr Thomas Hobbes of Malmesbury (who knew him) say, that he was like a lusty fellow that did drive his enemies before him, but would often give his own party smart back-blows.

When Doctor Kettell (the President of Trinity College, Oxford) died, which was in 1643, Dr Chillingworth was competitor for the presidentship, with Dr Hannibal Potter and Dr Roberts. Dr Potter had been formerly chaplain to the Bishop of Winchester, who was so much Dr Potter's friend, that though (as Will Hawes has told me) Dr Potter was not lawfully elected, upon referring themselves to their visitor (the Bishop of Winchester) the bishop (Curle) ordered Dr Potter possession; and let the fellows get him out if they could. This was shortly after the Lord Falkland was slain, who had he lived, Dr Chillingworth assured Will Hawes, no man should have carried it against him: and that he was so extremely discomposed and wept bitterly for the loss of his dear friend, yet notwithstanding he doubted not to have a consolation for it.

John Cleveland
1613–58

Cavalier poet.

John Cleveland was born in Warwickshire. He was a fellow of St John's College in Cambridge, where he was more taken notice of for his being

---

* Greek philosopher of the second–third centuries AD; one of the sceptic school. *Ed.*

an eminent debater than a good poet. Being turned out of his fellowship for a malignant (being a Royalist) he came to Oxford, where the king's army was, and was much caressed by them. He went thence to the garrison at Newark upon Trent, where upon some occasion when articles were drawn up, or some other writing, he would needs add a short conclusion, 'and hereunto we annex our lives, as a label to our trust'. After the king was beaten out of the field, he came to London and retired in Grays Inn. He and Samuel Butler etc of Gray's Inn, had a club [drinking-bout] every night. He was a comely plump man, good curled hair, dark brown.

George Clifford
Third Earl of Cumberland, 1558–1605

After losing much of his estate by his extravagance, George Clifford tried to recover his fortune by adventures against the Spanish. His bravado made him popular at court, and he was a favourite of the queen: Aubrey's story of the council depriving him of his booty is largely untrue, though he did lose a lawsuit over prize-money in 1592.

This George, Earl of Cumberland, built the greatest fleet of shipping that ever any subject did. He had a vast estate, and could then ride in his own lands from Yorkshire to Westmoreland.

The best account of his expedition with his fleet to America is to be found in *Purchas his Pilgrims*. He took from the Spaniards to the value of seven or eight hundred thousand pounds; when he returned with this rich cargo (the richest without doubt that every subject brought), the queen's council (where he had some that envied him—envy is virtue's companion) laid their heads together and concluded 'twas too much for a subject to have, and confiscated it all to the queen, even ships and all, and to make restoration to the Spaniards, so that he was forced to sell lands worth fifteen thousand pounds per annum. My lady Thanet told me she saw the accounts in writing. The armada of the Argonauts was but a trifle compared to this. As I take it, Sir Walter Raleigh went this brave voyage with his lordship; and Mr Edmund Wright, the excellent navigator; and not unlikely, Mr Harriot too.

This was the breaking of that ancient and noble family; but Robert Earl of Salisbury (who was the chiefest enemy) afterwards married his daughter, as he might well be touched in conscience, to make some recompense after he had done so much mischief. That he was an acquaintance of Sir Walter Raleigh, I remember by this token, that Sir

James Long told me that one time he came to Draycot with Sir Walter Raleigh from Bath, and hunting a buck in the park there, his horse made a false step in a rabbit-hole and threw him and broke his collarbone.

Henry Clifford
Fifth Earl of Cumberland, 1591–1643

A friend of Strafford, neither his political career nor his military exploits in the Royalist cause were particularly distinguished: with him the line of the earls of Cumberland came to an end.

Henry, earl of Cumberland, was a poet: the countess of Cork and Burlington has still his verses. He was of Christ Church, Oxford. Nicholas, earl of Thanet, was wont to say that the mare of Fountains Abbey did dash, meaning that since they got that estate (given to the church) they did never thrive, but still declined.

¶ He was an ingenious gentleman for those times and a great acquaintance of the Lord Chancellor Bacon's; and often wrote to one another, which letters the countess of Cork and Burlington, my lady Thanet's mother, daughter and heir of that family, keeps as reliques; and a poem in English that her father wrote upon the Psalms and many other subjects, and very well, but the language now being something out of fashion, like Sir Philip Sidney's, they will not print it.

Sir Edward Coke
1552–1634

The greatest practising lawyer of the seventeenth century, Coke quickly made a reputation for himself after he qualified as a barrister in 1578. He married one of the wealthy Paston family of Norfolk in 1582. Besides his practice as a barrister, he was also an MP, and became Speaker of the House of Commons in 1592–3. As attorney-general from 1593 onwards he was the prosecutor in the trials of Essex, of the gunpowder plotters and of Sir Walter Raleigh; but he distinguished himself only by the abuse he heaped on the defendants. With his appointment as Chief Justice of the common pleas in 1606, his greatest work began, the defence of the common law against the claims of the church to try cases under its own law, and against James I's attempts to establish royal authority as being above the law. As Lord Chief Justice after 1613, the conflict continued, ending only with Coke's dismissal in 1616, largely at the instigation of his opponent, Francis Bacon. In 1620, however, he returned to public life as an MP, and continued his attack on royal tyranny until his retirement in 1628. His Reports of Cases and Institutes are basic texts of English common law.

Sir Edward Coke, knight, Lord Chief Justice of the King's Bench, was born in Norfolk. I heard an old lawyer (Dunstable) of the Middle Temple, 1646, who was his countryman, say that he was born but to £300 land per annum, and I have heard some of his country say again that he was born but to £40 per annum. What shall one believe?

Ask Roger Coke at what college he was in Cambridge, or if ever at the University.

Old John Tussell (that was my attorney), has told me that he got a hundred thousand pounds in one year, viz the first year of King James's reign, being then attorney-general. His advice was that every man of estate (right or wrong) should sue out his pardon, which cost five pounds which was his fee.

He left an estate of eleven thousand pounds per annum. Sir John Danvers told me (who knew him) that when one told him his sons would spend the estate faster than he got it, he replied 'They cannot take more delight in spending of it than I did in the getting of it.' He was chamber-fellow to the Lord Chief Baron Wyld's father (Sergeant Wyld). He built the black buildings at the Inner Temple (now burnt) which were above the walk towards the west end, called then 'Coke's buildings'.

After he was put out of his place of Lord Chief Justice of the King's Bench, they made him sheriff of Buckinghamshire; at which time he caused the sheriff's oath to be altered, which till that time was, amongst other things, to enquire after and apprehend all Lollards. He was also chosen, after he was displaced, a burgess to sit in parliament.

He was of wonderful painstaking, as appears by his writings. He was short-sighted, but never used spectacles to his dying day, being then 83 years of age. He was a very handsome proper man and of a curious complexion, as appears by his picture at the Inner Temple, which his grandson gave them about 1668, full length, in his attorney-general's fustian gown, which the Inner Temple has turned into judge's robes.

He married, his second wife, Elizabeth the relict of Sir William Hatton, who was with child when he married her: laying his hand on her belly (when he came to bed) and finding a child stir, 'What,' said he, 'flesh in the pot?' 'Yes,' quoth she, 'or else I would not have married a cook.'* (From Elizabeth Lady Purbeck; see B. Jonson's *Masque of the Gipsies*.)

* A pun on the name Coke, pronounced Cook. *Ed.*

76

He showed himself too clownish and bitter in his attitude to Sir Walter Raleigh at his trial, where he says 'thou traitor' at every word, and 'thou liest like a traitor'.

His rule:

> *Sleep for six hours, give as much to just laws,*
> *Pray for four hours, give two to your mealtimes.*
> *What is left is the time to devote to the Muses.*

He plays with his case as a cat would with a mouse, and is so fulsomely pedantic that a schoolboy would be nauseated by it. But when he comes to matter of law, all acknowledge him to be admirable. When Mr Cuff, secretary to the Earl of Essex, was arraigned, he would dispute with him in specious arguments, till at last one of his brethren said 'Prithee, brother, leave off; thou dost dispute scurvily.' Cuff was a smart man and a great scholar, and baffled him. Said Coke:

> *Know thy lord.*

Cuff replied, 'My lord, you leave out the former part of the verse, which you should have repeated,

> *I am Actaeon,'*

reflecting on his being a cuckold.*

¶ The world expected from him a commentary on Littleton's *Tenures* [a legal text]; and he left them his commonplace book, which is now so much made use of.

Sir Edward Coke did envy Sir Francis Bacon, and was wont to undervalue his law; see on this in the Lord Bacon's letters, where he expostulates this thing with Sir Edward Coke, and tells him that he may grow when that others do stand at a stay.

Memorandum: he was of Cliffords Inn before he was of the Inner Temple, as the fashion then was first to be of an Inn of Chancery.

Memorandum: when the play called *Ignoramus* (made by one Ruggle of Clare Hall†) was acted with great applause before King James, they dressed Sir Ignoramus like Chief Justice Coke and cut his beard like him and feigned his voice. Mr Peyton, our vicar of Chalk, was then a scholar at King's College and saw it. This drollery did lead to serious evil: it set all the lawyers against the clergy, and shortly after this Mr Selden wrote of tithes that they were not according to God's laws.

---

* A cuckold was traditionally horned; the line (from Ovid's *Metamorphoses*) is addressed by Actaeon to his own hounds, after Venus had transformed him into a stag (because he had accidentally seen her naked). In this horned shape, Actaeon was torn to pieces by his own pack. *Ed.*
† Clare College, Cambridge. *Ed.*

Jean Baptiste Colbert
1619–83

Chief minister to Louis XIV, and successor to Cardinal Mazarin, Colbert was responsible for putting the finances of France on a sound practical footing, though his economic theories were often misguided. He does not seem to have been a merchant, contrary to Aubrey's story, but to have worked his way up through the royal service, starting as a clerk in the war office.

Monsieur Colbert was a merchant and an excellent accountant, i.e. for the double-entry system. He is of Scottish extraction, and that obscure enough, his grandfather being a Scottish bagpiper to the Scottish regiment [in France].

Cardinal Mazarin found that his stables were very expensive to him, and that he was imposed upon in accounts. He hearing of this merchant Colbert to be a great master in this art, sends for him and desires him to make an inspection into his accounts and put him into a better method to avoid being abused. Which he did, and that so well that he employed him in ordering the accounts of all his estate and found him so useful that he also made use of him to methodise and settle the accounts of the king. This was his rise.—From Dr John Pell.

John Colet
?1467–1519

Dean of St Paul's and founder of St Paul's School. He was a close friend of Erasmus.

After the conflagration, his monument being broken, his coffin, which was lead, was full of a liquor which conserved the body. Mr Wyld and Ralph Greatorex tasted it and 'twas of a kind of insipid taste, something of an ironish taste. The body felt, to the probe of a stick which they thrust into a chink, like brawn. The coffin was of lead and laid in the wall about two and a half feet above the surface of the floor.

Henry Coley
1633–?95

My friend Mr Henry Coley was born in Magdalen parish in the city of Oxford, October 18, 1633. His father was a joiner, with a shop over against the Theatre. He is a tailor in Gray's Inn Lane. He is a man of admirable parts, and more to be expected from him every day; and as good a natured man as can be. And comes by his learning merely by the strong impulse of his genius. He understands Latin and French; yet never finished learning his grammar.

He was a women's tailor: took to the love of astrology, in which he grew in a short time to a good proficiency; and in Mr W. Lilly's later time, when his sight grew dim, was his amanuensis. He has great practice in astrology, and teaches mathematics. He has published *The Key to Astrology*, wherein he has compiled clearly the whole science out of the best authors.

Thomas Cooper
?1517–94

Dr Edward Davenant told me that this learned man had a shrew to his wife, who was irreconcilably angry with him for sitting up so late at night, compiling his Latin dictionary. When he had half-done it, she had the opportunity to get into his study, took all his pains out in her lap, and threw it into the fire and burnt it. Well, for all that, that good man had so great a zeal for the advancement of learning, that he began it again, and went through with it to that perfection that he hath left it to us a most useful work. He was afterwards made bishop of Winchester.

Richard Corbet
1582–1635

Bishop of Oxford and later of Norwich, Richard Corbet was a bon viveur and wit, and a staunch anti-puritan. His best known poem is 'Farewell rewards and fairies'.

Richard Corbet, DD, was the son of Vincent Corbet, who was a gardener at Twickenham, as I have heard my old cousin Whitney say. See in Ben Jonson's *Underwoods* an epitaph on this Vincent Corbet, where he speaks of his nurseries.

He was a Westminster scholar; old parson Bussey of Alscott in Warwickshire went to school with him—he would say that he was a very handsome man, but something apt to abuse, and a coward.

He was a student of Christ Church in Oxford. He was very facetious, and a good fellow. One time he and some of his acquaintance being merry at 'Friar Bacon's Study' (where was good liquor sold), they were drinking on the leads of the house, and one of the scholars was asleep, and had a good pair of silk stockings on. Dr Corbet (then MA if not BD) got a pair of scissors and cut them full of little holes, but when the other awoke, and perceived how and by whom he was abused, he did chastise him, and made him pay for them.

After he was Doctor of Divinity, he sang ballads at the cross at Abingdon on a market-day. He and some of his comrades were at the tavern by the cross* (which by the way was then the finest of England; I remember it when I was a freshman; it was admirable curious Gothic architecture, and fine figures in the niches; 'twas one of those built by King Edward for his queen). The ballad singer complained he had no custom, he could not get rid of his ballads. The jolly doctor puts off his gown, and puts on the ballad singer's leather jacket, and being a handsome man, and had a rare full voice, he at once sold a great many, and had a great audience.

After the death of Dr Goodwyn, he was made dean of Christ Church: he had a good interest with great men, as you may find in his poems, and with the then great favourite, the Duke of Buckingham; his excellent wit was letters of recommendation to him. I have forgotten the story, but at the same time that Dr Fell thought to have carried the deanship, Dr Corbet put a pretty trick on him to let him take a journey on purpose to London for it, when he already had the grant of it.

He preached a sermon before the king at Woodstock (I suppose King James, query) and no doubt with a very good grace; but it happened he was broke down, on which occasion there were made these verses:

> A reverend dean
> With his ruff starched clean
>   Did preach before the king;
> In his band string was spied
> A ring that was tied,
>   Was that not a pretty thing?
>
> This ring without doubt
> Was the thing put him out,
>   So oft he forgot what was next;

* 'Twas after the fashion of the cross in High Street in Bristol, but more curious work. Query if not marble?

> For all that were there,
> On my conscience dare swear
> That he handled it more than his text.

His conversation was extremely pleasant. Dr Stubbins was one of his cronies; he was a jolly fat doctor and a very good host; parson of Ambrosden in Oxfordshire. As Dr Corbet and he were riding in Lob Lane, in wet weather ('tis an extraordinary deep dirty lane) the coach fell; and Dr Corbet said that Dr Stubbins was up to the elbows in mud, and he was up to the elbows in Stubbins.

In 1628 he was made Bishop of Oxford, and I have heard that he had an admirable, grave and venerable aspect.

One time, as he was confirming, the country people pressing in to see the ceremony, said he, 'Bear off there, or I'll confirm you with my staff.' Another time, being about to lay his hand on the head of a man very bald, he turns to his chaplain (Lushington) and said 'Some dust, Lushington' (to keep his hand from slipping). There was a man with a great venerable beard; said the bishop, 'You behind the beard'.

His chaplain, Dr Lushington, was a very learned and ingenious man, and they loved one another. The bishop sometimes would take the key of the wine-cellar, and he and his chaplain would go and lock themselves in and be merry. Then first he lays down his episcopal hat— 'There lies the bishop'. Then he puts off his gown 'There lies the doctor'. Then 'twas 'Here's to thee, Corbet', and 'Here's to thee, Lushington'.—From Josias Howe, BD, Trinity College, Oxford.

He built a pretty house near the causeway beyond 'Friar Bacon's Study'.

He married Alice Hutton, whom 'twas said he begot. She was a very beautiful woman, and so was her mother. He had a son (I think Vincent) that went to school at Westminster with Ned Bagshawe; a very handsome youth, but he is run out of all, and goes begging up and down to gentlemen.

He was made Bishop of Norwich, in 1632. He died 28 July 1635. The last words he said were 'Good night, Lushington'.

His poems are pure natural wit, delightful and easy. It appears by his verses to Master of the Requests Ailesbury, 9 December 1618, that he had knowledge of analytical learning, being so well acquainted with him and the learned Mr Thomas Hariot.

Memorandum: his antagonist Dr Price, the anniversarist*, was made dean of the church at Hereford. Dr Watts, canon of that church, told me, 1656, that this dean was a mighty pontifical proud man, and that

---

* Perhaps because he observed the Roman Catholic custom of offering prayers on the anniversary of a man's death. *Ed.*

one time when they went in procession about the cathedral church, he would not do it the usual way in his surplice, hood, etc on foot, but rode on a mare, thus habited, with the Common Prayer book in his hand, reading. A stallion happened to break loose, and smelled the mare, and ran and leapt her, and held the reverend dean all the time so hard in his embraces, that he could not get off till the horse had done his business. But he would never ride in procession afterwards.

Abraham Cowley
1618–67

Cowley was the son of a London stationer, and wrote poetry from the age of ten, when he was a Westminster scholar. Although he took up other employment, and was at one point a doctor, his real enthusiasm remained poetry and the theatre. He was one of the founders of the Royal Society. His poetry was in the metaphysical tradition of Donne; only his less high-flown pieces have stood the test of time.

He was born in Fleet Street, London near Chancery Lane; his father a grocer.

He was secretary to the Earl of St Alban's (then Lord Jermyn) at Paris. When his majesty returned, the Duke of Buckingham, hearing that at Chertsey was a good farm, belonging to the queen mother, goes to the Earl of St Albans and the commissioners to take a lease of it. The answer that 'twas beneath his grace to take a lease of them. That was all one, he would have it, paid for it, and had it, and freely and generously gave it to his dear and ingenious friend Mr Abraham Cowley, for whom purposely he bought it.

He lies interred at Westminster Abbey, next to Sir Geoffrey Chaucer, where the Duke of Buckingham has put a neat monument of white marble, viz. a fair pedestal, with an inscription. Above that a very fair urn, with a kind of garland of ivy about it.

By Sir J. Denham:

> Had Cowley ne'er spoke nor Tom Killigrew writ,
> They'd both have made a very good wit.

A. Cowley discoursed very ill and with hesitation.

He wrote when a boy at Westminster poems and a comedy called *Love's Riddle*, dedicated to Sir Kenelm Digby.

Abraham Cowley:—vide his will, that is, for his true and lasting charity, that is, he settles his estate in such a manner that every year so much is to be paid for the release of poor prisoners cast into gaol by cruel creditors for some debt. This I had from Mr Dunning of London, a scrivener, who is an acquaintance of Dr Cowley's brother. I do think this memorable benefaction is not mentioned in his life in print before his works; and it is certainly the best method of charity.

Thomas Cromwell
?1485–1540

Cromwell rose from being a clothier and lawyer, through service under Cardinal Wolsey, to being Henry VIII's chief minister. He was the architect of the Act of Supremacy (1534) by which the king became head of the English Church.

Over against Fulham, on the bank of the river Thames, is situated Putney, a small village, and famous for little, but giving birth to that remarkable instance of the inconstancy of fortune, Thomas Cromwell, son of a blacksmith of this place, raised from the anvil, and forge to the most beneficial places and highest of honours in the nation, insomuch that though a layman, he presumed to exercise an ecclesiastical authority over the clergy, and assumed an office, which began and ended in him; to his advice we owe the destruction of religious houses in this nation, and the sacrilegious alienations consequent on it. But the justice of divine providence soon overtook this favourite of fortune, and not only despoiled him of his upstart honours, but of his life, and so for some time retarded the happy Reformation, begun upon so bad principles.

Curtin

Madam Curtin, who had a good fortune of £3000, daughter to Sir William Curtin, the great merchant, lately married her footman, who not long after marriage, beats her, gets her money, and ran away.

The Danvers Family

The Danvers were local magnates in Wiltshire. The murder of Henry Long by Henry and Charles Danvers was one of the great scandals of the 1590s, which Aubrey's older neighbours remembered vividly. Both brothers obtained pardons in 1598; Henry had a distinguished military and governmental career in the 1610s and 1620s, despite the fact that his brother had been executed for treason, and was created Earl of Danby in 1626. Aubrey also gives biographies of their mother Elizabeth, their father, Sir John, and their younger brother, Sir John the younger. The family were distant cousins of Aubrey's, through his great-grandfather.

Sir Charles Danvers was beheaded on Tower Hill with Robert, Earl of Essex, 6 February 1601. I find in the register of the Tower Chapel only the burial of Robert, Earl of Essex, that year: wherefore I am induced to believe that his body was carried to Dauntsey in Wiltshire to lie with his ancestors. See Stowe's Chronicle, where is a full account of his and the earl's deportment at their death on the scaffold.

His familiar acquaintances were the Earl of Oxford; Sir Francis and Sir Horace Vere; Sir Walter Raleigh, etc—the heroes of those times.

¶ Of Sir Charles Danvers, from my lady Viscountess Purbeck:—Sir Charles Danvers advised the Earl of Essex either to treat with the queen—using hostages, whom Sir Ferdinando Gorges did let go; or to make his way through the gate at Essex House, and then to hasten away to Highgate, and so to Northumberland (the Earl of Northumberland married his mother's sister) and from thence to the King of Scots, and there they might make their peace; if not, the queen was old and could not live long. But the earl followed not his advice and so they both lost their heads on Tower Hill.

¶ Henry Danvers, Earl of Danby: ask my brother William, and J. Stokes for the examination order of the murder of Henry Long, by Charles Danvers at Cosham in North Wilts. R. Wisdom was then lecturer and preached that day, and Henry Long expired in his arms. My great-grandfather, R. Danvers, was in some trouble about it, his horse and men being in that action. His servants were hanged and so were Long of Linet's.

He perfected his Latin when a man by Parson Oldham of Dodmerton. He was a perfect master of the French; a historian; tall and spare; temperate; sedate and solid; a very great favourite of Prince Henry; lived most at Cornbury; a great improver of his estate, to £11,000 per annum income at the least; sold the Seven Downs in Wiltshire and turned the freehold into lease; afterwards bought fee-simple near Cirencester.

He was a great economist. All his servants were sober and discreet in their respective places.

He was page to Sir Philip Sidney—from my cousin Elizabeth Villiers. With all their failings, Wiltshire cannot show two such brothers.

Sir Henry Danvers, knight, Earl of Danby and Baron of Dauntsey, was born at Dauntsey 28 June 1573. He was of a magnificent and generous spirit, and made that noble physic-garden at Oxford, and endowed it I think with £30 per annum. In the epistles of Degory Wheare, History Professor of Oxford, in Latin, are several addressed to his lordship that do recite his worth. He allowed three thousand pounds per annum for his kitchen alone. He bred up several brave young gentlemen and preferred [assisted] them; e.g. Colonel Legge, and several others, of which enquire further of my lady Viscountess Purbeck.

He was made a Knight of the Garter AD 1633. For many years before, St George's Feast had not been more magnificently kept than when this earl, with the Earl of Morton, were installed Knights of the Garter. One might then have beheld the epitome of English and Scottish in their attendance. The Scottish Earl (like Zeuxis' picture) adorned with all art and costliness: whilst our English earl (like to the plain sheet of Apelles) by the gravity of habit, got the advantage of the gallantry of his co-rival in the eyes of judicious beholders.

Elizabeth Danvers. His mother, an Italian, prodigious parts for a woman. I have heard my father's mother say that she had Chaucer at her fingers' ends. A great politician; great wit and spirit, but revengeful. Knew how to manage her estate as well as any man; understood jewels as well as any jeweller.

Very beautiful, but shortsighted. To obtain pardons for her sons [over the murder of Long] she married Sir Edmund Carey, cousin-german to Queen Elizabeth, but kept him to hard meat.

The secret, handed down like a torch in the family of Latimer of poisoning King Henry VIII [? i.e. that he was poisoned]—from my lady Purbeck.

Sir John Danvers, the father, a most beautiful and good and even-tempered person. His picture yet extant—my cousin John Danvers has it. Memorandum, George Herbert's verses on the curtain:

> Pass not by; search and you may
> Find a treasure worth your stay.
> What makes a Danvers, would you find?
> In a fair body, a fair mind.
> Sir John Danvers' earthly part
> Here is copied out by art:

85

But his heavenly and divine
In his progeny doth shine.
Had he only brought them forth,
Know that much had been his worth.
There's no monument to a son:
Read him there, and I have done.

He was of a mild and peaceable nature, and his sons' sad accident [the murder of Long] broke his heart.

Sir John Danvers (the younger). Sir John, his son, was then a child about six [at his father's death]. An ingenious person, e.g. Chelsea House and garden and Lavington garden. A great friend of the king's party and a patron to distressed and cashiered cavaliers, e.g. Captain Gunter, he served Christopher Gibbons (organist), captain Peters, etc—Lord Bacon's friend. But to revenge himself of his sister, the Lady Gargrave, to ingratiate himself more with the Protector, to nullify his brother, Earl of Danby's, will, he, contrary to his own natural inclination did sit in the high court of justice at the king's trial.

Dauntsey ([an estate worth] £2500 per annum), not entailed, was forfeited and given to the Duke of York.

¶ His first wife was the Lady Herbert, a widow, mother of the Lord Edward Herbert of Cherbury and George Herbert, orator. By her he had no issue; she was old enough to have been his mother. He married her for love of her wit. The Earl of Danby was greatly displeased with him for this disagreeable match.

¶ Sir John Danvers told me that when he was a young man, the principal reason of sending their sons to travel was to wean them from their acquaintance and *familiarity* with the *serving-men*: for then parents were so austere and grave, that the sons must not be company for their father; and *some* company men must have: so they contracted a familiarity with the serving-men, who got a hold upon them they could hardly after claw off. Nay, parents would suffer their servants to domineer over their children: and some in what they found their child to take delight, in that would be sure to cross them.

¶ The pleasure and use of gardens were unknown to our great-grandfathers: they were contented with pot-herbs: and did mind chiefly their stables. But in the time of Charles II, gardening was much improved, and became common. 'Twas Sir John Danvers of Chelsea (brother and heir to Henry Danvers, Earl of Danby) who first taught us the way of Italian gardens. He had well travelled France and Italy, and made good observations. He had in a fair body an harmonical mind: in his youth his complexion was so exceedingly beautiful and fine that Thomas Bond esquire (who was his companion in his travels) did say, that the people would come after him in the street to admire him. He had a very fine fancy which lay (chiefly) for gardens, and architecture. The gardens at Chelsea in Middlesex (as likewise the house there) do remain monuments of his ingenuity. He was a great acquaintance of the Lord Chancellor Bacon, who took much delight in that elegant garden.

Sir John, being my relation and faithful friend, was wont in fair mornings in the summer to brush his beaver-hat on the hyssop and thyme, which did perfume it with its natural spirit, and would last a morning or longer.

Edward Davenant

?–1680

Edward Davenant, Doctor of Theology, was the eldest son of Davenant, merchant of London, who was elder brother to the right reverend father in God, the learned John Davenant, bishop of Salisbury.

I will first speak of the father, for he was a rare man in his time, and deserves to be remembered. He was of a healthy complexion, rose at 4 or 5 in the morning, so that he followed his studies till 6 or 7, the time that other merchants go about their business; so that, stealing so much and so quiet time in the morning, he studied as much as most men. He understood Greek and Latin perfectly, and was a better Grecian than the bishop. He wrote as rare a Greek character as ever I saw. He was a great mathematician, and understood as much of it as was known in his time. Dr Davenant, the son, has excellent notes of his father's, in mathematics, as also in Greek, and it was no small advantage to him to have such a learned father to imbue arithmetical knowledge into him when a boy, night times when he came from school (Merchant Taylors'). He understood trade very well, was a sober and good manager, but the winds and seas crossed him. He had such great losses that he went bankrupt, but his creditors knowing that it was no fault of his, and also that he was a person of great virtue and justice, used not extremity towards him; but I think gave him more credit, so that he went into Ireland, and did set up a fishery for pilchards at Wythy Island, in Ireland, where in some years he got £10,000; he satisfied and paid his creditors; and over and above left a good estate to his son. His picture bespeaks him to be a man of judgement and parts, and gravity extraordinary. He slipped coming down the stone stairs at the palace at Salisbury, which bruise caused his death. He lies buried in the south aisle of the choir in Salisbury Cathedral behind the bishop's stall.

Dr Edward Davenant was born at his father's house at Croydon in Surrey (the farthest handsome great house on the left hand as you ride to Banstead Downs). I have heard him say, he thanked God his father did not know the hour of his birth, for that it would have tempted him to have studied astrology, for which he had no esteem at all.

He went to school at Merchant Taylors' school, from thence to Queeen's College in Cambridge, of which house his uncle, John Davenant (after bishop of Salisbury) where he was fellow.

When his uncle was preferred to the church of Salisbury, he made his nephew treasurer of the church, which is the best dignity, and gave him the vicarage of Gillingham in Dorset, and then Paulsholt parsonage, near Devizes, which last in the late troubles [under the Commonwealth] he resigned to his wife's brother, William Grove.

He was to his dying day of great diligence in study, well versed in all kinds of learning, but his genius did most strongly incline him to the mathematics, wherein he has written, (in a hand as legible as print) manuscripts in quarto, a foot high at least. I have often heard him say (jestingly) that he would have a man knocked on the head that should write anything in mathematics that had been written of before. I have heard Sir Christopher Wren say that he does believe he was the best mathematician in the world about thirty or thirty-five years ago. But being a divine he was unwilling to print, because the world should not know how he had spent the greatest part of his time.

He very rarely went any farther than the church, which is hard by his house. His wife was a very discreet and excellent housewife, so that he troubled himself about no mundane affairs, and it is a private place, so that he was but little diverted with visits.

I have written to his executor, that we may have the honour and favour to conserve his manuscripts in the Library of the Royal Society, and to print what if fit. I hope I shall obtain my desire. And the bishop of Exeter (Lamplugh) married the doctor's second daughter Katherine, and he was tutor to Sir Joseph Williamson, our President. He had a noble library, which was the aggregate of his father's, the bishop's and his own.

He was of middling stature, somewhat spare; and weak, feeble legs; he had sometimes the gout; was always of great temperance, he always drank his beer at meals with a piece of toast, winter and summer, and said it made the beer better.

He was not only a man of vast learning, but of great goodness and charity; the parish and all his friends will have a great loss in him. He took no interest for money upon bond. He was my singular good friend, and to whom I have been more obliged than to anyone besides; for I borrowed five hundred pounds of him for a year and a half, and I could not fasten any interest on him.

He was very ready to teach and instruct. He did me the favour to inform me first in algebra. His daughters were algebrists.

His most familiar learned acquaintance was Lancelot Morehouse, parson of Pertwood. I remember when I was a young Oxford scholar, that he could not endure to hear of the *New* (Cartesian etc) *Philosophy*; 'for,' said he, 'if a new philosophy is brought in, a new divinity will shortly follow' (or 'come next'); and he was right.

He died at his house at Gillingham aforesaid, where he and his predecessor, Dr Jessop, had been vicars one hundred and more years, and lies buried in the chancel there.

He was heir to his uncle, John Davenant, bishop of Salisbury. Memorandum: when bishop Coldwell came to this bishopric (1591–6), he did let long leases which were but newly expired when bishop Davenant came to this see; so that there tumbled into his coffers vast sums. His predecessor Dr Tounson, married Davenant's sister, continued in the see but a little while, and left several children unprovided for, so the king or rather the duke of Buckingham gave bishop Davenant the bishopric out of pure charity. Sir Antony Weldon says (in his *Court of King James*) it was the only bishopric that he disposed of without simony, all others being made merchandise of for the advancement of his kindred. Bishop Davenant being invested, married all his nieces to clergymen, so he was at no expense for their preferment. He granted to his nephew (this Doctor) the lease of the great manor of Poterne, worth about £1000 per annum; made him treasurer of the church of Salisbury, of which the endowment is the parsonage of Calne, which was esteemed to be of like value. He made several purchases of property, all which he left him; insomuch as the churchmen of Salisbury say, that he gained more by this church than ever any man did by the church since the Reformation, and take it very unkindly that, at his death, he left nothing (or but £50) to that church which was the source of his estate. How it happened I know not, or how he might be worked on in his old age, but I have heard several years since, he had set down £500 in will for the Cathedral Church of Sarum.

He had six sons and four daughters. There was a good school at Gillingham: at winter nights he taught his sons arithmetic and geometry; his two eldest daughters, especially Mrs Ettrick, was a notable algebrist. Memory: He had an excellent way of improving his children's memories, which was thus: he would make one of them read a chapter or etc, and then they were at once to repeat what they remembered, which did exceedingly profit them; and so for sermons, he did not let them write notes (which jaded their memory), but gave a verbal account. When his eldest son, John, came to Winchester school (where the boys were enjoined to write sermon-notes) he had not written (any) and the master asked him for his notes—he had none, but said, 'If I do not give you as good an account of it as they that do, I am much mistaken.'

Sir William Davenant

1606–68

Poet Laureate from 1638–68 and a much-esteemed playwright immediately after the Restoration. Aubrey's account is the main source for his life, though there is a good deal of gossip in it as well as fact. His best-known 'play' was The Siege of Rhodes, *which was in effect the first opera produced in England; it was also the first stage play to use scenery, and the first in which a woman appeared on the English stage.*

Sir William Davenant, knight, Poet Laureate, was born about the end of February (baptised 3 March) 1606, in the city of Oxford, at the Crown tavern.

His father was John Davenant, a vintner there, a very grave and discreet citizen: his mother was a very beautiful woman, and of very good wit, and of conversation extremely agreeable. They had three sons, viz 1 Robert*, 2 William, and 3, Nicholas (an attorney): and two handsome daughters, one married to Gabriel Bridges (BD, fellow of Corpus Christi College, beneficed in the Vale of the White Horse), another to Dr Sherburne (minister of Pembridge in Hereford, and a canon of that church).

Mr William Shakespeare was wont to go into Warwickshire once a year, and did commonly in his journey lie at this house in Oxford, where he was exceedingly respected. (I have heard parson Robert say that Mr W. Shakespeare has given him a hundred kisses.) Now Sir William would sometimes, when he was pleasant over a glass of wine with his most intimate friends, e.g. Sam Butler (author of *Hudibras*), etc—say, that it seemed to him that he wrote with the very spirit that Shakespeare [wrote], and seemed contented enough to be thought his son: he would tell them the story as above, in which way his mother had a very light report.

He went to school at Oxford to Mr Sylvester (Charles Wheare, son of Degory Wheare, was his schoolfellow), but I fear he was drawn from school before he was ripe enough: he was preferred to the first Duchess of Richmond to wait on her as a page. I remember he told me, she sent him to a famous apothecary for some unicorn's-horn, which he was resolved to try with a spider which he encircled in it, but without the expected success; the spider would go over, and through and through, unconcerned.

He was next a servant (as I remember, a page also) to Sir Fulke

* Robert was a fellow of St John's College in Oxford: then preferred to the parsonage of West Kington by Bishop Davenant, whose chaplain he was.

Greville, Lord Brooke, with whom he lived until his death, which was that a servant of his—that had long waited on him and his lordship had often told him that he would do something for him, but did not, but still put him off with delays—as he was trussing up his lord's points coming from the lavatory (for then their breeches were fastened to the doublets with points: then came in hooks and eyes, which not to have fastened was in my boyhood a great crime) stabbed him. This was at the same time that the Duke of Buckingham was stabbed by Felton, and the great noise and report of the duke's stabbing, Sir William told me, quite drowned this of his lord's, that it was scarce taken notice of. This Sir Fulke Greville was a good wit, and had been a good poet in his youth. He wrote a poem in folio, which he printed not till he was old, and then, as Sir William said, with too much judgement and refining, spoiled it, which was at first a delicate thing.

He wrote a play or plays, and verses, which he did with so much sweetness and grace, that by it he got the love and friendship of his two Maecenases, Mr Endymion Porter, and Mr Henry Jermyn (since Earl of St Albans), to whom he has dedicated his poem called *Madagascar*. Sir John Suckling also was his great and intimate friend. After the death of Ben Jonson he was made in his place Poet Laureate.

He got a terrible clap of a dark-haired handsome wench that lay in Axe Yard, Westminster, whom he thought on when he speaks of Dalga in *Gondibert*, which cost him his nose, with which unlucky mischance many wits were too cruelly bold, e.g. Sir John Minnes, Sir John Denham etc . . .

In 1641, when the troubles began, he was fain to fly into France, and at Canterbury he was seized on by the mayor—vide Sir John Minnes' verse—

> For Will had in his face the flaws
> And marks received in country's cause:
> They flew on him like lions passant
> And tore his nose as much as was on't,
> And call'd him superstitious groom,
> And Popish Dog, and Cur of Rome
> . . .'Twas surely the first time
> That Will's religion was a crime.

In the civil wars in England he was in the army of William, Marquess of Newcastle (since duke), where he was general of the ordinance. I have heard his brother Robert say, for that service there was owing to him by King Charles the First £10,000. During that war, it was his hap to have two aldermen of York his prisoners, who were something stubborn, and would not give the ransom ordered by the council of war. Sir William used them civilly, and treated them in his tent, and sat them at the upper end of his table *à la mode de France* and having done so a good while to his charge, told them (privately and friendly) that he was not able to keep such expensive guests and bade them take an opportunity to escape, which they did; but having been gone a little way they considered with themselves that in gratitude they ought to go back and give Sir William their thanks; which they did, but it was likely to have been to their great danger of being taken by the soldiers; but they happened to get safe to York.

The king's party being overcome, Sir William Davenant (who received the honour of knighthood from the Duke of Newcastle by commission) went into France; resided chiefly in Paris where the Prince of Wales then was. He then began to write his romance in verse, called *Gondibert*, and had not written more than the first book, but being very fond of it, prints it (before a quarter finished), with an epistle of his to Mr Thomas Hobbes and Mr Hobbes' excellent epistle to him printed before it. The courtiers with the Prince of Wales could never be at quiet about this piece, which was the occasion of a very witty but satirical little book of verses in octavo, about four sheets, written by George Duke of Buckingham, Sir John Denham, etc—

'That thou forsak'st thy sleep, thy diet,
And which is more than that, *our quiet*.'

This last word Mr Hobbes told me was the occasion of their writing.

Here he laid an ingenious design to carry a considerable number of artificers (chiefly weavers) from hence to Virginia; and by Mary the queen mother's means, he got favour from the King of France to go into the prisons and pick and choose. So when the poor damned wretches understood what the design was, they cried with one voice: '*Tous tisserans!*' i.e. *We are all weavers!* Will took 36, as I remember, if not more, and shipped them; and as he was in his voyage towards Virginia, he and his *tisserans* were all taken by the ships then belonging to the Parliament of England. The slaves I suppose they sold, but Sir William was brought prisoner to England. Whether he was first a prisoner at Carisbrooke Castle in the Isle of Wight, or at the Tower of London, I have forgotten: he was a prisoner at both. His *Gondibert*, quarto, was finished at Carisbrooke Castle. He expected no mercy from the parliament, and had no hopes of escaping with his life. It pleased God that the two aldermen of York aforesaid, hearing that he was taken and brought to London to be tried for his life, which they understood was in extreme danger, they were touched with so much generosity and goodness, as, upon their own accounts and mere notion, to try what they could to save Sir William's life who had been so civil to them and a means to save theirs, to come to London: and acquainting the parliament with it, upon their petition etc, Sir William's life was saved.*

Being freed from imprisonment (because plays, i.e. tragedies and comedies, were in those Presbyterian times scandalous) he contrives to set up an Opera, in the reciting manner, wherein Serjeant Maynard and several citizens were backers. It began at Rutland House, in Charterhouse Yard; next (that is in 1656) at the Cockpit in Drury Lane where were acted very well, *stylo recitativo*, *Sir Francis Drake* and *The Siege of Rhodes* (first and second part). It did affect the eye and ear extremely. This first brought scenery in fashion in England; before, at plays, only a hanging.

In 1660 was the happy restoration of his majesty Charles II. Then was Sir William made Master of the Revels; and the Tennis Court† in Little Lincoln's Inn Field was turned into a playhouse for the Duke of York's players, where Sir William Davenant had lodgings and where he died, 7 April 1668.

I was at his funeral. He had a coffin of walnut tree. Sir John Denham said it was the finest coffin that ever he saw. His body was carried in a hearse from the playhouse to Westminster Abbey, where, at the great west door, he was received by the singing men and choristers, who sang the service of the church to his grave, which is in the south cross aisle, on which, on a paving stone of marble, is written, in imitation of that on Ben Jonson, '*O rare Sir Will Davenant*'.

Sir William has written about 25 (query) plays; the romance called *Gondibert*; and a little poem called *Madagascar*.

His private opinion was that religion at last—e.g. a hundred years hence—would come to settlement, and that in a kind of ingenious Quakerism.

¶ Sir William was poet laureate; and Mr John Dryden has his place. But methought it had been proper that a laurel should have been set on his coffin—which was not done.

* It was Harry Martyn that saved Sir William Davenant's life in the House—when they were talking of sacrificing one, then said Henry that 'in sacrifices they always offered pure and without blemish: now you talk of making a sacrifice of an old rotten rascal'. See H. Martyn's Life, where by this *very jest*, then forgotten, Lord Falkland saved H. Martyn's life.

† It is now a tennis court again, upon the building of the duke's theatre in Dorset Garden.

Michael Davy

?–1679

Michael Davy, mathematician, and a gunner of the Tower (by profession, a tobacco-cutter) an admirable algebrician, was buried in the churchyard near Bedlam on May Day 1679. With writing in the frosty weather, his fingers rotted and gangrened.

John Dee

1527–1608

John Dee, as a famous astrologer and mathematician, was particularly interesting to Aubrey, whose own studies had been chiefly in these fields. Dee also had the reputation of being a conjurer, which began when he produced a play at Cambridge in 1548, in which extraordinary stage effects were used; but this reputation was later entirely justified by his alchemical experiments. He was a great book collector, and was interested in subjects such as writing in cipher: but he also studied alchemy, and tried to communicate with spirits by means of a crystal ball. However, the 'skryer' whom he employed was probably a fraud, though Dee failed to detect this and retained him for a quarter of a century. Dee is the last of the medieval alchemists, lacking the critical attitude of Aubrey's contemporaries, the founders of the Royal Society.

I have left about 1674 with Mr Elias Ashmole three pages in folio concerning him.

The father of this John Dee was a vintner in London (from Elias Ashmole who has it from this Dee's grandson. Memorandum: Mr Meredith Lloyd tells me that his father was Roland Dee, a Radnorshire gentleman, and that he has his pedigree, which he has promised to lend to me. He was descended from Rees, prince of South Wales. My great-grandfather, William Aubrey (LlD), and he were cousins, and intimate acquaintance. Mr Ashmole has letters between them, under their own hands, viz one of Sr William Aubrey to him (ingeniously and learnedly written) touching the *Sovereignty of the Sea*, of which John Dee wrote a book which he dedicated to Queen Elizabeth and desired my great-grandfather's advice upon it. Dr Aubrey's country-house was at Kew, and John Dee lived at Mortlake, not a mile distant. I have heard my grandfather say they were often together.

Arthur Dee, MD, his son, lived and practised at Norwich, an intimate friend of Sir Thomas Browne, MD, who told me that Sir William Boswell, the Dutch ambassador, had all John Dee's manuscripts: ask his executors for his papers. He lived then somewhere in Kent.

Ask A. Wood for the manuscripts in the Bodleian library of Doctor Gwyn, wherein are several letters between him and John Dee, and Doctor Davies, of chemistry and of magical secrets, which my worthy friend Mr Meredith Lloyd has seen and read: and he tells me that he has been told that Dr Barlowe gave it to the Prince of Tuscany.

Meredith Lloyd says that John Dee's printed book of spirits is not above the third part of what was written, which were in Sir Robert Cotton's library; many whereof were much perished by being buried, and Sir Robert Cotton bought the field to dig after it.

Memorandum: he told me of John Dee conjuring at a pool in Brecknockshire, and that they found a wedge of gold; and that they were troubled and indicted as conjurers at the assizes; that a mighty storm and tempest was raised in harvest time, the country people had not known the like.

His picture in a wooden cut is at the end of Billingsley's Euclid but Mr Elias Ashmole has a very good painted copy of him from his son Arthur. He has a very fair, clear sanguine complexion (like Sir Henry Savile); a long beard as white as milk. A very handsome man.

Old goodwife Faldo (a native of Mortlake in Surrey), aged eighty or more (1672), did know Dr Dee, and told me he died at his house in Mortlake, next to the house where the tapestry hangings are made, viz west of that house; and that he died aged about sixty or more, eight or nine years since, and lies buried in the chancel, and had a stone (marble) upon him. Her mother tended him in his sickness. She told me that he did entertain the Polish ambassador at his house in Mortlake, and died not long after; and that he showed the eclipse by means of a *camera obscura* to the said ambassador.* She believes that he was eighty years old when he died. She said, he kept a great many stills going; that he laid the storm by magic: that the children dreaded him because he was accounted a conjurer. He recovered the basket of clothes stolen when she and his daughter (both girls) were negligent: she knew this.

A daughter of his (I think Sarah) is married to a flax-dresser in Southwark: ask for her name.

He built the gallery in the church at Mortlake. Goody Faldo's father was the carpenter that worked on it.

* *A Brief History of Muscovia* by Mr John Milton, London 1682: 'Dr Giles Fletcher went ambassador from the queen to Feodor then emperor; whose relations, being judicious and exact, are best read entirely by themselves. This emperor, upon report of the great learning of the mathematician, invited him to Moscow, with offer of two thousand pounds a year, and from Prince Boris one thousand marks; to have his provision from the emperor's table, to be honourably received, and accounted as one of the chief men in the land. All of which Dee accepted not.'

A stone was on his grave, which is since removed. At the upper end of the chancel then were steps, which in Oliver's days were levelled by the minister, and then it was removed. The children when they played in the church would run to Dr Dee's grave stone. She told me that he forewarned Queen Elizabeth of Dr Lopez' attempt against her (the doctor betrayed it, beshit himself).

He used to distil eggshells, and it was from hence that Ben Jonson had his hint of the alchemist, whom he meant.

He was a great peacemaker; if any of the neighbours fell out, he would never let them alone till he had made them friends.

He was tall and slender. He wore a gown like an artist's gown, with hanging sleeves, and a slit.

A mighty good man he was.

He was sent ambassador for Queen Elizabeth (she thinks) into Poland.

Memorandum: his regaining of the plate for a certain gentleman's butler, who coming from London by water with a basket of plate, mistook another basket that was like his. Mr J. Dee bid them go by water on such a day, and he would see the man that had his basket, and he did so. But he would not get lost horses, though he was offered several angels (pieces of money). He told a woman (his neighbour) that she laboured under the evil tongue of an ill neighbour (another woman) who came to her house, who, he said, was a witch.

Gideon de Laune
?1565–69

He was apothecary to Mary the queen mother [?Henrietta Maria]. He was a very wise man, and as a sign of it left an estate of £80,000.

Sir William Davenant was his great acquaintance, and told me of him, and that after his return into England he went to visit him, being then in his eighties, and very decrepit with the gout, but had his sight and understanding. He had a place made for him in the kitchen chimney; and even though he was master of such an estate, Sir William saw him slighted not only by his daughter-in-law, but by the cook-maid, which much affected him—misery of old age.

He wrote a book of prudent advice, in English verse, which I have seen, and there are good things in it.

Sir John Denham

1615–69

*Sir John Denham's youthful reputation was as a rake and gambler, but in
1641 his first play was a great and unexpected success. Cooper's Hill, a
pastoral poem, followed in 1642. During the Civil War he was active in
royalist diplomacy, and was later banned from living in London under the
Commonwealth. His last years were overshadowed by the death of his second
wife in 1667; Aubrey's story is more charitable than that of Pepys and many
other writers, who lay her death at Denham's door. (The post-mortem
revealed no traces of poison.) Denham himself died two years later.*

Sir John Denham, Knight of the Bath, was born at Dublin in Ireland,
in 1615.

Ask Dr Busby if he was a Westminster Scholar—I have forgotten. He
was admitted of Trinity College in Oxford; I have heard Mr Josias
Howe say that he was the most dreamy young fellow; he never expected
such things from him as he has left the world. When he was there he
would game extremely; when he had played away all his money, he
would play away his father's wrought rich gold cups.

His father was Sir John Denham, one of the Barons of the Exchequer.
He had been one of the Lords Justices in Ireland; he married Eleanor,*
one of the daughters of Sir Garrett Moore, knight, lord baron of
Mellifont in the Kingdom of Ireland; whom he married during his
service in Ireland in the place of Chief Justice there.

From Trinity College he went to Lincoln's Inn, where (as Judge
Wadham Windham, who was his contemporary, told me) he was as
good a student as any in the house. He was not suspected to be a wit.

At last, viz 1640, his play of *The Sophy* came out, which was a great
success: Mr Edmund Waller said then of him, that he 'broke out like
the Irish Rebellion†—three-score thousand strong, before anybody was
aware'.

He was much cheated by gamesters, and fell acquainted with that
unsanctified crew, to his ruin. His father had some suspicion of it, and
chided him severely, whereupon his son John (only child) wrote a little
essay in octavo, printed, *Against gaming and to shew the vanities and
inconveniences of it,‡* which he presented to his father to let him know

---

* She was a beautiful woman, as appears by her monument at Egham. Sir John, they
say, did much resemble his father.　　　　　　　　　　† His play came out at that time.

‡ See Justus Turcaeus, *On the deception of dice*, where he proves it is a disease and that it
proceeds from pride, and that the Spaniards (the proudest nation) are most addicted to it.

his detestation of it. But shortly after his father's death (who left £2,000 or £1,500 in ready money, two houses well furnished, and much plate) the money was played away first, and next the plate was sold. I remember about 1646 he lost £200 one night at New Cut. (I guess in 1642) he was high sheriff of the county of Surrey.

At the beginning of the civil war he was made governor of Farnham Castle for the king, but he was but a young soldier, and did not keep it. In 1643 after Edgehill fight, his poem called *Cowper's Hill* was printed at Oxford, in a sort of brown paper, for then they could get no better.

1646 (query) he conveyed, or stole away, the two Dukes, of York and Gloucester, from St James's (from the tuition of the Earl of Northumberland), and conveyed them into France, to the Prince of Wales and queen mother. King Charles II sent him and the Lord Culpeper envoys to the King of Poland.

In 1652 he returned into England, and being in some straits was kindly entertained by the Earl of Pembroke at Wilton, where I had the honour to contract an acquaintance with him. Here he translated a book of Virgil's *Aeneid*, and also burlesqued it; and burnt it, saying that it was not fit that the best poet should be so abused—From Mr Christopher Wace, who was then there, tutor to William Lord Herbert. He was, as I remember, a year with my lord of Pembroke at Wilton and London; he had then sold all the lands his father had left him.

His first wife was the daughter and heir of one Cotton, of Gloucestershire, by whom he had £500 per annum, one son and two daughters.

He was much beloved by King Charles the First, who much valued him for his ingenuity. He granted him the reversion of the office of surveyor of his majesty's buildings, after the decease of Mr Inigo Jones; which place, after the restoration of King Charles II, he enjoyed until his death, and got £7,000, as Sir Christopher Wren told me of, to his own knowledge. Sir Christopher Wren was his deputy.

In 1665 he married his second wife, Margaret Brookes, a very beautiful young lady; Sir John was ancient and limping. The Duke of York fell deeply in love with her, though (I have been morally assured) he never had carnal knowledge of her. This occasioned Sir John Denham's distemper of madness, which first appeared when he went from London to see the famous freestone quarries at Portland in Dorset, and when he came within a mile of it, turned back to London again, and would not see it. He went to Hounslow, and demanded rents of lands he had sold many years before; went to the king, and told him he was the Holy Ghost. But it pleased God that he was cured of this distemper, and wrote excellent verses, particularly on the death of Mr Abraham Cowley, afterwards. His second lady had no child; was poisoned by the hands of the Countess of Rochester with chocolate.

At the coronation of King Charles II he was made a Knight of the Bath.

He died at the house of his office (which he built, as also the brick buildings next the street in Scotland Yard) and was buried on 23 March 1669 in the south cross aisle of Westminster Abbey, near Sir Geoffrey Chaucer's monument, but hitherto (1680) without any memorial for him.

Memorandum:—the parsonage house at Egham (vulgarly called The Place) was built by Baron Denham; a house very convenient, not great, but pretty, and pleasantly situated, and which his son, Sir John (though he had better seats) did take most delight in. He sold it to John Thynne esquire. In this parish is a place called Camomile Hill, from the camomile that grows there naturally; as also west of it is Prunewell Hill (formerly part of Sir John's possessions) where was a fine tuft of trees, a clear spring, and a pleasant prospect to the east, over the level of Middlesex and Surrey. Sir John took great delight in this place, and was wont to say (before the troubles) that he would build there a retiring place to entertain his muses; but the wars forced him to sell that as well as the rest. He sold it to Mr Anstey. In this parish, west and by north (above Runnymede) is Cowper's Hill, which is incomparably well described by that sweet swan, Sir John Denham.

Memorandum: he delighted much in bowls, and did bowl very well.

He was of the tallest, but a little incurvetting at his shoulders, not very robust. His hair was but thin and flaxen, with a moist curl. His gait was slow, and was rather a stalking (he had long legs), which was wont to put me in mind of Horace, *De Arte Poetica*:

He, with head upraised, splutters verses, and off he strays; then like a fowler with his eyes upon blackbirds, he falls into a well . . . (454–9)

His eye was a kind of light goose-grey, not big; but it had a strange piercingness, not as to shining and glory, but (like a Momus) when he conversed with you he looked into your very thoughts.

He was generally temperate as to drinking; but one time when he was a student of Lincoln's Inn, having been merry at the tavern with his comrades, late at night, a frolic came into his head, to get a plasterer's brush and a pot of ink, and blot out all the signs between Temple Bar and Charing Cross, which made a strange confusion the next day, and it was in term time. But it happened that they were discovered and it cost them and him some moneys. This I had from R. Estcott, esquire, that carried the inkpot.

In the time of the civil wars, George Withers, the poet, begged Sir John Denham's estate at Egham of the Parliament, in whose cause he was a captain of horse. It happened that G. W. was taken prisoner, and was in danger of his life, having written severely against the king. Sir John Denham went to the king, and desired his majesty not to hang him, for that whilst G. W. lived he should not be the worst poet in England.

Memorandum: in the verses against Gondibert, most of them are Sir John's. He was satirical when he had a mind to it.

René Descartes
1596–1650

French philosopher and mathematician, whose most famous dictum 'I think, therefore I am', has become a commonplace. His chief work was the Discourse of Method *(1637). Though his ideas were much esteemed in Europe, he had few English disciples.*

How he spent his time in his youth, and by what method he became so knowing, he tells the world in his treatise entitled *Of Method*. The Jesuits glory in that their order had the educating of him. He lived several years at Egmont (near The Hague), from whence he dated several of his books. He was too wise a man to encumber himself with a wife; but as he was a man, he had the desires and appetites of a man; he therefore kept a good conditioned handsome woman that he liked, and by whom he had some children (I think two or three). 'Tis a pity, but coming from the brain of such a father, they should be well cultivated. He was so eminently learned that all learned men made visits to him, and many of them would desire him to show them his store of instruments (in those days mathematical learning lay much in the knowledge of instruments, and as Sir Henry Savile said, in doing of tricks). He would draw out a little drawer under his table and show them a pair of compasses with one of the legs broken; and then for his ruler, he used a sheet of paper folded double. This from Alexander Cooper (brother of Samuel), limner to Christina, Queen of Sweden, who was familiarly acquainted there with Descartes.

¶ Mr Hobbes was wont to say that had Descartes kept himself wholly to geometry, that he had been the best geometer in the world. He did very much admire him, but said that he could not pardon him for writing in the defence of transubstantiation which he knew to be absolutely against his judgment.

Sir Everard Digby
1578–1606

Sir Everard Digby inherited large estates in the Midlands from his father, who died when he was fourteen. He came to court while still a youth, but in 1599 was converted to Roman Catholicism by Father Gerard. His disappointment at James I's attitude towards Catholics led him to join the Gunpowder Plot of 1605.

Sir Everard suffered as a traitor in the gunpowder treason (1605); but King James restored his estate to his son and heir.

¶ When his heart was plucked out by the executioner (who, according to the custom cried 'Here is the heart of a traitor!'), it is credibly reported, he replied, 'Thou liest!' This my lord Bacon speaks of, but not mentioning his name, in his *History of life and death*.

¶ His second son was Sir John Digby, as valiant a gentleman and as good a swordsman as was in England, who died (or was killed) in the king's cause at Bridgewater, about 1644. It happened in 1647 that a grave was opened next to Sir John Digby's (who was buried in summertime, it seems), and the flowers on his coffin were found fresh, as I heard Mr Harcourt (that was executed) attest that very year. Sir John died a bachelor.

Sir Kenelm Digby
1603–65

Sir Kenelm Digby, courtier and virtuoso, had a remarkable and varied career. He became engaged to Venetia Stanley at the age of seventeen, but his mother disapproved, and he was sent abroad, where he travelled in France and Italy, and finally joined Prince Charles' entourage at Madrid, where Charles was seeking the hand of the Infanta. He was knighted on their return to England in 1623. He married Venetia Stanley in 1625. His career at court was blocked by the Duke of Buckingham, so in 1627 he set out as a privateer to the Mediterranean, where his exploits included the defeat of the French and Venetian ships at Scanderoon in the Adriatic. In 1633 Venetia died, and he retired from public life for two years, but after this resumed his place at court. He was imprisoned in 1642–3 for his French and Roman Catholic sympathies. He was exiled in 1643 and lived in France for most of the next ten years. After the Restoration, he was one of the founders of the Royal Society.

101

He was born on the eleventh of June: see Ben Jonson, second volume:

'Witness thy actions done at Scanderoon
Upon thy birthday, the eleventh of June'

(Memorandum: in the first impression in octavo it is thus; but in the folio it is *my*, instead of *thy*.)

Mr Elias Ashmole assures me, from two or three nativities by Dr Napier, that Ben Jonson was mistaken and did it for the rhyme's sake.

He was the eldest son of Sir Everard Digby, who was accounted the handsomest gentleman in England.

Sir Kenelm Digby was held to be the most accomplished cavalier of his time. He went to Gloucester Hall in Oxford in 1618. The learned Mr Thomas Allen (then of that house) was wont to say that he was the marvel of his age. He was not a member of the University, as I have heard my cousin Whitney say.

There was a great friendship between him and Mr Thomas Allen; whether he was his scholar I know not. Mr Allen was one of the learnedest men of this nation in his time, and a great collector of good books, which collection Sir Kenelm bought (Mr Allen enjoying the use of them for his life) to give to the Bodleian Library, after Mr Allen's decease, where they now are.

He was a great traveller, and understood ten or twelve languages. He was not only master of a good and graceful judicious style, but he also wrote a delicate hand, both fast-hand and Roman. I have seen tracts of his writing to the father of the present Earl of Pembroke, who much respected him.

He was such a goodly handsome person, gigantic and great voice, and had so graceful elocution and noble address, that had he been dropped out of the clouds in any part of the world, he would have made himself respected. But the Jesuits spoke spitefully, and said it was true, but then he must not stay there above six weeks. He was *envoyé* from Henrietta Maria (then queen mother) to the Pope, where at first he was mightily admired; but after some time he grew high, and hectored with His Holiness and gave him the lie. The pope said he was mad.

He was well versed in all kinds of learning. And he also had this virtue, that no man *knew better how to abound, and be abased*, and either was indifferent to him. No man became grandeur better; sometimes again he would live only with a lackey, and horse with a foot-cloth [ride on a splendidly-equipped horse].

He was very generous, and liberal to deserving persons. When Abraham Cowley was but thirteen years old, he dedicated to him a comedy, called *Love's Riddle*, and concludes in his epistle—'The Birch that whip't him then would prove a Bay'. Sir Kenelm was very kind to him.

Much against his mother's consent, he married that celebrated beauty and courtesan, Mrs Venetia Stanley, whom Richard Earl of Dorset kept as his concubine, had children by her, and settled on her an annuity of £500 per annum; which after Sir Kenelm Digby married her was unpaid by the earl; and for which annuity Sir Kenelm sued the earl, after marriage, and recovered it. He would say that a handsome lusty man that was discreet might make a virtuous wife out of a brothel-house. This lady carried herself blamelessly, yet (they say) he was jealous of her. She died suddenly, and hard-hearted women would censure him severely.

After her death, to avoid envy and scandal, he retired into Gresham College at London, where he diverted himself with his chemistry, and the professors' good conversation. He wore there a long mourning cloak, a high crowned hat, his beard unshorn, looked like a hermit, as signs of sorrow for his beloved wife, to whose memory he erected a sumptuous monument, now quite destroyed by the great conflagration. He stayed at the college two or three years.

The fair houses in Holborn, between King Street and Southampton Street (which broke off the continuance of them) were, about 1633, built by Sir Kenelm; where he lived before the civil wars. Since the restoration of Charles II he lived in the last fair house westward in the north portico of Covent Garden, where my lord Denzil Holles lived since. He had a laboratory there. I think he died in this house.

He was, 1643, prisoner for the king [Charles I] at Winchester House, where he practiced chemistry and made artificial gems, and wrote his book of Bodies and Soul, which he dedicated to his eldest son Kenelm, who was slain (as I take it) in the Earl of Holland's rising [July 1648].

In the time of Charles I he received the sacrament in the chapel at Whitehall, and professed the Protestant religion, which gave great scandal to the Roman Catholics; but afterwards he *looked back*.

He was a person of very extraordinary strength. I remember one at Sherborne (related to the Earl of Bristol) protested to us, that as he, being a middling man, being sat in a chair, Sir Kenelm took up him, chair and all, with one arm.

He was of an undaunted courage, yet not apt in the least to give offence. His conversation was both ingenious and innocent.

As for that great action of his at Scanderoon, see the Turkish History. Sir Edward Stradling of Glamorganshire, was then his vice-admiral, at whose house is an excellent picture of his, as he was at that time: by him is drawn an armillary sphere broken, and underneath is written *They would smite him undismayed* (Horace). See excellent verses of Ben Jonson (to whom he was a great patron) in his second volume.

There is in print in French, and also in English (translated by Mr James Howell) a speech that he made at a philosophical assembly at

Montpellier, *Of the sympathetique powder*. He made a speech at the beginning of the meeting of the Royal Society, *Of the vegetation of plants*.

He was born to three thousand pounds per annum. His ancient seat (I think) is Gayhurst in Buckinghamshire. He had a fair estate also in Rutlandshire. What by reason of the civil wars, and his generous mind, he contracted great debts, and I know not how (there being a great falling out between him and his *then* only son, John) he settled his estate upon Cornwallis, a subtle solicitor, and also a member of the House of Commons, who did put Mr John Digby to much charge at law; ask what became of it.

Mr John Digby had a good estate of his own, and lived handsomely at what time I went to him two or three times in order to your *Oxford Antiquities**; and he then brought me a great book, as big as the biggest Church Bible that ever I saw, and the richliest bound, bossed with silver, engraved with escutcheons and crest (an ostrich); it was a curious vellum. It was the history of the family of Digbys, which Sir Kenelm either did, or ordered to be done. There was inserted all that was to be found anywhere relating to them, out of records of the Tower, rolls, etc. All ancient church monuments were most exquisitely drawn by some rare artist. He told me that the compiling of it cost his father a thousand pounds. Sir John Fortescue said he did believe it was more. When Mr John Digby did me the favour to show me this rare manuscript, 'This book,' said he, 'is all that I have left of all the estate that was my father's!' He was almost as tall and as big as his father; he had something of the sweetness of his mother's face. He was bred by the Jesuits, and was a good scholar.

Sir John Hoskyns informs me that Sir Kenelm Digby did translate Petronius Arbiter† into English.

¶ Sir Kenelm Digby, that renowned knight, great linguist, and magazine of arts, was born and died on the eleventh of June, and also fought fortunately at Scanderoon the same day. Hear his epitaph, composed by Mr Ferrar:

> Under this stone the matchless Digby lies,
> Digby the great, the valiant and the wise:
> This age's wonder for his noble parts;
> Skill'd in six tongues, and learn'd in all the arts.
> Born on the day he died, th'eleventh of June,
> On which he bravely fought at Scanderoon.
> 'Tis rare that one and self-same day should be
> His day of birth, of death, of victory.

* Aubrey's *Lives* were written for Anthony Wood (see introduction), and here he addresses Wood directly. *Ed.*   † Petronius' *Satyricon*. *Ed.*

Venetia Digby

1600–33

Wife of Sir Kenelm Digby: Aubrey's account of her indiscretions is borne out by other writers, as is his praise of her behaviour after her marriage.

Venetia Stanley was daughter of Sir Edward Stanley. She was a most beautiful desirable creature; and being of a mature age was let by her father to live with a tenant and servants at Eynsham Abbey* (his land, or the Earl of Derby's) in Oxfordshire; but as private as that place was, it seems her beauty could not lie hid. The young eagles had espied her, and she was sanguine and tractable, and of much suavity (which to abuse was great pity).

In those days Richard Earl of Dorset (grandson and heir to the Lord Treasurer) lived in the greatest splendour of any nobleman of England. Among other pleasures that he enjoyed, Venus was not the least.† This pretty creature's fame quickly came to his lordship's ears, who made no delay to catch at such an opportunity.

I have now forgotten who first brought her to town, but I have heard my uncle Danvers say (who was her contemporary) that she was so commonly courted, and that by grandees, that it was written over her lodging one night in uncial letters,

> Pray come not near,
> for Dame Venetia lodgeth here.

The Earl of Dorset, aforesaid, was her greatest gallant, who was extremely enamoured of her, and had one if not more children by her. He settled on her an annuity of £500 per annum.‡

Among other young sparks of that time, Sir Kenelm Digby grew acquainted with her, and fell so much in love with her that he married her, much against the good will of his mother; he would say that 'a wise man, and lusty, could make an honest woman out of a brothel house'. Sir Edmund Wyld had her picture (and you may imagine was very familiar with her), which picture is now at Droitwich in Worcestershire, at an inn, where now the town keep their meetings. Also at Mr Rose's, a jeweller in Henrietta Street in Covent Garden, is an excellent piece of her, drawn after she was newly dead.

She had a most lovely and sweet-turned face, delicate dark brown

---

* At the west end of the church here were two towers as at Wells or Westminster Abbey, which were standing till about 1656. The rooms of the abbey were richly wainscotted, both sides and roof.

† Samual Daniel: 'Cheeks of roses, locks of amber, To b'enprisoned in a chamber' etc.

‡ In fact probably his brother Edward, who succeeded him in the earldom in 1624. *Ed.*

105

hair. She had a perfect healthy constitution; strong; good skin; well proportioned; much inclining to a wanton (near altogether). Her face, a short oval; dark brown eyebrow, about which much sweetness, as also in the opening of her eyelids. The colour of her cheeks was just that of the damask rose, which is neither too hot nor too pale. She was of a just stature, not very tall.

Sir Kenelm had several pictures of her by Vandyke etc. He had her hands cast in plaster, and her feet and her face. See Ben Jonson's second volume, where he had made her live in poetry, in his drawing of her, both body and mind:

> 'Sitting, and ready to be drawn,
> What makes these tiffany, silks, and lawn,
> Embroideries, feathers, fringes, lace,
> When every limb takes like a face!'—etc.

When these verses were made she had three children by Sir Kenelm, who are there mentioned, viz Kenelm, George and John.

Her picture drawn by Sir Anthony Vandyke hangs in the queen's drawing room, at Windsor Castle, over the chimney.

She died in her bed suddenly. Some suspected that she was poisoned. When her head was opened there was found but little brain, which her husband imputed to her drinking of viper wine; but spiteful women would say it was a viper-husband who was jealous of her, that she would steal a leap. I have heard some say,—e.g. my cousin Elizabeth Faulkner—that after her marriage she redeemed her honour by her strict living. Once a year the Earl of Dorset invited her and Sir Kenelm to dinner, where the earl would behold her with much passion, and only kiss her hand.

Sir Kenelm erected to her memory a sumptuous and stately monument at Christ Church (near Newgate Street) in the east end of the south aisle, where her body lies in a vault of brickwork, over which are three steps of black marble, on which was a stately altar of black marble with four inscriptions in copper gilt affixed to it: upon this altar her bust of copper gilt, all which (except only the vault, which was only opened a little by the fall) is utterly destroyed by the great conflagration. Among the monuments in the book mentioned in Sir Kenelm Digby's life is to be seen a curious drawing of this monument, with copies of the several inscriptions.

About 1676 or 5, as I was walking through Newgate Street, I saw Dame Venetia's bust standing at a stall at the Golden Cross, a brazier's shop. I perfectly remembered it, but the fire had got off the gilding: but taking notice of it to one that was with me, I could never see it afterwards exposed to the street. They melted it down. How these curiosities would be quite forgotten, did not such idle fellows as I am put them down!

Michael Drayton

1563–1631

Drayton's reputation as a poet stood very high with his contemporaries, but has varied from total neglect to a more modest place among the Elizabethan and Jacobean poets since then. His chief works were historical and patriotic poems, the most famous being Poly-Olbion, a description of England. He also contributed texts for many of the Jacobean masques.

Michael Drayton esq., born in Warwickshire at Atherston on Stour (ask Thomas Mariett). He was a butcher's son. Was a squire, that is, one of the esquires to Sir Walter Aston, Knight of the Bath, to whom he dedicated his poem. Sir J. Brawne was a great patron of his. He lived at the bay-window house next to the east end of St Dunstan's church in Fleet Street.

Sir Edward Bysshe, Clarenceux herald, told me he asked Mr Selden once (jestingly) whether he wrote the commentary to his 'Polyolbion' and 'Epistles' or Mr Drayton made these verses to his notes.

See his inscription (on his monument in Westminster Abbey) given by the countess of Dorset. Mr Marshal, the stone-cutter, of Fetter Lane, told me that these verses were made by Mr Francis Quarles, who was his great friend, and whose head he wrought curiously in plaster, and valued for his sake. 'Tis pity it should be lost. Mr Quarles was a very good man.

Saint Dunstan

924–988

Dunstan, son of a Somerset nobleman, became a monk at Glastonbury, though he retained close connections with the court. As abbot of Glastonbury, he reformed the monastery, while as archbishop of Canterbury he played an important role in political life.

I find in Mr Selden's verses before Hopton's *Concordance of Years* that he was a Somersetshire gentleman. He was a great chemist.

The story of his pulling the devil by the nose with his tongs as he was in his laboratory, was famous in church windows.

He was a Benedictine monk at Glastonbury, where he was afterwards abbot, and after that was made Archbishop of Canterbury. He preached the coronation sermon at Kingston, and crowned King Edwy. In his sermon he prophesied, which the Chronicle mentions.

Mr Meredith Lloyd tells me that there is a book in print of his on the philosopher's stone; ask its title.

Edwardus Generosus give a good account of him in a manuscript which Mr Ashmole has.

Meredith Lloyd had, about the beginning of the civil wars, a manuscript of this saint's concerning chemistry, and says that there are several manuscripts of his up and down in England: ask Mr Ashmole.

Edwardus Generosus mentions that he could make a fire out of gold, with which he could set any combustible matter on fire at a great distance.

Meredith Lloyd tells me that, three or four hundred years ago, chemistry was in a greater perfection much, than now; their process was then more seraphic and universal: now they look only after medicines.

Several churches are dedicated to him: two at London: ask if one at Glastonbury.

Sir John Dunstable

He calls the cellar his library. Parliament men prepare themselves for the business of the nation with all in the morning. Some justices sleep on the bench every assizes.

At Chippenham the Deputy Lieutenants met to see the order of the militia, but there were as many Deputy Lieutenants as officers. After a lengthy sitting (at dinner and drinking after dinner) the drums beat and the soldiers went to march before the window to be seen by the Deputy Leiutenant. Sir John Dunstable (colonel) had not marched before them many yards, but down he falls full length in the dirt. His myrmidons [troops], with much effort, heaved him up, and then he cried out, 'Some drink, ho!' and so there was an end of that business.

Sir Edward Dyer
?–1607

Sir Edward Dyer of Somersetshire (Sharpham Park, etc) was a great wit, poet and acquaintance of Mary, countess of Pembroke, and Sir Philip Sidney. He is mentioned in the preface of the *Arcadia*. He had four thousand pounds income per annum, and was left £80,000 in money; he wasted it almost all. This I had from Captain Dyer, his great-grandson, or brother's great-grandson. I thought he was the son of Lord Chief Justice Dyer, as I have inserted in one of these papers, but that was a mistake. The judge was of the same family, the captain tells me.

Thomas Egerton, Lord Ellesmere
1540–1617

Lord Keeper under Elizabeth and James I (1596–1604) and Lord Chancellor 1604–17.

Sir Thomas Egerton, Lord Chancellor, was the natural son of Sir Richard Egerton of Ridley in Cheshire. This information I had thirty years since from Sir John Egerton, of Egerton in Cheshire, baronet, the chief of that family.

He was of Lincoln's Inn, and I have heard Sir John Danvers say that he was so hard a student that for three or four years he was not out of the house. He had good parts (a good mind), and early came into good practice.

My old father, Colonel Sharinton Talbot,* told me that (Gilbert, I think) earl of Shrewsbury, desired him to buy that noble manor of Eldesmere for him, and delivered him the money. Egerton liked the bargain and the seat so well, that truly he even kept it for himself, and afterwards made it his barony (took his title from it), but the money he restored to the earl of Shrewsbury again.

He was a great patron to Ben Jonson, as appears by several epistles to him.

His son and heir, since earl of Bridgewater, was an indefatigable bell-ringer—see the ballad.

---

* He had, I believe, 200 adopted sons.

Desiderius Erasmus

1466–1536

The first great man of letters of the Renaissance, and friend of Sir Thomas More. Born in Holland, he spent much time in England, and his tracts and letters were an important, moderate influence in the Reformation: he refused to declare for either side, though he was himself ordained a Roman Catholic priest. In Praise of Folly, a satire, is his best-known individual work.

He loved not fish, though born in a fish town—from Sir George Ent, MD.

He was of the order of Augustine, whose habit was the same, that the pest-house master at (I think, Pisa; ask Dr John Pell) in Italy wore, and walking in that town, people beckoned him to go out of the way [for fear of infection] taking him to be the master of the pest-house; and he not understanding the meaning, and keeping on his way, was there by one well beaten. He made his complaint when he came to Rome, and had a dispensation from wearing his habit.

His name was Gerard Gerard, which he altered into Desiderius Erasmus. He was begot (as they say) *behind doors*—see an Italian book in octavo, *Of famous bastards*. His father (as he says in his life written by himself) was the tenth and youngest of his grandfather, who was therefore designed to be dedicated to God. The father of Gerard lived with Margaret (daughter of a certain Doctor Peter) as man and wife (and some would say that they were married).

His father took great care to send him to an excellent school, which was at Dusseldorf, in the Duchy of Cleves. He was a tender chit, and his mother would not entrust him at board, but took a house there, and made him cordials, etc.—from J. Pell, DD.

He studied sometime in Queen's College in Cambridge, his chamber was over the water. Ask Mr Paschal for more details; and if a fellow: Mr Paschal had his study when a young scholar there.

'The stairs which rise up to his study at Queen's College in Cambridge do bring first into two of the fairest chambers in the ancient building; in one of them, which looks into the hall and chief court, the vice-president kept in my time; in that adjoining, it was my fortune to be, when fellow. The chambers over are good lodging rooms; and to one of them is a square turret adjoining, in the upper part of which is that study of Erasmus; and over it a lead roof on which one could walk. To that belongs the best prospect about the college, viz upon the river, into the cornfields, and country adjoining, etc; so that it might very well consist with the civility of the College to that great man (who was no fellow, and I think stayed not long there) to let him have that study. His sitting-room might be either the vice-president's, or, to be near to him, the next. The room for his servitor that above over it; and through it he might go to that study, which for the height, and neatness, and prospect, might easily take his fancy.' This from Mr Andrew Paschal, Rector of Chedzoy in Somerset, 15 June 1680.

He mentions his being there in one of his *Epistles*, and criticizes the beer there. One long since, wrote in the margin of the book in the College library in which that comment is made *As it was in the beginning etc*, and all Mr Paschal's time they found fault with the brewer.

He had the parsonage of Aldington in Kent, which is about three degrees perhaps a healthier place than Dr Pell's parsonage in Essex. I wonder they could not find out for him better preferment; but I see that the Sun and Aries being in the second house [in his horoscope], he was not born to be a rich man.

He built a school at Rotterdam, and endowed it, and ordered the institution [laid down its regulations]. Sir George Ent was educated there. A statue in brass is erected to his memory on the bridge at Rotterdam.

Sir Charles Blount, of Mapledurham in Oxfordshire, near Reading, was his scholar (in his *Epistles* there are some to him), and desired Erasmus to do him the favour to sit for his picture, and he did so, and it is an excellent piece. Which picture my cousin John Danvers of Baynton (Wiltshire), has: his wife's grandmother was Sir Charles Blount's daughter or granddaughter. It was a pity such a rarity should have been alienated from the family, but the issue male is lately extinct. I will sometime or other endeavour to get it for Oxford Library.

They were wont to say that Erasmus was suspended between Heaven and Hell, till about the year 1655 the Conclave at Rome damned him for a heretic after he had been dead a hundred and twenty years.

His deepest divinity is where a man would least expect it: viz in his colloquies in a dialogue between a butcher and a fishmonger.

Memorandum: Julius Scaliger contested with Erasmus, but got nothing by it, for, as Fuller saith, he was like a badger, that never bit unless he made his teeth meet. He was the scout of our knowledge, and the man that made the rough and untrodden ways smooth and easy.

¶ John Dryden, esq, poet laureate, tells me that there was a great friendship between his great-grandfather's father and Erasmus of Rotterdam, and Erasmus was godfather to one of his sons, and the name of Erasmus has been kept in the family ever since. The poet's second son is Erasmus. And at the seat of the family is a chamber called Erasmus's chamber.

Thomas Fairfax
1612–71

A professional soldier who became the leading general of the parliamentary army, and victor of the battle of Naseby. He played a lessening part in military and political affairs from 1647 onwards, apart from a brief period of activity in 1659–60, when he did much to further the restoration of Charles II.

Thomas, Lord Fairfax of Cameron, Lord General of the Parliament Army: memorandum, when Oxford was surrendered (24 June 1646) the first thing General Fairfax did was to set a good guard of soldiers to preserve the Bodleian Library. It is said there was more hurt done by the cavaliers (during their garrison) by way of embezzling and cutting off chains of books, than there was since. He was a lover of learning, and had he not taken this special care, that noble library had been utterly destroyed—which N.B.; for there were ignorant senators enough who would have been contented to have had it so. This I do assure you from an ocular witness.

George Feriby
1573–?

In King James's time, one Mr George Feriby was parson of Bishop Cannings in Wiltshire: an excellent musician, and no ill poet. When Queen Anne* came to Bath, her way lay to traverse the famous Wansdyke, which runs through his parish. He made several of his neighbours good musicians, to play with him in consort and to sing. Against her majesty's coming, he made a pleasant pastoral, and gave her an entertainment, with his fellow songsters in shepherds' weeds and bagpipes, he himself like an old bard. After that wind music was over, they sang their pastoral eclogues (which I have, to insert in the other book).

* Wife of James I.

He was one of the King's chaplains. 'Twas he caused the eight bells to be cast there, being a very good ringer.

He has only one sermon in print that I know of, at the funeral of Mr Drew of Devizes, called *Life's Farewell*. He was demy [scholar], if not fellow, of Magdalen College, Oxford.

He gave another entertainment in Cotefield to King James, with carters singing, with whips in their hands; and afterwards a football play. This parish would have challenged all England for music, ringing and football play.

Sir William Fleetwood
1535–94

An energetic administrator, recorder of London from 1571 to 1591. Aubrey seems to have confused him with Sir Miles Fleetwood, receiver of the court of wards (d. 1641), as the dates given (1603, 1646) are clearly impossible.

Sir William Fleetwood, Recorder of London, was of the Middle Temple; was Recorder of London, when King James came into England; made his harangue to the City of London: 'When I consider your wealth, I do admire your wisdom, and when I consider your wisdom I do admire your wealth.' It was a two-handed piece of rhetoric, but the citizens took it in the best sense.

He was a very severe hanger of highwaymen, so that the fraternity was resolved to make an example of him: which they executed in this manner. They lay in wait for him not far from Tyburn, when he was coming from his house in Buckinghamshire; had a halter in readiness; brought him under the gallows, fastened the rope about his neck and on the tree, his hands tied behind him (and servants bound) and then left him to the mercy of his horse, which he called Ball.* So he cried 'Ho, Ball! Ho, Ball!' and it pleased God that his horse stood still, till somebody came along, which was half a quarter of an hour or more. He ordered that this horse should be kept as long as he would live, and it was so—he lived till 1646—from Mr Thomas Bigge, of Wycombe.

One day, going on foot to the guildhall with his clerk behind him, he was surprised in Cheapside with a sudden and violent looseness, near the Standard. He turned up his breech against the Standard and bade his man hide his face; 'For they shall never see my arse again,' said he.

---

* i.e. standing on his horse's back. *Ed.*

Samuel Foster

?–1652

From Mr Beyes, the watchmaker, his nephew: Mr Samuel Foster, was born at Coventry (as I take it); he was sometime usher of the school there. Was professor at Gresham College, London: where, in his lodging, on the wall in his chamber, is, of his own hand drawing, the best sundial I do verily believe in the whole world. Among other things it shows you what o'clock 'tis at Jerusalem, Gran Cairo etc. It is drawn very skilfully.

John Florio

?1553–1625

Elizabethan literature drew heavily on the Italian, and John Florio's great work was an Italian–English dictionary, published in 1598; but he is chiefly remembered for his translation of Montaigne's Essays. He knew many of the literary figures of London.

John Florio was born in London in the beginning of the reign of Edward VI, his father and mother flying from the Valtolin (it is somewhere in Piedmont or Savoy) to London for religion: Waldenses.* (The family is originally of Siena, where the name is to this day.) King Edward dying, upon the persecution of Queen Mary, they fled back again to their own country, where he was educated. Afterwards he came into England, and was by King James made informator [tutor] to Prince Henry for the Italian and French tongues, and clerk to the closet of Queen Anne. He wrote: *First* and *Second Fruits*, being two books of the instruction to learn the Italian tongue: *Dictionary*; and translated Montagne's *Essays*. He died of the great plague at Fulham in 1625.

---

* i.e. they fled because they were persecuted as heretics belonging to the Waldensian sect, an old dualist heresy. *Ed.*

Thomas Fuller
1608–61

Fuller was one of the first authors to make an income by writing: he published more than twenty books, both religious and historical, the most famous being The History of the Worthies of England, *printed after his death.*

Thomas Fuller, DD, born at Orwincle* in Northamptonshire. His father was minister there, and married one of the sisters of John Davenant, bishop of Salisbury. From Dr Edward Davenant.

He was a boy of pregnant wit, and when the bishop and his father were discoursing, he would be nearby and hearken and now and then join in, and sometimes beyond expectation, or his years (what would be expected of someone his age).

He was of a middle stature; thickset; curled hair; a very working head, in so much that, walking and meditating before dinner, he would eat up a penny loaf, not knowing that he did it. His natural memory was very great, to which he had added the art of memory: he would repeat to you forwards and backwards all the signs from Ludgate to Charing Cross.

He was fellow of Sidney Sussex College in Cambridge, where he wrote his *Divine Poems*. He was first minister of Broad Windsor in Dorset, and prebendary of the church of Salisbury. He was sequestered, being a royalist, and was afterwards minister of Waltham Abbey, and preacher of the Savoy, where he died, and is buried.

William Gascoigne
?1612–44

A brilliant astronomer, and inventor of the micrometer as used in astronomy.

There was a most gallant gentleman that died in the late wars, one Mr Gascoigne, of good estate in Yorkshire; from whom Sir Jonas Moore acknowledged to have received most of his knowledge. He was bred up by the Jesuits. I thought to have taken memoirs of him; but deferring it, death took away Sir Jonas. But I will set down what I remember.

William Gascoigne esq, of Middleton, near Leeds, Yorkshire, was

---

* J. Dryden, poet, was born here.

killed at the battle of Marston Moor, about the age of 24 or 25 at most.

Mr Towneley, of Towneley in Lancashire, esquire, has his papers.—
From Mr Edmund Flamsteed* who says he found out the way of improving telescopes before Descartes.

Mr Edmund Flamsteed tells me, September 1682, that 'twas at York fight he was slain.

John Graunt
1620–74

One of the first students of statistics.

He was born at the Seven Stars in Burchin Lane, London, in the parish of St Michael's, Cornhill. He wrote *Observations on the bills of mortality* very ingeniously (but I believe, and partly know, that he had his hint from his intimate and familiar friend Sir William Petty), to which he made some *Additions*, since printed. And he intended, had he lived, to have written more on the subject.

He wrote also some *Observations on the advance of excise*, not printed; ask his widow for them.

To give him his due praise, he was a very ingenious and studious person, and generally beloved, and rose early in the morning to his study before shop-time. He understood Latin and French. He was a pleasant facetious companion, and very hospitable.

He was brought up (as the fashion then was) in the Puritan way; wrote shorthand dextrously; and after many years constant hearing and writing sermon notes, he fell to buying and reading of the best Socinian books, and for several years continued of that opinion. At last he turned a Roman Catholic; of which religion he died a great zealot.

He was admitted a fellow of the Royal Society, about 1663.

He went bankrupt. He had one son, a man, who died in Persia; one daughter, a nun at, I think, Ghent. His widow yet alive.

He was by trade a haberdasher of small wares, but was freeman of the drapers' company. A man generally beloved; a faithful friend. Often chosen for his prudence and justness to be an arbitrator; and he was a great peacemaker. He had an excellent working head, and was very facetious and fluent in his conversation.

He had gone through all the offices of the city so far as common council man. He was common council man for two years. Captain of the

* The Astronomer Royal. *Ed.*

trained band, several years; major of it, two or three years, and then laid down trade and all other public employment for his religion, being a Roman Catholic.

He was my honoured and worthy friend—God have mercy on his soul, Amen.

His death is lamented by all good men that had the happiness to know him; and a great number of ingenious persons attended him to his grave. Among others, with tears, was that ingenious great virtuoso, Sir William Petty, his old and intimate acquaintance, who was sometime a student at Brasenose College.

Henry Gellibrand
1597–1637

Henry Gellibrand was born in London. He was of Trinity College in Oxford. Dr Potter and Dr William Hobbes knew him. Dr Hannibal Potter was his tutor, and preached his funeral sermon in London. They told me that he was good for little a great while, till at last it happened accidentally that he heard a geometry lecture. He was so taken with it that he immediately fell to studying it, and quickly made great progress in it. The fine sundial over the College Library is of his own doing. He was astronomy professor in Gresham College, London. He being one time in the country showed the tricks of drawing what card you touched, which was by combination with his confederate, who had a string that was tied to his leg, and the leg of the other, by which his confederate gave him notice by the touch, but by this trick he was reported to be a conjuror.

See *Canterbury's Doom* about Protestant martyrs, inserted in the almanac: he held prayer-meetings in Gresham College.

Alexander Gill

There were two men of this name, father and son, who were high master of St Paul's from 1608–35 and 1635–9 respectively. Although Aubrey appears to impute the whipping stories to the father, it was in fact the son who was renowned for this, and was finally dismissed for maltreating a boy.

Dr Gill, the father, was a very ingenious person, as may appear by his writings. Notwithstanding, he had moods and humours, as particularly his whipping fits:

117

As pedants out of schoolboys' breeches
Do claw and curry their own itches

Samuel Butler, *Hudibras*

This Dr Gill whipped Duncombe, who was not long after a colonel of dragoons at Edgehill-fight, taken pissing against the wall. He had his sword by his side, but the boys surprised him: somebody had thrown a stone in at the window; and they seized on the first man they lighted on. I think his name was Sir John Duncombe (Sir John Denham told me the story), and he would have cut the doctor, but he never went abroad except to church, and then his army went with him. He complained to the council, but it became ridicule and his revenge sank.

Dr Triplett came to give his master a visit, and he whipped him. The Dr (i.e. Triplett) got Pitcher of Oxford, who had a strong and a sweet bass, to sing a song against him under the school windows, and got a good guard to secure him with swords, and he was preserved from the test of the little myrmidons [troops] which issued out to attack him; but he was so frightened that he beshit himself most fearfully.

¶ At Oxford (and I do believe the like at Cambridge) the rod was frequently used by the tutors and deans on their pupils, till (they were) bachelors of arts; even gentlemen commoners. One Dr I knew (Dr Hannibal Potter, Trinity College, Oxford) right well that whipped his scholar with his sword by his side when he came to take his leave of him to go to the Inns of Court.

Robert Glover
1544–88

Somerset herald and one of the greatest collectors of heraldic and genealogical material in the Elizabethan period.

I have heard Sir William Dugdale say that, though Mr Camden had the name, yet Mr Glover was the best herald that did ever belong to the office. He took a great deal of pains in searching the antiquities of several counties. He wrote a most delicate hand and portrayed [drew] finely.

There is (or late was) at a coffee-house at the upper end of Bell Yard (or Shire Lane) in his own hand, a visitation of Cheshire, a most curious piece, which Sir William Dugdale wished one to see; and he told me that at York, at some ordinary house (I think a house of entertainment) he saw a similar elaborate piece on Yorkshire. But several counties he surveyed, and that with great exactness, but after his death they were all scattered abroad, and fell into ignorant hands.

Jonathan Goddard

1617–75

Physician to Oliver Cromwell, and warden of Merton College during the Commonwealth. He was on the council of the Royal Society from its foundation in 1663.

Jonathan Goddard, MD, born at Greenwich (or Rochester, where his father commonly lived; but to my best remembrance, he told me at the former). His father was a ship-carpenter.

He was of Magdalen Hall, Oxford. He was one of the College of Physicians in London; Warden of Merton College, Oxford during the Commonwealth; physician to Oliver Cromwell, protector; went with him into Ireland. Enquire if not also sent to him into Scotland, when he was so dangerously ill there of a kind of high fever, which made him mad that he pistolled one or two of his commanders that came to visit him in his delirious rage.

He was professor of medicine at Gresham College; where he lived and had his laboratory for chemistry. He was an admirable chemist.

He had three or four medicines wherewith he did all his cures; a great ingredient was serpent's root. From Mr Michael Weeks, who looked after his stills.

He intended to have left his library and papers to the Royal Society, had he made his will, and had not died so suddenly. So that his books (a good collection) are fallen into the hands of a sister's son, a scholar at Caius College, Cambridge. But his papers are in the hand of Sir John Bankes, fellow of the Royal Society. There were his lectures at Surgeons' Hall; and two manuscripts, thick volumes, ready for the press. One was a kind of Pharmacopocia (his nephew has this). 'Tis possible his invaluable universal medicines aforesaid might be retrieved amongst his papers. My Lord Brouncker has the recipe but will not impart it.

He was fellow of the Royal Society, and a zealous member for the improvement of natural knowledge amongst them. They made him their drudge, for when any curious experiment was to be done they would lay the task on him.

He loved wine and was most curious in his wines; was hospitable; but drank not to excess; but it happened that coming from his club at the Crown tavern in Bloomsbury, on foot, eleven o'clock at night, he fell down dead of an apoplexy in Cheapside, at Wood Street End, March 24, Anno Domini 1675, age 56.

Thomas Goffe
1591–1629

Goffe's reputation was as an orator and playwright rather than poet; three of his plays survive.

Thomas Goffe the poet was rector here; his wife, it seems, was not so kind. His wife pretended to fall in love with him, by hearing of him preach: upon which said one Thomas Thimble (one of the esquire beadles in Oxford (a university officer) and his confidant) to him: 'Do not marry her: if thou dost, she will break thy heart.' He was not obsequious [did not follow] to his friend's sober advice, but for her sake altered his condition, and cast anchor here. One time some of his Oxford friends made a visit to him; she looked upon them with an ill eye, as if they had come to eat her out of her house and home (as they say); she provided a dish of milk and some eggs for supper and nothing more. They perceived her niggardliness, and that her husband was inwardly troubled at it, (she wearing the breeches) so they were resolved to be merry at supper, and talk all in Latin, and laughed exceedingly. She was so vexed at their speaking Latin, that she could not hold, but fell out a-weeping, and rose from the table. The next day, Mr Goffe ordered a better dinner for them, and sent for some wine: they were merry, and his friends took their final leave of him. 'Twas no long time before this *Xantippe*★ made Mr Thimble's prediction good; and when he died the last words he spoke were: 'Oracle, oracle, Tom Thimble,' and so he gave up the ghost.

Edward Gunter
1581–1626

Captain Ralph Greatorex, mathematical instrument maker in London, said that he was the first that brought quadrant, sector, and cross-staff to perfection. His book of the mathematical instruments did open men's understandings and made young men in love with that study. Before, the mathematical sciences were locked up in the Greek and Latin tongues and so lay untouched, kept safe in some libraries. After

★ Socrates' proverbially shrewish wife. *Ed.*

Mr Gunter published his book, these sciences sprang up amain, more and more to that height it is at now (1690).

When he was a student at Christ Church, it fell to his lot to preach the Good Friday sermon, which some old divines that I knew did hear, but they said that 'twas said of him then in the University that our Saviour never suffered so much since his passion as in that sermon, it was such a lamentable one—*we cannot all do all things.*

The world is much indebted to him for what he has done well.

Gunter is originally a Brecknockshire family, of Tregunter. They came thither under the conduct of Sir Bernard Newmarch, when he made the conquest of that county (Camden says). 'Aubrey, Gunter, Waldbeof, Harvard, Pichard' (which is falsely expressed in all Mr Camden's books as Prichard, which is nonsense).

John Hales
1584–1656

John Hales' reputation rests almost entirely on his contemporaries' opinion of him as a brilliant thinker and preacher. He left very little published work, and lived for most of his life quietly at Eton.

Mr John Hales was born at Wells (I think I have heard Mr John Sloper say (vicar of Chalk; his mother was Mr Hales' sister, and he bred him at Eton)).

His father was a steward to the family of the Horners:

> Hopton, Horner, Smyth and Thynne
> When abbots went out, they came in

Went to school at Bath (as I take it). Fellow of Merton College. Assisted Sir Henry Savile in his edition of Chrysostom* with others. Afterwards fellow of Eton College. Went as chaplain to Sir Dudley Carlton (ambassador to [the Hague]). I think was at the Synod of Dort. When the Court was at Windsor, the learned courtiers much delighted in his company, and were wont to grace him with their company.

---

* St John Chrysostom (345–407) 'the golden-mouthed', one of the greatest of the early Greek Christian writers. *Ed.*

I have heard his nephew, Mr Sloper, say that he much loved to read Stephanus, who was a *familist*,* I think that first wrote of that sect of the Family of Love: he was mightily taken with it, and was wont to say that sometime or other those fine notions would take in the world. He was one of the first Socianians in England, I think the first. He was a general scholar, and I believe a good poet: for Sir John Suckling brings him into the session of the Poets:
Poets:

> 'Little Hales all the time did nothing but smile
> To see them, about nothing, keep such a coil.'

He had a noble library of books, and those judicially chosen; which he sold to Cornelius Bee, bookseller, in Little Britain (as I take it, for £1000), which was his maintenance after he was ejected out of his fellowship at Eton College. He had then only reserved some few for his private use, to wind up his last days withal. The Lady Salter (near Eton) was very kind to him after the sequestration; he was very welcome to her ladyship, and spent much of his time there. At Eton he lodged (after his sequestration) at the next house to the Christopher Inn, where I saw him, a pretty little man, sanguine, of a cheerful countenance, very gentle and courteous; I was received by him with very much humanity: he was in a kind of violet coloured cloth gown, with buttons and loops (he wore not a black gown), and was reading Thomas à Kempis; it was within a year before he deceased. He loved canary;‡ but moderately, to refresh his spirits. He had a bountiful mind. I remember in 1647, a little after the visitation [of Oxford by the Parliamentary Commission], when Thomas Mariett esquire, Mr William Radford and Mr Edward Wood (all of Trinity College) had a frolic from Oxford to London, on foot, having never been there before, they happened to take Windsor in their way, and made their address to this good gentleman, being then fellow. Mr Edward Wood was the spokesman, and remonstrated that they were Oxford scholars; he treated them well and put into Mr Wood's hands ten shillings.

He lies buried in the churchyard at Eton, under an altar monument of black marble, erected at the sole charge of Mr Curwyn, with a too long epitaph. He was no kith or kin to him.

¶ He died at Mrs Powney's house, a widow woman, in Eton, opposite to the churchyard, adjoining to the Christopher Inn southwards. 'Tis the house where I saw him. She is a very good woman and of a grateful spirit. She told me that when she was married Mr Hales was very

---

* Member of the sect called the Family of Love, who held that religion consisted in loving each other. *Ed.*

† Followers of Socinus—see p. 70 above. *Ed.*

‡ Wine from the Canaries: light and sweet. *Ed.*

bountiful to them in setting them up to live in the world. She was very grateful to him and respectful to him.

She told me that Mr Hales was the common godfather there, and it was pretty to see, as he walked to Windsor, how his godchildren asked him blessing. When he was bursar, he still gave away all his groats for the rents he collected to his godchildren; and by that time he came to Windsor Bridge, he would have never a groat left. This Mrs Powney assures me that the poor were more relievable, that is to say, that he received more kindness from them than from the rich. That that I put down of my lady Salter (sister to Brian Duppa, Bishop of Salisbury) from his nephew John Sloper, vicar of Chalk, is a mistake. She had him to her house indeed, but it was to teach her son, who was such a blockhead he could not read well. Cornelius Bee bought his library for £700, which cost him not less than £2,500. Mrs Powney told me that she was much against the sale of them, because she knew it was his life and joy. He might have been restored to his fellowship again, but he would not accept the offer. He was not at all covetous, and desired to leave only £10 to bury him. He bred up our vicar, who, she told me, never sent him a token; and he is angry with her, thinks he left her too much. She is a woman primitively good, and deserves to be remembered. I wish I had her Christian name. Her husband has an inscription on a gravestone in Eton College chapel towards the south wall. She has a handsome dark old-fashioned house. The hall, after the old fashion, above the wainscot, painted cloth, with godly sentences out of the Psalms, etc, according to the pious custom of old times; a convenient garden and orchard. She has been handsome: a good understanding, and cleanly.

Francis Hall
1595–1675

Professor of Hebrew and mathematics at the Jesuit College at Liège. He was in England from 1656–72 as a missionary priest.

Father Franciscus Linus, i.e. Hall, was born in London—which captain Robert Pugh, SJ, assured me, who was his acquaintance.

He was of the Society of Jesus and lived most at Liège, where he died.

He wrote a learned discourse, on colours, which Sir Kenelm Digby quotes with much praise in his philosophy.

He printed a discourse of sundials in quarto, Latin, and made the Jesuits' College there the finest dials in the world, which are described in that book. The like dials he made (which resemble something a branch of candlesticks) in the garden at Whitehall which were one night, in 1674 (as I take it), broken all to pieces (for they were of glass spheres) by the earl of Rochester, Lord Buckhurst, Fleetwood Shepherd, etc, coming in from their revels. 'What!' said the earl of Rochester, 'dost thou stand here to tell time?' Dash, they fell to work. There was a watchman always stood there to guard it.

He wrote a piece of philosophy in Latin in octavo, called . . .

He had great skill in the optics, and was an excellent philosopher and mathematician, and a person of exceeding suavity, goodness and piety, insomuch that I have heard Father Manners, SJ, say that he deserved canonisation.

Memorandum—he wrote a little tract, about half a sheet or not much more, of Transubstantiation, proving it metaphysically and by natural reason—which I have seen.

Edmund Halley

1656–1742

One of the youngest of Aubrey's contemporaries to be given a place in the Lives, Halley made his reputation by his voyage to St Helena at the age of twenty-one, when he laid the foundations for the astronomy of the southern hemisphere. His later career, after Aubrey's death, included the posts of Savilian Professor of Geometry at Oxford, and, later, of Astronomer Royal. Halley's Comet, which returns every seventy-six years, commemorates his discovery that the comets of 1531, 1607 and 1682 were in fact one and the same body.

Mr Edmund Halley, Master of Arts, the eldest son of Mr Halley, a soap-boiler, a wealthy citizen of the city of London; of the Halleys of Derbyshire, a good family.

He was born in Shoreditch parish, at a place called Haggerston, the backside of Hogsdon.

At nine years old, his father's apprentice taught him to write, and arithmetic. He went to Paul's school, to Dr Gale: while he was there, he was very perfect in the celestial globes, insomuch that I heard Mr

Moxon (the globe-maker) say that if a star were misplaced he would at once find it. He studied geometry, and at 16 could make a dial, and then, he said, thought himself a brave fellow.

At 16 went to Queen's College in Oxford, well versed in Latin, Greek and Hebrew: where at the age of nineteen, he solved this useful problem in astronomy, never done before, viz 'from three distances given from the sun, and angles between, to find the orb': (mentioned in the *Philosophical Transactions*, Aug. or Sept. 1676, No. 115), for which his name will be ever famous.

Left Oxford, and lived at London with his father until 1676; at which time he got leave and a money for his travels from his father, to go to the island of Saint Helena, purely upon the account of advancement in astronomy, to make the globe of the Southern Hemisphere right, which before was very erroneous, as being done only after the observations of ignorant seamen. At his return, he presented his planisphere, with a short description, to his majesty, who was very well pleased; but received nothing but praise. I have often heard him say that if his majesty would only pay for sending out a ship, he would take the longitude and latitude, right ascensions and declinations of many southern fixed stars.

In 1678, he added a spectacle glass to the shadow-vane of the lesser arch of the sea-quadrant (or back-staff); which is of great use, for that that spot of light will be manifest when you cannot see any shadow.

He went to Danzig to visit Hevelius; 1 December 1680, went to Paris.

¶ Cardinal D' Estrée caressed him and sent him to his brother the admiral with a letter of recommendation. He hath contracted an acquaintance and friendship with all the eminentest mathematicians of France and Italy, and holds a correspondence with them.

He returned into England, 24 January 1682.

¶ Mr Edmund Halley, FRS was carried on with a strong impulse to take a voyage to St Helena, to make observations of the southern constellations, being then about twenty-four years old. Before he undertook his voyage, he dreamt that he was at sea, sailing towards the place, and saw the prospect of it from the ship in his dream, which he declared to the Royal Society, to be the perfect representation of that island, even as he had it really when he approached to it.

Thomas Hariot
1560–1621

Mathematician and astronomer.

Sir Robert Moray (from Francis Stuart) declared at the Royal Society—
'twas when the comet appeared before the Dutch war—that Sir Francis
had heard Mr Harriot say that he had seen nine comets, and had
predicted seven of them, but did not tell them how. 'Tis very strange;
let the astronomers work it out.

Mr Hariot went with Sir Walter Raleigh into Virginia, and has
written the Description of Virginia which is since printed in Mr
Purchas's Pilgrims.

Dr Pell tells me that he finds among his papers (which are now, 1684,
in Dr Busby's hands) an alphabet he had contrived for the American
language, like devils.*

When Henry Percy, ninth earl of Northumberland and Sir Walter
Raleigh were both prisoners in the Tower, they grew acquainted, and
Sir Walter Raleigh recommended Mr Hariot to him, and the earl settled
an annuity of two hundred pounds a year on him for life, which he
enjoyed. But to Hues (who wrote *On the Use of Globes*) and to Mr
Warner, he gave an annuity of but sixty pounds per annum. These
three were usually called '*the earl of Northumberland's three Magi*'. They
had a table at the earl's expense, and the earl himself had them to
converse with, singly or together.

He was a great acquaintance of Master Ailesbury, to whom Dr
Corbet sent a letter in verse, December 9, 1618, when the great blazing
star appeared:

> Now for the peace of Gods and men advise,
> (Thou that hast wherewithal to make us wise),
> Thine own rich studies, and deep Harriot's mine,
> In which there is no dross, but all refine.

The bishop of Salisbury (Seth Ward) told me that one Mr Haggar (a
fellow-countryman of his), a gentleman and a good mathematician, was
well acquainted with Mr Thomas Hariot, and was wont to say, that he
did not like (or valued not) the old story of the Creation of the World.
He could not believe the old position he would say 'Nothing is made out
of nothing.' But, said Mr Haggar, a nothing killed him at last; for in the
top of his nose came a little red speck (exceeding small) which grew

---

* Andrew Clark notes in his edition of 1898: 'Perhaps because the letters ended in
tridents' (like devils' traditional pitchforks). *Ed.*

126

bigger and bigger, and at last killed him. I suppose it was that which surgeons call a *noli me tangere*.

He made a philosophical theology, wherein he cast off the Old Testament, and then the New one would (consequently) have no foundation. He was a Deist. His doctrine he taught to Sir Walter Raleigh, Henry, earl of Northumberland, and some others. The divines of those times looked on his manner of death as a judgement upon him for valuing the Scripture at nothing.

James Harrington
1611–77

In a period of experiments with different kinds of government, James Harrington's Oceana *was a model for the ideal commonwealth, drawing on Machiavelli but with great emphasis on elections and ballots. Harrington was a theorist rather than a practical politician, and did not take sides in the Civil War; but his projects were suspect to the newly-restored monarchy, and he was imprisoned for a time from 1661 onwards.*

He was a commoner of Trinity College in Oxford. He travelled France, Italy and the Netherlands. His genius lay chiefly towards the politics and democratical government.

He was much respected by the Queen of Bohemia [Princess Elizabeth, daughter of James I], who was bred up by the Lord Harrington's lady, and she acknowledged the kindness of the family.

In 1647 he was by order of parliament made one of his majesty's bedchamber at Holmeby. The king loved his company; only he would not endure to hear of a commonwealth: and Mr Harrington passionately loved his majesty. Mr Harrington and the king often disputed about government. He was on the scaffold with the king when he was beheaded; and I have at these meetings [of his club, below] oftentimes heard him speak of King Charles I with the greatest zeal and passion imaginable, and that his death gave him so great grief that he contracted a disease by it; that never anything did go so near to him [affect him so much]. Memorandum: Mr Herbert, the traveller, was the other of his bedchamber by order of parliament, and was also on the scaffold. He gave them both there some watches.

He made several essays in poetry, viz love-verses, and translated a book of Virgil's *Aeneid*; but his music was rough, and Mr Henry Nevill, an ingenious and well-bred gentleman, a member of the House of Commons, and an excellent (but concealed) poet, was his great familiar and confident friend, and dissuaded him from tampering in poetry, which he did despite Minerva, and to improve his proper talent, viz political reflections, whereupon he wrote his *Oceana*, printed London [in 1656]. Mr T. Hobbes was wont to say that Henry Nevill had a finger in that pie; and it is likely enough. That ingenious tract, together with his and H. Nevill's smart discourses and inculcations, daily at coffee-houses, made many proselytes. In so much that, in 1659, the beginning of Michaelmas Term, he had every night a meeting at the (then) Turk's Head, in the New Palace Yard, where they take water [where people hire boats on the Thames], the next house to the stairs, at one Miles's, where was made purposely a large oval table, with a passage in the middle for Miles to deliver his coffee. About it sat his disciples and the virtuosi. The discourses in this kind were the most ingenious, and smart, that ever I heard, or expect to hear, and bandied with great eagerness: the arguments in the Parliament House were but flat to it.

He now printed a little pamphlet (quarto) called *Divers Models of Popular Government*, printed by Daniel Jakeman; and then his party desired him to print another little pamphlet called *The Rota*, quarto.

Here we had (very formally) a ballotting-box, and ballotted how things should be carried, by way of experiments. The room was every evening full as it could be crammed. I cannot now recount the whole number. Mr Cyriack Skinner, an ingenious young gentleman, scholar to John Milton, was chairman. There was Mr Henry Nevill; Major John Wildman; Mr Woolseley of Staffordshire; Mr Coke, grandson of Sir Edward; Sir William Poultney (chairman); Sir John Hoskins; J. Arderne; Mr Maximilian Petty (a very able man in these matters, and who had more than once turned the councilboard to Oliver Cromwell his kinsman); Mr Michael Malett; Mr Carteret of Guernsey; Cradoc, a merchant; Mr Henry Ford; Major Venner; Mr Edward Bagshaw; Thomas Mariett esquire; Croon, MD; with many others now slipped out of my memory. Besides which were, as listeners, several: e.g. the Lord Tirconnel; Sir John Penruddock; Mr John Birkenhead; myself. Stafford esquire: opponents. Several soldiers.*

We many times adjourned to the Rhenish wine-house. One time Mr Stafford and his gang came in, drunk, from the tavern, and affronted the junto. The soldiers offered to kick them downstairs, but Mr Harrington's moderation and persuasion hindered it. Mr Stafford tore their orders and numbers.

The doctrine was very taking, and the more because, as to human foresight, there was no possibility of the king's return. But the greatest part of the parliament-men perfectly hated this design of *rotation by*

* Some names are crossed out; Aubrey added a note to Wood saying that 'Sir John Hoskyns, etc., Dean Arderne etc., would not like to have their names seen', as the Rota had been republican and therefore suspect after the Restoration. *Ed.*

ballotting: for they were cursed tyrants, and in love with their power, and it was death to them, except eight or ten, to admit of this way, for H. Nevill proposed it in the House, and made it out to them, that except [unless] they embraced that model of government they would be ruined—but *whom God would destroy He first sends mad.*

Pride of senators for life is insufferable; and they were able to grind any one they owed ill will to to powder; they were hated by the army and their country they represented, and their name and memory stinks. 'Twas worse than tyranny. Now this model upon rotation was:—that the third part of the House should rote out by ballot every year, so that every ninth year the House would be wholly altered; no magistrate to continue above three years, and all to be chosen by ballot, than which manner of choice, nothing can be invented more fair and impartial.

Well: this meeting continued November, December, January till February 20 or 21; and then, upon the unexpected turn upon general Monk's coming in, all these airy models vanished. Then it was not fit, nay treason, to have done such; but I well remember Harrington several times (at the breaking-up) said, 'Well, the king will come in. Let him come in, and call a parliament of the greatest cavaliers in England, if they be men of estates, and let them sit but seven years, and they will all turn Commonwealth's men.'

He was wont to find fault with the constitution of our government, that it was by jumps, and told a story of a cavaliero he saw at the carnival in Italy, who rode on an excellent managed horse that with a touch of his toe would jump quite round. One side of his habit was Spanish, the other French; which sudden alteration of the same person pleasantly surprised the spectators. 'Just so,' said he, 'it is with us. When no parliament, then absolute monarchy; when a parliament, then it runs to a commonwealth.'

In 1660 he was committed prisoner to the Tower, where he was kept for a time; then to Portsea castle. His durance in these prisons (he being a gentleman of a high spirit and hot head) was the direct cause of his deliration or madness; which was not outrageous, for he would discourse rationally enough and be very facetious company, but he grew to have a fancy that his perspiration turned to flies, and sometimes to bees—but sober as to all else; and he had a timber *versatile** built in Mr Hart's garden (opposite to St James's Park) to try the experiment. He would turn it to the sun, and sit towards it; then he had his fox-tails there to chase away and massacre all the flies and bees that were to be found there, and then shut his windows. Now this experiment was only to be tried in warm weather, and some flies would lie so close in the crannies and the cloth (with which it was hung) that they would not at

* Aubrey perhaps means that it could be altered for the purposes of the experiments. *Ed.*

129

once show themselves. A quarter of an hour after, perhaps, a fly or two or more might be drawn out of the lurking holes by the warmth; and then he would cry out, 'Do not you see it plainly that these come from me?' It was the strangest sort of madness that ever I found in anyone: talk of anything else, his discourse would be very ingenious and pleasant.

He married to his old sweet-heart Mrs Dayrell, a comely and discreet lady. It happening so, from some private reasons, that he could not enjoy his dear in the flower and heat of his youth, he would never lie with her, but loved and admired her dearly; for she was rising in years when he married her, and had lost her sweetness.

He was of a middling stature, stocky man, strong and thick, well set, sanguine, quick-hot-fiery hazel eye, thick moist curled hair, as you may see by his picture. In his conversation very friendly, and facetious, and hospitable.

For above twenty years before he died (except his imprisonment) he lived in the Little Aumbry (a fair house on the left hand), which looks into the Dean's Yard in Westminster. In the upper storey he had a pretty gallery, which looked into the yard where he commonly dined, and meditated and took his tobacco.

His friends were: Henry Nevill esquire, who never forsook him to his dying day. Though a whole year before he died, his memory and discourse were taken away by a disease (it was a sad sight to see such a sample of mortality, in one whom I lately knew a brisk lively cavaliero), this gentleman, whom I must never forget for his constant friendship, paid his visits as duly and respectfully as when his friend was in the prime of his understanding—a true friend: Sir Thomas Dolman, Mr Roger l'Estrange, Dr John Pell, John Aubrey.

He was wont to say that 'Right reason in contemplation is virtue in action, *et vice versa*. To live according to nature is to live virtuously; the divines [clergy] will not have it so; and that 'when the divines would have us be an inch above virtue, we fall an ell below it'.

These verses he made:

> The state of nature never was so raw,
> But oaks bore acorns and there was a law
> By which the spider and the silkworm span;
> Each creature had her birthright, and must man
> Be illegitimate! have no child's part!
> If reason had no wit, how came in art?

Mr Andrew Marvell made a good epitaph for him, but it would have given offence.

William Harvey
1578–1657

William Harvey is famous as the discoverer of the principle of the circulation of the blood, which he first outlined in a series of lectures in 1616, and published in 1628. His work was not immediately accepted, as it was based on dissection and observation rather than 'ancient authority', but gradually came to be recognised as a major physiological discovery.

William Harvey, MD, born at Folkestone in Kent: born at the house which is now the post-house, a fair stone-built house, which he gave to Caius College in Cambridge, with some lands there: vide his will. His brother Eliab would have given any money or exchange for it, because 'twas his father's, and they all born there; but the doctor (truly) thought his memory would better be preserved this way, for his brother has left noble seats, and about £3000 per annum at least.

Dr Harvey added (or was very bountiful in contributing to) a noble building of Roman architecture (of rustic work, with Corinthian pilasters) at the Physician's College, viz a kind of convocation house for the fellows to meet in, below; and a library, above. All these remembrances and building was destroyed by the general fire [of 1666].

He was always very contemplative, and the first that I hear of that was curious in anatomy in England. He had made dissections of frogs, toads, and a number of other animals, and had curious observations on them, which papers (together with his goods, in his lodgings at Whitehall) were plundered at the beginning of the Rebellion, he being for the king, and with him at Oxford; but he often said, that of all the losses he sustained, no grief was so crucifying to him as the loss of these papers, which for love or money he could never retrieve or obtain. When Charles I by reason of the tumults left London, he attended him, and was at the fight of Edgehill with him; and during the fight, the prince and Duke of York were committed to his care: he told me that he withdrew with them under a hedge, and took out of his pocket a book and read; but he had not read very long before a bullet from a great gun grazed on the ground near him, which made him remove his station. He told me that Sir Adrian Scrope was dangerously wounded there, and left for dead amongst the dead men, stripped; which happened to be the saving of his life. It was cold, clear weather, and a frost that night; which staunched his bleeding, and about midnight, or some hours after his hurt, he awoke, and was glad to draw a dead body upon himself for warmth's sake.

After Oxford was surrendered, which was 24 June 1646, he came to

London, and lived with his brother Eliab (a rich merchant in London) opposite to St Lawrence Poultry Church, where was then a high leaden steeple (there were but two, viz this and St Dunstan's in the East), and at his brother's country house at Roehampton.

His brother Eliab bought, about 1654, Cockaine House, now (1680) the Excise office, a noble house, where the doctor was wont to contemplate on the leaded roof of the house, and had his several sitting-places in regard of the sun, or wind.

He did delight to be in the dark, and told me he could then best contemplate. He had a house heretofore at Combe, in Surrey, with a good air and prospect where he had caves made in the earth, in which in summertime he delighted to sit and meditate. He was pretty well versed in the mathematics, and had made himself master of Mr Oughtred's *Key to Mathematics* in his old age; and I have seen him perusing it, and working problems, not long before he died, and that book was always in his meditating apartment.

His chamber was that room that is now the office of Elias Ashmole esquire; where he died, being taken with a stroke which took away his speech. As soon as he saw he was attacked, he at once sent for his brother, and nephews, and gave one a watch, another another thing, etc as remembrances of him. He died worth £20,000, which he left to his brother Eliab. In his will he left to his old friend Mr Thomas Hobbes £10 as a token of his love.

His sayings:—He was wont to say that man was but a great mischievous baboon.

He would say that we Europeans knew not how to order or govern our women, and that the Turks were the only people who used them wisely.

He was far from bigotry.

He had been physician to the Lord Chancellor Bacon, whom he esteemed much for his wit and style, but would not allow him to be a great philosopher. 'He writes philosophy like a Lord Chancellor,' said he to me, speaking in derision; 'I have cured him.'

About 1649 he travelled again into Italy, Dr George (now Sir George) Ent then accompanying him.

At Oxford, he grew acquainted with Dr Charles Scarborough, then a young physician (since, by King Charles II, knighted), in whose conversation he much delighted; and whereas before, he marched up and down with the army, he took him to himself and made him lie in his chamber, and said to him, 'Prithee leave off they gunning, and stay here; I will bring thee into practice.'

I remember he kept a pretty young wench to wait on him, which I guess he made use of for warmth's sake as King David did, and took care of her in his will, as also of his man servant. For twenty years before he died he took no manner of care about his worldly concerns, but his brother Eliab, who was a very wise and prudent manager, ordered all not only faithfully, but better than he could have done himself. He was, as all the rest of the brothers, very choleric; and in his young days wore a dagger (as the fashion then was; nay I remember my old schoolmaster Mr Latimer at 70, wore a dagger with a wooden hilt, with a knife, and short pointed dagger as also my old grandfather Lyte, and Alderman Whitson of Bristol, which I suppose was the common fashion in their young days) but this doctor would be too apt to draw out his dagger upon every slight occasion.

He was not tall; but of the lowest stature, round faced, olive complexion; little eye, round, very black, full of spirit; his hair was black as a raven, but quite white twenty years before he died.

I first saw him at Oxford, 1642, after Edgehill fight, but was then too young to be acquainted with so great a doctor. I remember he came several times to Trinity College, to George Bathurst, BD, who had a hen to hatch eggs in his chamber, which they daily opened to see the progress and way of generation. I had not the honour to be acquainted with him till 1651, being my she cousin Montague's physician and friend. I was at that time bound for Italy (but to my great grief dissuaded by my mother's importunity). He was very communicative, and willing to instruct any that were modest and respectful to him. And, for the purpose of my journey, he gave me, i.e. dictated to me, what to see, what company to keep, what books to read, how to manage my studies: in short, he bid me go to the fountain-head, and read Aristotle, Cicero, Avicenna, and did call the modern authors shit-breeches. He wrote a very bad hand, which (with use) I could pretty well read.

I have heard him say, that after his book of the *Circulation of the Blood* came out, that he fell mightily in his practice, and that it was believed by the vulgar that he was crack-brained; and all the physicians were against his opinion, and envied him; many wrote against him as Dr Primige, Paracisanus etc (see Sir George Ent's book). With much ado at last, in about twenty or thirty years' time, it was received in all the universities in the world; and, as Mr Hobbes says in his book *De Corpore [On the Body]*, *he is the only man, perhaps, that ever lived to see his own doctrine established in his life time.*

He understood Greek and Latin pretty well, but was no critic, and he wrote very bad Latin. The *Circulation of the Blood* was, as I take it, done into Latin by Sir George Ent (query), as also his book *On the Reproduction of Animals*, but a little book in duodecimo against Riolani (I think), wherein he makes out his doctrine clearer, was written by himself, and that, as I take it, at Oxford.

His majesty King Charles I gave him the Wardenship of Merton

College in Oxford, as a reward for his service, but the times suffered him not to receive or enjoy any benefit by it.

He was physician, and a great favourite of the Lord High Marshal of England, Thomas Howard, Earl of Arundel and Surrey, with whom he travelled as his physician in his embassy to the Emperor at Vienna, in 1636. Mr W. Hollar (who was then one of his excellency's gentlemen) told me that, in his voyage, he would still be making of excursions into the woods, making observations of strange trees, and plants, earth, etc, of that country and sometimes likely to be lost, so that my lord ambassador would be really angry with him, for there was not only danger of thieves, but also of wild beasts.

He was much and often troubled with the gout, and his way of cure was thus; he would then sit with his legs bare, if it were frost, on the lead roof of Cockaine House, put them into a pail of water, till he was almost dead with cold, and betake himself to his stove, and so 'twas gone.

He was hot-headed, and his thoughts working would many times keep him from sleeping; he told me that then his way was to rise out of nis bed and walk about his chamber in his shirt till he was pretty cool, i.e. till he began to have a shiver, and then return to bed, and sleep very comfortably.

I remember he was wont to drink coffee; which he and his brother Eliab did, before coffee-houses were in fashion in London.

All his profession would allow him to be an excellent anatomist, but I never heard of any that admired his therapeutic way. I knew several practisers in London that would not have given threepence for one of his prescriptions; and that a man could hardly tell by one of his bills what he did aim at.

He did not care for chemistry, and was wont to speak against chemists with an undervalue.

It is now fit, and but just, that I should endeavour to undeceive the world in a scandal that I find strongly runs of him, which I have met amongst some learned young men: viz that he made himself a way to put himself out of his pain, by opium: not but that, had he laboured under great pains, he had been ready enough to have done it; I do not deny that it was not according to his principles upon certain occasions to . . . . : but the manner of his dying was really, and *bona fide*, thus, viz the morning of his death, about 10 o'clock, he went to speak, and found that he had a stroke in his tongue; then he saw what was to become of him, he knew there was then no hopes of his recovery, so presently sends his young nephews to come up to him, to whom he gives one his watch (it was a minute watch with which he made his experiments); to another, another remembrance, etc; made sign to Sambroke, his apothecary (in Blackfriars) to let him blood in his tongue, which did little or no good; and so he ended his days. His practise was not very great towards his later end; he declined it, unless to a special friend, e.g. my lady Howland, who had a cancer in her breast, which he did cut off and seared, but at last she died of it.

He rode on horseback with a foot-cloth* to visit his patients, his man following on foot, as the fashion then was, which was very decent, now quite discontinued. The judges rode also with their footcloths to Westminster Hall, which ended at the death of Sir Robert Hyde, Lord Chief Justice. Anthony Earl of Shaftesbury would have revived it, but several of the judges, being old and poor horsemen, would not agree to it.

The scandal aforesaid [about Harvey's taking of opium] is from Sir Charles Scarborough's saying that he had, towards his latter end, a preparation of opium and I know not what, which he kept in his study to take, if occasion should serve, to put him out of his pain, and which Sir Charles promised to give him; this I believe to be true; but do not at all believe that he really did give it him. The palsy did give him an easy passport.

He lies buried in a vault, at Hempstead in Essex, which his brother Eliab Harvey built; he is lapped in lead, and on his breast in great letters Dr William Harvey. I was at his funeral, and helped to carry him into the vault.

¶ Dr Harvey told me, and any one if he examines himself will find it to be true, that a man could not fancy—truthfully—that he is imperfect in any part that he has. Nature tends to perfection, and in matters of generation we ought to consult more with our sense and instinct, than our reason, and prudence, fashion of the country and interest. We see what contemptible products are those of the prudent politics [those who have married for status or wealth], weak, fools and ricketty children, scandals to nature and their country. The heralds are fools—they are completely on the wrong track. A blessing goes with a marriage for love upon a strong impulse.

Richard Head
?1637–?1686

Mr Meriton—his true name was Head. Mr Bovey knew him. He was a bookseller in Little Britain (in London).

He had been amongst the gipsies. He looked like a knave with his goggling eyes. He could transform himself into any shape. Went bank-

---

* A long cloth covering most of the horse's back and falling nearly to the ground on either side. Aubrey notes: 'I have seen him ride (like this) in 1654 or 5.' Ed.

rupt two or three times. Was at last a bookseller, or towards his later end. He maintained himself by scribbling. He was paid 20s. per (printed) sheet. He wrote several pieces, viz *The English Rogue, The Art of Wheedling* etc.

He was drowned going to Plymouth by the long sea route about 1676 being about fifty years of age.

Edward Herbert
Lord Cherbury, 1583–1648

Traveller, soldier and courtier, Edward Herbert spent much of his early life abroad, and was ambassador to France in 1619–21. He took a neutral attitude in the Civil War, though he had been at court as late as 1640, and his sons were active in the royalist cause. In his later years he wrote his autobiography, his best-known work; his philosophical works were also important.

Usher, Lord Primate of Ireland, was sent for by him, when in his death-bed, and he would have received the sacrament. He said indifferently of it that 'if there was good in anything it was in that', or 'if it did not good it would do no hurt'. The primate refused it, for which many blamed him. He died at his house in Queen Street, very serenely; asked what o'clock it was, and was told: 'then', said he, 'an hour hence I shall depart'. He then turned his head to the other side and expired. In his will he gave special order to have his white stallion (which he loved) to be well fed and carefully looked after as long as he lived. He had two libraries, one at London, the other at Montgomery; the former whereof he gave to Jesus College, Oxford.

¶ Mr Fludd tells me he had constantly prayers twice a day in his house, and Sundays would have his chaplain read one of Smyth's sermons.

I have seen him several times with Sir John Danvers; he was a dark-haired man.

Memorandum: the castle of Montgomery was a most romancy seat. It stood upon a high promontory, the north side thirty feet or more high. From hence is a most delightsome prospect, four different ways. Southwards, outside the castle, is Primrose Hill: see Donne's *Poems*.

> Upon this Prim-rose-hill,
> Where, if Heaven would distill
> A shower of rain, each several drop might go
> To his own prim-rose, and grow manna so;
> And where their form and their infinity

Make a terrestrial galaxy
As the small stars do in the sky;
I walk to find a true-love, and I see
That 'tis not a mere woman that is she,
But most, or more, or less than woman be, etc.

In this pleasant solitude did this noble lord enjoy his muse. Here he wrote his *De veritate* [*On Truth*]. Dr Coote (a Cambridge scholar and a learned) was one of his chaplains. Mr Thomas Masters, of New College, Oxford, lived with him till 1642.

This stately castle was demolished since the late wars at the charge of the country.

In Brecknockshire, about three miles from Brecknock, is a village called Penkelly (in English Hazelwood), where is a little castle. It is an ancient seat of the Herberts. Mr Herbert of this place came, by the mother's side, of Ŵgan. The Lord Cherbury's ancestor came by the second venter [the wife of a second marriage] who was a miller's daughter. The greatest part of the estate was settled on the issue by the second venter, viz Montgomery castle, and Aberystwyth. Upon this match with the miller's daughter are to this day recited, or sung, by the Welsh, these verses: viz:—

O gway vinney (dhyw) râg wilidh
Vôd vinhad yn velinidh
A 'vôd vy mam yn velinidhes
A 'môd inney yn arglwydhes.

To this sense:

O God! Woe is me miserable, my father was a miller, and my mother a milleress, and I am now a lady.

George Herbert
1593–1633

Brother of Edward Herbert, Lord Cherbury, Herbert became public orator for Cambridge University soon after taking his degree there. His speeches found favour with James I, and he was often in attendance at court. But on James's death he turned away from 'the painted pleasures of court life' and took holy orders. He was vicar, first at Leighton Bromswold in Huntingdonshire, then at Bemerton in Wiltshire, and, despite his own slender means, restored the churches in both places. His poetry was printed after his death, the second edition appearing only three weeks later: The Temple, as the

137

volume was called, was an immediate success and was frequently reprinted in the next fifty years.

Mr George Herbert was kinsman (remote) and chaplain to Philip, Earl of Pembroke and Montgomery, and Lord Chamberlain. His lordship gave him a benefice at Bemerton (between Wilton and Salisbury) a pitiful little chapel of ease to Foughelston. The old house was very ruinous. Here he built a very handsome house for the minister, of brick, and made a good garden and walks. He lies in the chancel, under no large, nor yet very good, marble grave-stone, without any inscription.

He wrote: Sacred Poems, called *The Church*, printed, Cambridge, 1633; a book entitled *The Country Parson*, not printed till about 1650, octavo. He also wrote a folio in Latin, which because the parson of Hincham could not read, his widow (then wife to Sir Robert Cooke) condemned to the uses of good housewifery.

He was buried (according to his own desire) with the singing service for the burial of dead, by the singing men of Salisbury. Francis Sambroke (attorney) then assisted as a chorister boy; my uncle, Thomas Danvers, was at the funeral. Look in the register book at the office where he died, for the parish register is lost.

He married Jane, the third daughter of Charles Danvers, of Baynton in Wiltshire, but had no issue by her. He was a very fine complexion and consumptive. His marriage, I suppose, hastened his death. My kinswoman was a handsome wanton and ingenious. When he was first married he lived a year or better at Dauntsey House. H. Allen, of Dauntsey, was well acquainted with him, who has told me that he had a very good hand on the lute, and that he set his own lyrics or sacred poems. It is an honour to the place, to have had the heavenly and ingenious contemplation of this good man, who was pious even to prophecy:

> Religion now on tip-toe stands
> Ready to go to the American strands.

Mary Herbert
Countess of Pembroke, 1561–1621

Mary Sidney married the second Earl of Pembroke, twenty-seven years her senior, in 1577. She made Wilton into one of the great centres of poetry and learning, and collaborated with her brother Sir Philip Sidney on many of his literary projects. After the earl's death in 1601, she was left without the means to continue her patronage.

Mary Countess of Pembroke, was sister to Sir Philip Sidney; married to Henry the eldest son of William Earl of Pembroke aforesaid; but this subtle old earl did foresee that his fair and witty daughter-in-law. would horn [cuckold] his son: and told him so and advised him to keep her in the country and not to let her frequent the court.

She was a beautiful lady and had an excellent wit, and had the best education that that age could afford. She had a pretty sharp-oval face. Her hair was of a reddish yellow.

She was very salacious, and she had a contrivance that in the spring of the year, when the stallions were to leap the mares, they were to be brought before such a part of the house where she had a *vidette* to look on them and please herself with their sport; and then she would act the like sport herself with *her* stallions. One of her great gallants was crook-backed Cecil, Earl of Salisbury.

In her time Wilton House was like a college, there were so many learned and ingenious persons. She was the greatest patroness of wit and learning of any lady in her time. She was a great chemist and spent yearly a great deal in that study. She kept for her helper in the house Adrian Gilbert (vulgarly called Dr Gilbert) (half-brother to Sir Walter Raleigh) who was a great chemist in those days*. It was he that made the curious wall about Rowlington Park, which is the park that adjoins to the house at Wilton. Mr Henry Sanford was the earl's secretary, a good scholar and poet, and who did pen part of the *Arcadia* dedicated to her (as appears by the preface). He has a preface before it with the two letters of his name. It is he that has verses before Bond's Horace. She also gave an honourable yearly pension to Dr Mouffett, who has written a book *On Insects*. Also one Boston, a good chemist, a Salisbury man born, who did undo himself by studying the philosopher's stone, and she would have kept him but he would have all the gold to himself and so died I think in a gaol.

At Wilton is a good library which Mr Christopher Wase can give you the best account of of any one; which was collected in this learned lady's time. There is a manuscript very elegantly written, viz all the Psalms of David translated by Sir Philip Sidney, curiously bound in crimson velvet. There is a MS written by Dame Marian† of hunting and hawking, in English verse, written in King Henry the Eighth's time (ask Mr Christopher Wase for more details). There is the ledger

---

* Aubrey notes elsewhere: 'He was a man of great parts, but the greatest buffoon in England; cared not what he said to man or woman of what quality soever. Some curious ladies of our country have rare receipts of his.' *Ed.*

† In fact Juliana Berners; the date of her treatise is 1486. *Ed.*

book of Wilton, one page Saxon and the other Latin, which Mr Dugdale perused.

This curious seat of Wilton and the adjacent country is an Arcadian place and a paradise. Sir Philip Sidney was much here, and there was so great love between him and his fair sister that I have heard old gentlemen (old Sir Walter Long of Draycot and old Mr Tyndale) say that they lay together, and it was thought that the first Philip Earl of Pembroke was begot by him, but he inherited not the wit of either brother or sister.

This countess, after her lord's death, married‡ to Sir Matthew Lister, knight, one of the College of Physicians, London. He was, they say, a learned and a handsome gentleman. She built then a curious house called Houghton Lodge near Ampthill. The architects were sent for from Italy. It is built according to the description of Basilius' house in the first book of the *Arcadia* (which is dedicated to her). It is most pleasantly situated and has four vistas, each prospect twenty-five or thirty miles. This was sold to the Earl of Elgin. The house did cost £10,000 in the building of it.

I think she was buried in the vault in the choir at Salisbury, by Henry Earl of Pembroke, her first husband: but there is no memorial of her, nor of any of the rest except some pennons and escutcheons.

¶ An epitaph on the lady Mary, Countess of Pembroke, in print somewhere, by William Browne, who wrote the *Pastorals* (whom William Earl of Pembroke preferred to be tutor to the first Earl of Caernarvon which was worth to him £5 or 6000 i.e. he bought £300 p.a. land)—from old Jack Markham—

> Underneath this sable hearse
> Lies the subject of all verse:
> Sydney's sister, Pembroke's mother
> Death! erst thou shalt kill such another
> Fair and good and learn'd as SHE
> Time will throw his dart at thee.

¶ I shall now pass to the illustrious Lady Mary, Countess of Pembroke, whom her brother has eternised by his *Arcadia*; but many or most of the verses in the *Arcadia* were made by her Honour, and they seem to have been written by a woman. 'Twas a great pity that Sir Philip had not lived to put his last hand to it. He spent much, if not most part of his time here, and at Ivychurch, near Salisbury, which did then belong to this family, when he was in England; and I cannot imagine that Mr Edward Spenser could be a stranger here.

Her Honour's genius lay as much towards chemistry as poetry. The

‡ Aubrey notes: 'Jack Markham says they were not,' *Ed.*

140

learned Dr Mouffett, that wrote of insects and of meats, had a pension hence. In a catalogue of English plays set forth by Gerard Langbain, is thus, viz: 'Lady Pembroke, Antonius, 4to.'

There lived in Wilton, in those days, one Mr Boston, a Salisbury man (his father was a brewer there), who was a great chemist, and did great cures by his art. The lady Mary, Countess of Pembroke did much esteem him for his skill, and would have had him to have been her operator, and live with her, but he would not accept of her ladyship's kind offer. But after long search after the philosopher's stone, he died at Wilton, having spent his estate. After his death they found in his laboratory two or three baskets of egg shells, which I remember Geber says is a principal ingredient of that stone.

Philip Herbert
Fourth Earl of Pembroke, 1584–1650

Favourite of James I, renowned for his erratic temper and extravagant living. He was interested in the settlements in the New World, though he achieved relatively little there. In the Civil War, he played a fairly neutral part, though he preferred the parliament to the king, and from 1642 onwards held parliamentary office. In 1649 he was elected to the House of Commons, but died early the following year.

The genius of Philip fourth Earl of Pembroke lay much to painting and building, and he had the best collection of paintings of the best masters of any peer of his time in England; and, besides those pictures before mentioned, collected by his ancestors, he adorned the rooms above stairs with a great many pieces of Giorgione, and some of Titian, his scholar. His lordship was the great patron of Sir Anthony Vandyke, and had the most of his paintings of any one in the world; some whereof, of his family, are fixed now in the great panels of the wainscot in the great dining room, or room of state;* which is a magnificent, stately room; and his majesty, King Charles the Second was wont to say, 'twas the best proportioned room that ever he saw.

Upon the coming of the Scots, in 1634, Sir . . . Fenwyck and another fearing their breeds of horses would be taken away by the Scots, did sell their breeds of horses and mares to Philip fourth Earl of Pembroke. His lordship had also Arab horses, and for race horses, besides Peacock and

---

* The famous 'Double-cube' room. *Ed.*

Delavill, he had a great many more kept at the park at Ramsbury and at Rowlington. Then for his stag-hunting, fox-hunting, brook-hawking, and land-hawking, what number of horses were kept to be fit at all seasons for it, I leave the reader to guess, besides his horses for at least half a dozen coaches. Mr Chr. Wroughton guesses not less than a hundred horses.

It is certain that Peacock used to run the four-miles course in five minutes and a little more; and Delavill since came but little short of him. Peacock was first Sir Thomas Thynne's of Longleat; who valued him at £1000. Philip Earl of Pembroke gave £5 but to have a sight of him: at last his lordship had him; I think by gift. Peacock was a half-Arab. He was the most beautiful horse ever seen in this last age, and was as fleet as handsome. He died about 1650.

His lordship had all sorts of hounds, for several disports: that is, great hounds to harbour the stags, and also small bull dogs to break the bays of the stag; fox-hounds, finders, harriers and others. His lordship had the choicest tumblers that were in England, and the same tumblers that rode behind him he made use of to retrieve the partridges. The setting-dogs for supper-flights for his hawks. Greyhounds for his hare warren, as good as any were in England. When they returned from hawking the ladies would come to see the hawks at the highest flying, and then they made use of their setting dogs to be sure of a flight. His lordship had two hawks, one a falcon called Shrewsbury, which he had of the Earl of Shrewsbury, and another called the little tercel, which would fly quite out of sight, that they knew not how to show the fowler till they could see which way the head pointed. They had not little telescopes in those days; those would have been of great use for the discovery which way the hawk's head stood.

'Tis certain that the Earls of Pembroke were the most popular peers in the west of England; but one might boldly say, in the whole kingdom. The revenue of his family was, till about 1652, £16,000 per annum, but with his offices and all, he had £30,000 per annum, and, as the revenue was great, so the greatness of his retinue and hospitality was corresponded to it. One hundred and twenty family uprising and down lying, whereof you take out six or seven, and all the rest servants and retainers.

It was the Right Honourable Philip Earl of Pembroke, that was the great hunter. It was in his lordship's time, that is in the time of James I and Charles I, a serene calm of peace, that hunting was at its greatest height that ever was in this nation. The Roman governors had not, I think, that leisure. The Saxons were never at quiet; and the barons' wars, and those of York and Lancaster, took up the greatest part of the time since the Conquest: so that the glory of English hunting breathed its last with this earl, who deceased about 1644 [1650], and shortly after the forests and parks were sold and converted into arable etc.

'Twas after his lordship's decease that I was a hunter; that is to say, with the Right Honourable William, Lord Herbert of Cardiff, the aforesaid Philip's grandson. Mr Christopher Wace then taught him Latin and hunted with him; and 'twas then that he translated Gratius' *Cynegeticon*, and dedicated it to his lordship, which will be a lasting monument for him.

Philip Earl of Pembroke, his brother, did not delight in books or poetry; but exceedingly loved painting and building, in which he had singular judgement, and had the best collection of any peer in England. He had a wonderful sagacity in the understanding of men, and could discover whether an ambassador's message was real or feigned; and his majesty King James made great use of this talent of his. Mr Tonars, an ingenious gentleman, who understood painting well, and did travel beyond sea to buy rare pieces for his lordship, had a pension of £100 per annum. Mr Richard Gibson, the dwarf, whose marriage Mr Edmund Waller has celebrated in his poems, that is, 'The Marriage of the Dwarfs', a great master in miniature, has a pension of a hundred pounds per annum. Mr Philip Massinger, author of several good plays, was a servant to his lordship, and had a pension of £20 or £30 per annum, which was paid to his wife after his decease. She lived at Cardiff, in Glamorganshire. There were others also had pensions, that I have forgotten.

William Herbert
First Earl of Pembroke, 1501–70

Despite his youthful adventures, with which Aubrey is chiefly concerned, William Herbert proved a skilful politician under Edward VI and Mary, managing to retain favour under both. He played some part in the restoration of Protestantism under Elizabeth. His chief service to the crown during this whole period was as a military commander, though he saw action only in France in 1557.

William Earl of Pembroke (the first earl of that family) was born (I think I have heard my cousin Whitney say) in Monmouthshire. Herbert, of Colbrooke in Monmouthshire, is of that family.

He was (as I take it) a younger brother, a mad fighting fellow. 'Tis certain he was a servant to the house of Worcester, and wore their blue-coat and badge. My cousin Whitney's great aunt gave him a golden angel [coin worth 6s 8d] when he went to London. One time being at Bristol, he was arrested, and killed one of the sheriffs of the city; he made his escape through Back Street, through the (then great) gate, into the marsh, and got into France.

Memorandum: upon this action of killing the sheriff, the city ordered the gate to be walled up, and only a little postern gate or door, with a turnstile for a foot-passenger, which continued so till Bristol was a garrison for the king, and the great gate was then opened, in 1644, or 1645. When I was a boy there, living with my father's mother, who was married to alderman John Whitson* (who was my god-father), the story was as fresh as but yesterday. He was called 'black Will Herbert'.

In France he betook himself into the army, where he showed so much courage, and readiness of wit in conduct, that in a short time he became eminent, and was favoured by the king, who afterwards recommended him to Henry VIII of England, who much valued him, and heaped favours and honours upon him. Upon the dissolution of the abbeys, he gave him the abbey of Wilton, and a *country* of lands and manors thereabouts belonging to it. He gave him also the abbey of Remesbury in Wilts, with much lands belonging to it. He gave him Cardiff Castle in Glamorganshire, with the ancient crown lands belonging to it. Almost all the country held of this castle. It was built by Sir Robert Fitzhamond the Norman, who lies buried at Tewkesbury Abbey with a memorial: and he built the abbey of Gloucester. It afterwards came to Jasper Duke of Bedford; so to the crown.

He married Anne Parr, sister of Queen Katherine Parr, daughter and co-heir of Thomas Parr, by whom he had two sons, Henry Earl of Pembroke, and the ancestor of the Lord Powys.

He was made Privy Councellor and conservator of King Henry the Eighth's will. He could neither write nor read: but had a stamp for his name. He was of good natural parts; but very choleric. He was strong set but bony, reddish-favoured, of a sharp eye, stern look.

In Queen Mary's time, upon the return of the Catholic religion, the nuns came again to Wilton Abbey, and this William Earl of Pembroke came to the gate (which looks towards the court by the street, but is now walled up) with his cap in hand and fell upon his knee to the lady abbess† and the nuns, crying 'I have sinned'. Upon Queen Mary's death the earl came to Wilton (like a tiger) and turned them out, crying 'Out, you whores, to work, to work, you whores, go spin.'

He being a stranger in our country, and an upstart, was much envied.

* He was the greatest benefactor to the city that has been since the Reformation. He gave £500 per annum at least to the city to maintain blue-coats, boys and maids. He died about 1629.

† The last lady abbess here was Gawen of Norrington, belonging to Chalke where that family has been four hundred years (sold about 1665 to Judge Wadham Windham).

And in those days (of sword and buckler), noblemen (and also great knights, such as the Longs), when they went to the assizes or sessions at Salisbury, etc, had a great number of retainers following them; and there were (you have heard in those days) feuds (i.e. quarrels and animosities) between great neighbours. Particularly this new earl was much envied by the then Lord Sturton, who would, when he went or returned from Salisbury (by Wilton was his road) sound his trumpets and give reproachful challenging words; it was a relic of knighthood-errantry.

From my great-uncles, the Brownes of Broad Chalke:—in Queen Elizabeth's time, some bishop (I have forgot who) that had been his chaplain, was sent to him from the queen and council, to take interrogatories of him [to question him on his beliefs]. So he takes out his pen and ink, examines and writes. When he had written a good deal, said the earl, 'Now let me see it'. 'Why?' said the bishop, 'your lordship cannot read it.' 'That's all one: I'll see it' said he and takes it and tears it to pieces: 'Zounds, you rascal', said he, 'do you think I will have my throat cut with a penknife?' It seems they had a mind to have picked a hole in his coat and to have got his estate. 'Tis reported that he caused himself to be let blood and bled so much that it was his death, and that he should say as he was expiring, 'They would have Wilton—they would have Wilton', and so gave up the ghost.

Memorandum:—this William (the founder of this family) had a little cur-dog which loved him, and the earl loved the dog. When the earl died the dog would not go from his master's dead body, but pined away, and died under the hearse; the picture of which dog is under his picture, in the Gallery at Wilton. Which puts me in mind of a paralleled story in Appian (Syrian War):—Lysimachus being slain, a dog that loved him stayed a long time by the body and defended it from birds and beasts till such time as Thorax, King of Pharsalia, finding it out, gave it burial. And I think there is another such story in Pliny.

William Herbert
Third earl of Pembroke, 1580–1630

Courtier, poet, patron of the arts and supporter of several expeditions to America. He was banished from the court by Elizabeth for seducing one of her ladies. The first folio of Shakespeare's works is dedicated to him and his brother Philip.

145

His nativity was calculated by old Mr Thomas Allen: his death was foretold, which happened true at the time foretold. Being well in health, he made a feast; ate and drank plentifully; went to bed; and found dead in the morning.

He was a most magnificent and brave peer, and loved learned men. He was a poet. There is a little book which contains his wife's and Sir Benjamin Rudyer's (verses) who was his friend and contemporary.

¶ As I remember he was Lord High Steward of his Majesty's Household, Justice in Eyre of all his Majesty's Forests, etc on this side Trent, Chancellor of the University of Oxford, one of his Majesty's Privy Council, and Knight of the Garter. He was a most noble person, and the glory of the court in the reigns of King James and King Charles. He was handsome, and of an admirable presence. He was the greatest Maecenas [patron] to learned men of any peer of his time or since. He was very generous and open handed. He gave a noble collection of choice books and manuscripts to the Bodleian Library at Oxford, which remain there as an honourable monument of his munificence. 'Twas thought, had he not been suddenly snatched away by death, to the grief of all learned and good men, that he would have been a great benefactor to Pembroke College in Oxford, whereas there remains only from him a great piece of plate that he gave there. His lordship was learned, and a poet; there are yet remaining some of his lordship's poetry in a little book of poems written by his lordship and Sir Benjamin Ruddyer. He had his nativity calculated by a learned astrologer, and died exactly according to the time predicted therein, at his house at Baynard's Castle in London. He was very well in health, but because of the fatal direction which he lay under, he made a great entertainment (a supper) for his friends, and died in his sleep, April 10, 1630.

He was of an heroic and public spirit, bountiful to his friends and servants, and a great encourager of learned men.

John Heydon
1629–?

From Elias Ashmole esq.: he had the book called *The way to bliss* from his adoptive father Backhouse at Swallowfield in Berkshire, a manuscript written in queen Elizabeth's time, hand and style anonymous.

Mr Heydon married Nicholas Culpepper's widow, and lights there (among Culpepper's papers) on the aforesaid manuscript, and prints a book with a great deal of *The way to bliss* word for word, and verses that are printed in the commendation of other books; and instead of such and such old philosophers (named in the MS) he puts down John Bowker's and William Lilly's name, which they never heard of; and is so impudent in one of his books since as to say Mr Ashmole borrowed of him.

Nicholas Hill
1570–?1610

This Nicholas Hill was one of the most learned men of his time: a great mathematician and philosopher and traveller, and a poet. His writings had the usual fate of those not printed in the author's lifetime. He was so eminent for knowledge that he was the favourite of the great earl of Oxford,* who had him to accompany him on his travels (he was his steward), which were so splendid that he kept at Florence a greater court than the Grand Duke. This earl spent in travelling the inheritance of ten or twelve thousand pounds per annum.

Old Serjeant Hoskins (the poet, grandfather to the present Sir John Hoskins, baronet, my honoured friend) knew him (was well acquainted with him) by which means I have this tradition which otherwise had been lost.

I fancy that his picture (i.e. head) is at the end of the Long Gallery of pictures at Wilton; it has the most philosophical aspect that I have seen, very much of Mr T. Hobbes of Malmesbury, but rather in the antique fashion. 'Tis pity that in noblemen's galleries the names are not written on, or behind, the pictures.

In his travels with his lord (I forget whether in Italy or Germany, but I think the former) a poor man begged him a penny. 'A penny!' said Mr Hill, 'what do you say to ten pounds?' 'Ah, ten pounds' said the beggar, 'that would make a man happy.' Mr Hill gave him immediately £10, and put it down in the accounts: 'Item, to a beggar, ten pounds, to make him happy.'

Mr Thomas Henshaw bought from Nicholas Hill's widow, in Bow Lane, some of his books; among which is a manuscript *On the Infinity and Eternity of the World*. He finds by his writings that he was (or leaning) a Roman Catholic. Mr Henshaw believes he died about 1610; he died an old man. He flourished in queen Elizabeth's time. I will search the register at Bow.

¶ I have searched the register at Bow, where I did not find Nicholas Hill.

* 'Twas that earl of Oxford that let the f. . . . before queen Elizabeth; whereupon he travelled. (See p. 307 below.)

Thomas Hobbes

1588–1679

*Aubrey's life of Hobbes is his most ambitious attempt, occupying a separate
manuscript: hence the elaborate introduction. Besides the text given here, he
also included some source material, such as Hobbes' Latin poems on his own
career. Aubrey was particularly proud of his acquaintance with him, and
often calls him* Malmesburiensis, *of Malmesbury, underlining their shared
Wiltshire birth. Little needs to be added by way of introduction to Aubrey's
fairly complete account, except to underline the utilitarian, agnostic tone of
the* Leviathan, *which explains the clergy's hatred of his works. The
universities, dominated by clergy, likewise attacked him over it, and much of
his time after its publication was taken up in controversy. Only in the
nineteenth century did his ideas attract any great following; in his own
lifetime, he had few if any supporters.*

The writers of the lives of the ancient philosophers used to, in the first
place, to speak of their lineage; and they tell us that in process of time
several illustrious great families accounted it their glory to be branched
from such or such a wise man. Why now should that method be omitted
in this little history of our Malmesbury philosopher? Who though but
of plebeian descent, his renown has and will give brightness to his name
and family, which hereafter may arise glorious and flourish in riches
and may justly take it an honour to be of kin to this worthy person, so
famous, for his learning, both at home and abroad.

Thomas Hobbes, then, whose life I write, was second son of Mr
Thomas Hobbes, vicar of Charlton and Westport next to Malmesbury,
who married Midleton of Brokenborough (a yeomanly family), by
whom he had two sons and one daughter. Thomas, the father, was one
of the ignorant 'Sir Johns' of Queen Elizabeth's time; could only read
the prayers of the church and the homilies; and disesteemed learning
(his son Edmund told me so), as not knowing the sweetness of it.* As to
his father's ignorance and clownery, it was as good metal in the ore,

---

* A letter from Aubrey's brother William adds the following:

'The old vicar Hobbes was a good fellow and had been at cards all Saturday night, and
at church in his sleep he cries out "Trafells is trumps" (viz clubs). Then quoth the clerk,
"Then master, he that have ace takes the trick". He was a choleric man, and a parson
(which I think succeeded him at Westport) provoked him (on purpose) at the church
door, so Hobbes struck him and was forced to fly for it and lived in obscurity beyond
London; died there, it was about eighty years since.

Mr William Hobbes . . . was first and second cousin to the philosopher. He went
bankrupt and had £1000 left and was £1000 in debt; and at London challenged one to
throw with him one throw on the dice for £1000, and won, paid his debt, and afterwards
flourished in his trade . . .'

which wants excoriating and refining. A wit requires much cultivation, much pains, and art and good conversation to perfect a man.

His father had an elder brother whose name was Francis, a wealthy man, and had been alderman of the borough; by profession a glover†, which is a great trade here, and in times past much greater. Having no child, he contributed much to or rather altogether maintained his nephew Thomas at Magdalen Hall in Oxford; and when he died gave him a mowing ground called the Gasten ground, lying near to the horse-fair at Malmesbury, worth £16 or £18 per annum; the rest of his lands he gave to his nephew Edmund.

Edmund was near two years older than his brother Thomas, and something resembled him in aspect, not so tall, but fell much short of him in his intellect, though he was a good plain understanding country-man. He had been bred at school with his brother; and could have made theme, and verse, and understood a little Greek to his dying day. This Edmund had only one son named Francis, and two daughters married to countrymen in the neighbourhood. This Francis pretty well resembled his uncle Thomas, especially about the eye; and probably had he had good education might have been ingenious; but he drowned his wit in ale.*

Westport is the parish without the west gate (which is now demolished), which gate stood on the neck of land that joins Malmesbury to Westport. Here was before the late wars a very pretty church, consisting of a nave and two aisles, dedicated to St Mary; and a fair spire-steeple, with five tuneable bells, which, when the town was taken (about 1644) by Sir W. Waller, were converted into ordnance, and the church pulled down to the ground, that the enemy might not shelter themselves against the garrison. The steeple was higher than that now standing in the borough, which much adorned the prospect. The windows were well painted, and in them were inscriptions that declared much antiquity; now is here rebuilt a church like a stable.

Thomas Hobbes of Malmesbury, philosopher, was born at his father's house in Westport, being that extreme house that points into, or faces, the Horse-Fair; the farthest house on the left hand as you go to Tedbury, leaving the church on your right. To prevent mistakes, and that hereafter may rise no doubt what house was famous for this famous man's birth, I do here testify that in April 1659, his brother Edmund went with me into this house, and into the chamber where he was born. Now things begin to be antiquated, and I have heard some guess it might be at the house where his brother Edmund lived and died. But this is so, as I here deliver it. This house was given by Thomas, the

† Shall I express or conceal this? The philosopher would acknowledge it.
* This part much given to drunkenness.

149

vicar [Hobbes' father] to his daughter, whose daughter or grand-daughter possessed it when I was there. It is a firm house, stone-built, and tiled, of one room (besides a buttery, or the like, within) below, and two chambers above. It was in the innermost where he first drew breath.

The day of his birth was 5 April 1588, on a Friday morning, which that year was Good Friday. His mother fell in labour with him upon the fright of the invasion of the Spaniards.

At four years old he went to school in Westport Church, till eight; by that time he could read well, and number four figures. Afterwards he went to school to Malmesbury, to Mr Evans, the minister of the town; and afterwards to Mr Robert Latimer, a young man of about nineteen or twenty, newly come from the University, who then kept a private school in Westport, where the broad place is, next door north from the smith's shop, opposite to the Three Cups (as I take it). He was a bachelor and delighted in his scholar's company, and used to instruct him, and two or three ingenious youths more, in the evening till nine o'clock. Here T.H. so well profited in his learning, that at fourteen years of age, he went away a good school-scholar to Magdalen Hall in Oxford. It is not to be forgotten that before he went to the University, he had turned Euripides' *Medea* out of Greek into Latin iambics, which he presented to his master. Mr H. told me he would fain have had them, to have seen how he did grow; and twenty odd years ago I searched all old Mr Latimer's papers, but could not find them; the oven (pies) had devoured them. I have heard his brother Edmund and Mr Wayte (his schoolfellow) say that when he was a boy he was playsome enough, but withal he had even then a contemplative melancholiness; he would get himself into a corner, and learn his lesson by heart at once. This Mr Latimer was a good Graecian Greek scholar, and the first that came into our parts hereabout since the Reformation. He was after-wards minister of Malmesbury, and from thence preferred to a better living of £100 per annum or more, at Leigh Delamere within this hundred.

At Oxford Mr T.H. used, in the summer time especially, to rise very early in the the morning, and would tie the leaden counters (which they used in those days at Christmas at 'post and pair') with packthreads, which he did besmear with birdlime, and bait them with parings of cheese, and the jackdaws would spy them a vast distance up in the air,* and as far off as Osney Abbey, and strike at the bait, and so be entangled in the string, which the weight of the counter would make cling about their wings. He did not much care for logic, yet he learned it, and thought himself a good disputant. He took great delight there to

* This story he happened to tell me, discoursing of the optics, to instance such sharpness of sight in so little an eye.

150

go to the bookbinders' shops and lie gaping on maps.

After he had taken his bachelor of arts degree, the then principal of Magdalen Hall (Sir James Hussey) recommended him to his young lord when he left Oxford, who did believe that he should profit more in his learning if he had a scholar of his own age to wait on him than if he had the information of a grave doctor. He was his lordship's page, and rode a-hunting and hawking with him, and kept his privy purse. By this way of life he had almost forgotten his Latin. He therefore bought him books of an Amsterdam print that he might carry in his pocket (particularly Caesar's *Commentaries*), which he did read in the lobby, or ante-chamber, whilst his lord was making his visits.

¶ Before Thucydides, he spent two years in reading romances and plays, which he has often repented and said that these two years were lost of him—wherein perhaps he was mistaken too, for it might furnish him with copy of words [? broaden his vocabulary].

The Lord Chancellor Bacon loved to converse* with him. He assisted his lordship in translating several of his essays into Latin, one, I well remember, is that *Of the Greatness of Cities*. The rest I have forgotten. His lordship was a very contemplative person, and was wont to contemplate in his delicious walks at Gorhambury, and dictate to Mr Thomas Bushell, or some other of his gentlemen, that attended him with ink and paper ready to set down presently [at once] his thoughts. His lordship would often say that he better liked Mr Hobbes's taking his thoughts, than any of the others, because he understood what he wrote, which the others not understanding, my lord would many times have a hard task to make sense of what they wrote.

It is to be remembered that about these times, Mr T.H. was much addicted to music, and practised on the bass viol.

1634: this summer—I remember it was in venison season (July or August)—Mr T.H. came into his native country to visit his friends, and amongst others he came then to see his old schoolmaster, Mr Robert Latimer, at Leigh Delamere, where I was then at school† in the church, newly entered in my grammar by him: here was the first place and time that ever I had the honour to see this worthy, learned man, who was then pleased to take notice of me, and the next day visited my relations. He was then a proper man, brisk, and in very good habit. His hair was then quite black. He stayed at Malmesbury and in the neighbourhood a week or better; 'twas the last time that ever he was in Wiltshire.

He was forty years old before he looked on geometry; which happened

* This, I believe, was after his first lord's death.
† I had then a fine little horse and commonly rode—(but this is irrelevant)—i.e. I was not a vulgar boy and carried not a satchel at my back. But this between ourselves.

accidentally. Being in a gentleman's library Euclid's *Elements* lay open, and 'twas the forty-seventh proposition in the first book. He read the proposition. 'By G——‡,' said he, 'this is impossible!' So he reads the demonstration of it, which referred him back to such a proof; which referred him back to another, which he also read. And so forth, that at last he was demonstratively convinced of that truth. This made him in love with geometry. I have heard Sir Jonas Moore (and others) say that it was a great pity he had not begun the study of the mathematics sooner, for such a working head would have made great advancement in it. So had he done [if he had done so] he would not have lain so open to his learned mathematical antagonists. But one may say of him, as one says of Jos. Scaliger, that where he errs, he errs so ingeniously, that one had rather err with him than hit the mark with Clavius. I have heard Mr Hobbes say that he was wont to draw lines on his thigh and on the sheets, abed, and also multiply and divide. He would often complain that algebra (though of great use) was too much admired, and so followed after, that it made men not contemplate and consider so much the nature and power of lines, which was a great hindrance to the growth of geometry; for that though algebra did rarely well and quickly in right lines, yet it would not *bite* in *solid* geometry.

Memorandum: after he began to reflect on the interest of the King of England as touching his affairs between him and the parliament, for ten years together his thoughts were much, or almost altogether, unhinged from the mathematics; but chiefly intent on his *De Cive* [*On the State*] and after that on his *Leviathan*: which was a great putback to his mathematical improvement, which N.B.—for in ten years' (or better) discontinuance of that study (especially) one's mathematics will become very rusty.

Memorandum: he told me that Bishop Manwaring (of St David's) preached *his doctrine*: for which, among others, he was sent prisoner to the Tower. Then thought Mr Hobbes, it is time now for me to shift for myself, and so withdrew into France, and resided at Paris. As I remember, there were others likewise did preach his doctrine. This little MS treatise grew to be his book *De Cive*, and at last grew there to be the so formidable *Leviathan*; the manner of writing of which book (he told me) was thus. He walked much and contemplated, and he had in the head of his cane a pen and ink-horn, carried always a note-book in his pocket, and as soon as a thought darted, he at once entered it into his book, or otherwise he might perhaps have lost it. He had drawn the design of the book into chapters etc so he knew whereabout it would come in. Thus that book was made.

During his stay at Paris he went through a course of chemistry with

‡ He would now and then swear, by way of emphasis.

Dr Davison; and he there also studied Vesalius' *Anatomy*. This I am sure was before 1648; for that Sir William Petty (then Dr Petty, physician) studied and dissected with him.

In 1650 or 1651 he returned into England, and lived most part in London, in Fetter Lane, where he wrote, or finished his book *De Corpore* [*On the Body*], in Latin and then in English; and wrote his lessons against the two Savilian professors at Oxford.

He was much in London till the restoration of his majesty, having here convenience not only of books, but of learned conversation, as Mr John Selden, Dr William Harvey, John Vaughan etc. I have heard him say, that at his lord's house in the country there was a good library, and that his lordship stored the library with what books he thought fit to be bought; but he said, the want of learned conversation* was a very great inconvenience, and that though he conceived he could order his thinking as well perhaps as another man, yet he found a great defect.

Amongst other of his acquaintance I must not forget our common friend, Mr Samuel Cowper, the prince of limners of this last age, who drew his picture as like as art could afford, and one of the best pieces that ever he did; which his majesty, at his return, bought of him, and conserves as one of his great rarities in his closet at Whitehall.

1659. In 1659, his lord was—and some years before—at Little Salisbury House (now turned to the Middle Exchange), where he wrote, among other things, a poem in Latin hexameter and pentameter, of the encroachment of the clergy (both Roman and reformed) on the civil power. I remember I saw then over five hundred verses (for he numbered every tenth as he wrote). I remember he did read Cluverius's *Historia universalis* [*Universal History*], and made up his poem from this.

His manner of thinking:—His place of meditation was then in the portico in the garden. He said that he sometimes would set his thoughts upon researching and contemplating, always with this rule that he very much and deeply considered one thing at a time (namely, a week or sometimes a fortnight).

There was a report (and surely true) that in parliament, not long after the king was settled [at the Restoration], some of the bishops made a motion to have the good old gentleman burnt for a heretic. Which he hearing, feared that his papers might be searched by their order, and he told me he had burnt part of them.

1660. The winter-time of 1659 he spent in Derbyshire. In March following was the dawning of the coming in of our gracious sovereign, and in April the Aurora [i.e. dawn itself]. I then sent a letter to him in

* Methinks, in the country, in long time, for want of good conversation, one's understanding (wit, invention) grows mouldy.

the country to advertise him of the advent of his master the king and desired him by all means to be in London before his arrival; and knowing his majesty was a great lover of good painting I must needs presume he could not but suddenly see Mr Cooper's curious pieces† of whose fame he had so much heard abroad and seen some of his work, and likewise that he would sit to him for his picture, at which place and time he would have the best opportunity of renewing his majesty's graces to him. He returned me thanks for my friendly intimation and came to London in May following.

It happened about two or three days after his majesty's return, that, as he was passing in his coach through the Strand, Mr Hobbes was standing at Little Salisbury House gate (where his lord then lived). The king espied him, put off his hat very kindly to him, and asked him how he did. About a week after he had oral conference with his majesty at Mr S. Cowper's, where, as he sat for his picture, he was diverted by Mr Hobbes' pleasant discourse. Here his majesty's favours were renewed to him, and order was given that he should have free access to his majesty, who always much delighted in his wit and smart repartees.

The wits at court were wont to bait him, but he feared none of them, and would make his part good. The king would call him *the bear*:* 'here comes the bear to be baited.'

Repartees. He was marvellous happy and ready in his replies, and that without rancour (except provoked)—but now I speak of his readiness in replies as to wit and drollery. He would say that he did not care to give, neither was he adroit at, an immediate answer to a serious query: he had as lief they should have expected an extemporary solution to an arithmetical problem, for he turned and winded and compounded in philosophy, politics, etc, as if he had been at analytical work. He always avoided, as much as he could, to conclude hastily.

Memorandum: from 1660 till the time he last went into Derbyshire, he spent most of his time in London at his lord's (viz at Little Salisbury House; then, Queen Street; lastly, Newport House), following his contemplation and study. He contemplated and invented (set down a hint with a pencil or so) in the morning, but compiled in the afternoon.

1664. In 1664 I said to him 'Methinks it is a pity that you that have such a clear reason and active mind did never take into consideration the learning of the laws'; and I endeavoured to persuade him to it. But he answered that he was not likely to have life enough left to go through with such a long and difficult task. I then presented him with the Lord Chancellor Bacon's *Elements of the Law* (a thin quarto) in order thereunto and to draw him on; which he was pleased to accept, and perused;

---

† i.e. Samuel Cooper's miniatures. *Ed.*

* This is *too low* wit to be published.

154

and the next time I came to him he showed therein two clear faulty arguments in the second page (one, I well remember, was in page 2), which I am heartily sorry are now out of my remembrance.

I desponded, for his reasons, that he should make any attempt towards this design; but afterwards, it seems, in the country, he wrote his treatise *De Legibus* [*On Laws*] (unprinted) of which Sir John Vaughan, Lord Chief Justice of the Common Pleas, had a transcript, and I do affirm that he much admired it.

1665. This year he told me that he was willing to do some good to the town where he was born; that his majesty loved him well, and if I could find out something in our country [Wiltshire] that was in his gift, he did believe he could beg it of his majesty, and seeing he was bred a scholar, he thought it most proper to endow a free school there; which is wanting *now* (for, before the Reformation, all monasteries had great schools attached to them; e.g. Magdalen School and New College School). After enquiry I found out a piece of land in Braydon forest (of about £25 per annum value) that was in his majesty's gift, which he hoped to have obtained of his majesty for a salary for a schoolmaster; but the queen's priests smelling out the design and being his enemies hindered this public and charitable intention.

1675, he left London with a mind never to come back and spent the remainder of his days in Derbyshire, with the Earl of Devonshire at Chatsworth and Hardwick in contemplation and study.

Then his sickness, death, burial and place, and epitaph, which send for.*

From a letter to John Aubrey from James Wheldon, 16 January 1679.

'He fell sick about the middle of October last. His disease was the strangury, and the physicians judged it incurable by reason of his great age and natural decay. About the 20th of November, my lord being about to remove from Chatsworth to Hardwick, Mr Hobbes would not be left behind; and therefore with a feather bed laid into the coach; upon which he lay warm clad, he was conveyed safely, and was in appearance as well after that little journey as before it. But seven or eight days after, his whole right side was taken with the dead palsy, and at the same time he was made speechless. He lived after this seven days, taking very little nourishment, slept well, and by intervals endeavoured to speak, but could not. In the whole time of his sickness he was free from fever. He seemed therefore to die rather for want of the fuel of life (which was spent in him) and mere weakness and decay, than by power of his disease, which was thought to be only an effect of his age and weakness

---

* The letter which follows is the information which Aubrey received on sending for details. *Ed.*

. . . He was put into a woollen shroud and coffin, which was covered with a white sheet, and upon that a black hearse cloth, and so carried upon men's shoulders, a little mile to church. The company, consisting of the family and neighbours that came to his funeral, and attended him to his grave, were very handsomely entertained with wine, burned and raw, cake, biscuit, etc . . .'

His complexion. In his youth he was unhealthy, and of an ill complexion (yellowish).

His lord, who was a waster, sent him up and down to borrow money, and to get gentlemen to be bound for him, being ashamed to speak himself: he took colds, being wet in his feet (then were no hackney coaches to stand in the streets), and trod both his shoes aside the same way. Notwithstanding, he was well-beloved: they loved his company for his pleasant facetiousness and good nature. From forty, or better, he grew healthier, and then he had a fresh, ruddy complexion. He was *sanguineo-melancholicus**; which the physiologers say is the most ingenious complexion. He would say that 'there might be good wits of all complexions; but good-natured, impossible'.

Head. In his old age he was very bald (which claimed a veneration); yet within door, he used to study, and sit, bareheaded, and said he never took cold in his head, but that the greatest trouble was to keep off the flies from pitching on the baldness.

Skin. His skin was soft and of that kind which my Lord Bacon in his *History of Life and Death* calls a goose-skin, i.e. of a wide texture:

A wide skin, a wide skull, a wide wit

Face not very great, ample forehead; whiskers yellowish-reddish, which naturally turned up—which is a sign of a brisk wit. Below he was shaved close, except a little tip under his lip. Not but that nature could have afforded a venerable beard, but being naturally of a cheerful and pleasant humour, he affected not at all austerity and gravity and to look severe. He desired not the reputation of his wisdom to be taken from the cut of his beard, but from his reason—*A beard does not make a philosopher. 'He consists of no more than the point of his beard and his two moustaches; as a result all that is needed to demolish him is three scissor cuts.'*—Balzac, *Lettres*.

Eye. He had a good eye, and that of a hazel colour, which was full of life and spirit, even to the last. When he was earnest in discourse, there shone (as it were) a bright live-coal within it. He had two kinds of looks: when he laughed, was witty, and in a merry humour, one could scarce see his eyes; by and by, when he was serious and positive, he opened his

---

* i.e. according to the medical theory of the 'four humours'. *Ed.*

eyes round (i.e. his eyelids). He had middling eyes, not very big, nor very little.

Stature. He was six foot high, and something better, and went indifferently erect, or rather, considering his great age, very erect.

Sight; wit. His sight and wit continued to the last. He had a curious sharp sight, as he had a sharp wit, which was also so sure and steady (and contrary to that which men call *broadwittedness*) that I have heard him oftentimes say that in multiplying and dividing he never mistook a figure: and so in other things. He thought much, and with excellent method and steadiness, which made him seldom make a false step.

Though he left his native country at fourteen, and lived so long, yet sometimes one might find a little touch of our pronunciation. Old Sir Thomas Malet, one of our judges of the King's Bench, knew Sir Walter Raleigh, and said that, notwithstanding his great travels, conversation, learning, etc, he still spoke broad Devonshire to his dying day.

His books. He had very few books. I never saw (nor Sir William Petty) above half a dozen about him in his chamber. Homer and Virgil were commonly on his table; sometimes Xenophon, or some probable history, and Greek Testament, or so.

Reading. He had read much, if one considers his long life; but his contemplation was much more than his reading. He was wont to say that if he had read as much as other men, he should have known no more than other men.

His physic. He seldom used any physic. What it was I have forgotten, but will enquire of Mr Shelbrooke his apothecary at the Black Spread-Eagle in the Strand. He was wont to say that he had rather have the advice or take physic from an experienced old woman, that had been at many sick people's bedsides, than from the learned but unexperienced physician.   •

Temperance and diet. He was, even in his youth, (generally) temperate, both as to wine and women. I have heard him say that he did believe he had been drunk in his life, a hundred times; which, considering his great age, did not amount to above once a year: when he did drink, he would drink to excess to have the benefit of vomiting, which he did easily; by which benefit neither his wit was disturbed (longer than he was spewing) nor his stomach oppressed; but he never was, nor could not endure to be, habitually a good fellow, i.e. to drink every day wine with company, which, though not to drunkenness, spoils the brain.

For his last thirty or more years, his diet, etc, was very moderate and regular. After sixty he drank no wine, his stomach grew weak, and he did eat most fish, especially whitings, for he said he digested fish better than flesh. He rose about seven, had his breakfast of bread and butter; and took his walk, meditating till ten; then he did put down the minutes of his thoughts.

157

He had an inch thick board about sixteen inches square, whereon paper was pasted. On this board he drew his lines (schemes). When a line came into his head, he would, as he was walking, take a rough memorandum of it, to preserve it in his memory till he came to his chamber. He was never idle; his thoughts were always working.

His dinner was provided for him exactly by eleven, for he could not now stay till his lord's hour—that is, about two: that his stomach could not bear.

After dinner he took a pipe of tobacco, and then threw himself immediately on his bed, with his neckband off, and slept (took a nap of about half an hour).

In the afternoon he penned his morning thoughts.

Exercises. Besides his daily walking, he did twice or thrice a year play at tennis (at about 75 he did it); then went to bed there and was well rubbed.* This he did believe would make him live two or three years the longer.

In the country, for want of a tennis court, he would walk up hill and down hill in the park, till he was in a great sweat, and then give the servant some money to rub him.

Prudence. He gave to his amanuensis, James Wheldon (the Earl of Devonshire's baker; who writes a delicate hand), his pension at Leicester, yearly, to wait on him, and take a care of him, which he did perform to him living and dying, with great respect and diligence: for which consideration he made him his executor.

Clothing. In cold weather he commonly wore a black velvet coat, lined with fur; if not, some other coat so lined. But all the year he wore a kind of leggings of Spanish leather, laced or tied along the sides with black ribbons.

Singing. He had always books of written music lying on his table— e.g. of H. Lawes', etc, *Songs*—which at night, when he was abed, and the doors made fast, and was sure nobody heard him, he sang aloud (not that he had a very good voice, but for his health's sake); he did believe it did his lungs good and conduced much to prolong his life.

Shaking palsy. He had the shaking palsy in his hands; which began in France before the year 1650, and has grown upon him by degrees, ever since, so that he has not been able to write very legibly since 1665 or 1666, as I find by some of his letters to me.

Charity. His brotherly love to his kindred has already been spoken of. He was very charitable according to his means to those that were true objects of his bounty. One time, I remember, going into the Strand, a poor and infirm old man craved his alms. He beholding him with eyes

---

* Memorandum: there was no Turkish bath in his time. That in Newgate Street was built about the time of his death.

of pity and compassion, put his hands in his pocket, and gave him 6d. Said a divine (that is Dr Jasper Mayne) that stood by—'Would you have done this, if it had not been Christ's command?' 'Yes,' said he. 'Why?' said the other. 'Because,' said he, 'I was in pain to consider the miserable condition of the old man; and now my alms, giving him some relief, doth also ease me.'

¶ His goodness of nature and willingness to instruct anyone that was willing to be informed and modestly desired it, which I am a witness of as to my own part and also to others.

Aspersions and envy. His work was attended with envy, which threw several aspersions and false reports on him. For instance, one (common) was that he was afraid to lie alone at night in his chamber, (I have often heard him say that he was not afraid of *sprites*, but afraid of being knocked on the head for five or ten pounds, which rogues might think he had in his chamber); and several other tales, as untrue.

I have heard some positively affirm that he had a yearly pension from the King of France—possibly for having recommended such a monarchy as the King of France exercises, but for what other grounds I know not, unless it be for that the present King of France is reputed an encourager of choice and able men in all faculties who can contribute to his greatness. I never heard him speak of any such thing; and, since his death, I have enquired of his most intimate friends in Derbyshire who write to me they never heard of any such thing. Had it been so, he, nor they, ought to have been ashamed of it, and it had been becoming the munificence of so great a prince to have done it.

Atheism. For his being branded with atheism, his writings and virtuous life testify against it. And that he was a Christian, it is clear, for he received the sacrament of Dr Pierson, and in his confession to Dr John Cosins, on his (as he thought) death-bed, declared that he liked the religion of the Church of England best of all other.

He would have the worship of God performed with music (he told me).

¶ It is of custom in the lives of wise men to put down their sayings. Now if truth (uncommon) delivered clearly and wittily may go for a saying, his common discourse was full of them, and which for the most part were sharp and significant.

He said that if it were not for the gallows, some men are of so cruel a nature as to take a delight in killing men more than I should to kill a bird. I have heard him inveigh much against the cruelty of Moses for putting so many thousands to the sword for bowing to the golden calf.

I have heard him say that Aristotle was the worst teacher that ever was, the worst politician and teacher of ethics—a country fellow that could live in the world would be as good; but his rhetoric and discourse of animals was rare.

159

When Mr T. Hobbes was sick in France, the divines came to him, and tormented him (both Roman Catholic, Church of England and Calvinist). Said he to them 'Let me alone, or else I will detect all your cheats from Aaron to yourselves!' I think I have heard him speak something to this purpose.

Insert the love verses he made not long before his death:

1.

Tho' I am past ninety, and too old
T'expect preferment in the court of Cupid,
And many winters made me ev'n so cold
I am become almost all over stupid,

2.

Yet I can love and have a mistress too,
As fair as can be and as wise as fair;
And yet not proud, nor anything will do
To make me of her favour to despair.

3.

To tell you who she is were very bold;
But if i' th' character your self you find
Think not the man a fool tho' he be old
Who loves in body fair a fairer mind.

*Catalogue of his learned familiar friends and acquaintances, besides those already mentioned, that I remember him to have spoken of.**

Mr Benjamin Jonson, poet-laureate, was his loving and familiar friend and acquaintance.

[Sir Robert] *Aytoun*, a Scotsman, a good poet and critic and good scholar. He was nearly related to his lord's lady (Bruce). And he desired Ben Jonson, and this gentleman, to give their judgement on his style in his translation of Thucydides.

Lucius Cary, Lord Falkland was his great friend and admirer and so was *Sir William Petty*; both which I have here enrolled amongst those friends I have heard him speak of, but Dr Blackburne left them both out of his life of Hobbes (to my astonishment). I asked him why he had done so. He answered, because they were both unknown to foreigners. His acquaintance with Sir William Petty began at Paris, 1648 or 1649, at which time Mr Hobbes studied Vesalius' *Anatomy*, and Sir William with him. He then assisted Mr Hobbes in drawing his schemes for his book of optics, for he had a very fine hand in those days for drawing,

---

* Aubrey lists a large number of names; only those where he adds comments which throw light on Hobbes himself have been included here. *Ed.*

which drafts Mr Hobbes did much commend. His excellency in this kind conciliated them the sooner to the familiarity of our common friend Mr S. Cowper.

When he was at Florence he contracted a friendship with the famous *Galileo Galileo*, whom he extremely venerated and magnified; and not only as he was a prodigious wit, but for his sweetness of nature and manners. They pretty well resembled one another, as to their countenances, as by their pictures doth appear; were both cheerful and melancholic-sanguine; and had both a consimility of [the same] fate, to be hated and persecuted by the ecclesiastics.

Descartes and he were acquainted and mutually respected one another. He would say that had he kept himself to geometry he had been the best geometer in the world but that his head did not lie for philosophy.

When his *Leviathan* came out he sent by his stationer's (Andrew Crooke) man a copy of it, a well-bound, to *Mr John Selden* in the Carmelite Buildings. Mr Selden told the servant, he did not know Mr Hobbes, but had heard much of his worth, and that he should be very glad to be acquainted with him. Whereupon Mr Hobbes waited on him. From which time there was a close friendship between them to his dying day. He left by his will to Mr Hobbes, a legacy of ten pounds.

Sir Jonas Moore, mathematician, surveyor of his majesty's ordnance, who had a great veneration for Mr Hobbes and was wont much to lament, he fell to the study of the mathematics so late.

Edmund Waller esquire of Beconsfield: 'but what he was most to be commended for was that he being a private person threw down the strongholds of the Church, and let in light.'

Robert Stevens, serjeant at law, was wont to say of him, and that truly, that 'no man had so much, so deeply, seriously and profoundly considered human nature as he'.

Memorandum: he hath no countryman living who hath known him so long (since 1634) as myself, or of his friends, who knows so much about him.

Now as he had these ingenious and learned friends, and many more, no question, that I know not or now escape my memory; so he had many enemies (though undeserved; for he would not provoke, but if provoked, he was sharp and bitter): and as a prophet is not esteemed in his own country, so he was more esteemed by foreigners than by his countrymen.

His chief antagonists were:

Seth Ward, DD, now Bishop of Salisbury, who wrote against him in his *Vindicia Academiarum* anonymously with whom though formerly he had some contest, for which he was sorry, yet Mr Hobbes had a great veneration for his worth, learning and goodness.

John Wallis, DD, a great mathematician, and that has deserved exceedingly of the commonwealth of learning for the great pains etc, was his great antagonist in mathematics. It was a pity, as is said before, that Mr Hobbes began so late, else he would not have lain so open.

To conclude, he had a high esteem for the Royal Society, having said that 'Natural Philosophy was removed from the universities to Gresham College', meaning the Royal Society that meets there; and the Royal Society (generally) had the like for him: and he would long since have been ascribed a member there, but for the sake of one* or two persons, whom he took to be his enemies. In their meeting room at Gresham College is his picture, drawn from the life, 1663, by a good hand, which they much esteem, and several copies have been taken.

William Holder

1616–98

Holder's most memorable achievement was the teaching of a deaf-mute to speak, which Aubrey describes, though he contributed other papers to the meetings of the Royal Society, of which he was one of the first fellows. He also composed music, and was sub-dean of the Chapel Royal, the royal singing-school.

He was born in Nottinghamshire; went to Pembroke Hall in Cambridge, where he had a Greek scholar's place. About 1640 he married the daughter of Christopher Wren, dean of Windsor and rector of Knoyle in Wiltshire. In 1642, he had his institution and induction for the rectory of Bletchington in Oxfordshire. In the troublesome times he was with his father-in-law Wren at the garrison of Bristol. After the surrender of it to the parliament, he lived some years at Knoyle with him. About 1646, he went to Bletchington to his parsonage, where his hospitality and learning, mixed with great courtesy, easily conciliated the love of all his neighbours to him. The dean came with him thither, and died and is buried there.

He was very helpful in the education of his brother-in-law, Mr Christopher Wren, now knighted (a youth of a prodigious inventive wit), and of whom he was as tender as if he had been his own child. He gave him first instructions in geometry and arithmetic, and when he was a young scholar at the University of Oxford, was a very necessary and kind friend. The parsonage-house at Bletchington was Mr Christopher

* Dr Wallis (surely their Mercuries are in opposition) and Mr Boyle. I might add Sir Paul Neile, who disobliges everybody.

Wren's home, and retiring-place; here he contemplated, and studied, and found out a great many curious things in mathematics. About this house he made several curious dials, with his own hands, which are still to be seen.*

But to return to this honest worthy gentleman, he is a good poet. I have some very good verses (about 100) in Latin on St Vincent's Rocks and the hot well, near Bristol. He is very musical, both in theory and practically, and he had a sweet voice. He has written an excellent treatise of music, in English, which is written both for the learned and unlearned, and ready for the press. He is extremely well qualified for his place of sub-dean of the King's Chapel: to which he was preferred in 1674, as likewise of the sub-almoner, being a person abhorring covetousness, and full of pity.

The only son of Edward Popham (admiral for the parliament), being born deaf and dumb, was sent to him to learn to speak, which he taught him to do: by what method, and how soon, you may see in the appendix concerning it to his *Elements of Speech*, octavo, London, printed [1669]. It is a most ingenious and curious discourse, and untouched by any other; he was beholding to no author; did only consult with nature. This book I sent to Mr Anthony Lucas at Liège, who very much admires it and I have desired him to translate it into French. Dr John Wallis unjustly arrogates the glory of teaching the said young gentleman to speak, in the *Philosophical Transactions*, and in Dr Robert Plot's *History of Oxfordshire*; which occasioned Dr Holder to write against him a pamphlet in quarto.†

He is a handsome, graceful person, and of a delicate constitution, and of an even and smooth temper; so that, if one would go about to describe a perfect good man, one would draw this doctor's character. Of a just stature; grey eye; tall and well set; sanguine; thin skin; roundish face; graceful elocution; his discourse so gentlemanly and obliging; clear reason.

They say that a likeness in morals leads to friendship; then it will not be found strange that there should be such a close friendship between this worthy gentleman and the right reverend father in God, Seth Ward, Lord Bishop of Salisbury, his contemporary in Cambridge.

It ought not to be forgotten, the great and exemplary love between this

---

* Aubrey notes: 'Which see, as well worthy to be seen.' *Ed.*

† Thomas Hobbes, in a letter which Aubrey kept with his notes for Hobbes' life, commented: 'As for the matter itself, I mean the teaching of a man born deaf and dumb to speak, I think it impossible. But I do not count him deaf and unteachable that can hear a word spoken as loud as possible at the very entrance to his ear, for of this I am assured that a man born absolutely deaf must of necessity be made to hear before he can be made to speak, much less to understand. And that he could make him hear (being a great and common good) would well deserve both to be honoured and to be enriched. He that could make him speak a few words only deserved nothing. But he that brags of this and cannot do it, deserves to be whipped.' *Ed.*

163

doctor and his virtuous wife, who is not less to be admired, in her sex and station, than her brother Sir Christopher; and (which is rare to be found in a woman) her excellences do not inflate her. Amongst many other gifts she has a strange sagacity as to curing of wounds, which she does not do so much by precedents and receipt books, as by her own thinking-out, considering the causes, effects and circumstances. His majesty Charles II had hurt his hand, which he entrusted his surgeons to make well; but they ordered him so that they made it much worse, so that it swelled, and pained him up to his shoulder; and pained him so extremely that he could not sleep, and began to be feverish. Someone told the king what a rare she-surgeon he had in his house; she was at once sent for at eleven o'clock at night. She presently made ready a poultice, and applied it, and gave his majesty sudden ease, and he slept well; next day she dressed him, and in a few days perfectly cured him, to the great grief of all the surgeons, who envy and hate her.

Hugh Holland
?–1633

From Sir John Penrudock: Hugh Holland, poet: he was descended of the family of the earls of Kent, etc, and was a Roman Catholic. The lady Elizabeth Hatton (mother to the lady Purbeck) was his great patroness (see Ben Jonson's masque of the Gipsies for these two beauties).

Sir J.P. asked him his advice as he was dying (or he then gave it) that, the best rule for him to govern his life was to read St Jerome's Epistles.

He was of a Lancashire family.

Philemon Holland
1552–1637

He is best known for his translations of Pliny, Suetonius and of William Camden's Britannia.

Philemon Holland was schoolmaster of the free school at Coventry, and that for many years. He made a great many good scholars. He translated Livy with one and the same pen, which the lady (see at the end of his translation of Suetonius) embellished with silver, and kept amongst her heirlooms. He wrote a good hand, but a rare Greek character; witness the manuscript of Euclid's Harmonics in the library belonging to the school. He translated several Latin authors, e.g. Livy, Pliny's Natural History, Suetonius Tranquillus.

One made this epigram on him:

> Philemon with 's translations doeth so fill us
> He will not let Suetonius be Tranquillus.*

Wenceslaus Hollar

1607-77

Hollar's maps and views of London are our most vivid record of the seventeenth century city. He came to England about 1636, and in the Civil War fought in the Royalist cause; but about 1643 he fled to Antwerp, returning to England in 1652. Over 2,500 engravings by him survive, as well as many drawings.

Aubrey's story about his father appears to be mere gossip.

Wenceslaus Hollar, a Bohemian, was born at Prague; his father was a knight of the Empire: which is granted by letters patent under the imperial seal (as our baronets). I have seen it. The seal is bigger than the broad seal of England: in the middle is the Imperial coat of arms; and, round about it, are the coats of the princes electors. His father was a Protestant, and either for keeping a private prayer-meeting, or being taken at one, forfeited his estate, and was ruined by the Roman Catholics.

He told me that when he was a schoolboy he took a delight in drawing of maps; which drafts he kept, and they were pretty. He was designed by his father to have been a lawyer, and was put to that profession, when his father's troubles, together with the wars, forced him to leave his country. So that what he did for his delight and recreation only when a boy, proved to be his livelihood when a man.

I think he stayed some time in Northern Germany, then he came into England, where he was very kindly entertained by that great patron of painters and draughtsmen, the Lord High Marshal, Earl of Arundel

* i.e. quiet. *Ed.*

and Surrey, where he spent his time in drawing and copying rarities, which he did etch (i.e. eat with aqua fortis in copper plates). When the lord marshal went ambassador to the Emperor of Germany to Vienna, he travelled with much grandeur; and among others, Mr Hollar went with him (very well clad) to take views, landscapes, buildings, etc remarkable in their journey, which we see now at the print shops. He has done the most in that way that ever anyone did, insomuch that I have heard Mr John Evelyn, FRS, say that at sixpence a print his labour would come to many pounds. He was very shortsighted, and did work in so much detail that the curiosity of his work is not to be judged without a magnifying glass. When he drew his landscapes, he, then, had a glass to help his sight.

At Arundel House, he married my lady's waiting woman, Mrs Tracy, by whom he has a daughter, that was one of the greatest beauties I have seen; his son by her died in the plague, an ingenious youth, who drew delicately.

When the Civil Wars broke out, the lord marshal had leave to go beyond sea, to Italy. Mr Hollar went into the Low Countries, where he stayed till about 1649.

I remember he told me that when he first came into England (which was a serene time of peace) that the people, both poor and rich, did look cheerfully, but at his return, he found the countenances of the people all changed, melancholy, spiteful, as if bewitched.

I have said before that his father was ruined upon the account of the Protestant religion. Wenceslaus died a Catholic, of which religion, I suppose, he might be ever since he came to Arundel House.

He was a very friendly good natured man as could be, but careless in his affairs and died not rich. He married a second wife, 1665, by whom he as several children. He died on Lady Day, 25 March 1677. Had he lived till the thirteenth of July following, he had been just seventy years old.

Robert Hooke

1635–1703

Aubrey's life needs little additional explanation: Hooke was probably the best experimental scientist among the first Fellows of the Royal Society, and certainly one of the most wide-ranging of the 'philosophers'.

Mr Robert Hooke, curator of the Royal Society at London, was born at Freshwater in the Isle of Wight; his father was minister there, and of the family of the Hookes of Hooke in Hants, in the road from London to Salisbury, a very ancient family and in that place for many (three or more) hundred years. His father, Mr John Hooke, had two or three brothers, all ministers.

John Hoskyns, the painter, being at Freshwater, to draw pictures, Mr Hooke* observed what he did, and, thought he, 'Why cannot I do so too?' So he gets him chalk, and red ochre, and coal, and grinds them, and puts them on a trencher [flat wooden plate] got a pencil, and to work he went, and made a picture: then he copied (as they hung up in the parlour) the pictures there, which he made like. Also, being a boy there, at Freshwater, he made a sundial on a round trencher; never having had any instruction. His father was not mathematical at all.

When his father died, his son Robert was but 13 years old, to whom he left one hundred pounds, which was sent up to London with him, with an intention to have him bound to Mr Lely† the painter, with whom he was a little while upon trial; who liked him very well, but Mr Hooke quickly perceived what was to be done, so, thought he, 'why cannot I do this by myself and keep my hundred pounds?' He also had some instructions in drawing from Mr Samuel Cooper (prince of portrait painters of this age); but whether from him before or after Mr Lely, query?

Query when he went to Mr Busby's the schoolmaster of Westminster, at whose house he was; and he made very much of him. With him he lodged his hundred pounds. There he learned to play twenty lessons on the organ. He there in one week's time made himself master of the first six books of Euclid, to the admiration of Mr Busby (now doctor of theology), who introduced him. At school here he was very mechanical, and (amongst other things) he invented thirty different ways of flying, which I have not only heard him say but also Dr Wilkins (at Wadham College at that time), who gave him his *Mathematical Magic*, which did him a great kindness. He was never a King's Scholar [i.e. at Westminster School] and I have heard Sir Richard Knight (who was his schoolfellow) say that he seldom saw him in the school.

In 1658 he was sent to Christ Church in Oxford, where he had a chorister's place (in those days when the church music was put down‡), which was a pretty good maintenance. He was there assistant to Dr Thomas Willis in his chemistry; who afterwards recommended him to the honourable Robert Boyle esq, to be useful to him in his chemical operations. Mr Hooke then read to him (i.e. Robert Boyle) Euclid's Elements and made him understand Descartes' philosophy.

In 1662 Mr Robert Boyle recommended Mr Robert Hooke to be Curator of the experiments of the Royal Society, wherein he did an

* This episode refers to Hooke's boyhood: Aubrey meant to give his age, but left a blank for it to be inserted later.
† i.e. Sir Peter Lely.
‡ i.e. suppressed under the Commonwealth. *Ed.*

admirable good work to the commonwealth of learning in recommending the fittest person in the world to them. In 1664 he was chosen geometry professor at Gresham College. Sir John Cutler, knight, endowed a lecture on mechanics, which he read.

In 1666 the great conflagration of London happened, and then he was chosen one of the two surveyors of the city of London; by which he has got a great estate. He built Bedlam, the Physician's College, Montagu House, the Monument on Fish Street Hill and Theatre there; and he is much made use of in designing buildings.

He is but of middling stature, something crooked, pale faced, and his face but little below, but his head is large; his eye full and popping, and not quick; a grey eye. He has a delicate head of hair, brown, and of an excellent moist curl. He is and ever was very temperate, and moderate in diet etc.

As he is of prodigious inventive head, so is a person of great virtue and goodness. Now when I have said his inventive faculty is so great, you cannot imagine his memory to be excellent, for they are like two buckets, as one goes up, the other goes down. He is certainly the greatest expert on mechanics this day in the world. His head lies much more to geometry than to arithmetic. He is a bachelor, and, I believe, will never marry. His elder brother left one fair daughter, which is his heir. In fine, (which crowns all) he is a person of great suavity and goodness.

It was Mr Robert Hooke that invented the pendulum watches, so much more useful than the other watches.

He has invented an engine for the speedy working out of division, etc or the speedy and immediate finding out of the divisor.

¶ (From a letter to Anthony Wood)*: About nine or ten years ago, Mr Hooke wrote to Mr Isaac Newton of Trinity College, Cambridge, to make a demonstration of this theory (of gravity), not telling him, at first, the proportion of the gravity to the distance, nor what was the curved line that was thereby made. Mr Newton, in his answer to this letter, did express that he had not known of it; and in his first attempt about it, he calculated the curve by supposing the attraction to be the same at all distances: upon which, Mr Hooke sent, in his next letter, the whole of his hypothesis, that is, that the gravitation was reciprocal to the square of the distance . . . which is the whole celestial theory, concerning which Mr Newton has a demonstration, not at all owning he received the first intimation of it from Mr Hooke. Likewise Mr Newton has in the same book printed some other theories and experiments of Mr Hooke's, as that about the oval figure of the earth and sea: without acknowledging from whom he had them. . . .

* The letter was corrected by Robert Hooke, and some of his technical details have been omitted.

Mr Wood! This is the greatest discovery in nature that ever was since the world's creation. It never was so much as hinted by any man before. I know you will do him right. I hope you may read his hand. I wish he had written plainer and afforded a little more paper.

Yours,

J. Aubrey

Before I leave this town, I will get of him a catalogue of what he has written; and as much of his inventions as I can. But there are many hundreds; he believes not fewer than a thousand. It is such a hard matter to get people to do themselves right.

John Hoskyns
1566–1638

John Hoskyns, serjeant-at-law, was born at Monnington in the county of Hereford. Monnington belonged to the priory of Llantony near Gloucester, where his ancestors had the office of cupbearer (or 'pocillator') to the prior. I have heard there was a window given by one Hoskyns there, as by the inscription did appear.

Whether the serjeant were the eldest brother or no, I have forgotten; but he had a brother, John, DD, a learned man, rector of Ledbury and canon of Hereford, who, I think, was eldest, who was designed to be a scholar, but this John (the serjeant) would not be quiet, but he must be a scholar too. In those days boys were seldom taught to read that were not to be of some learned profession. So, upon his insistence, being then ten years of age, he learned to read, and, at the year's end, entered into his Greek grammar. This I have heard his son, Sir Benet Hoskyns, knight and baronet, several times say. Charles Hoskyns was brother to the Serjeant and the Doctor, a very ingenious man, who would not have been inferior to either, but killed himself with hard study.

He was of a strong constitution, and had a prodigious memory. He went to Winchester school, where he was the flower of his time. I remember I have heard that one time he had not made his exercise (verse) and spoke to one of his form to show him his, which he saw. The schoolmaster presently calls for the exercises, and Hoskyns told him that he had written it out but lost it, but he could repeat it, and repeated the other boy's exercise (I think twelve or sixteen verses) having read them once only. When the boy who really had made them showed the master the same, and could not repeat them he was whipped for stealing Hoskyns' exercise. I think John Owen and he were schoolfellows.

There were many pretty stories of him when a schoolboy, which I have forgotten. I have heard his son say that he was a year at Westminster; and not doing well there, he was sent to Winchester.

The Latin verses in the quadrangle at Winchester College, at the taps where the boys wash their hands, were of his making, where there is the picture of a good servant, with hind's feet, asses' ears, a padlock on his lips etc. The Latin verses describe the properties of a good servant.

When he came to New College, he was *Terrae filius*;* but he was so bitterly satirical that he was expelled and put to his shifts.

He went into Somersetshire and taught a school for about a year at Ilchester. He compiled there a Greek lexicon as far as M, which I have seen. He married (near there) a rich widow; she was a Moyle of Kent; by whom he had only one son and one daughter.

After his marriage, he admitted himself at the Middle Temple. He wore good clothes and kept good company. His excellent wit gave him letters of commendation to all ingenious persons. At his first coming to London, he got acquainted with the under-secretaries at court, where he was often useful to them in writing their Latin letters.

His great wit quickly made him be taken notice of. Ben Jonson called him 'father'. Sir Benet (bishop Bennet of Hereford was his godfather) told me that one time desiring Mr Jonson to adopt him for his son, 'No,' said he, 'I dare not; it is honour enough for me to be your brother: I was your father's son, and it was he that polished me.' In short, his acquaintances were all the wits about the town; e.g. Sir Walter Raleigh, who was his fellow-prisoner in the Tower, where he was Sir Walter's critic and editor, to review and polish Sir Walter's style; John Donne, DD; John Owen; Marbyn, recorder of London; Sir Benjamin Ruddyer, with whom it was once his fortune to have a quarrel and fought a duel with him and hurt him in the knee, but they were afterwards friends again; Sir Henry Wotton, provost of Eton College; and many others.

His conversation was exceedingly pleasant, and on the road he would make anyone good company to him. He was a great master of the Latin and Greek language; a great divine. He understood the law well, but he was worst at that.

His verses on the fart in the Parliament house are printed in some of the *Drolleries*. He had a book of poems, neatly written by one of his clerks, bigger than Dr Donne's poems, which his son Benet lent to he knows not who, about 1653, and could never hear of it since. Mr Thomas Henshaw has an excellent Latin copy in rhyme in the praise of ale of his.

---

* i.e. he had to make an amusing, traditionally satirical, speech on graduation day. *Ed.*

He was a very strong man and active. He did the pomado* in the saddle of the third horse in his armour, (which Sir John Hoskyns has still) before William, earl of Pembroke. He was about my height.

He had a very ready wit, and would make verses on the road, where he was the best company in the world. In Sir H. Wotton's *Remaynes* are verses (dialogue) made on the road by him and Sir Henry. He made an anthem in English to be sung at Hereford Minster at the assizes; but Sir Robert Harley (a great Puritan) was much offended at it. He made the epitaph on Woodgate in New College cloisters. He made the best Latin epitaphs of his time; amongst many others an excellent one on Finch, the earl of Winchelsea's grandfather, who has a noble monument at Eastwell in Kent. Besides his excellent natural memory, he acquired the artificial way of memory.

He wrote his own life (which his grandson Sir John Hoskyns, knight and baronet, has) which was to show that whereas Plutarch etc had written the lives of many generals, etc, grandees, that he, or an active man might, from a private fortune by his wit and industry attain to the dignity of a serjeant at law. But he should have said that they must have qualities like his too. This life I cannot borrow.

He was a close prisoner in the Tower, in king James's time, for speaking too boldly in the Parliament house of the king's profuse liberality to the Scots. He made a comparison of a conduit, whereunto water came, and ran out afar off. 'Now', said he, 'this pipe reaches as far as Edinburgh.' He was kept a 'close prisoner' there, i.e. his windows were boarded up. Through a small chink he once saw a crow, and another time, a kite; the sight whereof, he said, was a great pleasure to him. He, with much ado, obtained at length the favour to have his little son Bennet to be with him; and he then made a Latin distich, thus Englished by him:

> My little Ben, whilst thou art young,
> And know'st not how to rule thy tongue,
> Make it thy slave whil'st thou art free,
> Lest it, as mine, imprison thee.

I have heard that when he came out of the Tower, his crest was granted him, viz, 'a lion's head couped or, breathing fire'. The serjeant would say jocosely that it was the only lion's head in England that took tobacco.

Not many months before his death (being at the assizes sessions at Hereford) a massive country fellow trod on his toe, which caused a

---

* A vault over the horse, done by placing one hand on the pommel of the saddle. *Ed.*

171

gangrene which was the cause of his death. One Mr Dighton* of Gloucester (an experienced surgeon who had formerly been surgeon in the wars in Ireland) was sent for to cure him; but his skill and care could not save him. His toes were first cut off. The minister of his parish had a club foot or feet (I think his name was Hugh). Said he, 'Sir Hugh',—after his toes were cut off—'I must be acquainted with your shoemaker.'

Sir Robert Bye, attorney of the court of wards, was his neighbour, but there was no great goodwill between them—Sir Robert was haughty. He happened to die on Christmas Day: the news being brought to the serjeant, said he, 'The devil has a Christmas pie.'

He was a very strong man and valiant, and an early riser in the morning (that is at four in the morning). He was black-eyed and had black hair.

He lies buried under an altar monument on the north side of the choir of Dore Abbey in Herefordshire.

(In this abbey church of Dore are two *frustum's* or remainders of mailed and cross-legged monuments, one said to be of a lord Chandos, the other, the lord of Ewyas Lacy. A little before I saw them a mower had taken one of the arms to whet his scythe).

He was wont to say that all that came to London were either carrion or crows.

Edward Hyde
Earl of Clarendon, 1609–74

Charles II's most trusted councillor from 1651–67. He was disgraced in 1667, and ended his life in exile. The History of the Rebellion *was eventually published in 1702–4.*

I think I told you that the present earl of Clarendon told me his father was writing the history of our late times. He begins with King Charles I and brought it to the restoration of King Charles II, when, as he was writing, the pen fell out of his hand: he took it up again to write: it fell out again. So then he perceived he was attacked by death, that is, the dead palsy [a stroke].—They say it is very well done; but his son will not print it.

---

* Mr Dighton would oftentimes say that he generally observed in the Irish wars that those men that went to their wenches the day before the battle either did die upon the spot or came under his hands. The finger of God!

Henry Isaacson
1581–1654

Mr Henry Isaacson was secretary to Lancelot Andrewes, lord bishop of Westminster.

Memorandum: Bourman, Doctor of Divinity, of Kingston upon Thames, did know Mr Isaacson, and told me that he was a learned man, which I easily believed when I heard he was secretary to that learned prelate, who made use of none but for merit. The Doctor told me that when he presented his *Chronology* to his majesty King Charles the First, it was in the matted gallery of Whitehall.* The king presently discerned the purpose of the treatise, and turned to his own birth: said the King, 'Here's one lie to begin with.' It seems that Mr Isaacson had taken it out of a foreigner, who used the other account.† Poor Mr Isaacson was so ashamed at this unlucky encounter, that he immediately sneaked away and stayed not for praise or reward, both of which perhaps he might have had, for his majesty was well pleased with it. He wrote several little books besides his *Chronology*. He was of Pembroke Hall in Cambridge. He was there about Master of Arts standing.

Dr Jaquinto

Physician to the Pope, then to King James. He went into the marshes of Essex, where they put their sheep to cure them of the rot, where he lived sometime purposely to observe what plants the sheep did eat, of which herbs he made his medicine for the consumption, which Mr Edmund Wyld has.

---

* It was presented in an ill hour. An astrologer would give something to know *that day and hour*. He wanted a good election [i.e. choice of an astrologically favourable moment].

† i.e. the Gregorian, not the Julian calendar. The Gregorian calendar was only adopted in England in 1752, by which time there was a difference of eleven days between English and Continental reckoning. *Ed.*

David Jenkins

1582–1663

An independent and obstinate character, Jenkins opposed Charles I's policies in the 1630s, and his quarrel with the methods of one of the bishops led to three separate excommunications in 1640. His zealous support of the royal cause in 1643 is therefore surprising, as is a story that when he was captured in 1645, he had £6000 in gold on him, which he refused to use in the king's support. It is certain that he never submitted to the authority of the Commonwealth.

The story of Jenkins' refusal to bribe Clarendon was the main reason for Aubrey's breach with Anthony Wood. Wood printed the tale in the second volume of his Athenae Oxoniensis, *and was prosecuted for libel by the second Earl of Clarendon, despite the fact that his father had been dead for nearly thirty years, and that this very charge of corruption had been made against him in parliament. Wood let it be known that Aubrey was the source of the story, and although Aubrey came to no harm by it, Wood's unnecessary indiscretion angered Aubrey. Wood was expelled from Oxford, and the second volume of the* Athenae *publicly burnt, as a result of Clarendon's prosecution.*

Judge Jenkins, prisoner in the Tower of London, Windsor, etc, eleven years for his loyalty.* He would have taken it kindly to have been made one of the judges in Westminster Hall, but would give no money for it, so the Lord Chancellor Hyde never preferred him.

He was of very good courage. Rode in the Lord Gerard's army in Pembrokeshire, in the forlorn hope, with his rapier drawn holding it on end.

¶ He was one of the judges of the Carmarthen, Cardigan and Pembrokeshire circuit before the wars. In the wars he was taken prisoner at Hereford. He was long time prisoner in the Tower, Newgate, Wallingford, and Windsor. He never submitted to the usurping power (I think, the only man). All his estate was confiscated; and was always excepted from pardons by the parliament, in the first rank of delinquents.

In his circuit in Wales at the beginning of the wars, he caused to be indicted several men of those parts (that were parliament, etc, engaged against the king) for high treason; and the grand jury indicted them. Afterwards, when he was prisoner in Newgate, some of these grandees came to him to triumph over him, and told him that if they had been

---

* To the king under the Commonwealth. *Ed.*

174

thus in his power, he would have hanged them. 'God forbid else!'†
replied he—which undaunted return they much admired.

The parliament intended to have hanged him; and he expected no
less, but resolved to be hanged with the Bible under one arm and
Magna Carta under the other. And hanged he had been, had not Harry
Martyn told them in the house that

The blood of martyrs is the seed of the church

and that that way would do them more mischief. So his life was saved,
and they removed him out of the way to Wallingford Castle.

He died upwards of fourscore years of age at Cowbridge in the county
of Glamorgan. It is a pity he was not made one of the judges of
Westminster Hall for his long sufferings; and he might have been, he
told me, if he would have given money to the Chancellor—but he
scorned it. He needed it not, for he had his estate again £1500 per
annum and being old and broken by imprisonment. Mr Thomas Hobbes
told him one day at dinner that 'that hereafter would not show well for
somebody's honour in history'.

Sir Leoline Jenkins

1623–85

*Leoline (or Llewellyn) Jenkins' early career was as a teacher; he then
became a church lawyer, and finally a civil servant and diplomat. He
represented Britain at the Congress of Nijmwegen in 1676–79, where a
general European peace settlement was attempted. His reputation was of an
efficient but unimaginative 'secretary', with a vast knowledge of legal and
diplomatic forms and procedures.*

Sir Leoline Jenkins, knight, was born at Llantrithyd in the county of
Glamorgan. His father (whom I knew) was a good plain countryman, a
copyholder of Sir John Aubrey, knight and baronet (eldest son of Sir
Thomas) whose manor it is. He went to school at Cowbridge, not far
off. David Jenkins, that was prisoner in the Tower (married a sister of
Sir John Aubrey) was some remote kin to him; and looking on him as a
boy promising, diligent and good, he contributed something towards
his education.

In 1641, he was matriculated of Jesus College in Oxford, where he

† That I should have done otherwise. *Ed.*

175

stayed till (I think) he took his degree of BA. About that time Sir John Aubrey sent for him home to inform his eldest son Lewis Aubrey (since deceased, 1659) in grammar; and that he might take his learning the better, he was taught in the church-house where several boys came to school, and there were six or seven gentlemen's sons (Sir Francis Maunsell, bart; Mr Edmund Thomas) boarded in the town. The young gentlemen were all near of an age, and ripe for the university together; and to Oxford they all went under Mr Jenkins' care about the year 1649 or 50, but by reason of the disturbances of those times, Sir John would not have his son of any college. But they all studied at Mr (now Sir) Sampson White's house, a grocer, opposite to University College. Here he stayed with my cousin about three years or better, and then in 165– (see Mr Hobbes' *De Corpore*, it was that year), he travelled with my cousin and two or three of the other gentlemen into France, where they stayed about three years, and made themselves masters of that language. He first studied the civil law, that is bought *Vinnius on Justinian*, 1653. When he brought home Mr Lewis Aubrey, he returned to Jesus College (ask if he was of the foundation). After his majesty's restoration Dr Maunsell was restored to his principalship of that house, but being very old and weary of worldly cares, he kept it not long before he resigned it to Mr Jenkins.

Gilbert Sheldon, Archbishop of Canterbury, and Sir John Aubrey were contemporaries, and contracted a great friendship at Oxford in their youth, which continued to their deaths. In the troublesome times after Dr Sheldon was expelled, he was a year (I think) or two with Sir John at Llantrithyd, where he took notice of the virtue and assiduity of the young man Mr Jenkins. After the king's restoration Sir John Aubrey recommended Mr Jenkins to him; made his fortune. In [1668] he was Archbishop of Canterbury; Sir William Meyric LlD and judge of the Prerogative Court of Canterbury died, and the archbishop conferred that place on Mr Jenkins. In 1670, he had the honour of knighthood.

In 1673, he was sent with Sir Joseph Williamson, plenipotentiaries, to Nijmwegen: I remember that very time they went away was opposition to Saturn and Mars. I said then to the Earl of Thanet that if that embassy came to any good I would never trust to astrology again.

March 25, 1680, he was made Principal Secretary of State. When I came to wait on him to congratulate for the honour his majesty had been pleased to bestow on him, he received me with his usual courtesy and said that 'it had pleased God to raise up a poor worm to do his majesty humble service'.

He has a strong body for study, indefatigable, temperate and virtuous. God bless him.

When Mary the queen-mother died at Paris, the King of France

176

caused her jewels and treasures to be locked up and sealed. His majesty of Great Britain sent Sir Llewellyn (which is Leoline in Latin) to Paris concerning the administration.

George Johnson

It pleased God at Whitsuntide last to bereave me of a dear, useful and faithful friend, Mr Johnson who had the reversion of the place of Master of the Rolls;* who generously, for friendship and neighbourhood sake (we were born the same week and within four miles and educated together) gave me the grant to be one of his secretaries—which place is worth £500 per annum. He was a strong lusty man and died of a malignant fever, infected by the earl of Abingdon's brother, making of his will. It was such an opportunity that I shall never have the like again.

Mr Vere Bertie† was his chamber-fellow (at the Inner Temple) in 1655, the wintertime, which was his rise.

Inigo Jones
1573–1652

The greatest architect of the period and designer of the sets and costumes for many of the masques of the Stuart court.

Inigo Jones' monument—this tomb is on the north side of the church, but his body lies in the chancel about the middle. The inscription mentions that he built the banqueting house and the portico at (old) St Paul's. Mr Marshall in Fetter Lane took away the bust here to his house, which see. Ask Mr Oliver about this.

Mr Oliver, the city surveyor, has all his papers and designs, not only of St Paul's Cathedral etc and the banqueting house, but his design of all Whitehall, in the same style as the Banqueting House; a rare thing, which see.

Memorandum: Mr Emanuel De Critz (sergeant painter to King Charles I) told me in 1649, that the catafalque of King James at his

---

* He would have succeeded to the office on the death of the then holder. *Ed.*
† Later Justice of the Common Pleas, and Baron of the Exchequer. *Ed.*

funeral (which is a kind of bed of state erected in Westminster Abbey, as Robert, earl of Essex, had, Oliver Cromwell and general Monck) was very ingeniously designed by Mr Inigo Jones, and that he made the four heads of the caryatids (which bore up the canopy) of plaster of paris, and made the drapery of them of white calico, which was very handsome and cheap, and showed as well as if they had been cut out of white marble.

Ben Jonson
?1573–1637

Ben Jonson seems to have come from an old Border family: his early career was turbulent, and in Aubrey's day some of the incidents had become confused—for instance, he did indeed kill a fellow-actor, but it was not Christopher Marlowe. His plays rank second only to Shakespeare's, but some of his best work is to be found in the court masques which he wrote for James I and Charles I, and for which Inigo Jones provided designs.

I remember when I was a scholar at Trinity College, Oxford, 1646, I heard Dr Ralph Bathurst, now Dean of Wells, say that Ben Jonson was a Warwickshire man—but ask about this. 'Tis agreed that his father was a minister; and by his epistle dedicatory of *Every Man in his Humour* to Mr William Camden that he was a Westminster scholar and that Mr W. Camden was his schoolmaster.

Anthony Wood in his *History* says he was born in Westminster: that (at riper years) after he had studied at Cambridge he came of his own accord to Oxford and there entered himself in Christ Church and took his Master's degree in Oxford (or it was conferred on him) in 1619.

His mother, after his father's death, married a bricklayer; and 'tis generally said that he wrought some time with his stepfather (and particularly on the garden wall of Lincoln's Inn next to Chancery Lane—from old Parson Hill, of Stretton, Herefordshire, 1646) and that a knight, a bencher,* walking through and hearing him repeat some Greek verses out of Homer, discoursing with him, and finding him to have a wit extraordinary, gave him some exhibition to maintain him at Trinity College in Cambridge.

Then he went into the Low Countries, and spent some time (not very long) in the army, not to the disgrace of himself, as you may find in his *Epigrams*.

---

* Member of the governing body of Lincoln's Inn. *Ed.*

Then he came over into England, and acted and wrote, but both ill, at the Green Curtain, a kind of nursery or obscure playhouse, some where in the suburbs (I think towards Shoreditch or Clerkenwell)— from J. Greenhill.

Then he undertook to write a play and did hit it admirably well, viz *Every Man in his Humour* which was his first good one.

Serjeant John Hoskins, of Herefordshire, was his *father*. I remember his son (Sir Bennet Hoskins, baronet, who was something poetical in his youth), told me, that when he desired to be adopted his son: 'No,' said he, ''tis honour enough for me to be your brother; I am your father's son, 'twas he that polished me, I do acknowledge it.'

He was (or rather had been) of a clear and fair skin; his habit was very plain. I have heard Mr Lacy, the player, say that he was wont to wear a coat like a coachman's coat, with slits under the armpits. He would many times exceed in drink: canary was his beloved liquor; then he would tumble home to bed, and, when he had thoroughly perspired, then to study. I have seen his studying chair, which was of straw, such as old women used, and as Aulus Gellius is drawn in.

When I was in Oxford, Bishop Skinner (of Oxford) who lay at our college, was wont to say that he understood an author as well as any man in England.

He mentions in his *Epigrams* a son that he had, and his epitaph.

Long since, in King James's time, I have heard my uncle Danvers say (who knew him) that he lived without Temple Bar, at a comb-maker's shop about the Elephant and Castle. In his later time he lived in Westminster, in the house under which you pass as you go out of the churchyard into the old palace; where he died.

He lies buried in the north aisle of Westminster Abbey in the path of square stone (the rest is lozenge), opposite to the scutcheon of Robertus de Ros, with this inscription only on him, in a pavement square of blue marble, about 14 inches square

O RARE BENN IOHNSON

which was done at the charge of Jack Young (afterwards knighted) who, walking there while the grave was covering, gave the fellow eighteen pence to cut it.

His motto before his (bought) books was, *Like an Explorer*. I remember 'tis in Seneca's *Epistles*.

He was a favourite of the Lord Chancellor Egerton, as appears by several verses to him. In one he begs his lordship to do a friend of his a favour.

'Twas an ingenious [clever] remark of my Lady Hoskins, that B.J. never writes of love, or if he does, does it not naturally.

He killed Mr Marlowe, the poet, on Bunhill, coming from the Green

Curtain play-house—from Sir Edward Shirburn.*

¶ Ben Johnson had £50 per annum for many years together to prevent Sir W. Wiseman of Essex from being sheriff. At last King James pricked him,† and Ben came to his majesty and told him that he 'had pricked him to the heart' and then explained himself (meaning Sir W.W. being pricked sheriff) and got him struck off.

See his *Execration against Vulcan*. See *None-such-Charles*. When B.J. was dying King Charles sent him but £10. Ask T. Shadwell for notes of B.J. from the Duke of Newcastle; and also ask Thomas Henshawe (as also about the stones in Ireland).‡ Ask my Lord Clifford of the gentleman that cut the grass under Ben Jonson's feet, of whom he said: 'Ungrateful man! I showed him Juvenal.'

¶ Ben Jonson had one eye lower than t'other, and bigger, like Clun, the player; perhaps he begot Clun. He took a catalogue from Mr Lacy (the player) of the Yorkshire dialect. 'Twas his hint for clownery to his comedy called *The Tale of a Tub*. This I had from Mr Lacy.

King James made him write against the Puritans who began to be troublesome in his time.

A Grace by Ben Johnson, *extempore*, before King James

> Our king and queen, the Lord-God bless
> The Paltzgrave,§ and the Lady Bess,
> And God bless every living thing
> That lives, and breathes, and loves the king,
> God bless the Council of Estate,
> And Buckingham, the fortunate.
> God bless them all, and keep them safe,
> And God bless me, and God bless Raph.

The king was mighty inquisitive to know who this Raph was. Ben told him 'twas the drawer at the Swan tavern, by Charing Cross, who drew him good canary. For this drollery his majesty gave him a hundred pounds.

This account I received from Mr Isaac Walton (who wrote Dr John Donne's etc Life), 2 December 1680, he being then eighty-seven years of age. This is his own handwriting.

I hardly knew Ben Jonson; but my lord the Bishop of Winchester knew him very well, and says that he was in the 6th, that is the uppermost form in Westminster School. At which time, his father died, and his mother married a bricklayer, who made him (much against his

* Elsewhere Aubrey attributes the story to John Lacy, the actor, and notes above it 'false'. *Ed.*

† Sheriffs were chosen by pricking a list with a bodkin, a custom still continued today. *Ed.*

‡ Aubrey was interested in stone circles and megaliths. *Ed.*

§ Pfalzgraf (Elector of the Rhine-Palatinate). *Ed.*

will) to help him in his trade. But in a short time, his schoolmaster, Mr Camden, got him a better employment, which was to attend or accompany a son of Sir Walter Raleigh's in his travels. Within a short time after their return, they parted (I think not in cool blood) and with a love matching what they had in their travels (not to be commended); and then, Ben began to set up for himself in the trade by which he got his subsistence and fame, of which I need not give any account. He got in time to have £100 a year from the king, also, a pension from the City, and the like from many of the nobility, and some of the gentry, which was well paid for love or fear of his railing in verse or prose, or both. My lord of Winchester told me, he told him he was (in his long retirement, and sickness, when he saw him, which was often) much afflicted that he had profaned the scripture in his plays; and lamented it with horror; yet, that at that time of his long retirement, his pensions (so much as came in) was given to a woman that governed him, with whom he lived and died near the Abbey in Westminster; and that neither he nor she took much care for next week, and would be sure not to want wine; of which he usually took too much before he went to bed, if not oftener and sooner. My lord tells me, he knows not, but thinks he was born in Westminster. The question may be put to Mr Wood very easily upon what grounds he is positive as to his being born there? He is a friendly man and will resolve it. So much for brave Ben.

Ralph Kettell

1563–1643

President of Trinity College from 1599 to 1643. Aubrey, who came to the college in 1642, remembered him as a vivid link with the Elizabethan past, and as a great character in a rather conservative mould. He was a good administrator rather than a great scholar.

Ralph Kettell, DD, president of Trinity College, Oxford, was born at King's Langley in Hertfordshire. The Lady Elizabeth Pope brought him in to be a scholar of the house at eleven years of age (as I have heard Dr Ralph Bathurst say). I have heard Dr Whistler say that he wrote good Latin, and Dr Ralph Bathurst (whose grandmother he married) that he scolded the best in Latin of anyone that ever he knew. He was of an admirable healthy constitution. He died a year or more after I came to the college, and he was then a good deal above 80, and he had then a

181

fresh ruddy complexion. He was a very tall well grown man. His gown and surplice and hood being on, he had a terrible gigantic aspect with his sharp gray eyes. The ordinary gown he wore was a russet cloth gown. He was, they say, white-haired very soon; he had a very venerable presence, and was an excellent governor. One of his maxims of governing was to keep down the youthful enthusiasm.* He was chosen president in 1599 the second after the foundation of the College.

He was a right Church of England man, and every Tuesday, in term time, in the morning, the undergraduates (I have forgotten if BAs as well) were to come into the chapel and hear him expound on the Thirty-Nine Articles of the Church of England. I remember he was wont to talk much of the rood loft, and of the wafers: he remembered those times. On these days, if anyone had committed a fault, he should be sure to hear of it in the chapel before his fellow collegiates: [he would] have at him that had a white cap on; for he concluded him to have been drunk, and his head to ache. Sir John Denham had borrowed money of Mr Whistler, the recorder, and after a great while, the recorder asked him for it again. Mr Denham laughed at it, and told him he never intended that. The recorder acquainted the president, who, at a lecture in the chapel, reproved him, and told him: 'Thy father,' (the judge), 'has hanged many an honester man.' In my time Mr Anthony Ettrick and some others frightened a poor young freshman of Magdalen College with conjuring, which when the old doctor heard of, on the next Tuesday, said he: 'Mr Ettrick,' (who is a very little man) 'will conjure up a jackanapes to be his great-grandfather.'

Memorandum: till Oxford was surrendered (after the siege of 1646) we sang the reading psalms on Sundays, holy-days, and holy-day eves; and one of the scholars of the house sang the gospel for the day in the hall, at the latter end of dinner, and concluded *Here endeth the gospel according to St John; Lord have mercy upon us.*

Kettell sang a shrill high treble; but there was one (J. Hoskyns) who had a higher, and would play the wag with the doctor to make him strain his voice up to his.

He saw how the factions in religion in those days drew,† and he kept himself unconcerned. W. Laud, Archbishop of Canterbury, sent him one time a servant of his with venison, which the old doctor with much earnestness refused, and said that he was an old man, and his stomach weak, and he had not eaten of such meat in a long time, and by no means would accept it; but the servant was as much pressing it on him on the other side, and told the president that he dared not carry it back again. Well, seeing there was no avoiding it, the president asked the

* 'Tis Seneca's expression.
† How people were taking sides in religious matters. *Ed.*

182

servant seriously, if the Archbishop of Canterbury intended to put in any scholars or fellows into his college.

One of the fellows (in Mr Francis Potter's time) was wont to say, that Dr Kettell's brain was like a hasty pudding, where there was memory, judgement and fancy all stirred together. He had all these faculties in great measure, but they were all just so jumbled together. If you had to do with him, taking him for a fool, you would have found in him great subtlety and reach: on the other hand if you treated with him as a wise man, you would have mistaken him for a fool. A neighbour of mine (Mr Laurence St Low) told me he heard him preach once in St Mary's Church, at Oxford. He began thus: 'Being my turn to preach in this place, I went into my study to prepare myself for my sermon, and I took down a book that had blue strings, and looked in it, and 'twas sweet St Bernard. I chanced to read such a part of it, on such a subject, which has made me to choose this text—.' I know not whether this was the only time or no that he used this following way of conclusion: 'But now I see it is time for me to shut up my book, for I see the doctor's men come in wiping of their beards from the alehouse.' (He could from the pulpit plainly see them, and 'twas their custom in sermon to go there, and about the end of sermon to return to wait on their masters.)

He had two wives, if not three, but no child. His second wife was a Villiers, or rather (I think) the widow of a Villiers, who had two beautiful daughters, co-heirs. The eldest, whom several of good estate would gladly have wedded, he would needs dispose of himself, and he thought nobody so fit a husband for this angelic creature as one Mr Bathurst, of the college, a second brother, and of about £300 per annum, but an indifferent scholar, red faced, not at all handsome. But the doctor's fashion was to go up and down the college, and peep in at the keyholes to see whether the boys did follow their books or no. He seldom found Bathurst minding of his book, but mending of his old doublet or breeches. He was very thrifty and penurious, and upon this reason he carried away this curious creature. But she was very happy in her issue; all her children were ingenious and prosperous in the world, and most of them beautiful.

Near seventy years since, I suppose, one Mr Isham (elder brother to Sir Justinian Isham) a gentleman-commoner of this house, died of the smallpox. He was a very fine gentleman, and very well beloved by all the college, and several of the fellows would have preached his funeral sermon, but Dr Kettell would not permit it, but would do it himself; which the fellows were sorry for, for they knew he would make a ridiculous piece of work of it. But preach the doctor did: takes a text and preaches on it a little while; and then takes another text, for the satisfaction of the young gentleman's mother; and anon he takes another text, for the satisfaction of the young gentleman's grandmother. When he came to the panegyric, said he: 'He was the finest sweet young gentleman; it did do my heart good to see him walk along the quadrangle. We have an old proverb that "Hungry dogs will eat dirty puddings"; but I must needs say for this young gentleman that he always loved* *sweet*'—he spoke it with a squeaking voice—'things'— and there was an end.

He observed that the houses that had the poorest beer had most drunkards, for it forced them to go into the town to comfort their stomachs; wherefore Dr Kettell always had in his college excellent beer, not better to be had in Oxford; so that we could not go to any other place but for the worse, and we had the fewest drunkards of any house in Oxford.

He was constantly at lectures and exercises in the hall to observe them, and brought along with him his hour-glass; and one time, being offended at the boys, he threatened them, that if they would not do their exercises better he 'would bring an hour-glass two hours long'. He was irreconcilable to long hair; called them hairy scalps, and as for periwigs (which were then very rarely worn) he believed them to be the scalps of men cut off after they were hanged, and so tanned and dressed for use. When he observed the scholars' hair longer than ordinary (especially if they were scholars of the house) he would bring a pair of scissors in his muff (which he commonly wore) and woe be to them that sat on the outside of the table.† I remember he cut Mr Radford's hair with the knife that clips the bread on the buttery-hatch, and then he sang (this is in the old play—Henry VIII—of *Gammer Gurton's Needle*),

> And was not Grim the collier finely trimm'd?
> Tonedi, Tonedi.

'Mr Lydall,' said he, 'how do you decline *tondeo* [*I cut hair*]? *Tondeo, tondes, tonedi?*‡'

One time, walking by the table where the logic lecture was read, where the reader was telling the boys that a syllogism might be true as to the form but not as to the substance; said the president (who would interrupt sometimes), 'There was a fox had spied a crow upon a tree, and he had a great mind to have him, and so gets under the tree in this hope, and lays out his tail crooked like a horn, thinking the crow might come and peck at it, and then he would seize him. Now come we' (this was his favourite word), 'I say the fox's tail is a horn: is this a true proposition or no?' (to one of the boys). 'Yes,' said he (the doctor

---

* They were wont to mock me with this. (Perhaps because Aubrey had a sweet tooth? *Ed.*)

† The tables were arranged down the sides of the hall, one bench being against the wall. *Ed.*

‡ It should be *tondet. Ed.*

184

expected he should have said 'No'; for it put him out of his design*);
'Why then,' said he, 'take him and—toot him'; and away he went.

He dragged with one foot a little, by which he gave warning (like the rattlesnake) of his coming. Will Egerton (Major-General Egerton's younger brother) a good wit and mimic, would go so like him, that sometimes he would make the whole chapel rise up, imagining he had been entering in.

As they were reading of inscribing and circumscribing figures, said he, 'I will show you how to inscribe a triangle in a quadrangle. Bring a pig into the quadrangle, and I will set the college dog at him, and he will take the pig by the ear; then come I and take the dog by the tail, and the hog by the tail, and so there you have a triangle in a quadrangle; *quod erat faciendum.*'

He preached every Sunday at his parsonage at Garsington (about five miles off). He rode on his bay gelding, with his boy Ralph before him, with a leg of mutton (commonly) and some college bread. He did not care for the country revels, because they tended to debauchery. Said he, at Garsington revel, 'Here is Hey for Garsington! and Hey for Cuddesdon! and Hey Hockley! but here's nobody cries, Hey for God Almighty!'

Upon Trinity Sunday (our festival day) he would commonly preach at the college, whither a number of the scholars of other houses would come, to laugh at him. In his prayer (where he was of course to remember Sir Thomas Pope, our founder, and the lady Elizabeth his wife, deceased) he would many times make a wilful mistake, and say, 'Sir Thomas Pope our *Confounder*',† but then at once recall himself.

He was a person of great charity. In his college, where he observed diligent boys that he guessed had but a slender allowance from their friends he would many times put money in at their windows; that his right hand did not know what his left did. Servitors that wrote good hands he would set on work to transcribe for him and reward them generously, and give them good advice. Mrs Howe, of Grendon, sent him a present of hippocras and some fine cheese-cakes, by a plain country fellow, her servant. The doctor tastes the wine: 'What,' said he, 'didst thou take this drink out of a ditch?' and when he saw the cheese-cakes: 'What have we here, *crinkum, crankum*‡?' The poor fellow stared on him, and wondered at such a reception of such a handsome present; but he shortly made him amends with a good dinner and half a crown. The parsonage of Garsington (which belongs to the college) is

* He was going to explain that the fox's tail had the form, but not the substance, of a horn. *Ed.*

† Instead of co-founder. *Ed.*

‡ Meaning unclear: perhaps 'something with the pox', *crincum* being a name for this disease. *Ed.*

185

worth many pounds per annum, and this good old doctor, when one of his parish, that was an honest industrious man, happened by any accident to be in decay and low in the world, would let his parsonage to him for a year, two or three, forty pounds a year under value.

In his younger years, he had been chaplain to Bilson, Bishop of Winchester.

In August 1642, the Lord Viscount Say and Sele came (by order of the parliament) to visit the colleges, to see what of new Popery they could discover in the chapels. In our chapel, on the backside of the screen, had been two altars (of painting well enough for those times, and the colours were admirably fresh and lively). That on the right hand as you enter the chapel was dedicated to St Katharine, that on the left was of the taking our Saviour off from the cross. My Lord Say saw that this was done of old time, and Dr Kettell told his lordship, 'truly, my lord, we regard them no more than a dirty dish-cloth': so they remained untouched, till Harris' time,† and then were coloured over with green. The windows of the chapel were good Gothic painting, in every column a figure:—e.g. St Cuthbert, St Leonard, St Oswald. I have forgotten the rest. 'Tis pity they should be lost. I have note of all the escutcheons in glass about the house. 'Twas pity Dr Bathurst took the old painted glass out of the library. Anciently, in the chapel, was a little organ over the door of the screen. The pipes were, in my time, in the bursary.

'Tis probable this venerable doctor might have lived some years longer, and finished his century, had not those civil wars come on; which much grieved him, that was wont to be absolute in the college, to be affronted and disrespected by rude soldiers. I remember, being at the rhetoric lecture in the hall, a foot-soldier came in and broke his hour-glass. The doctor indeed was just stepped out, but Jack Dowch pointed at it. Our grove was the Daphne for the ladies and their gallants to walk in, and many times my Lady Isabella Thynne would make her entry with a theorbo or lute played before her. I have heard her play on it in the grove myself, which she did rarely; for which Mr Edmund Waller has in his *Poems* for ever made her famous. One may say of her as Tacitus said of Agrippina, *All qualities she had, save a pure mind.* She was most beautiful, most humble, charitable, etc but she could not subdue one thing. I remember one time this lady and fine Mrs Fenshawe* (her great and intimate friend, who lay at our college) would have a frolic to make a visit to the president. The old doctor quickly perceived that they came to tease him; he addressed his discourse to

---

† President, 1648–58. *Ed.*

* She was wont, and my Lady Thynne, to come to our chapel, mornings, half-dressed, like angels.

Mrs Fenshawe, saying 'Madam, your husband and father I bred up here, and I knew your grandfather; I know you to be a gentlewoman, I will not say you are a whore; but get you gone for a very woman.' The dissoluteness of the times, as I have said, grieving the good old doctor, his days were shortened and he died in 1643, and was buried at Garsington.

Seneca's scholar Nero found fault with his style, saying 'twas mortar without lime: now Dr Kettell was wont to say that 'Seneca writes, as a boar does piss' that is, by jerks.

I cannot forget a story that Robert Skinner, Lord Bishop of Oxford, has told us: one Slymaker, a fellow of this college long since, a fellow of great impudence and little learning—the fashion was in those days to go, every Saturday night (I think) to Joseph Barnes' shop, the book-seller (opposite to the west end of St Mary's), where the news was brought from London, etc: this impudent clown would always be hearkening to people's whisperings and overlooking their letters, that he was much taken notice of. Sir Isaac Wake, who was a very witty man, was resolved he would put a trick upon him, and understood that on such a Sunday Slymaker was to preach at St Mary's. So Sir Isaac, the Saturday before, reads a very formal letter to some person of quality, that Cardinal Baronius was turned Protestant, and was marching with an army of 40,000 men against the Pope. Slymaker hearkened with greedy ears, and the next day in his prayer before his sermon, beseeched God of his infinite mercy and goodness to give a blessing to the army of Cardinal Baronius, who was turned Protestant and now marching with an army of forty thousand men, and so runs on: he had a stentorian voice, and thundered it out. The auditors all stared and were amazed: Abbot was then vice-chancellor, and when Slymaker came out of the pulpit, sends for him and asked his name: 'Slymaker' said he; 'No', said the vice-chancellor, ''tis *Liemaker*.'

Dr Kettell, when he scolded at the idle young boys of his college, he used these names, viz *Turds*, *Tarrarags* (these were the worst sort, rude rake-hells), *Rascal Jacks*, *Blindcinques*, *Scobberlotchers* (these did no hurt, were sober, but went idling about the grove with their hands in their pockets, and telling the number of trees there, or so).

Memorandum: there was in my time a rich pall to lay on a coffin, of crimson velvet, with a large plain cross on it of white silk or satin.

¶ To make you merry, I'll tell you a story that Dr Henry Birkhead told us the other day at his cousin Marriott's, that is that about 1638 or 1640 when he was of Trinity College, Dr Kettell, preaching as he was wont in Trinity Sunday, told them that they should keep their bodies chaste and holy: 'but', said he, 'you fellows of the college here eat good commons and drink good double-beer . . . and that will get out.' How would the good old doctor have ranted and beat up his kettledrum, if he had seen such luxury in the College as there is now, Times are changed.

¶ You must know that there was a great faction between Dr Kettell and the fellows, and one time at a scrutiny, the doctor upbraiding them for their disrespect to him said: 'Oh! you are brave gallant gentlemen, and *learned* men; you despise and snort and fart, at your poor president: I am an old stager: but who was it proposed you to be fellows, from poor rascal-jacks, and servitors? Was it not your president: and yet name one of your friends were ever so grateful as to present me with so much as a wrought night-cap. I cry you mercy (Mr Dr Hobbs!) indeed, I remember your mother sent me once a gammon of bacon.'

Ludolph van Keulen
?1554–1610

Ludolph van Keulen was first, by profession, a fencing-master; but becoming deaf, he betook himself to the study of the mathematics wherein he became famous.

He wrote a learned book, of the proportion of the diameter of a circle to the periphery: before which is his picture, and round about it in the compartment are swords and bucklers and halberds etc—weapons: the reason whereof I understood not until Dr John Pell gave the aforesaid account, who had it from Sir Francis Godolphin, who had been his scholar as to fencing and boarded at his house.

Richard Knolles
?1550–1610

Knolles' General History of the Turks, *published in 1603, was very popular, and his style was praised by Dr Johnson for its clarity.*

The author of the *Battle of Lepanto* was hanged at Tyburn; he was reduced to such necessity.

The lord Burleigh, when he read Knolles' Turkish history, was particularly extremely pleased at the description of the battle of Lepanto; sent for Knolles, who told him that an ingenious young man came to him, hearing what he was about, and desired that he might write that, having been in that action. I think he has taught in a school near Sandwich.

My lord hunted after him, and traced him from place to place, and at last to Newgate. He was hanged but a fortnight before. He unluckily lost a good opportunity of being preferred—from Mr Smyth, Magdalen College.

John Lacy

?–1681

Chief actor of the King's Company, under Tom Killigrew, from 1661 to his death; he also wrote a number of plays. Pepys often refers to him, and admired his acting.

John Lacy, player, of the King's House, born near Doncaster in Yorkshire. Came to London to the playhouse 1631. Apprentice to Mr John Ogilby.

B. Jonson took a note of his Yorkshire words and proverbs for his *Tale of a Tub*, several 'Gad kettlepins!'

1642 or 3, lieutenant and quartermaster to the Lord Gerard. See Dr Earles' *Character of a Player*.

He was of an elegant shape, and fine complexion.

His majesty (Charles II) has several pictures of this famous comedian at Windsor and Hampton Court in the postures of several parts that he acted, e.g. Teague, Lord Vaux, the Puritan.

He made his *exit* on Saturday, 17 September 1681.

Sir Henry Lee

1530–1610

Master of the Ordnance under Elizabeth, Sir Henry Lee was one of the last enthusiasts of chivalry. He was largely responsible for the Accession Day tilts in which he and his companions held the field against all comers in honour of Elizabeth on the anniversary of her accession. His entertainment of the queen at Ditchley in 1575 was a memorable occasion.

Sir Henry Lee of Ditchley in Oxfordshire was a gentleman of a good estate, and a strong and valiant person. He was ranger of Woodstock

Park, and (I have heard my old cousin Whitney say) would many times in his younger years walk at nights with his keepers. Sir Gerard Fleetwood succeeded him in this place; as his nephew Sir William Fleetwood did him, and him the Earl of Rochester.

This Sir Henry Lee's nephew and heir* (whom I remember very well; he often came to Sir John Danvers') was called *Whip-and-away*. The occasion of it was thus: this old hero declining in his strength by age and so not being able to be a righter of his own wrongs as heretofore—

> *Age undermines and destroys the strength of former years.*
> *Milon, grown old, weeps to see those arms hanging limp*
> *and thin, whose massive knotted muscles once rivalled*
> *those of Hercules* (Ovid, *Metamorphoses*, XV.3)

Some person of quality had affronted him. So he spoke to Sir Henry Lee his heir to lie in wait for him about the Bell Inn in the Strand with half a dozen or more lusty fellows at his back and as the party passed along to give him a good blow with his cane and *whip and away*, the tall fellows should finish the revenge. Whether 'twere nicety of conscience or cowardice, but Sir Henry the younger absolutely refused it. For which he was disinherited, and old Sir Henry settled his whole estate upon a keeper's son of Witchwood Forest of his own name, no kin to him, from whom the Earl of Lichfield now is descended, as also the Lady Norris and Lady Wharton.

He was never married, but kept women to read to him when he was abed. One of his readers was Parson Jones' wife of Wotton. I have heard her daughter (who had no more wit) glory what a brave reader her mother was and how Sir Harry's worship much delighted to hear her. But his dearest dear was Mrs Anne Vavasour. He erected a noble altar monument of marble (—see it) wherein his effigy in armour lay; at the feet was the effigy of his mistress Mrs Anne Vavasour. Which occasioned these verses:

> Here lies good old knight Sir Harry
> Who loved well, but would not marry,
> While he lived, and had his feeling,
> She did lie, and he was kneeling,
> Now he's dead and cannot feel
> He doth lie, and she doth kneel.

Memorandum: some bishop did threaten to have this monument defaced (at least to remove Mrs Vavasour's effigy).

Old Sir Henry Lee was knight of the Garter and was supposed brother of Queen Elizabeth. He ordered that all his family should be christened *Harry's*.

* Also called Sir Henry Lee. *Ed.*

190

William Lee
?–?1610?

Mr William Lee, MA, was of Oxford (I think, Magdalen Hall). He was the first inventor of the weaving of stockings by an engine of his contrivance. He was a Sussex man born, or else lived there. He was a poor curate, and observing how much pains his wife took in knitting a pair of stockings, he bought a stocking and a half, and observed the contrivance of the stitch, which he designed in his loom, which (though some of the instruments attached to the engine be altered) keeps the same to this day. He went into France, and there died before his loom was made there. So the art was, not long since, in no part of the world but England. Oliver [Cromwell, the] Protector made an act that it should be felony to transport this engine overseas. See Stowe's Chronicle and Baker's Chronicle, if any mention of it. This information I took from a weaver (by this engine) in Pear-pool Lane, 1656. Sir John Hoskyns, Mr Stafford Tundale and I went purposely to see it.

William Lilly
1602–81

'The last of the astrologers', Lilly's almanacs reached a wide public, though even in his lifetime his claims to be a serious scientific investigator were frequently attacked.

He was born on May Day 1601; had he lived till next May he had been full fourscore (eighty). He settled his estate at Hersham, £200 per annum, on the son of the Lord Commissioner Whitlocke (who was his great patron).

He wrote his own life very largely, which Elias Ashmole Esq has. Memorandum, he predicted the great comet which appeared in 1680 in his almanac 1677, which was the last that he wrote himself with his own hands; for afterwards he fell blind. Memorandum, to bind up the almanac aforesaid with other octavo pamphlets, for 'tis exceeding considerable.

Sir Matthew Lister
?1571–1656

Sir Matthew Lister was born at Thornton in Craven in Yorkshire. His nephew Martin Lister, MD, FRS, from whose mouth I have this information, tells me he was of Oriel College in Oxford; he thinks he was a fellow.

He built that stately house at Ampthill in Bedfordshire (now the earl of Aylesbury's). He sent for the architects from Italy.

He died at Burwell near Louth in Lincolnshire about 1656 or 1657, aged 92 years.

He was physician to queen Anne (queen of king James). See the list of the names of the physicians before *The London Dispensatory;* as I remember, he was then president of the Physician's College in London.

He printed nothing that Dr Martin Lister knows of (Sir Matthew Lister bred him up).

Mr Wyld says Sir Matthew Lister built the house (Ampthill) for Mary, countess of Pembroke. He was her surveyor, and managed her estate. The seat at Ampthill is now in the possession of the earl of Aylesbury, whose grandfather (the earl of Elgin) bought it of the countess of Pembroke. That he was president of the Physicians College appears by the dedication of *The London Dispensatory* to him, being then president.

Sir James Long
1617–92

A Wiltshire neighbour of Aubrey's. His career as a royalist colonel was chequered.

Sir James Long, baronet: I should now be both orator and soldier to give this honoured friend of mine 'a gentleman absolute in all numbers', his due character.

Only son of Sir W. Long; born at South Wraxhall in Wilts. Westminster scholar; of Magdalene College, Oxford; Fisher there. Went to France. Married Dorothy Leich, a most elegant beauty and wit, daughter of Sir E. Leich, aged 25. In the civil wars, colonel of horse in Sir F. Dodington's brigade. Good sword-man; horseman; admirable extempore orator for a harangue; great memory; great historian and romancer; great falconer and for horsemanship; for insects; exceeding curious and searching long since, in natural things.

Oliver, Protector, hawking at Hounslow Heath, discoursing with him, fell in love with his company, and commanded him to wear his sword, and to meet him a-hawking, which made the strict cavaliers look on him with an evil eye.

He wrote 'History and Causes of the Civil War' or 'Reflections' (enquire); 'Examination of witches at Malmesbury'.

¶ My honoured and faithful friend Colonel James Long of Draycot, since baronet, was wont to spend a week or two every autumn at Avebury in hawking, where several times I have had the happiness to accompany him. Our sport was very good, and in a romantic country, that is, the prospects noble and vast, the downs stocked with numerous flocks of sheep, the turf rich and fragrant with thyme and burnet. Nor are the nut-brown shepherdesses without their graces. But the flight of the falcon was but a parenthesis to the colonel's facetious discourse, who was as much the son of Mercury as of Mars; and the muses did accompany him with his hawks and spaniels.

Richard Lovelace
1618–58

Poet and royalist soldier: his most famous lyric, written in prison at Westminster in 1642, is Stone walls do not a prison make/Nor iron bars a cage. *His imprisonment was the result of his enthusiasm for the royalist cause. He regained his freedom soon afterwards, joined the royal army in 1645. He was imprisoned again in 1648, and wrote the volume called* Lucasta, *published in 1649. He had spent all his money in support of the king, and Aubrey records his poverty-stricken end.*

Richard Lovelace, esquire: he was a most beautiful gentleman. *The twin stars that were his eyes, at his flowing locks, worthy of Bacchus or Apollo, his smooth cheeks, his ivory neck, his lovely face where a rosy flush stained the snowy whiteness of his complexion.* (Ovid, *Metamorphoses* III: Echo and Narcissus)

He died in a cellar in Long Acre, a little before the restoration of his majesty. Mr Edmund Wyld, etc have made collections for him and given him money.

One of the handsomest men of England. He was of Kent, and had

£500 per annum and more (ask E.W.).

He was an extraordinary handsome man, but proud. He wrote a poem called *Lucasta*, octavo, printed London by Thomas Harper to be sold at the Gun in Ivy Lane, 1649.

He was of Gloucester Hall, Oxford, as I have been told.

He had two younger brothers, viz Colonel Francis Lovelace and another brother that died at Carmarthen.

George Petty, haberdasher, in Fleet Street, carried 20s to him every Monday morning from Sir [John?] Many and Charles Cotton esquire, for many months, but was never repaid.

Henry Lyte
?1529–1607

A distant connection of Aubrey's, whose mother's father was a Lyte. His work as an antiquary was mostly on the fabulous history of Britain; he also translated an important book on plants.

I will enquire at Lyte's Cary when Henry Lyte, esq, died—He translated Dodantus' *Herbal*, and wrote a little pamphlet, which I have, called '*The Light of Britaine*, being a short summary of the old English history', dedicated to queen Elizabeth.

He began the genealogy of King James, derived from Brute; which his eldest son Thomas Lyte, of Lyte's Cary aforesaid, finished, and presented to King James. It is most rarely done and exquisitely limned by a miniature painter—all the king's pictures etc. King James, after it had hung some time at Whitehall, ordered him to have it again and to get it engraved, which was done. Mr Humble of Pope's-Head Alley had the plates before the fire: I hope they are not lost—it is most curiously done by Hole. It is as big as the greatest map of England that ever I saw.

T. Lyte wrote the best print hand that ever yet I saw. The original, which is now in the parlour of Lyte's Cary, was written with his hand, and painted by a famous artist.

Henry Marten

1602–80

*Henry Marten was one of the more unusual characters on the parliamentary
side, apparently opposed to the king on theoretical grounds (though Aubrey
suggests that there were personal reasons). Simon D'Ewes grouped him with
those 'fiery spirits who, accounting their own position desperate, did not care
how they hazarded the whole kingdom to save themselves'. Aubrey's view of
him is more favourable than most; though his straightforwardness and
opposition to tyranny of any kind earned him great popularity.*

Henry Marten, esquire, son and heir of Sir Henry Martin, knight,
Judge of the Arches, was born at Oxford.

Sir Henry Marten, LID was born at Stoke Poges in the county of
Bucks; his father a copy-holder there of about £60 per annum. He was
formerly a fellow of New College, Oxford. He left his son £3000 per
annum.

Henry, the son, was of the University of Oxford; travelled France,
but never Italy. His father found out a rich wife for him, whom he
married something unwillingly. He was a great lover of pretty girls, to
whom he was so liberal that he spent the greatest part of his estate.

He lived from his wife a long time. If I am not mistaken, she was
sometime driven mad by his unkindness to her. He was very hospitable:
and exceedingly popular in Berks, the whole county.

King Charles I had complaint against him for his wenching. It
happened that Henry was in Hyde Park one time when his majesty was
there, going to see a race. The king espied him, and said aloud, 'Let
that ugly rascal be gone out of the park, that whoremaster, or else I will
not see the sport.' So Henry went away patiently, but it remained
indelibly stamped on his mind. That sarcasm raised the whole county of
Berkshire against the king: Henry Marten was as far from a Puritan as
light from darkness. Shortly after (1641), he was chosen knight of the
shire of that county, unopposed, and proved a deadly enemy to the
king.

He was a great and faithful lover of his country, and never got a
farthing by the parliament. He was of an incomparable wit for repartees;
not at all covetous; humble, not at all arrogant, as most of them were; a
great cultivator of justice, and did always in the house take the part of
the oppressed.

In 1660 he was in extreme disfavour for having been one of the late
king's judges, and he was in very great danger to have suffered as the
others did (he pleaded only the king's act or proclamation at Breda,

which he showed in his hand) but (as he was a wit himself) so the Lord Falkland saved his life by wit, saying, 'Gentlemen, you talk here of making a sacrifice; it was the old law, all sacrifices were to be without spot or blemish; and now you are going to make an old rotten rascal a sacrifice.' This wit took in the house, and saved his life.

He was first a prisoner at the Tower; then at Windsor (removed from thence because he was an eyesore to his majesty etc); from thence to Chepstow, where he is now (1680). During his imprisonment his wife relieved him out of her personal fortune but she died.

Sir Edward Baynton was wont to say that his company was incomparable, but that he would be drunk too soon. When he had found a married woman that he liked (and he had his emissaries, male and female, to look out) he would contrive such and such a good bargain, £20 or £30 per annum under rent, to have her near him.

His speeches in the house were not long, but wondrous poignant, pertinent and witty. He was exceeding happy in apt instances. He alone has sometimes turned the whole house. His stature was but middling: his habit moderate; his face not good. Making an invective speech one time against old Sir Henry Vane, when he had done with him, he said, *But for young Sir Harry Vane*—and so sat him down. Several cried out—'What have you to say to young Sir Harry?' He rises up: 'Why! if young Sir Harry lives to be old; he will be old Sir Harry!' and so sat down and set the house a-laughing, as he oftentimes did. Oliver Cromwell once in the house called him, jestingly or scoffingly, '*Sir Harry Martin.*' H.M. rises and bows, 'I thank your majesty, I always thought that when you were king, that I should be knighted.'—A godly member made a motion to have all profane and unsanctified persons expelled from the Houses. H.M. stood up and moved that all the fools might be put out likewise, and then there would be a thin house. H.M. said that he had 'seen the Scripture fulfilled—Thou hast exalted the humble and meek; thou hast filled the empty with good things, and the rich hast thou sent empty away.' See a pretty speech of his in print about the coming in of the Scots to assist us—He was wont to sleep much in the house (at least cat-nap): Alderman Atkins made a motion that such scandalous members as slept and minded not the business of the house should be put out. H.M. starts up—'Mr Speaker, a motion has been to turn out the *Nodders*; I desire the *Noddees** may also be turned out.'

Insert the song of

Oliver came to the house like a sprite etc

He died at Chepstow, a prisoner, September (about the middle) 1680.

* Those who made the others go to sleep. *Ed.*

Memorandum: when his study was searched they found letters to his concubine, which was printed 4to. There is wit and good nature in them.

Becket in the parish of Shrineham his chief seat: in the Vale of White Horse: now Major Wildman's.

H. Martin esquire, his letters in 4to to his miss, printed 1685, but 'tis not to his disgrace: evidence of real natural wit and *bon naturel*.

¶ Henry Marten made the motion in the house to call the *addressers* to account (viz these that addressed to Richard Cromwell, Protector, to stand by him with their lives and fortunes) and that all the addressers that were of it (of the house) might be turned out as enemies to the Commonwealth of England and betrayers of their trust to bring in government by a single person. Had not Dick Cromwell sneaked away, then it is certain that the Rump would have cut off his head, as I am well assured from a dear friend of mine.

Memorandum that Dr Wilkins (who married Richard Cromwell's aunt) was very instrumental in persuading persons of quality and corporations to address: but what did it signify?

Henry Marten esquire; 'you have already made your little less'.

¶ His short letter to his cousin Stonehouse of Radley by Abingdon that 'if his majesty should take the advice of his gun-smiths and pow-dermen he would never have peace'—from Sir John Lenthall: as also of his drawing up the remonstrance of the parliament when 'twas formed a Commonwealth—within five or six lines of the beginning he says 'restored to its ancient government of a *Commonwealth*.' When 'twas read Sir Henry Vane stood up and reprimanded and 'wondered at his impudence to affirm such a notorious lie'. H.M. standing up, meekly replied that 'there was a text had much troubled his spirit for several days and nights of the man that was blind from his mother's womb whose sight was restored at last', i.e. was restored to the sight which he should have had.

Richard Martin
1570–1618

Wit and orator, friend of several poets of the period.

Insert his picture which I sent to Mr A. Wood.

He was of the ancient family of the Martins of Athelminston in the county of Dorset, a very fair seat. The name was lost about fifty years since by a daughter and heiress, who was married to Mr Bruen, who had a daughter and heiress married to Sir Ralph Banks, who sold it to Sir Robert Long (1668). In the church are several noble monuments. Their crest is an ape; men use to say 'a Martin ape'.

(In queen Elizabeth's time, one Penry of Wales wrote a book* called *Martin Mar-prelate*, on which there was this epigram:

> Martin the ape, the drunk and the mad,
> The three Martins are whose works we have had.
> If a fourth Martin comes after Martins so evil,
> He can be no man, he must be a devil.)

He was a very handsome man, a graceful speaker, facetious and well-beloved. I think he died of a merry symposiac [drinking party].

He was recorder but (only for) a month before his death.

¶ Ben Jonson dedicates his comedy called the Poetaster to him:

'A thankful man owes a courtesy ever, the unthankful but when he needs. For whose innocence, as for the author's, you were once a noble and timely undertaker to the greatest justice of this kingdom.'

Died of a symposiac excess with his fellow wits. Was not recorder above quarter of a year: ask Sir John Hoskyns.

Andrew Marvell
1621–78

Poet and civil servant. He started his career as a civil servant in 1653 on Milton's recommendation, and his poetry reflects his close association with the Commonwealth. He became MP for Hull in 1659; his poems to Cromwell had never been published, and he was able to continue his parliamentary career undisturbed at the Restoration, though he was never a very active member. His satires were enjoyed by a large audience, including the king himself.

Mr Andrew Marvell: his father was minister of, I think, Hull (enquire).

He had good grammar education: and was after sent to Cambridge.

In the time of Oliver the Protector he was Latin secretary. He was a great master of the Latin tongue; an excellent poet in Latin or English: for Latin verses there was no man would come into competition with him. The verses called *The Advice to the Painter* were of his making. His native town of Hull loved him so well that they elected him for their representative in parliament, and gave him an honourable pension to maintain him.

* He was hanged for it. He was kin to my great-grandfather.

He was of a middling stature, pretty strong set, roundish faced, cherry-cheeked, hazel eye, brown hair. He was in his conversation very modest, and of very few words: and though he loved wine he would never drink hard in company, and was wont to say that, he would not play the good-fellow in any man's company in whose hands he would not trust his life.

He kept bottles of wine at his lodging, and many times he would drink liberally by himself to refresh his spirits, and exalt his muse. I remember I have been told (by Mr Haak and Dr Pell) that a learned High German scholar was wont to keep bottles of good Rhenish wine in his study, and when he had exhausted himself he would drink a good rummer of it.

James Harrington, esquire (the author of Oceana) was his intimate friend. John Pell, DD, was one of his acquaintance. He had not a general acquaintance.

He died in London, 18 August, 1678. Some suspect that he was poisoned by the Jesuits, but I cannot be positive.

I remember I heard him say that the Earl of Rochester was the only man in England that had the true vein of satire.

Thomas May
1595–1650

May's plays and poems found favour at Charles I's court, but he was never rewarded by the king. Perhaps for this reason, he joined the parliamentary party in the Civil War, and his History of the Long Parliament *is an important account of the period. He seems to have been a free-thinker and atheist: hence the rumours of his 'debauchery in all things'.*

He stood candidate for Poet Laureate after B. Jonson; but Sir William Davenant carried it—it remains indelibly stamped on his mind perhaps.

A great acquaintance of Tom Chaloner. Would, when in his cups speak slightingly of the Trinity.

Shammed.*

Friend: Sir Richard Fanshawe. Mr De Critz was present at the debate at their parting before Sir Richard went to the king, where both camps were most rigorously divided.

Had venereal disease. Came of his death after drinking with his chin tied with his cap (being fat); suffocated.

¶ Mr Edmund Wyld told me that he was acquainted with him when

* Aubrey means that he would tell tall stories in order to take people in. *Ed.*

199

he was young, and then he was as other young men of the town are, that is, he said he was debauched in all things; but do not by any means take notice of it—for we have all been young. But Mr Marvell in his poems upon Tom May's death falls very severe upon him.

He was of the Sussex Mays, as appears by his coat of arms; but where born or of what university I know not, and cannot find out.

Nicholas Mercator
1640–87

Mathematician and expert on algebra and calculus.

Mr Nicholas Mercator: Philip Melancthon was his great-grandmother's brother.

He is of little stature, perfect; black hair, of a delicate moist curl; dark eye, but of great vivacity of spirit. He is of a soft temper, of great temperance (he loves Venus a little): of a prodigious invention, and will be acquainted (familiarly) with nobody. His true German name is Nicolas Kauffmann, i.e. chapman, i.e. Mercator.

Memorandum: Mr Nicholas Mercator made and presented to King Charles II a clock ('twas of a foot diameter) which showed the inequality of the sun's motion from the apparent motion, which the king did understand by his informations, and did commend it, but he never had a penny of him for it.

Well! This curious clock was neglected, and somebody of the court happened to become master of it, who understood it not; he sold it to Mr Knibb, a watch-maker, who did not understand it neither, who sold it to Mr Fromanteel (that made it) for £5 who asks now (1683) for it £200.

In February 1682, Mr N. Mercator left London; went with his family to Paris, being invited thither by Monseigneur Colbert.

John Milton
1608–74

Milton was originally intended for a career in the church, but disliking Laud's high church policy, decided instead to earn his living by his pen.

After a journey to Italy in 1638–9, he returned to England, and became tutor to his two nephews, on whose memories of him Aubrey drew. His early works were pamphlets, on divorce (his first marriage ran a chequered course) and on the freedom of the press. Under the Commonwealth he was Latin secretary, and an active propagandist of republican ideas. Despite his increasing blindness, he retained his post until the Restoration. His activities in the previous years now brought him into danger, but although reduced to poverty, he escaped with a small fine. He now (1663) completed Paradise Lost, *begun in 1658, and wrote* Paradise Regained, *published in 1671.*

Mr John Milton was of an Oxfordshire family.

His grandfather (a Roman Catholic) was of Holton, in Oxfordshire, near Shotover.

His father was brought up in the University of Oxford, at Christ Church, and his grandfather disinherited him because he kept not to the Catholic religion.* So thereupon he came to London, and became a writer or clerk (trained by a friend of his; was not an apprentice) and got a plentiful estate by it, and left it off many years before he died.— He was an ingenious man; delighted in music; composed many songs now in print, especially that of *Oriana*.

I have been told that the father composed a song of fourscore parts for the Prince of Hesse, for which his highness sent a medal of gold, or a noble present. He died about 1647; buried in Cripplegate Church, from his house in the Barbican.

His son John was born in Bread Street, in London, at the Spread Eagle, which was his house (he had also in that street another house, the Rose; and other houses in other places). Ask Mr Christopher Milton to see the date of his brother's birth. John Milton was born 9 December 1608, Friday, half an hour after 6 in the morning.

In 1619, he was ten years old, as by his picture; and was then a poet.

His schoolmaster then was a Puritan, in Essex, who cut his hair short.

He went to school to old Mr Gill, at St Paul's School. Went, at his own expense, to Christ's College in Cambridge at fifteen, where he stayed eight years at least. Then he travelled into France and Italy (he had Sir H. Wotton's commendatory letters). At Geneva he contracted a great friendship with the learned Dr Deodati of Geneva: see his poems. He was acquainted with Sir Henry Wotton, ambassador at Venice, who delighted in his company. He was several years beyond sea, and returned to England just upon the breaking out of the Civil Wars.

From his brother, Christopher Milton:—When he went to school, when he was very young, he studied very hard, and sat up very late,

* Enquire about this: he found a Bible in English, in his chamber.

201

commonly till 12 or 1 o'clock at night, and his father ordered the maid to sit up for him, and in those years (10) composed many sets of verses which might well become a riper age. And was a very hard student in the university, and performed all his exercises there with good applause. His first tutor there was Mr Chapell; from whom receiving some unkindness,† he was afterwards (though it seemed contrary to the rules of the college) transferred to the tuition of one Mr Tovell, who died parson of Lutterworth.

He went to travel about the year 1638 and was abroad about a year's space, chiefly in Italy. Immediately after his return he took a lodging at Mr Russell's, a tailor, in St Bride's Churchyard, and took into his tuition his sister's two sons, Edward and John Phillips, the first 10, the other 9 years of age; and in a year's time made them capable of interpreting a Latin author at sight etc. And within three years they went through the best of Latin and Greek poets—Lucretius and Manilius,* of the Latins; Hesiod, Aratus, Dionysus Afer, Oppian, Apollonii *Argonautica*, and Quintus Calaber. Cato, Varro and Columella *De re rustica* were the very first authors they learned.—As he was severe on one hand, so he was most familiar and free in his conversation to those to whom he was most sour in his way of education. N.B. he made his nephews songsters, and sing, from the time they were with him.

He married his first wife, Mary Powell of Fosthill at Shotover in Oxford; by whom he had four children. He has two daughters living: Deborah was his amanuensis (he taught her Latin, and to read Greek to him when he had lost his eyesight). She [Mary] went from him to her mother's in the king's quarters, near Oxford; and [he] wrote the *Triplechord* about divorce.

Two opinions do not well on the same bolster. She was a royalist and went to her mother to the king's quarters, near Oxford. I have perhaps so much charity to her that she might not wrong his bed: but what man (especially contemplative) would like to have a young wife environed and stormed by the sons of Mars, and those of the enemy party?

¶ His first wife (Mrs Powell, a royalist) was brought up and lived where there was a great deal of company and merriment, dancing etc. And when she came to live with her husband, at Mr Russell's, in St Bride's churchyard, she found it very solitary; no company ever came to her; oftentimes heard his nephews beaten and cry. This life was irksome to her, and so she went to her parents at Fost Hill. He sent for her, after some time; and I think his servant was roughly handled: but as for that matter of wronging his bed, I never heard the least suspicion; nor had he, of that, any jealousy.

† He whipped him.
* And with him the use of the globes, and some rudiments of arithmetic and geometry.

¶ He had a middle wife, whose name was (he [? Edward Phillips] thinks, Katherine) Woodcock. No child living by her.

He married his second [third] wife, Elizabeth Minshull, the year before the sickness [1664]: a genteel person, a peaceful and agreeable humour.

He was Latin secretary to the parliament.

His sight began to fail him at first upon his writing against Salmasius, and before 'twas fully completed one eye absolutely failed. Upon the writing of other books, after that, his other eye decayed.

His eye-sight was decaying about twenty years before his death: enquire, when stark blind? His father read without spectacles at 84. His mother had very weak eyes, and used spectacles as soon as she was thirty years old.

After he was blind, he wrote the following books, viz *Paradise Lost, Paradise Regained, Grammar, Dictionary* (imperfect)—ask if there were more.

I heard that after he was blind that he was writing a Latin Dictionary (in the hands of Moyses Pitt*). His widow states that she gave all his papers (among which this dictionary, imperfect) to his nephew, a sister's son, that he brought up, Phillips who lives near the Maypole in the Strand (enquire). She has a great many letters in her possession from learned men, his acquaintance, both of England and beyond the sea.

He lived in several places, e.g. Holborn, near King's Gate. He died in Bunhill, opposite to the Artillery Garden wall.

He died of the gout struck in, the 9th or 10th of November 1674, as appears by his apothecary's book.

His harmonical and ingenious soul did lodge in a beautiful and well-proportioned body:

Nowhere on his body was there a blemish   Ovid, *Amores*, 15, 18

He was a spare man. He was scarce so tall as I am—question, how many feet I am high: answer, of middle stature. He had light brown hair. His complexion exceeding fair—he was so fair that they called him *the lady of Christ's College*. Oval face. His eye a dark gray.

He had a *delicate tuneable* voice, and had good skill: his father instructed him: he had an organ in his house: he played on that most.

Of a very cheerful humour.

He was very healthy and free from all diseases: seldom took any physic (only sometimes he took manna): only towards his latter end he was visited with the gout, spring and fall. He would be cheerful even in his gout-fits, and sing.

---

* A London bookseller. *Ed.*

203

He had a very good memory; but I believe that his excellent method of thinking and disposing did much to help his memory.

He pronounced the letter R (*littera canina*) very hard—a certain sign of a satirical wit—from John Bryden.

Write his name in red letters on his pictures, with his widow, to preserve.

His widow has his picture, drawn very well and like, when a Cambridge scholar.

She has his picture when a Cambridge scholar, which ought to be engraven; for the pictures before his books are not *at all* like him.

His exercise was chiefly walking.

He was an early riser (that is at 4 o'clock in the morning); yea, after he lost his sight. He had a man read to him: the first thing he read was the Hebrew Bible, and that was at half past four. Then he contemplated.

At seven his man came to him again, and then read to him again, and wrote till dinner: the writing was as much as the reading. His second daughter, Deborah, could read to him Latin, Italian and French, and Greek. She married in Dublin to one Mr Clarke (sells silk, etc); very like her father. The other sister is the first, Mary, more like her mother.

After dinner he used to walk three or four hours at a time (he always had a garden where he lived); went to bed about nine.

Temperate man, rarely drank between meals. Extreme pleasant in his conversation, and at dinner, supper, etc; but *satirical*.

From Mr E. Phillips:—All the time for writing his *Paradise Lost*, his vein began at the autumnal equinoctial, and ceased at the vernal (or thereabouts: I believe about May): and this was four or five years of his doing it. He began about two years before the king came in, and finished about three years after the king's restoration.

In the fourth book of *Paradise Lost* there are about six verses of Satan's exclamation to the sun, which Mr E. Phillips remembers about fifteen or sixteen years before ever his poem was thought of. Which verses were intended for the beginning of a tragedy which he had designed, but was diverted from it by other business.

*Whatever he wrote against monarchy was out of no animosity to the king's person, or out of any faction or interest, but out of a pure zeal to the liberty of mankind, which he thought would be greater under a free state than under a monarchical government. His being so conversant in Livy and the Roman authors, and the greatness he saw done by the Roman commonwealth, and the virtue of their great commanders induced him to.

From Mr Abraham Hill:—Memorandum: his sharp writing against Alexander More, of Holland, upon a mistake, notwithstanding he had

* This paragraph is in an unknown hand, not Aubrey's. *Ed.*

204

given him by the ambassador† all satisfaction to the contrary: viz that the book called *Clamor* was written by Peter du Moulin. Well, that was one; he having written it, it should go into the world; one of them was as bad as the other.

¶ Mr John Milton made two admirable panegyrics, as to sublimity of wit, one on Oliver Cromwell, and the other on Thomas, Lord Fairfax, both which his nephew Mr Phillips has; but he has hung back these two years, as to imparting copies to me for the collection of mine with you. Wherefore I desire you in your next to intimate your desire of having these two copies of verses aforesaid, were they made in commendation of the devil, 'twere all one to me: 'tis the summit that I look after. I have been told 'tis beyond Waller's or anything in that kind.

¶ He was visited much by learned men; more than he did desire. He was mightily implored to go into France and Italy. Foreigners came much to see him, and much admired him, and offered to him great preferments to come over to them: and the only inducement of several foreigners that came into England, was chiefly to see Oliver Protector and Mr John Milton; and would see *the house and chamber* where *he* was born. He was much more admired abroad than at home.

His familiar learned acquaintance were Mr Andrew Marvell, Mr Skinner, Dr Paget, MD; Mr Skinner, who was his disciple; John Dryden esquire, Poet Laureate, who very much admires him, and went to him to have leave to put his *Paradise Lost* into a drama in rhyme. Mr Milton received him civilly, and told him he would give him leave to tag his verses.

His widow assures me that Mr T. Hobbes was not one of his acquaintance, that her husband did not like him at all, but he would acknowledge him to be a man of great parts, and a learned man. Their interests and tenets did run counter to each other: see in Hobbes' *Behemoth*.

George Monck
First Duke of Albemarle, 1608–70

George Monck began his military career on the continent, but at the outbreak of the Civil War was a commander in the royal army in Ireland. He joined the royalist forces and was captured in 1644. In 1646, the parliament needed

† Enquire the ambassador's name of Mr Hill? He answers, Newport, the Dutch ambassador.

205

officers with experience in Ireland, and Monck was chosen. He served there and in Scotland until 1652, when he was chosen as one of three generals of the fleet, despite his lack of experience at sea. His successes at sea virtually brought the war against the Dutch to an end, and in 1654 resumed his command in Scotland. His action early in 1660 in invading England with his army was decisive in securing Charles II's restoration, and he was rewarded with the lord-lieutenancy of Ireland. In 1665 he was given the command of the fleet, with Prince Rupert, which he retained until 1667.

George Monck was born in Devon (see Devon in Heralds' Office), a second son of an ancient family, and which had about Henry VIII's time £10,000 per annum (as he himself said).

He was a strong, lusty, well-set young fellow; and in his youth happened to slay a man,* which was the occasion of his flying into the Low Countries, where he learned to be a soldier.

At the beginning of the late Civil Wars, he came over to the king's side, where he had command (enquire in what part of England).

In 1644 he was prisoner in the Tower, where his seamstress, Nan Clarges (a blacksmith's† daughter) was kind to him; in a double capacity. It must be remembered that he then was in want,‡ and she assisted him. Here she was got with child. She was not at all handsome, nor cleanly. Her mother was one of the five women barbers.

In, as I remember, 1635, there was a married woman in Drury Lane that had clapped, i.e. given the pox to, a woman's husband, a neighbour of hers. She complained of this to her neighbour gossips. So they concluded on this revenge, viz to get her and whip her and to shave all the hair off her pudenda; which severities were executed and put into a ballad. 'Twas the first ballad I ever cared for the reading of: the burden of it was thus:

> Did ye ever hear the like
> Or ever heard the same
> Of five woman-barbers
> That lived in Drury lane?

Her brother Thomas Clarges came on shipboard to G.M. and told him his sister was brought to bed. 'Of what?' said he. 'Of a son.' 'Why then,' said he, 'she is my wife.' He had only this child.

In [1646] (I have forgotten by what means) he got his liberty, and an

* From Mrs Linden, his kinswoman, a Devon woman whose maiden name was Monck.

† The shop is still of that trade; the corner shop, the first turning on the right hand as you come out of the Strand into Drury Lane; the house is now built of brick.

‡ He was taken prisoner by the parliament forces, and kept in the Tower; and the truth was, he was forgotten and neglected at court, that they did not think of exchanging him, and he was in want.

employment under Oliver (I think) at sea, against the Dutch, where he did good service; he had courage enough. But I remember the seamen would laugh, that instead of crying *Tack about*, he would say *Wheel to the right* (or *left*).

In 1651 he had command in Scotland, where he was well beloved by his soldiers, and, I think, that country (for an enemy). Oliver, Protector, had a great mind to have him home, and sent him a find complimentary letter, that he desired him to come into England to advise with him. He sent his highness word, that if he pleased, he would come and wait upon him at the head of 10,000 men. So that design was spoiled.

In 1660, 10 February (as I remember), being then sent for by the parliament to disband Lambert's army, he came into London with his army about one o'clock P.M.* He then sent to parliament this letter, which, printed, I annex here. Shortly after he was sent for to the parliament house; where in the house a chair was set for him, but he would not (in modesty) sit down in it. The parliament (Rump†) made him odious to the city, purposely, by pulling down and burning their gates (which I myself saw). The Rump invited him to a great dinner in February, (shortly after); from whence it was never intended that he should have returned.‡ The members stayed till 1, 2, 3, 4 o'clock, but at last his excellency sent them word he could not come: I believe he suspected some treachery.

You must now know that long before these days, Colonel Massey and Thomas Mariett, of Whitchurch in Warwickshire, esquire, held correspondence with his majesty, who wrote them letters with his own hand, which I have seen. Both these were now in London privately. Tom Mariett lay with me (I was then of the Middle Temple); G.M. lay at Draper's Hall in Throgmorton Street. Col. Massey (Sir Edward afterwards), and T. Mariett every day were trying to persuade G.M., as also Col. Robinson (afterward Lieutenant of the Tower, whom I remember they counted not so wise as King Solomon); and they could not find any inclination or propensity in G.M. for their purpose, that is to be instrumental to bring in the king. Every night late, I had an account of all these transactions abed, which like a sot as I was, I did not, while fresh in memory, commit to writing, as neither has Tom Mariett: but I remember in the main, that they were satisfied he no more intended or designed the king's restoration, when he came into

* On a Saturday. On Sunday (the next day) Sir Ralph Sydenham (his countryman) went and dined with him, and told him that God had put a good opportunity into his hands, hinting at restoring the king; to which he gave an indefinite answer, and said he hoped he should do like an honest man. We that were Sir Ralph's acquaintance were longing for his coming home to supper for the general's answer, who kept him till 9 at night. He [Monck], after the king's restoration, made him master of the Charterhouse.

† *The rump of a house*: 'twas the wooden invention of General Browne (a woodmonger).

‡ Of this I am assured by one of that parliament.

England, or first came to London, than his horse did: but shortly after finding himself at a loss, and that he was (purposely) made odious to the city, as aforesaid—and that he was a lost man—by the parliament; and that the generality of the city and country were for the restoring of the king, having long groaned under the tyranny of other governments, he had no way to save himself but to close with the city, etc, again. Memorandum that Threadneedle Street was all day long and late at night crammed with multitudes, crying out *A free Parliament, a free Parliament*, that the air rang with their clamours. One evening in February, he coming out on horseback, they were so violent that he was almost afraid of himself, and so, to satisfy them (as one does to importunate children), *Pray be quiet, ye shall have a free Parliament.* This about 7, or rather 8 as I remember, at night. Immediately a loud holla and shout was given, all the bells in the city ringing, and the whole city looked as if it had been in a flame by the bonfires, which were prodigiously great and frequent and ran like a train over the city, and I saw some balconies that began to be kindled. They made little gibbets, and roasted rumps of mutton; nay, I saw some very good rumps of beef. Healths to the king, Charles II, were drunk in the streets by the bonfires, even on their knees; and this humour ran by the next night to Salisbury, where was the like joy. So to Chalk, where they made a great bonfire on the top of the hill; from hence to Blandford and Shaftesbury, and so to the Landsend: and perhaps it was so over all England. So that the return of his most gracious majesty was by the hand of GOD; but as by this person [Monck] merely accidental, whatever the pompous history in octavo says (printed opposite St Dunstan's Church; enquire if not written by Sir Thomas Clarges, brother to her grace, formerly an apothecary; and was physician to his army; and 1660 was created MD, who commonly at coffee houses uses to pretend strange things, of his contrivances, and bringing on of his brother-in-law etc).

Well! a free parliament was chosen, and met. Sir Harbottle Grimston, knight and baronet, was chosen Speaker. The first thing he put to the question was, 'Whether Charles Stuart should be sent for, or no?' 'Yea, yea.' unopposed. Sir John Greenvill (now Earl of Bath) was then in town, and posted away to Brussels; found the king at dinner, little dreaming of so good news, rises presently from dinner, had his coach immediately made ready, and that night got out of the King of Spain's dominions into the Prince of Orange's dominions, I think, Breda.*

Now, as the morn grows lighter and lighter, and more glorious, till it is perfect day, so it was with the joy of the people. Maypoles, which in the hypocritical times, 'twas forbidden to set up, now were set up in

---

* This I have heard bishop John Earles and his wife Bridget, then at Brussels, say, several times.

every cross-way; and at the Strand, near Drury Lane, was set up the most prodigious one for height, that (perhaps) was ever seen; they were fain (I remember) to have the assistance of the seamen's art to elevate it; that which remains (being broken with a high wind, I think about 1672) is but two parts of three of the whole height from the ground, besides what is in the earth. The juvenile and rustic folks at that time had so much their fullness of desires in this kind, but I think there have been very few set up since.

The honours conferred on G.M. everyone knows. His sense might be good enough, but he was slow, and heavy. He died in 1670 and had a magnificent funeral suitable to his greatness. His figure in his robes was very skilfully done, which lay in a catafalque under a canopy, in or near the east end of Westminster Abbey, a month or six weeks. Seth Ward, Lord Bishop of Salisbury (his great acquaintance) preached his funeral sermon, which is printed. His eldest brother died without children about the time of the king's return. His younger brother was made Bishop of Hereford. G.M. and his duchess died within a day or two of each other. The Bishop of Salisbury told me that he did the last office of a confessor to his grace; and closed his eyes, as his lordship told me himself.

Some months before G.M.'s coming into England, the king sent Sir Richard Grenville (since Earl of Bath) to him to negotiate with him that he would do him service, and to correspond with him. Said he, 'If opportunity be, I will do him service; but I will not by any means have any correspondence with him'; and he did like a wise man in it; for if he had he would certainly have been betrayed.

'Twas shrewd advice which Wyld, then Recorder of London, gave to the citizens, i.e. to keep their purse-strings fast; else the parliament would have paid the army, and kept out the king.

He was first an ensign, and after a captain, in the Low Countries, and for making false musters was like to have been [hanged?] which he afterwards did not forget:—from Major Cosh.

This underneath was written on the door of the House of Commons:

> Till it be understood
> What is under Monck's hood
>   The citizens put in their horns.
> Until the ten days are out
> The Speaker has the gout
>   And the Rump, they sit upon thorns.

Memorandum: Mr Baron Brampton invited me to his chamber to give me a farther account of general Monck. I let slip the opportunity, and my honoured friend is dead.

Sir Jonas Moore

1617–79

A distinguished mathematician, he made his reputation as a surveyor in the draining of the Fens. His survey of Tangier in 1663 led to an appointment as Surveyor-General of the Ordnance, and in 1674 he was able to arrange the foundation of the Royal Observatory at Greenwich. He was elected a fellow of the Royal Society in 1674.

Sir Jonas Moore was born at Whitelee in Lancashire, towards the bishopric of Durham. He was inclined to mathematics when a boy, which some kind friends of his (whom he mentions in the preface of his first edition of his *Arithmetic*, and Edmund Wyld esquire) and afterwards Mr Oughtred, more fully informed him; and then he taught gentlemen in London, which was his livelihood.

He was a clerk under Dr Burghill, Chancellor of Durham. Parson Milbourne, in the bishopric, put him upon the mathematics, and instructed him in it. Then he came to the Middle Temple, London, where he published his *Arithmetic*, and taught it in Stanhope Street. After this, he got in with the Lord Gorges, Earl of Bedford, and Sir Thomas Chichele, for the surveying of the Fens—from Captain Sherbourne.

Mr William Gascoigne (of the north, I think Yorkshire), a person of good estate, a most learned gentleman, who was killed in the Civil Wars in the king's cause, a great mathematician, and bred by the Jesuits at Rome, gave him good information in mathematical knowledge.

When the great level of the Fens was to be surveyed, Mr Wyld aforesaid who was his scholar and a member of parliament was very instrumental in helping him to the employment of surveying it, which was his rise, which I have heard him acknowledge with much gratitude before several persons of quality, since he became a knight, and which evidenced an excellent good nature in him.

Memorandum: when he surveyed the fens, he observed the line that the sea made on the beach, which is not a straight line (enquire what line?), by which means he got great credit in keeping out the sea in Norfolk: so he made his banks against the sea of the same line that the sea makes on the beach; and no other could do it, but that the sea would still break in upon it. Memorandum: he made a model of a citadel for Oliver Cromwell, to bridle the City of London, which Mr Wyld has; and this citadel was to have been the cross building of St Paul's church.

Upon the restoration of his majesty he was made Master Surveyor of his majesty's ordnance and armories. In 1663 he received the honour of knighthood. He was a good mathematician, and a good fellow.

He died at Godalming, coming from Portsmouth to London, and was buried at the Tower Chapel with a sixty-gun salute (equal to the number of his years). He was tall and very fat, thin skin, fair, clear grey eye.

He always intended to have left his library of mathematical books to the Royal Society, of which he was a member; but he happened to die without making a will, whereby the Royal Society have a great loss.

His only son, Jonas, had the honour of knighthood conferred upon him, 9 August 1680, at Windsor; 'his majesty being pleased to give him this mark of his favour as well in consideration of his own abilities, as of the faithful service of his father deceased' (*London Gazette*, no. 1537)— but young Sir Jonas, when he is old, will never be *old Sir Jonas*, for all the *Gazette*'s eulogy.

Memorandum: speak to Sir Christopher Wren, to get the wooden sphere that was made for Prince Henry by Mr Wright, out of young Sir Jonas Moore's hands, into the king's again.

I remember Sir Jonas told us that a Jesuit (I think 'twas Grenbergerus, of the Roman College) found out a way of flying, and that he made a youth perform it. Mr Gascoigne taught an Irish boy the way, and he flew over a river in Lancashire (or thereabouts), but when he was up in the air, the people gave a shout, whereat the boy being frightened, he fell down on the other side of the river, and broke his legs, and when he came to himself, he said that he thought the people had seen some strange apparition, which fancy amazed him. This was in 1635, and he spoke [about] it in the Royal Society, upon the account of the flying at Paris two years since. See the *Transactions*.

I remember I have heard Sir Jonas say that when he began mathematics, he wonderfully profited by reading Billingsley's *Euclid*, and that 'twas his excellent, clear, and plain exposition of the fourth proposition of the first book of the *Elements*, did first open and clear his understanding: which N.B.

¶ Sir Jonas Moore: Sciatica: he cured it by boiling his buttock. The Duke of York said that 'Mathematicians and physicians had no religion': which being told to Sir Jonas Moore, he presented his duty to the Duke of York and 'wished with all his heart that his highness were a mathematician too': this was since he was supposed to be a Roman Catholic.

Sir Robert Moray
?–1673

A founder-member of the Royal Society. His career was almost entirely abroad, until the Restoration, when he settled in London. Pepys called him 'a most excellent man of reason and learning, and understands the doctrine of music, and everything else I could discourse of, very finely'.

Sir Robert Moray, knight: he was of the ancient family of the Morays in Scotland. He was born, as I take it, in the Highlands. The Highlanders (like the Swedes) can make their own clothes; and I have heard Sir Robert say that he could do it.

He spent most of his time in France. After his juvenile education at school and the University he betook himself to military employment in the service of Louis XIII. He was at last Lieutenant-Colonel. He was a great master of the Latin tongue and was very well read. They say he was an excellent soldier.

He was far from the rough humour of the camp breeding, for he was a person the most obliging about the court and the only man that would do a kindness *gratis* upon an account of friendship. A lackey could not have been more obsequious and diligent. What I do now aver I know to be true upon my own score as well as others. He was a most humble and good man, and as free from covetousness as a Carthusian. He was abstemious and abhorred women. His majesty was wont to tease at him. 'Twas pity he was a Presbyterian.

He was the chief support of his countrymen and their good angel. There had been formerly a great friendship between him and the duke of Lauderdale, till, about a year or two before his death, he went to the duke on his return from Scotland and told him plainly he had betrayed his country.

He was one of the first contrivers and institutors of the Royal Society and was our first president, and performed his charge in the chair very well.

He was my most honoured and obliging friend, and I was more obliged to him than to all the courtiers besides. I had a great loss in his death, for had he lived, he would have got some employment or other for me before this time. He had the king's ear as much as anyone, and was indefatigable in his undertakings. I was often with him. I was with him three hours the morning he died; he seemed to be well enough. I remember he drank at least half a pint of fair water, according to his usual custom.

His lodging where he died was the leaded pavilion in the garden at Whitehall. He died suddenly July 4 about 8 pm, 1673. He had but one shilling in his pocket, i.e. in all. The king paid for his burial. He lies by Sir William Davenant in Westminster Abbey.

He was a good chemist and assisted his majesty in his chemical operations.

Sir Thomas More
1478–1535

Son of a London lawyer, More went to Oxford just as the new humanist learning was coming into fashion there. He nearly abandoned his studies for the Bar to enter the priesthood, but after four years' religious training, returned to legal studies. He quickly made a brilliant name as a lawyer and, later, as a writer. He was a particular favourite of Henry VIII, and on the fall of Thomas Wolsey, became Lord Chancellor, the first layman to hold that office. His work as Chancellor was remarkable for the way in which he dealt with cases at all hours of day and night, often with little formality, so that there were soon no cases on the waiting list at all. However, Henry's desire for a divorce from Katherine of Aragon was strongly opposed by More, as were all hints of heretical doctrines. When Henry declared himself head of the English Church, More refused to take the oath of allegiance; and he resigned soon afterwards. He was too popular a figure to be allowed to retire undisturbed, and on the pretext of his involvement with the Holy Maid of Kent, who was preaching against Henry, he was tried for high treason, and was executed in 1535. He was canonised in 1935.

Sir Thomas More, Lord Chancellor: his country-house was at Chelsea in Middlesex, where Sir John Danvers built his house. The chimney-piece of marble in Sir John's chamber, was the chimney-piece of Sir Thomas More's chamber, as Sir John himself told me: where the gate is now, adorned with two handsome pyramids, there stood anciently a gatehouse, which was flat on top, leaded, from whence is a most pleasant prospect of the Thames and the fields beyond. On this place the Lord Chancellor More was wont to recreate himself and contemplate. It happened one time that a Tom a Bedlam [madman] came up to him, and had a mind to have thrown him from the battlements, saying 'Leap, Tom, leap'. The chancellor was in his gown, and besides ancient, and not able to struggle with such a strong fellow. My lord had a little dog with him; said he, 'Let us first throw the dog down, and see what sport that will be'; so the dog was thrown over. 'This is very fine sport,' said my lord, 'let us fetch him up, and try once more.' While the madman was going down, my lord fastened the door, and called for help, but ever after kept the door shut.

Memorandum that in his *Utopia*, his law is that the young people are to see each other stark naked before marriage. Sir William Roper of Eltham in Kent, came one morning, pretty early, to my lord, with a proposal to marry one of his daughters. My lord's daughters were then both together a bed in a truckle bed in their father's chamber asleep. He carries Sir William into the chamber and takes the sheet by the corner and suddenly whips it off. They lay on their backs, and their smocks up as high as their armpits. This awakened them, and immediately they turned on their bellies. Quoth Roper, 'I have seen both sides', and so gave a pat on the buttock (to the one) he made choice of, saying, 'Thou art mine'. Here was all the trouble of the wooing. This account I had from my honoured friend old Mrs Tyndale, whose grandfather Sir William Stafford was an acquaintance of this Sir William Roper, who told him the story.

This Sir William Roper (from whose brother is descended the Lord Tenham) had in one piece, drawn by Hans Holbein, the pictures of Sir Thomas More, his lady, and all his children, which hung at his house aforesaid in Kent but about 1675 'twas presented as a rarity to King Charles II and hangs in Whitehall.

His discourse was extraordinarily facetious. Riding one night, upon the sudden he crossed himself with a great cross, crying out, 'Jesu Maria! do not you see that prodigious dragon in the sky?' They all looked up, and one did not see it, nor the other did not see it. At length one had spied it, and at last all had spied; whereas there was no such phantom; only he imposed on their fantasies.

After he was beheaded, his trunk was interred in Chelsea church, near the middle of the south wall. His head was upon London Bridge: there goes this story in the family, viz that one day as one of his daughters was passing under the bridge, looking on her father's head, said she, 'That head has lain many a time in my lap, would to God it would fall into my lap as I pass under.' She had her wish, and it did fall into her lap, and is now preserved in a vault in the cathedral church at Canterbury. The descendant of Sir Thomas, is Mr More, of Chilston, in Herefordshire, where, among a great many things of value plundered by the soldiers (in the Civil War) was his jaw, which they kept for a relic. Methinks 'tis strange that all this time he is not canonised, for he merited highly of the Church.

Memorandum: in the hall of Sir John Lenthall, at Bessils-Lye in Bucks, is an original of Sir Thomas and his father, mother, wife and children, done by Hans Holbein. There is an inscription in golden letters of about 60 lines, which I spoke to Mr Thomas Pigot of Wadham College to transcribe, and he had done it very carefully. Ask him for it.

Memorandum:—Sir Thomas More's father had a country house at Gubbins in Hertfordshire, which is in the family still, who are still Catholics, whether he was born there or no, he cannot say—Seth Ward, Bishop of Salisbury.

Lancelot Morehouse

?–1672

Mr Lancelot Morehouse, minister of Pertwood (£40 per annum), about six miles from Kilmanton, a very learned man, and a solid and profound mathematician, wrote against Mr Francis Potter's book of 666, and falls upon him, for that 25 is not the true root, but the approximate root; to which Mr Potter replied with some sharpness, and that it ought not to be the true root, for this agrees better with his purpose. The manuscript pro and con Mr Morehouse gave to Seth Ward, bishop of Salisbury, 1668; together with a MS in folio in French of alliances between the king of England and the king of France, and a prophecy concerning England, curiously written in Latin verse, one sheet in quarto, which he rescued from the tailor's shears.

Mr Morehouse (of Cambridge) is dead and left his many excellent mathematical notes to his ingenious friend John Graunt of Hindon.

He wrote on squaring the circle; wherein is a great deal of wit and learning; but at last Dr Davenant (his neighbour) convinced him of his paralogism. I would have it printed (for it is learnedly done) to show where and how great wits may err and be deceived.

He was a man of a very searching wit, and indefatigable at solving a question, as I have heard Dr Edward Davenant oftentimes say.

He was either of Clare Hall or King's College. Westmoreland by birth, Curate at Chalke to Mr Walker. He was preferred by bishop Hinchman to Little Langford, where he died about 1672.

Sir Thomas Morgan

?–?1679

A leading commander in the Parliamentary armies, first under Fairfax, later under Monck in Scotland. He was sent by Cromwell to Flanders in 1657 as

215

second in command of the English forces there. He rejoined Monck in Scotland in the autumn of 1659, and remained there as commander after Monck had marched south. In 1665 he was made governor of Jersey.

Sir Thomas Morgan: Sir John Lenthall told me that at the taking of Dunkirk, Marshal Turenne, and (I think Cardinal Mazarin too) had a great mind to see this famous warrior. They gave him a visit, and whereas they thought to have found an Achillean or gigantic person, they saw a little man, not many degrees above a dwarf, sitting in a hut of turves, with his fellow-soldiers, smoking a pipe about three inches (or near so) long, with a green hat-case on.* He spoke with a very thin tone, and did cry out to the soldiers, when angry with them, 'Sirrah, I'll cleave your skull!' as if the words had been spoken by an eunuch. He was of mean parentage in Monmouthshire. He went over to the Low Country wars about sixteen, being recommended by some friend of his to some commander there, who, when he read the letter, said, 'What! has my cousin recommended a *rattoon* to me?' at which he took offence and sought his fortune (as a soldier) in Saxon Weimar.

He spoke Welsh, English, French, German and Low Dutch, but never a one well. His seat was at Cheuston, in Herefordshire.

¶ See Mr Howe at Mr Griffin's house in York Buildings, below Mrs Kent, next house but one or two to the water: he was his secretary and has his memoirs.† He died about 1679.

Cardinal Morton
1410–1500

In my last I gave you some memoirs of Cardinal Morton, and that the tradition of the country people in Dorset, when I was a schoolboy there at Blandford, was that he was a shoemaker's son of Bere in the same county: but Sir William Dugdale says 'by no means I must put in writing hearsays.'

---

* Literally, hat-box. OED gives no other meaning: perhaps a piece of armour? Or has Aubrey absent-mindedly added -case? *Ed.*

† Published 1699. *Ed.*

Dr Thomas Mouffet
1553–1604

Doctor of medicine and expert on insects. He was persuaded to come to Wilton by Mary Herbert (q.v.) who arranged a pension for him.

Dr Mouffet lived in his later time at Bulbridge (at the west end of Wilton—it belongs to the earl of Pembroke) at the manor-house there, which is a fair old-built house. This Bulbridge is adjoining to Wilton: the river only parts it.

At this place he died and lies buried at Wilton. The earl of Pembroke's steward told me that he finds by the old books and accounts that a pension was paid him yearly. He was one of the learnedest physicians of that age. He wrote a book in Latin on insects which Dr John Pell told me (inquire) heretofore was first begun by a friar.

Robert Murray
1635–?1725

Murray wrote on trade and banking practice, and is said to have had the idea for a penny post in 1679.

Mr Robert Murray is a citizen of London, a milliner, of the company of clothworkers. His father a Scotchman; mother, English. Born in the Strand, 1633, December.

The penny-post was set up in 1680, our Lady Day (March 25), being Friday, a most ingenious and useful project. Invented by Mr Murray first, and then Mr Dockwra joined with him. It was set up February 1680.

Mr Murray was formerly clerk to the general company for the revenue of Ireland, and afterwards clerk to the committee of the grand excise of England; and was the first that invented and introduced into this city the club of commerce consisting of one of each trade, whereof there were after very many erected and are still continued in this city. *And also continued and set up the office or bank of credit at Devonshire house in Bishopsgate Street without, where men depositing their goods and

---

* What follows is not in Aubrey's hand. *Ed.*

217

merchandise were furnished with bills of current credit on two-thirds or three-quarters of the value of the said goods answering to the intrinsic value of money, whereby the deficiency of coin might be fully supplied: and for rendering the same current, a certain or competent number of traders (viz ten or twenty of each trade, whereof there be five hundred several trades within the city) were to be associated or formed into such a society or company of traders as might amongst them complete the whole body of commerce, whereby any possessed of the said current credit might be furnished among themselves with any kind of goods as effectually as they could do elsewhere for money.

Sir Hugh Myddelton
?1560–1631

Goldsmith and merchant-venturer of London. He first became interested in the 'New River' project when it was discussed in the House of Commons, of which he was a member, and in 1609 offered to take over the undertaking. It was completed in 1613, and provided London with a much-needed supply of pure water. Parts of Myddelton's original canal survive in Islington.

Mr Ingelbert was the first inventor or projector of the scheme for bringing the water from Ware to London called *Myddelton's water*. He was a poor man, but Sir Hugh Myddelton, alderman of London, financed the business; undertook it; and got the profit and also the credit of that most useful invention, for which there ought to have been erected a statue for the memory of this poor man from the City of London. From my honoured and learned friend Mr Fabian Philips, law official of London etc, who was in a commission about this water.

From Dr Hugh Chamberlain, MD—that King James took half of the profits of the New River from Sir Hugh Myddelton. Some say 'twas in consideration of money advanced by the king; but this is not certain. He did indeed reconvey this back to him and his heirs, etc for a rent of £500 per annum, which is duly paid, but I think granted back to him from his majesty.

This Sir Hugh Myddelton had his picture in Goldsmith's Hall with a waterpot by him, as if he had been the sole inventor. Mr Fabian Philips saw Ingelbert afterwards, in a poor rug-gown like an almsman, sitting by an apple-woman at the parliament stairs.

Memorandum that now (1682) London is grown so populous and big that the New River of Myddelton can serve the pipes to private houses but twice a week—which N.B.

Richard Napier

1559–1634

*Parson of Great Linford (Bucks) from 1590–1634. He was a pupil of
Simon Forman the astrologer (whose diaries have recently been published)
and he inherited Forman's papers. He was equally well known for his
medical skill, and was formally licensed to practise in 1604.*

Dr Richard Napier was a person of great abstinence, innocence, and
piety: he spent every day two hours in family prayer: when a patient or
someone seeking advice came to him, he at once went to his closet to
pray: and told to admiration the recovery, or death of the patient. It
appears, by his papers, that he did converse with the angel Raphael,
who gave him the responses. Elias Ashmole, esquire, had all his papers,
where is contained all his practice for about fifty years. Before the
responses stands this mark, viz *R.Ris*, which Mr Ashmole said was
Responsium Raphaelis [*Raphael's answer*].

The angel told him if the patient were curable or incurable. There are
also several other queries to the angel, as to religion, transubstantiation,
etc which I have forgot. I remember one is, whether the good spirits or
the bad be most in numbers. *R.Ris*: The good.

It is to be found there, that he told John Prideaux, DD, in 1621, that
twenty years hence (1641) he would be a bishop, and he was so, that is,
Bishop of Worcester.

R.Ris did resolve him, that Mr Booth, of Cheshire should have a son
that should inherit three years hence, viz from 1619. Sir George Booth
aforesaid was born 18 December 1622.

This I extracted out of Dr Napier's original diary, then in the
possession of Mr Ashmole.

When Edmund Wyld esquire was about eight years old, he was
troubled with the worms. His grandfather carried him to Dr Napier at
Linford. Mr E.W. peeped in at the closet at the end of the gallery, and
saw him upon his knees at prayer. The doctor told Sir Francis that at
fourteen years old his grandson would be freed from that distemper;
and he was so. The medicine he prescribed was, to drink a little draught
of sweet Muscat wine in the morning. 'Twas about 1625.

It is impossible that the prediction of Sir George Booth's birth could
be found any other way, but by angelical revelation.

This Dr Richard Napier was rector of Linford in Bucks, and did
practice physic; but gave most to the poor that he got by it. 'Tis certain
he told his own death to a day and hour; he died praying upon his
knees, being of a very great age, 1 April 1634. He was nearly related to

the learned Lord Napier of Merchiston in Scotland; I have forgotten whether he was his brother. His knees were horny with frequent praying. He left his estate to Sir Richard Napier, MD of the college of physicians, London, from whom Mr Ashmole had the doctor's picture, now in the Museum.

Dr Richard Napier, rector of Linford, was a good astrologer, and so was Mr Marsh of Dunstable; but Mr Marsh did seriously confess to a friend of mine, that astrology was but the countenance; and that he did his business by the help of the blessed spirits; with whom only men of great piety, humility and charity, could be acquainted; and such a one he was. He was an hundred years old when my friend was with him; and yet did understand himself very well.

Mr Ashmole told me, that a woman made use of a spell to cure an ague, by the advice of Dr Napier; a minister came to her, and severely reprimanded her, for making use of a diabolical help, and told her, she was in danger of damnation for it, and commanded her to burn it. She did so, and her distemper returned severely; insomuch that she was importunate with the doctor to use the same again; she used it, and had ease. But the parson hearing of it, came to her again, and thundered hell and damnation, and frightened her so, that she burnt it again. Whereupon she fell extremely ill, and would have had it a third time; but the doctor refused, saying, that she had despised and slighted the power and goodness of the blessed spirits (or angels), and so she died.

Sir William Neale
1609–91

'*Scoutmaster*', *i.e. commander of the scouts responsible for discovering the enemy's whereabouts, in prince Rupert's army.*

Sir William Neale, knight, scout-master general to king Charles the first, died on the 24th of March last, 1691, in Grays Inn Lane, being 81 years old. When he died, he was the oldest field-officer of king Charles the first.

He was not less than six foot high: very beautiful in youth. I remember him: and of great courage, but a great plunderer and cruel.

He lived in town ever since the Popish Plot (1679), and that worthy generous gentleman Edmund Wyld Esq, was much supporting to him. His mother and Sir William were cousins german. But for these five years last past his gouts etc emaciated him extremely; so that he did often put me in mind of that of Ovid, *Metamorphoses* (xv, 229) 'Milo, grown old,

weeps to see those arms hanging limp and thin, whose massive knotted muscles once rivalled those of Hercules.'

He died penitent.

He was the grandson of . . . Neale, Esq of Wollaston near Northampton, who married one of Sir Edmund Conquest's sisters, of Houghton Conquest, Bedfordshire. Sir Francis Clarke of Houghton Conquest aforesaid (father of Mr Edmund Wyld's mother, a daughter and heir) married another sister of Sir Edmund Conquest.

Sir William married major-general Egerton's sister, by whom he had issue, William, a lusty stout fellow, of the guards, who died about the abdication (1688), and two daughters.

John Newton
1622–78

Dr Newton, now parson of Ross in Herefordshire, told me that he was of St Edmund's Hall: yet living; and likely to live, for when his stomach is out of order, he cures himself by eating a piece of hot roast beef off the spit.

¶ Dr J. Newton: he told me he was born in Bedfordshire, but would not tell me where.

¶ He was against learning of Latin in a mathematical school.

John Norden
1548–1625

Surveyor and topographer. He projected a series of histories of the counties of England, of which Middlesex and Hertfordshire were published, and five others completed in manuscript. The maps he made in connection with this work are of the greatest historical value; he was the first English mapmaker to include roads.

John Norden—from Mr Bagford, a good antiquary, Mr Crump's acquaintance.

He lived at Fulham, and (perhaps) died there.

He made maps of Middlesex, Herefordshire, Surrey, and Hampshire, and also Cornwall; and he did not only make the maps aforesaid but has written descriptions of them, which Mr Bagford has. The description of

Cornwall (I think) was not printed; but Dr Gale of Paul's School has it in manuscript, which N.B.

Mr Morgan, the herald painter, gives us an account in his *Armorie*, that he had, in his custody, Kent, Essex, Isle of Man, Isle of Wight, and Hampshire.

In the end of Mr Gregory's posthumous works, he gives us an account of the excellency of Mr Norden's maps, and Saxton's too.

His dialogues I have, printed first, 1610; dedicated to Cecil, earl of Salisbury, whose servant he was, (I suppose) steward or surveyor.

Sometime or other I will look into the church at Fulham; he died ('tis thought) in King James the first's reign.

Mr Wood! pray add this to the rest of the lives.

Roger North
?1585–1652

North accompanied Raleigh on his ill-fated Guiana expedition of 1618, and in 1627 established a plantation in Guiana. He was forced to return to England for a lawsuit, and the plantation failed in his absence.

Captain Roger North was brother to Lord North. He was a great acquaintance of Sir Walter Raleigh's and accompanied him in his voyages. He was with him at Guiana, and never heard that word but he would fall into a passion for the miscarriage of that action.

He was a great algebrist, which was rare in those days; but he had the acquaintance of his fellow-traveller Mr Hariot.

He was a most accomplished gentleman.

He died in Fleet Street about 1656 or 1657.

He had excellent collections and remarks of his voyages, which were all unfortunately burnt in Fleet Street at the great conflagration of the city (1666)—From Sir Francis North, Lord Chief Justice of the Common Pleas, his nephew, and Edmund Wyld, esq, who knew him very well.

He died about the time of the fire (?); enquire again.

This family speaks not well of Sir Walter Raleigh, that Sir Walter designed to break with the Spaniard, and to make himself popular in England. When he came to (Guiana?) he could not show them where the mines of gold were. He would have then gone to the King of France (Louis XIII) but his own men brought him back.

Capt North: enquire if of Oxford: I think of University College.

Mr Thomas North, that translated Plutarch's Lives (my lord chief justice tells me) was great-uncle to his grandfather.

Richard Norwood
?1590–1675

A teacher of mathematics and surveyor, who was involved in the early settlement of the Bermudas; he lived there at intervals from 1640 onwards.

Mr Richard Norwood: whence he was born I cannot yet learn.

Norwood is an ancient family: about three hundred years since St Low married with a daughter and heir of them and quarters the coat in the margent. They flourish still in Gloucestershire, the manor of Lakehampton belonging to them.—'Tis probable that this learned Norwood was of that county.

He at his own charge, measured with a chain from Berwick to Christ Church (he says he came up in ten or eleven days) in order to the finding the quantity of a degree, and so the circumference of the earth and sea in our known measures—July 1 1636.

By a letter from Nicholas, earl of Thanet, to me, concerning his purchase in the Bermudas, not dated, but written about 1674 or 1675—thus: 'ao to old Mr Norwood, to whom the Royal Society would send some queries, he is lately dead as his son informs me, who lately went captain in that ship wherein I sent my gardener and vines to the Bermudas. He was aged above 90.'

William Noy
1577–1634

Attorney-general from 1631–4.

From Fabian Philips, esq:

Mr attorney-general Noy was a great lawyer and a great humorist. There is a world of merry stories of him.

He would play at span-counter* with the tavern bar-boy.

A country clown asked for a good inn, and he bids him ride into Lincoln's Inn, and asked if his horse went to hay or to grass.

He caused the breeches of a bencher of Lincoln's Inn to be taken in by a tailor, and made him believe he had the dropsy.

One time he met accidentally with Butler, the famous physician of

---

* 'A game in which the object of one player was to throw his counters so close to those of his opponent that the distance between them could be spanned with the hand.'—OED.

Cambridge, at the earl of Suffolk's (Lord Treasurer). They were strangers to each other, and both walking in the gallery (waiting for audience). Noy was wearied, and would be gone. Butler wanted to know his name. Noy had him to the Peacock Tavern in Thames Street and made him drunk all that day.

Another time Noy and Pine of Lincoln's Inn went afoot to Barnet with clubs in their hands, like country fellows. They went to the Red Lion inn; the people of the house were afraid to trust them, fearing they might not pay.

John Ogilby
1600–76

Writer, publisher and mapmaker. His translations and other books issued by him between 1654 and 1676 are among the very finest of the period. His talents ranged from verse translations of Virgil and Homer to the production of major atlases (some engraved by Hollar) and the arrangement of the procession for Charles II's coronation. He published an illustrated account of the festivities in 1661. His maps of London and the Home Counties are remarkable, as are his road atlases.

John Ogilby, esquire, was born in Scotland, 17 November 1600. He was of a gentleman's family, and bred to his grammar.

His father had spent his estate, and fell to decay, and was a prisoner in the King's Bench, whom, together with his mother, his son relieved by his own industry, being then but about the age of twelve or thirteen years. By the advantage of his son's industry, he raised a small sum of money, which he adventured on the lottery for the advancement of the plantation in Virginia, and he got out of prison by this means. His motto (of his lot)* was

> 'I am a poor prisoner, God wot
> God send me a good lot,
> I'll come out of prison, and pay all my debts

It so happened that he had a very good lot, that did pay his debts.

John (the son) bound himself apprentice to one Mr Draper, who kept a dancing-school in Gray's Inn Lane, and in short time arrived to so

---

* Printed on the ticket. *Ed.*

great excellency in that art, that he found means to purchase his time†
of his master and set up for himself. When the Duke of Buckingham's
great masque was represented at Court, he was chosen (among the rest)
to perform some extraordinary part in it, and high-dancing, i.e. vault-
ing and cutting capers, being then in fashion, he, endeavouring to do
something extraordinary, by misfortune of a false step when he came to
the ground, did sprain a vein on the inside of his leg, of which he was
lame ever after, which gave an occasion to say that 'he was an excellent
dancing master, and never a good leg'.

He taught two of the Lord Hopton's (then Sir Ralph) sisters to
dance, then at Witham in Somersetshire; and Sir Ralph taught him to
handle the pike and musket, namely all the postures.

He went over into Ireland to Thomas Earl of Strafford, lord lieutenant
there, and was there entertained to teach in that family. And here it was
that first he gave proof of his inclination to poetry, by paraphrasing
upon some of Aesop's fables. (He wrote a fine hand.) He had a warrant
from the lord lieutenant to be master of the ceremonies for that
kingdom; and built a little theatre in St Warburgh Street, in Dublin. It
was a short time before the rebellion broke out, by which he lost all,
and ran through many hazards, and particularly being likely to have
been blown up at the castle of Refarnum near Dublin.

He came into England about the year 1648 (see the date of his Virgil,
octavo). He printed Virgil, translated by himself into English verse,
dedicated to the right honourable William, Lord Marquis of Hertford,
who loved him very well.

After he had translated Virgil, he learned Greek of Mr Whitfield, a
Scotch bishop's son, and grew so great a proficient in it that he fell to
translate Homer's *Iliad*, 1660.

Next, as if by a prophetic spirit, foreseeing the restoration of King
Charles II and also the want there might be of Church Bibles, he
printed the fairest impression, and the most correct of English Bibles,
in royal and imperial paper sizes, that ever was yet done. He printed
and published his majesty's entertainment at his coronation, in folio
with engravings, 1662.

The same year, 1662 he went into Ireland again, being then by patent
(before, only by warrant) master of the revels, having disputed his right
with Sir William Davenant, who had got a grant; and built a noble
theatre at Dublin, which cost £2000, the former being ruined and
spoiled and a cowhouse made of the stage in the troubles.

His *Odyssey* came out in 1665. People did then suspect, or would not
believe that 'twas he was the author of the paraphrase upon Aesop, and
to convince them he published a second volume, which he calls his

† Buy himself out of his apprenticeship. *Ed.*

225

Aesopics, which he did during the plague of 1665 in his retirement at Kingston upon Thames, after he had published Homer's *Iliad* and *Odyssey*.

The general and dreadful conflagration [Great Fire, 1666] burnt all that he had, that he was fain to begin in the world again, being then at best worth £5. He had such an excellent inventive and prudential wit, and master of so good address, that when he was undone he could not only shift handsomely (which is a great mastery) but he would make such rational proposals that would be embraced by rich and great men, that in a short time he could gain a good estate again; and never failed in anything he ever undertook, but always went through with profits and honour.

Being thus utterly undone again by the fire, he made his proposals for the printing of a fair English *Atlas*, of which he lived to finish the histories of Africa, America, and part of Asia: and then, being encouraged by the king and the nobility to make an actual survey of England and Wales, he proceeded in it so far as to an actual survey of the roads both in England and Wales.

¶ The year before Lord Strafford went to Ireland as Deputy (1633) he kept a dancing school in the Black Spread Eagle court (then an inn) in Gray's Inn Lane. Mr John Lacy, the actor, from whom I take this information was his apprentice.

¶ He went into Ireland with the Lord Strafford (Deputy) and rode in his troop of guards, as one of my lord's gentlemen, which gave occasion of his writing an excellent copy of verses called *The description of a trooper*, which get.

Mr J.O. was in the lord lieutenant's troop of guards, and taught his lady and children to dance; that was his place. And he there made those excellent verses *of the Trooper* (enquire).

Upon this Mr Chantrel† put him upon learning the Latin tongue (in the age of forty or more) and taught him himself and took a good deal of pains with him. This was the first time he began his Latin. He stayed in Ireland a good while after the wars broke out.

He would not tell where in Scotland he was born: enquire about it. He said drollingly that he would have as great contests hereafter for the place of his birth as of Homer's. Mr Gadbury says that Mr Ogilby told him (he was very sure) that he was born either in or near Edinburgh. But however ask about this of Mr Morgan his grandson.

After John Ogilby had built the theatre at Dublin, he was wrecked at sea, and came to London very poor, and went on foot to Cambridge.

John Ogilby married the daughter of Mr Fox★ of Netherhampton,

---

† Servant to the Earl of Pembroke, a good livery.

★ Mr Chantrel, chaplain to Sir George Ratcliffe, favourite. Sir George Ratcliffe was afterwards the Duke of York's governor in France.

who was born as he was wont to say 'in the first Olympiad' that is when the first race was run at Salisbury in Henry Earl of Pembroke's time. She had only one daughter by him, married to Mr Morgan, who left a son, who now succeeds his grandfather as his majesty's cosmographer.

He wrote a play at Dublin, called *The Merchant of Dublin*, never printed.

William Oughtred
1575–1660

One of the best practical mathematicians of the generation before Aubrey. Aubrey's particular interest in mathematics led him to project a collection of the lives of the greatest English mathematicians, in which Oughtred would have been included. Oughtred's Clavis Mathematicae *(1631) was the best summary of algebra and arithmetic then available, including such innovations as the use of* × *for multiplication.*

Mr Oughtred: Mr Sloper tells me that his father was butler of Eton College: he remembers him, a very old man.

William Oughtred: see Henry Coley's *Astrologie.*—A note from my honoured and learned friend Thomas Fludd esquire, who had been High Sheriff of Kent, to the effect that he was Mr Oughtred's acquaintance. He told me that Mr Oughtred confessed to him that he was not satisfied how it came about that one might foretell by the stars, but so it was that it fell out true as he did often by his experience find.

Mr William Oughtred, BD, Cambridge, was born at Eton in Buckinghamshire near Windsor, 5 March 1574.

His father taught to write at Eton, and was a scrivener, and understood common arithmetic, and 'twas no small help and furtherance to his son to be instructed in it when a schoolboy. His grandfather came from the north for killing a man. The last knight of the family was one Sir Jeffrey Oughtred. I think a Northumberland family (enquire).

He was chosen to be one of the King's Scholars at Eton College. He went to King's College in Cambridge at the age of 23, he wrote there his *Horologiographia Geometrica*, as appears by the title page.

He was instituted and inducted into the rectory or parsonage of Albury in Surrey, worth £100 per annum; he was pastor of this place fifty years.

He married Miss Caryl (an ancient family in those parts) by whom he had nine sons (most lived to be men) and four daughters. None of his sons he could make scholars.

He was a little man, had black hair, and black eyes (with a great deal of spirit). His head was always working: he would draw lines and diagrams in the dust.

His oldest son Benjamin (who lives in the house with my cousin Boothby (who gives him his board and now an old man) he bound apprentice to a watchmaker; who did work pretty well, but his sight now fails for that fine work. He told me that his father did use to lie abed till eleven or twelve o'clock, with his doublet on, ever since he can remember. Studied late at night, went not to bed till eleven o'clock, had his tinder box by him, and on the top of his bedpost he had his inkhorn fixed. He slept but little. Sometimes he went not to bed in two or three nights, and would not come down to meals till he had found out what he sought.

He was more famous abroad for his learning, and more esteemed, than at home. Several great mathematicians came over into England on purpose to converse with him. His country neighbours (though they understood not his worth) knew that there must be extraordinary worth in him, that he was so visited by foreigners.

When Mr Seth Ward, MA, and Mr Charles Scarborough, MD, came (as in pilgrimage, to see him and admire him)—they lay at the inn at Shere (the next parish)—Mr Oughtred had against their coming prepared a good dinner, and also he had dressed himself thus: an old red russet cloth cassock that had been black in days of yore, girt with an old leather girdle, an old fashioned russet hat, that had been a beaver [hat] in the days of Queen Elizabeth. When learned foreigners came and saw how privately he lived, they did admire and bless themselves, that a person of so much worth and learning should not be better provided for.

Seth Ward, MA, a fellow of Sidney Sussex College in Cambridge (now Bishop of Salisbury) came to him and lived with him half a year (and he would not take a farthing for his board) and learned all his mathematics of him. Sir Jonas Moore was with him a good while, and learned; he was but an ordinary accountant before. Sir Charles Scarborough was his scholar; so Dr John Wallis was his scholar; so was Christopher Wren his scholar; so was Mr Smethwick, FRS. One Mr Austin (a most ingenious man) was his scholar, and studied so much that he became mad, fell a-laughing, and so died, to the great grief of the old gentleman. Mr Stokes, another scholar, fell mad, and dreamed that the good old gentleman came to him and gave him good advice, and so he recovered, and is still well. Mr Thomas Henshawe, FRS, was his scholar, then a young gentleman. But he did not so much like any, as those that tugged and took pains to work out questions. He taught all free. He could not endure to see a scholar write an ill hand; he taught them all at once to mend their handwriting. Amongst others Mr

T. Henshawe who when he came to him wrote a lamentable hand, he taught to write very well. He wrote a very elegant hand, and drew his schemes most neatly, as if they had been cut in copper. His father (no doubt) was an ingenious artist at the pen and taught him to write so well.

He was an astrologer, and very lucky in giving his judgements on nativities; he would say that he did not understand the reason why it should be so: but so it would happen: he did believe some genius or spirit did help. He has asserted the rational way of dividing the twelve houses according to the old way, which (the original) Elias Ashmole has of his own handwriting; which transcribe. Captain George Wharton has inserted it in his Almanac, 1658 or 1659. The country people did believe that he could conjure, and 'tis like enough that he might be well enough contented to have them think so. I have seen some notes of his own handwriting on Cattan's *Geomancy*.

He has told Bishop Ward, and Mr Elias Ashmole (who was his neighbour) 'on this spot of ground' or 'leaning against this oak' or 'that ash, the solution of such or such a problem came into my head, as if infused by a divine genius, after I had thought on it without success for a year, two or three'. Ben Oughtred told me that he had heard his father say to Mr Allen (the famous mathematical instrument maker) in his shop, that he had found out the longitude*; but I scarcely believe it.

Nicholas Mercator of Holstein went to see him few years before he died. 'Twas about midsummer, and the weather was very hot, and the old gentleman had a good fire, and used Mr Mercator with much humanity (being exceedingly taken with his excellent mathematical wit) and one piece of his courtesy was to be mighty importunate with him to sit on his upper hand next the fire; he being cold (with age) thought Mercator had been so too.

He was a great lover of chemistry, which he studied before his son Ben can remember, and continued it, and told John Evelyn of Deptford, FRS, not above a year before he died, that if he were but five years (or three years) younger, he doubted not to find out the philosopher's stone. He used to talk much of the maiden-earth for the philosopher's stone.‡ It was made of the harshest clear water that he could get, which he let stand to putrify, and evaporated by simmering. Ben tended his furnaces. He has told me that his father would sometimes say that he could make the stone. Quicksilver refined and strained, and gold as it came natural over†—

---

* The problem of reckoning longitude while at sea was not solved until the following century, when Harrison invented an accurate chronometer which gave a basis for calculations. *Ed.*

‡ Ask for what he said it was good.

† This line is imperfect. It is blurred in my notes.

The old gentleman was a great lover of heraldry, and was well known with the heralds at their office, who proved his descent.

Memorandum: he struck out above half of the grammar and wrote new instead. He taught a gentleman in half a year to understand Latin, at Mr Duncombe's, his parishioner. Ask his daughter Mrs Brookes at Oxford for it.

His wife was a penurious woman, and would not allow him to burn candle after supper, by which means many a good notion is lost, and many a problem solved; so that Mr Henshawe, when he was there, bought candle, which was a great comfort to the old man.

The right honourable Thomas Howard, Earl of Arundel and Surrey, Lord High Marshal of England, was his great patron, and loved him entirely. One time they were likely to have been killed together by the fall at Albury of a grotto, which fell down but just as they were come out. My lord had many grottos about his house, cut in the sandy sides of hills, wherein he delighted to sit and discourse.

In the time of the Civil Wars the Duke of Florence invited him over, and offered him £500 per annum; but he would not accept of it, because of his religion. For notwithstanding all that has been said of this excellent man, he was in danger to have been ejected from his living, and Onslow, that was a great stickler against the royalists and living not far from him—he translated his *Clavis* into English and dedicated it to him to gain favour with him, and it did so his business and saved him from sequestration. Now this Onslow was no scholar and hated by the county for bringing his countrymen of Surrey into the trap of slaughter when so many petitioners were killed at Westminster and on the roads in pursuit.

I have heard his neighbour ministers say that he was a pitiful preacher; the reason was because he never studied it, but bent all his thoughts on the mathematics; but when he was in danger of being sequestered for a royalist, he fell to the study of divinity, and preached (they said) admirably well, even in his old age.

He was a good Latinist and Grecian, as appears in a little treatise of his against one Delamain, a joiner, who was so saucy as to write against him (I think about his circles of proportion): upon which occasion I remember I have seen, many years since, twenty or more good verses made, which begin to this purpose:

> Thus may some mason or rude carpenter
> Put into the balance his rule and compasses
> 'Gainst learned Euclid's pen etc.

Enquire for them and insert them.

Before he died he burned a world of papers, and said that the world was not worthy of them; he was so proud. He burned also several printed books, and would not stir, till they were consumed. His son Ben was confident he understood magic. Mr Oughtred, at the Custom House (his grandson), has some of his papers; I myself have his *Pitiscus*, embellished with his excellent marginal notes, which I esteem as a great rarity. I wish I could also have got his Billingsley's *Euclid*, which John Collins says was full of his annotations.

He died 13 June 1660 in the year of his age eighty-eight and odd days. Ralph Greatorex his great friend, the mathematical instrument maker, said he conceived he died with joy for the coming in of the king which was the twenty-ninth of May before. 'And are you sure he is restored? Then give me a glass of sack to drink his sacred majesty's health': his spirits were then quite upon the wing to fly away. The fifteenth of June he was buried in the chancel at Albury, on the north side near the screen between the chancel and the body of the church. I had much ado to find the very place where the bones of this learned and good man lay (and 'twas but sixteen years after his death). When I first asked his son Ben, he told me that truly the great grief for his father's death was so great, that he did not remember the place: now I should have thought it would have made him remember it the better: but when he had put on his considering cap (which was never like his father's), he told as aforesaid, with which others did agree: there is not to this day any manner of memorial for him, which is a great pity. I have desired for Mr John Evelyn etc, to speak to our patron, the Duke of Norfolk, to bestow a decent inscription of marble on him, which will also perpetuate his grace's fame. I asked Ben concerning the report of his father's dying a Roman Catholic: he told me that 'twas true indeed that when he was sick some priests came from my lord duke's (then Mr Henry Howard, of Norfolk) to him to have discourse with him, in order to his conversion to their church, but his father was then past understanding. Ben was then by, he told me.

He wrote a little treatise of watchmaking for the use of his son Benjamin, who told me that Mr Horton of Whitehall, of the Woodyard, has the true copy of it.

I have heard Mr Hobbes say (and very truly) that with all his great skill in algebra, he did never add one proposition to geometry; he could bind up a bundle well.

John Overall

1560–1619

Although Aubrey's account of him hardly touches on his theological works, Overall was in fact one of the leading divines of his time, playing an important part in the convocation of 1606, and helping to revise the Old Testament translation for the Authorised Version. He later became Bishop of Coventry and then, in 1618, of Norwich.

Dr Overall and his wife: Dr Overall was Dean of St Paul's, London.

I see his picture in the rationale [reasoned essay] written by Sparrow, Bishop of Exeter, in the beginning whereof are the effigies of L. Andrews, Bishop of Winchester, Mr Hooker, and John Overall, Bishop of Norwich—before which is written *Defenders of the Anglican Church and Liturgy.* Ask if that this dean was that bishop.

I know not what they wrote or whether he was any more than a common-prayer doctor; but most remarkable by his wife, who was the greatest beauty in her time in England. That she was so I have it attested from the famous portrait painter Mr Hoskins and other old painters, besides old courtiers. She was not more beautiful than she was obliging and kind, and was so tender-hearted that (truly) she could scarce deny anyone. She had (they told me) the loveliest eyes that ever were seen, but wondrous wanton. When she came to court or to the playhouse, the gallants would so flock round her. Richard, the Earl of Dorset, and his brother Edward, since earl, both did mightily adore her. And by their report he must have had a hard heart that did not admire her. Bishop Hall says in his *Meditations* that 'there is none so old that a beautiful person loves not; nor so young whom a lovely feature moves not'.

The good old dean, notwithstanding he knew well enough that he was cuckolded, loved her infinitely: in so much that he was willing she should enjoy what she had a mind to. Among others who were charmed by her was Sir John Selby of Yorkshire. In 1656, old Mrs Tyndale (of the Priory near Easton Piers*), who knew her, remembers a song made of her and Sir John, part whereof was this, viz:

> The Dean of Paul's did search for his wife,
> And where d'ye thinke he found her?
> Even upon Sir John Selby's bed,
> As flat as any flounder.

* Aubrey's Wiltshire house. *Ed.*

On these two lovers was made this following copy of pastoral verses, e.g.

Down lay the shepherd swain
  So sober and demure,
Wishing for his wench again
  So bonny and so pure,
With his head on hillock low
  And his arms akimbo
And all was for the loss of his
  Hye nonny nonny no.

His tears fell as thin
  As water from the still,
His hair upon his chin
  Grew like thyme upon a hill,
His cherry cheeks pale as snow
  Did testify his mickle woe,
And all was for the loss of his
  Hye nonny etc.

Sweet she was, as kind a love
  As ever fettered swain;
Never such a dainty one
  Shall man enjoy again.
Set a thousand on a row
  I forbid that any show
Ever the like of her
  Hye nonny etc.

Face she had of filberd [hazel] hue
  And bosomed like a swan;
Back she had of bended yew,
  And waisted by a span.
Hair she had as black as crow
  From the head unto the toe
Down, down, all over her
  Hye nonny etc.

With her mantle tucked up high
  She foddered her flock
So buxom and alluringly,
  Her knee upheld her smock.
So nimbly did she use to go,
  So smooth she danced on tip-toe,
That all men were fond of her
  Hye nonny etc.

She smiled like a Holy-Day
  And simpered like the Spring,
She prancked it like a popinjay
  And like a swallow sing,
She tripped it like a barren doe,
  She strutted like a gor-crow,
Which made the men so fond of her
  Hye nonny etc.

To sport it on the merry down
  To dance the lively Hay
To wrestle for a green gown
  In heat of all the day
Never would she say me no
  Yet me thought I had tho'
Never enough of her
  Hye nonny etc.

But gone she is, the prettiest lass
  That ever trod on plain.
What ever hath betide of her
  Blame not the shepherd swain
For why? She was her own foe
  And gave her self the overthrow
By being so frank of her
  Hye nonny nonny no.

John Partridge
1644–1715

Partridge is best remembered as the subject of an attack by Swift, who published a mock-almanac similar to Partridge's own productions, in which he predicted Partridge's death on 29 March 1708. Swift then published a further pamphlet in which he announced the fulfilment of the prediction, including the following epitaph:

> *Here, five feet deep, lies on his back,*
> *A cobbler, starmonger and quack,*
> *Who to the stars in pure good will*
> *Does to his best look upward still:*
> *Weep, all you customers that use*
> *His pills, his almanacks or shoes.*

Partridge had the greatest difficulty in persuading the world at large that he was still alive.

John Partridge, astrologer, the son of [Mr] Partridge (yet living, 1680, an honest waterman at Putney in Surrey).

He was born, as by his scheme (of astrological signs) appears, January 18, 1644 in the latitude of London.

He was taught to read, and a little to write.

He was bound apprentice to a shoe-maker; where he was kept hard to his trade.

At 18 he got him a Lillie's grammar, and Goldman's dictionary, and a Latin bible, and Ovid's Metamorphoses.

He is of an excellent healthy constitution and great temperance, of indefatigable industry, and sleeps but [a few] hours.

In [a few] years he made himself a competent master of the Latin tongue, well enough to read any astrological book, and quickly became a master of that science. He then studied the Greek tongue, and also the Hebrew, to neither of which he is a stranger. He then studied good authors in physic, and intends to make that his profession and practice; but is yet (1680) a shoemaker in Covent Garden.

John Pell
1611–85

Another of the Lives of the Mathematicians *projected by Aubrey; this is an extensive example, corrected by Pell himself.*

John Pell was the son of John Pell, of Southwick in Sussex, in which parish he was born, on St David's Day (March 1) 1610.

His father was a divine but a kind of Non-conformist; of the Pells of Lincolnshire, an ancient family; his mother of the Hollands of Kent. His father died when his son John was but five years old and six weeks, and left him an excellent library.

He went to school at the free school at Steyning, a borough town in Sussex, at the first founding of the school; an excellent schoolmaster, John Jeffreys. At thirteen years and a quarter old he went as good a scholar to Cambridge, to Trinity College, as most Masters of Arts in the University (he understood Latin, Greek and Hebrew), so that he played not much (one must imagine) with his schoolfellows, for, when they had play-days, or after school time, he spent his time in the library aforesaid.

He never stood at any election of fellows or scholars (of the House at) Trinity College.

Of person he was very handsome, and of a very strong and excellent habit of body, melancholic, sanguine, dark brown hair with an excellent moist curl.

Before he went first out of England he understood these languages (besides his mother tongue, viz. Latin, Greek, Hebrew, Arabic, Italian, French, Spanish, German and Dutch.

In 1632 he married Ithamara Reginalds, second daughter to Mr Henry Reginalds of London. He had by her four sons and four daughters.

Dr Pell has said to me that he did believe that he solved some questions (not without God's help).

In 1643 he went to Amsterdam, in December; was there Professor of Mathematics, next after Martinus Hortensius, about two years.

1646, the prince of Orange called for him to be public professor of philosophy and mathematics at the High School at Breda, that was founded that year by His Highness; see the Doctor's inaugural oration there.

He returned into England, 1652.

In 1654, Oliver, Lord Protector, sent him envoyé [as envoy] to the Protestant cantons of Switzerland; he resided chiefly at Zurich. He was sent out with the title of legate but afterwards he had order to continue there with the title of Resident.

In 1658, he returned into England and so little before the death of Oliver Cromwell that he never saw him since he was Protector.

Memorandum—when he took his leave from Zurich, June 23, 1658, he made a Latin speech, which I have seen.

Memorandum that in his negotiation he did no disservice to King Charles II, nor to the church, as may appear by his letters which are in the Secretary of State's office.

¶ Richard Cromwell, Protector, did not fully pay him for his business in Piedmont, whereby he was in some want; and so when King Charles II was restored, Dr Sanderson, bishop of Lincoln, persuaded him to take Holy Orders. He was not adroit for preaching.

¶ When King Charles II had been at home ten months, Mr John Pell first took orders. He was made deacon upon the last of March, 1661, by bishop Sanderson of Lincoln, by whom he was made priest in June following.

Gilbert Sheldon, bishop of London procured for him the parsonage of Fobbing in Essex, 1661, and two years after (1663) gave him the parsonage of Laindon with the attached chapel of Bartlesdon in the same county, which benefices are in the infamous and unhealthy (feverish) hundreds of Essex.

Mr Edward Waller on the death of the countess of Warwick:

> Curst be alreadie those Essexian plaines
> Where . . . Death and Horrour reignes.—etc.

At Fobbing seven curates died within the first ten years; in sixteen years, six of these that had been his curates at Laindon are dead; besides these that went away from both places; and the death of his wife, servants and grandchildren.

Gilbert Sheldon being made archbishop of Canterbury, 1663, John Pell was made one of his Cambridge* chaplains; and complaining one day to his Grace at Lambeth of the unhealthiness of his benefice as abovesaid, said my Lord, 'I do not intend that you shall live there.' 'No', said Doctor Pell, 'I shall die there.'

Now by this time (1680) you doubt not but this great, learned man, famous both at home and abroad, has obtained some considerable dignity in the church. You ought not in modesty to guess at less that than a deanery.—Why, truly, he is staked to this poor preferment still. For though the parishes are large, yet (curates, etc. paid for) he clears not above three score pound (£60) per annum (hardly fourscore) and lives in an obscure lodging, three stories high, in Jermyn Street, next to the sign of the ship, wanting not only books but his own MSS which are many. Many of them are at Brereton at my lord Brereton's in Cheshire.

* He (the Archbishop) has two Oxford chaplains and two Cambridge.

Memorandum: Lord Brereton was sent to Breda to receive the instruction of this worthy person by his grandfather (George Goring, the earl of Norwich) in 1647, where he stayed for some years, where he became a good practitioner, especially in algebra to which his genius most inclined him and which he used to his dying day, which was 17 March 1680; lies buried in St Martin's church in-the-fields. I cannot but mention this noble lord but with a great deal of passion, for a more virtuous person (besides his great learning) I never knew. I have had the honour of his acquaintance since his coming from Breda into England. Never was there greater love between master and scholar than between Dr Pell and this scholar of his, whose death March 17, 1680 has deprived this worthy doctor of an ingenious companion and a useful friend.

Dr Pell has often said to me that when he solves a question he strains every nerve about him, and that now in his old age it brings him to a looseness.

Dr J. Pell was the first inventor of that excellent way or method of the marginal working in algebra.

He could not cringe and sneak for preferment, though otherwise no man more humble nor more communicative. He was cast into King's Bench prison for debt September 7, 1680.

¶ In March 1682 he was very kindly invited by Daniel Whistler, MD, to live with him at the Physicians College in London, where he was very kindly entertained. About the middle of June he fell extremely sick of a cold and removed to a grandchild of his married to one Mr Hastings in St Margaret's Churchyard, Westminster, near the tower, who now (1684) lives in Browlow Street in Drury Lane, where he was almost burnt in his bed by a candle. November 26, fell into convulsion fits which had almost killed him.

¶ Gilbert Sheldon, Lord Bishop of London, gave Dr Pell the parsonage of Laindon cum Basildon in the hundreds of Essex (they call it *kill-priest*, sarcastically); and king Charles the second gave him the parsonage of Fobbing, four miles distant. Both are of the value of two hundred pounds per annum (or so accounted); but the Doctor was a most shiftless man as to worldly affairs, and his tenants and relations cheated him of the profits and kept him so indigent that he lacked necessaries, even paper and ink, and he had not sixpence in his purse when he died, and was buried by the charity of Dr Richard Busby and Dr Sharp, Rector of St Giles in the fields and Dean of Norwich, who ordered his body to lie in a vault belonging to the Rector (the price of vault-burial is £10).

I could not persuade him to make a will; so his books and MSS fell by administratorship to Captain Raven, his son-in-law.

His son (John) is a Justice of Peace in New York and lives well. He intended to have gone over to him.

This learned person died in St Giles' parish aforesaid at the house of

Mr Cothorne the reader in Dyot Street on Saturday December 12, 1685, between 4 and 5 p.m. Dr Busby, schoolmaster of Westminster, bought all his books and papers of Captain Raven, among which is the last thing he wrote (which he did at my earnest request) viz. THE TABLES, which are according to his promise in the last line of his printed tables of squares and cubes (if desired) and which Sir Cyril Wych (then President of the Royal Society) did license for the press. There only wants a leaf or two for the explanation of the use of them, which his death has prevented. Sir Cyril Wych, only, knows the use of them. I do (imperfectly) remember something of his discourse of them, viz. whereas some questions are capable of several answers, by the help of these tables it might be discovered how many, and no more, solutions, or answers, might be given.

I desired Mr Theodore Haak, his old acquaintance, to make some additions to this short collection of memoirs of him, but he has done nothing.

He died of a broken heart.

Dr Whistler invited Dr Pell to his house in (1682), which the doctor liked and accepted of, loving good cheer and good liquor, which the other did also; where eating and drinking too much, was the cause of shortening his days.

Dr Pell had a brother, a surgeon and practitioner in physic, who purchased an estate of the natives of New York and when he died he left it to his nephew John Pell, only son of the Doctor. It was a great estate eight miles broad and—miles long (ask Capt Raven).

He had three or four daughters.

William Penn
1644–1718

Son of the admiral, Sir William Penn. He was sent down from Oxford as a non-conformist in 1661, but did not become a Quaker until 1667. A business interest in America led him to the idea of founding a commonwealth there with a wide degree of religious liberty, unlike the narrow conformity imposed by English law. He obtained the deeds of Pennsylvania in 1682, as settlement of a debt due to his father, who had died in 1670. The colony was successfully established in 1682, but Penn himself returned to England in 1684. He played a part in English religious politics, though his close association with James II meant that he was suspect after 1688. He returned to Pennsylvania from 1699–1701, but died in England in 1718.

William Penn, the eldest son of Sir William Penn, knight, admiral both of the English navy before the restoration of the king, and commanded as captain-general under the Duke of York in 1665 against the Dutch fleet, was born in London, at Tower Hill, the fourteenth day of October 1644. 'Twas upon a Monday he thinks; but 'twas about 7 o'clock in the morning.

(His father was a very good man, but no Quaker; was very much against his son.)

Went to school in London, a private school on that hill, and his father kept a tutor in the house: but first he went to school at Chigwell in Essex.

He was mighty lively, but with innocence; and extremely tender under rebuke; and very early delighted in retirement; much given to reading and meditating of the scriptures, and at 14 had marked over the Bible. Oftentimes at 13 and 14 in his meditations ravished with joy, and dissolved into tears.

The first sense he had of God was when he was 11 years old at Chigwell, being retired in a chamber alone. He was so suddenly surprised with an inward comfort and (as he thought) an external glory in the room that he has many times said that from thence he had the seal of divinity and immortality. That there was a God and that the soul of man was capable of enjoying his divine communications.—His schoolmaster was not of his persuasion.

To Christ Church in Oxford in 1660, aged 16; stayed there about two years.

About 1662, went into France, stayed there two years. Returned to London and was entered of Lincoln's Inn; about the plague [1665], growing entirely solitary, was again turned away (to worldly things). Was employed by his father in a journey into Ireland to the Duke of Ormond's court. The diversions of which not being able to keep down the stronger motions of his soul to a more religious and retired life, upon the hearing of one Th. Lowe, a tradesman, of Oxford, at Cork, 1667, was so thoroughly convinced of the simplicity and self-denial of the way of the people called Quakers that from thence he heartily espoused that judgement and belief.

Since which time he has passed a life of great variety of circumstances, both with respect to good and evil report, divers controversies oral and written*, several imprisonments† (one in Ireland, one in the Tower, third in Newgate). Travelled into Germany, Upper and Lower Holland, in 1671 and 1677, where several were affected with his way.‡

---

* Ben Clark the bookseller will give me a catalogue of all his writings.
† Ask the year and day of his imprisonments and his sicknesses and dangers.
‡ Did he gain any to him in France?

Notwithstanding those many odd adventures of his life, he has several times found favour from his majesty and also the Duke of York with divers of the nobility, and men of quality and learning in this kingdom.

His majesty owing to his father £10,000, 16— (which, with the interest of it, came not to less than £20,000) did, in consideration thereof, grant to him and his heirs a province in America which his majesty was pleased to name Pennsylvania, the fourth day of March 1681, to which he is now going this next September 1681.

His patent for Pennsylvania is from the beginning of the 40th degree to 43 degrees in latitude, and 5 degrees in longitude from Chesapeake Bay.

Edmund Wyld —two or three things, e.g. military, mighty necessary (for the settlement)—ask him for some proposals.

He speaks well the Latin and French tongues, and his own with great mastership. He often declaims in the assembles of his Friends, and that with much eloquence and fervency of spirit—by which, and his perpetual attendance on king and prince for the relief of his Friends, he often exposes his health to hazard.

He was chosen (ballotted) November 9, unopposed, admitted fellow of the Royal Society, London, with much respect.

26 August 1682, Saturday. This day about 4 o'clock p.m. W. Penn, esquire, went towards Deal to launch for Pennsylvania. God send him a prosperous and safe voyage.

Last Wednesday in August (namely 30 August 1682) about noon he took ship at Deal.

He returned into England, October (about the middle) 1684—ask the day.

W. Penn, esquire, married Gulielma Maria Springet, daughter of Sir William Springet, of the Springets of The Broyle in Sussex.

She was a posthumous daughter of her father, a young gentleman of religion and courage, who died at the siege of Arundel. His daughter was his image in person and qualities, virtuous, generous, wise, humble; generally beloved for these good qualities, and one more—the great cures she does, having great skill in physic and surgery, which she freely bestows.

She early espoused the same kind of person, about 1657. She was a great fortune to her husband, being worth a clear £10,000. Her fortune, quality, and good humour gave her the importunity of many suitors of extraordinary condition, e.g. Lord Brookes and Lord John Vaughan etc; but valuing the unity of belief and the self denial of her faith above the glories of the world, resisted their motions till Providence brought a man of equal condition and fortune to herself to the sincere embracing of the same faith, whose marriage has been crowned with a continued affection.

240

William Penn's father, was a man of excellent natural abilities, not equalled in his time for knowledge of naval affairs and instrumental to the raising of many families. Bred his son religiously; and, as the times grew loose, would have had his son of the fashion, and was therefore extremely bitter at his son's retirement. But this lasted not always; for, in the conclusion of his life, he grew not only kind, but doting; made him the judge and ruler of his family; was sorry he had no more to leave him (and yet, in England and Ireland, he left him £1500 per annum). But, which is most remarkable, he that opposed his son's way because of the opposition that was in it to the world's easy morals, did himself embrace this faith, recommending to his son the plainness and self denial of it, saying 'Keep to the plainness of your way, and you will make an end of the priests to the ends of the earth.' And so he deceased, desiring that none but his son William should close his eyes (which he did). He died aged 49 and 4 months.

Sir William Petty
1623–87

Petty is perhaps best known through the pages of Pepys' Diary. He was a largely self-made man, and owed his fortune to his success in surveying Ireland. His scientific interests were extensive, and Pepys, though he sometimes grumbled at his administrative work, delighted in his company. Like Pepys, he was a member of the Royal Society, and also of John Harrington's Rota Club at the end of the Commonwealth. He wrote a number of important papers on political economy, which mark the beginning of such studies. Aubrey called him 'my especial friend'.

His horoscope was done, and a judgement upon it, by Charles Snell esquire of Alderholt near Fordingbridge in Hampshire—'Jupiter in Cancer makes him fat at heart'. John Gadbury also says that vomits would be excellent good for him.

Sir William Petty knight was the son of Mr Petty of Rumsey in Hampshire.

His father was born on the Ash Wednesday before Mr Hobbes that is 1588; and died and was buried at Rumsey 1644, where Sir William intends to set up a monument for him. He was by profession a clothier, and also did dye his own clothes; he left little or no estate to Sir William.

He was born at his father's house aforesaid, on Monday, the twenty-sixth of May 1623, eleven hours 42′ 56″ afternoon (see scheme of astrological nativity): christened on Trinity Sunday.

Rumsey is a little haven port, but has most kinds of artificers in it: when he was a boy, his greatest delight was to be looking on the artificers, e.g. smiths, the watchmaker, carpenters, joiners, etc: and at twelve years old could have worked at any of these trades. Here he went to school, and learned by 12 years a competent smattering of Latin, and was entered into the Greek. He has had few sicknesses: about 8 in April very sick and so continued till towards Michaelmas. About 12 (or 13), i.e. before 15, he has told me, happened to him the most remarkable *accident of life* (which he did not tell me), and which was the foundation of all the rest of his greatness and acquiring riches.

He informed me that, about 15, in March, he went over into Normandy, to Caen, in a vessel that went hence, with a little stock, and began to merchandize; he began to play the merchant; and had so good success that he maintained himself, and also educated himself; this I guess was that most remarkable accident that he meant. Here he learned the French tongue, and perfected himself in the Latin, and had Greek enough to serve his turn. Here at Caen he studied the arts; at 18, he was (I have heard him say) a better mathematician than he is now: but when occasion is, he knows how to recur to more mathematical knowledge. Memorandum: he was sometime at La Fleche in the college of Jesuits. At Paris he studied anatomy, and read Vesalius with Mr Thomas Hobbes (see Mr Hobbes' life), who loved his company: Mr Hobbes then wrote his *Optics*. Sir W.P. then had a fine hand in drawing and figure-drawing, and drew Mr Hobbes' optical schemes for him which he was pleased to like. At Paris, one time, it happened that he was driven to great straits for money, and I have heard him say, that he lived a week on two pennyworth (or three, I have forgotten which, but I think the former) of walnuts. Enquire whether he was not sometimes a prisoner there?

In 1648 he came to Oxford and entered himself of Brasenose College. Here he taught anatomy to the young scholars; anatomy was then but little understood by the university; and I remember, he kept a body that he brought by water from Reading, a good while to study, some way preserved or pickled.

In 1650 happened that memorable accident and experiment of the reviving of Nan Green, which is to be ascribed and attributed to Dr William Petty, as the first discoverer of life in her, and author of saving her. Here at Oxford he lived and was beloved by all the ingenious scholars, particularly Ralph Bathurst of Trinity College (then Doctor of Physic); Dr John Wilkins, Warden of Wadham College; Seth Ward, DD, Professor of Astronomy; Dr Wood; Thomas Willis, MD etc. Memorandum:—about these times science first budded here and was cultivated by these virtuosi in that dark time.

In . . . (ask Edmund Wyld, esquire, when) the parliament sent surveyors to survey Ireland.

I remember there was a great difference between him and one of Oliver's knights about 1660. They printed one against the other. (This knight was wont to preach at Dublin.) The knight has been a soldier, and challenged Sir William to fight with him. Sir William is extremely short-sighted, and being the challengee it belonged to him to nominate place and weapon. He nominates for the place a dark cellar, and the weapon to be a great carpenter's axe. This turned the knight's challenge into ridicule, and so it came to nought.

He can be an excellent comedian (if he has a mind to it) and will preach *extempore* incomparably, either the Presbyterian way, Independent, Capucin friar, or Jesuit.

He has a natural daughter that much resembles him, no legitimate child so much, that acts at the Duke's playhouse, who has had a child by . . . about 1679. She is (1680) about 21.

The Kingdom of Ireland he has surveyed, and that with that exactness (ask Sir J.H. how), that there is no estate there to the value of threescore pounds per annum but he can show, to the value, and these that he employed for the geometrical part were ordinary fellows, some (perhaps) foot-soldiers, that circumambulated with their *box and needles*, not knowing what they did, which Sir William knew very right well how to make use of.

In 1676, March 18, he was reproved by the Lord Chancellor Finch, when the patent for the farming of Ireland* was sealed, to which Sir William would not seal. Monday, 20 March, he was affronted by Mr Vernon: Tuesday following, Sir William and his lady's brother (Mr Waller) hectored Mr Vernon and caned him.

Dr Petty was resident in Oxford 1648, 1649, and left it (if Anthony Wood is not mistaken) in 1652.

He was about 1650 (query) elected professor of music at Gresham College, by, and by the interest of, his friend Captain John Graunt (who wrote the *Observations on the Bills of Mortality*), and at that time was worth but forty pounds in all the world.

Shortly after (that is in 1652 in August), he had the patent for Ireland; he was recommended to the parliament, to be one of the surveyors of Ireland, to which employment Capt. J. Graunt's interest did also help to give him a lift, and Edmund Wyld, esquire, also, then a member of parliament, and a great patron of ingenious and good men,

---

* A grant of the tax payable in Ireland to an individual who paid the crown a fixed annual rent. *Ed.*

for mere merit's sake* (not being formerly acquainted with him) did him great service, which perhaps he knows not of. To be short, he is a person of so great worth and learning, and has such a prodigious working wit, that he is both fit for, and an honour to, the highest preferment. By this surveying employment he got an estate in Ireland (before the restoration of King Charles II) of £18,000 per annum, the greatest part whereof he was forced afterwards to refund, the former owners then declared innocents. He has still there £7 or 8,000 per annum, and can, from Mount Mangorton in the county of Kerry, behold 50,000 acres of his own land. He has an estate in every province of Ireland.

In 1667 he married on Trinity Sunday the widow of Sir Maurice Fenton, of Ireland, knight, daughter of Sir Hasdras Waller of Ireland, a very beautiful and ingenious lady, brown, with glorious eyes, by whom he has sons and daughters, very lovely children, but all like the mother.

He received the honour of knighthood in 1662.

He had his patent for Earl of Kilmore and Baron of . . . 166–, which he stifles during his life to avoid envy, but his son will have the benefit of the precedency.

I expected, that his son would have broken out a lord or earl: but it seems that he had enemies at the court of Dublin, which, out of envy, obstructed the passing of his patent.

In 1660 he came into England, and was at once received into good grace with his majesty, who was mightily pleased with his discourse.

In 1663 he made his double-bottomed vessel (launched about New Year's tide), of which he gave a model to the Royal Society made with his own hands, and it is kept in the repository at Gresham College. It did do very good service, but in 16— happened to be lost in an extraordinary storm in the Irish Sea. (Memorandum: there is yet a double-bottomed vessel in the Isle of Wight, which they say sails well: ask Capt. Lee.)

He is a person of an admirable inventive head, and practical parts. He has told me that he has read but little, that is to say, not since he was aged 25, and is of Mr Hobbes his mind, that had he read much, as some men have, he had not known as much as he does, nor should have made such discoveries and improvements.

He went towards Ireland in order to be a member of that parliament, 22 March 1680. God send him a prosperous journey.

I remember one St Andrew's Day (which is the day of the general meetings of the Royal Society for annual elections), I said, 'Methought

* Several made offers to the parliament to survey it (when the parliament ordered to have it surveyed) for £4000, £5000, £6000; but Sir William (then Dr) went *lower* than them and got it. Sir Jonas Moore condemned it as dangerous, loving to sleep in a whole skin: he was afraid of the Tories. From Edmund Wyld esquire.

'twas not so well that we should pitch on the Patron of Scotland's day, we should rather have taken St George or St Isidore' (a philosopher canonised). 'No,' said Sir William, 'I would rather have had it on St Thomas' day, for he would not believe till he had seen and put his fingers into the holes,' according to the motto *There is nothing in words*.

He has told me that he never got by legacies in his life, but only £10 which was not paid.

He has told me, that whereas some men have accidentally come into the way of preferment, by lying at an inn, and there contracting an acquaintance; on the road; or as some others* have done; he never had any such like opportunity, but hewed out his fortune himself—which N.B.

He is a proper handsome man, measured six foot high, good head of brown hair, moderately turning up: see his picture as Doctor of Physic. His eyes are a kind of goose-grey, but very short-sighted, and, as to aspect, beautiful, and promise sweetness of nature, and they do not deceive, for he is a marvellous good-natured person, and compassionate. Eyebrows thick, dark and straight (horizontal). His head is very large. He was in his youth very slender, but since these twenty years and more past he grew very plump, so that now (1680), he is sluggish. This last March, 1680, I persuaded him to sit for his picture to Mr Loggan, the graver, whom I forthwith went for myself, and he drew it just before his going into Ireland, and 'tis very like him. But about 1659, he had a picture in miniature drawn by his friend and mine, Mr Samuel Cooper (prince of portrait painters of his age) one of the likest that ever he drew.

I have heard Sir William Petty say more than once, that he knew not he was almost blind till his master† (a master of a ship) bade him climb up the rope ladder, and give notice when he espied such a steeple (somewhere upon the coast of England or France. I have forgotten where), which was a landmark for the avoiding to a shelf; at last the master saw it on the deck, and they fathomed and found they were but a few foot water, whereupon (as I remember) his master drubbed him with a cord.

Before he went into Ireland, he solicited, and no doubt he was an admirable good solicitor, I have heard him say that in soliciting (with the same pains) he could despatch several businesses, nay, better than one alone, for by conversing with several he should gain the more knowledge, and the greater interest.

In the time of the war with the Dutch, they concluded at the council-

---

* e.g. my cousin Rowland Plattes, when the Lord Cottington never having seen before, liked so well, that he made him his gentleman of the horse when he went to his embassy into Spain. This was on shipboard.

† He was first bound apprentice to a sea-captain.

board at London, to have so many seamen out of Ireland (I think 1500). Away to Ireland came one with a commission, and acquaints Sir William with it; says Sir William, 'You will never raise this number here'. 'Oh,' said the other, 'I warrant you, I will not abate you a man.' Now Sir William knew 'twas impossible, for he knew how many tons of shipping belonged to Ireland, and the rule is, to so many tons, so many men. Of these ships half were abroad, and of those at home so many men unfit. In fine, the commissioner with all his diligence could not possibly raise above 200 seamen there. So we may see how statesmen may mistake for want of this politic arithmetic.

Another time the council at Dublin were all in a great racket for the prohibition of coal from England and Wales, considering that all about Dublin is such a vast quantity of turf; so they would improve their rents, set poor men on work, and the city should be served with fuel cheaper. Sir William *prima facie* knew that this project could not succeed. Said he, 'If you will make an order to hinder the bringing in of coals by foreign vessels and bring it in vessels of your own, I approve of it very well: but for your supposition of the cheapness of turf, 'tis true 'tis cheap on the place, but consider carriage, consider the yards that must contain such a quantity for respective houses, these yards must be rented; what will be the charge?' They calculated it, and found that 'everything considered' 'twas much dearer than to fetch coal from Wales or etc.

Memorandum: about 1665 he presented to the Royal Society a discourse of his (in manuscript, of about a quire of paper) of building of ships, which the Lord Brouncker (then president) took away, and still keeps, saying ''Twas too great secret of state to be commonly perused'; but Sir William told me that Dr Robert Wood, MD, aforesaid, has a copy of it, which he himself has not; ask Dr Wood for it.

Sir William Petty died at his house in Piccadilly street (almost opposite to St James church) on Friday, 16 December 1687, of a gangrene in his foot, occasioned by the swelling of the gout, and is buried with his father and mother in the church at Rumsey in Hampshire.

My Lady Petty was created Baroness of Shelburn in Ireland, and her eldest son baron of the same, a little before the coming-in of the Prince of Orange (1688).

Sir William Petty had a brother, like him, who died *sine prole* [childless]: he has his picture. Query if I have mentioned Nan Green out of the printed narrative?

His picture by Fuller in his Dr of Medicine gown, a skull in his hand; then a spare man; wearing a little band; Vesalius' Anatomy by him. 'Twas he (Sir William) that put Fuller to draw the muscles as at Oxford Gallery [the Bodleian picture collection].

Enquire for the name of the knight his antagonist, Sir . . . . . ?

246

Answer:—'Twas Sir Hierome Sanchy that was his antagonist: against whom he wrote the octavo book, about 1662. He was one of Oliver's knights, a commander and preacher and no conjuror. He challenged Sir William to fight with him. Sir William being the challengee named the place, a dark cellar, the weapon, carpenter's great axe; so by this expedient Sir William (who is short-sighted) would be at an equal tourney with this doughty man.

Sir W. Petty was a Rota man, and troubled Mr James Harrington with his arithmetical proportions, reducing politics to numbers.

Sir William Petty wrote *A Political Anatomy of Ireland*. He assured me by letter from Dublin, 12 July 1681: 'I am not forward to print this Political Arithmetic, but do wish that what goes abroad were compared with the copy in Sir Robert Southwell's hands, which I corrected in March 1679.' He told me some years since, before the copy was dedicated to the Royal Society, that 'the doing of it will cost £50,000, but Ireland will be done'.

Sir William Petty had a boy that whistled incomparably well. He after waited on a lady, a widow, of good fortune. Every night this boy was to whistle his lady asleep. At last she could hold out no longer, but bids her chamber-maid withdraw: bids him come to bed, sets him to work, and marries him the next day. This is certain true; from himself and Mrs Grant.

Fabian Philips
1601–90

Fabian Philips—from himself, 1682—born hard by Prestbury in Gloucestershire, in 1601, in September, on Michaelmas Eve. His mother's name was Bagehot (an heir to a younger brother); his father was Andrew Philips, of an ancient family in Herefordshire, seven descents (generations), who sold £600 per annum in Herefordshire, in Leominster; some of it his son Fabian (of whom I write) bought again. He was of the Middle Temple, London; a filizer [law officer] of London, Middlesex, Cambridgeshire and Huntingdonshire of great assiduity, and reading, and a great lover of antiquities. He has a great memory, which holds still well now in his eightieth year. He told me St Augustine wrote at 90; judge Coke at 84; and bishop Hall, of Norwich, at over 80. His house is over against the middle of Lincoln's Inn garden, in Chancery Lane. Two days before King Charles I was beheaded, he wrote 'a protestation against the intended murder of the king', and printed it, and caused it to be put upon the posts [? hitching-posts in the streets]. When all the courts in Westminster Hall were voted down by Barebones Parliament, he wrote a book to justify the right use of them, and Lenthall (the speaker) and the Keepers of Liberty did send him thanks for saving of the courts.

He died the 17th of November 1690. His son will not pay for his father's epitaph to be set up. But I have spoken to his good daughter to set his name and date of death. His works 'will praise him in the gates'. [Proverbs xxxi, 31].

Old Fabian Philips has told me several times that it has cost him £800 in taking pains searching and writing to assert the king's prerogative and never got a groat. Only, when the regulation of the law was carried out, he was made one of the commissioners, which was worth £200 per annum—I think it lasted two years.

Katherine Philips
1631–64

A fashionable poetess who wrote under the pen-name 'Orinda'. Her contemporaries called her 'the matchless Orinda', but her reputation has not stood the test of time.

Orinda—From Mr J. Oxenbridge, her uncle (now prisoner in the Fleet on her account for a debt of her husband, that is, bound for him 28 years since), and Lady Montagu.

Mrs Katharine Fowler was the daughter of John Fowler of London, merchant, (an eminent merchant in Bucklersbury), and Katherine Oxenbridge, daughter of Dr Oxenbridge, MD, President of the Physicians' College—look this up in [the London] Dispensatory.

She was christened in St Mary Woolchurch. If alive now (July 1681), she might be 48 or 49.

She went to school at Hackney to Mrs Salmon, a famous schoolmistress, Presbyterian, who used Ball's catechism.* Friends: Mrs Mary Aubrey and Mrs Harvey, since Lady Deering. Loved poetry at school, and made verses there. She takes after her grandmother Oxenbridge, who was an acquaintance of Mr Francis Quarles, being much inclined to poetry herself.

Married to James Philips of the Priory at Cardigan, esquire, about 1647 (that is, the year after the army was at Putney), by whom she had one son, dead (mentioned in her book), and one daughter married to Mr Wgan, in some degree like her mother.

* A famous seventeenth century schoolbook. *Ed.*

She was very religiously devoted when she was young, prayed by herself an hour together, and took sermons down *verbatim* when she was but ten years old.

She died of the smallpox in Fleet Street. She lies buried at St Benet Shearhog at the end of Syth's Lane in London.

She was when a child much against the bishops, and prayed to God to take them to him, but afterwards was reconciled to them. Prayed aloud, as the hypocritical fashion then was, and was overheard—see Thomas Hobbes' *Civil Wars* and *Satire against Hypocrites*.

My cousin Montagu told me she had a red spotty face; wrote out verses in inns, or mottos in windows, in her table-book.

Memorandum: *La Solitude* de St Amant was translated by Mrs Katherine Philips. 'Tis 20 stanzas—I think not yet printed—I had them from Elizabeth Countess of Thanet, 1672.

She went into Ireland (after her marriage) with the Lady Dungannon (whom she calls *Lucasia*); and at Dublin she wrote *Pompey* [a tragedy].

Her husband had a good estate, but bought Crown lands [during the Commonwealth]; he mortgaged etc. His brother Hector took off the mortgages and has the lands.

From her cousin Blackett, who lived with her from her swaddling clothes to eight, and taught her to read:—She informs me viz when a child she was mighty apt to learn, and she assures me that she had read the Bible through before she was full four years old; she could have said I know not how many places of Scripture and chapters. She was a frequent hearer of sermons; had an excellent memory and could have brought away a sermon in her memory. Very good-natured; not at all proud; pretty fat; not tall; reddish faced.

Ask my cousin Montagu when she began to make verses. Ask how many children she had.

Major General Skippon was her mother's third husband.

Sir William Platers
?–1668

Sir William Platers, knight, was a Cambridgeshire (Suffolk) gentleman. He had a good estate (about £3,000 per annum). He was a very well bred gentleman, as most was of these times; had travelled France, Italy, etc. and understood well these languages. He was one of the Long Parliament in the time of the late wars.

He was a great admirer and lover of handsome women, and kept several. Henry Marten and he were great cronies, but one time (about

1644) there was some difference between them—Sir William had got away one of Henry's girls and Sir John Birkenhead inserted in the *Mercurius Aulicus** how the saints fell out. He was temperate and thrifty as to all other things.

He had only one son, who was handsome and ingenious, and whom he cultivated with all imaginable care and education, and, knowing that he was flesh and blood, took care himself to provide sound and agreeable females for him. He allowed his son liberally, but enjoined him still temperance, and to set down his expenses.

The father was a good linguist and a good antiquary. This beloved son of his dying shortened his father's days. He built the triumphal-like arch whereon the king's arms is in the partition between church and chancel at St Margaret's Westminster.

¶ Sir William Platers, knight and baronet; about £5,000 per annum. His son very ingenious, and made a very good return of his education. He was a colonel in the king's army and was killed in his service, which his father took so to heart that he enjoyed not himself afterwards.

Henry Marten, his crony, invited him to a treat, where Sir William fell in love with one of his misses and enticed her away—which Sir John Birkenhead put in the *Mercurius Aulicus*.

¶ I do not enter him here as a worthy, but he does fill a place. He was a merry man in the reign of the Saints. *Mercurius Aulicus* made a good sport with him and Henry Marten.

Sir Robert Pointz
1589–1665

Sir Robert Pointz of Iron-Acton in Gloucestershire, knight of the Bath, is the same family with Clifford (as may be seen by the pedigree), Clifford being called *de Pons* till he was lord of Clifford Castle in Herefordshire, adjoining to Breconshire.

In Henry III's reign they married with a daughter and heir of Acton, by whom they had the manor aforesaid and perhaps other lands.

Mr Player, Mr Anthony Ettrick's son-in-law, who bought this estate, June 1684, has all the old evidences and can further inform me.

¶ When I was sick of the smallpox at Trinity College, Mr Saul, who was an old servant of his, told me I think that he was of Lincoln (or, perhaps, that he lay there in the wars†).

---

* The Royalist newspaper: see p. 37 above. *Ed.*
† During the Royalist occupation of Oxford. *Ed.*

The family have had a great estate, and were men of note at court.

¶ Sir Robert, son of Sir John, Poyntz of whom I now write, and with whom I had some small acquaintance, was a loyal, sober and a learned person. His study, law; chiefly towards the civil law. Since the king's restoration he published in print, a pamphlet, about the bigness of a good play-book, entitled, *The Right of Kings* (or to that purpose; but to my best remembrance, that is the very title.†)

As I remember he told me when I was of Trinity College, Oxford, that he was of Lincoln College. He married first Grisel, one of the daughters and co-heirs of Mr Gibbons, of Kent, by whom he had only two daughters.

After her decease he had a natural son by Cicely Smyth, who had been his lady's chambermaid, whose name was John, as I remember, who married the daughter of Mr Caesar, in Herefordshire. He died without issue about four or five years since (1684) or less. So there is an end of this ancient family.

Memorandum: Newark (now the seat of Sir Gabriel Lowe) was built by Sir Robert's grandfather to keep his whores in.

Sir Thomas Pope
?1507–59

Privy councillor under Henry VIII; indirectly involved in the suppression of the monasteries. Trinity was established in the buildings of Durham College, which had belonged to the abbey of Durham.

Sir Thomas Pope, founder of Trinity College, Oxford, bought church lands* without money. His way was this. He contracted for them, and then at once sold long leases, for which he had great fines (premiums) and but a small rent. Those leases were expired in the reign of King James the first, and then the estate was worth £8000 per annum. He could have ridden in his own lands from Cogges (by Witney) to Banbury, about 18 miles.

I have a curious manuscript manual of Sir Thomas Pope, which if I so thought, would be chained in Trinity College library, I would give it there, but I know not how magistracy, etc have altered somebody.‡

† In fact it was 'A vindication of the monarchy . . .' *Ed.*
* At the Dissolution of the monasteries, in the 1540s. *Ed.*
‡ A reference to Ralph Bathurst (President of Trinity), recently appointed Vice-Chancellor. *Ed.*

Sir John Popham
?1531–1607

Lord Chief Justice from 1592–1607. He made his name as a lawyer and MP and was Speaker of the House of Commons in 1580. Aubrey's stories are largely local Wiltshire gossip about him, though the facts of the famous Littlecote murder itself are accurate enough.

Sir John Popham, Lord Chief Justice of the King's Bench, was the son of Alexander Popham of the county of Somerset.

He was of the Society of . . . . . and for several years addicted himself but little to the study of the laws, but to profligate company, and was wont to take a purse with them. His wife considered her and his condition, and at last prevailed with him to lead another life, and to stick to the study of the law; which, upon her importunity, he did, being then about thirty years old. He spoke to his wife to provide a very good entertainment for his comrades to take his leave of them; and after that day fell extremely hard to his study, and profited exceedingly. He was a strong, stout man, and could endure to sit at it day and night;* became eminent in his calling, had good practice; called to be a serjeant, then a judge; see *Origines Judiciales.*

Sir (John, I think) Dayrell, of Littlecote, in Wiltshire, having got his lady's waiting woman with child, when her labour came, sent a servant with a horse for a midwife, when he was to bring blindfold. She was brought, and laid the woman, but as soon as the child was born, she saw the knight take the child and murder it, and burnt it in the fire in the chamber. She having done her business was extraordinarily rewarded for her pains, and sent blindfold away. This horrid action did much run in her mind, and she had a desire to discover it, but knew not where 'twas. She considered with herself the time that she was riding, and how many miles might be ridden at that rate, and that it must be some great person's house, for the room was twelve feet high; and she could know the chamber if she saw it. She went to a Justice of the Peace, and search was made. The very chamber was found. The knight was brought to his trial; and to be short, the judge had this noble house, park and manor, and (I think) more, for a bribe to save his life.†

I have seen his picture; he is a huge, heavy, ugly man. He left a vast

---

* The picture of a common lawyer: He must have 'an iron head, a brazen face, and a leaden breech'.

† Sir John Popham gave sentence according to law; but being a great person and a favourite Dayrell procured a *noli prosequi* [*abandonment of proceedings*]. (Popham actually appears to have bought Littlecote late. *Ed.*)

estate to his son, Sir Francis (I think £10,000 per annum); he lived like a hog, but his son John was a great waster, and died in his father's time. He [John] was the greatest householder in England; would have at Littlecote, four or five or more lords at a time. His wife (Harvey) was worth to him, I think, £60,000, and she was as vain as he, and she said that she had brought such an estate, and she scorned to live otherwise than as high as he did; and in her husband's absence would have all the women of the county thither, and feast them, and make them drunk, as she would be herself. They both died by excess; and by luxury and cheating by their servants, there was, I think, £100,000 debt. Old Sir Francis, he lived like a hog, at Hounstreet in Somerset, all this while with a moderate pittance. Mr John would say that his wife's estate was ill-gotten, and that was the reason they prospered no better; she would say that the old judge got the estate unjustly, and thus they would reproach one another, and that with matter of truth.

I remember this epitaph was made on Mr John Popham:

> Here lies he, who, not long since,
> Kept a table like a prince,
> Till Death came, and took away.
> Then asked the old man, What's to pay?

Memorandum: at the hall in Wellington in the county of Somerset (the ancient seat of the Pophams), and which was this Sir John's, Lord Chief Justice (but enquire if he did not buy it?), did hang iron shackles, of which the tradition of the country is that, long ago, one of the Pophams (lord of this place) was taken and kept a slave by the Turks for a good while, and that by his lady's great piety, and continual prayers, he was brought to this place by an invisible power, with these shackles on his legs, which were hung up as a memorial, and continued till the house (being a garrison) was burnt. All the country people steadfastly believed the truth thereof.

¶ Lord Chief Justice Popham first brought in (i.e. revived) brick building in London (that is after Lincoln's Inn and St James's); and first set afoot the Plantations—e.g. Virginia (from Fabian Philips)—which he stocked or planted out of all the gaols of England.

Francis Potter
1594–1678

Clergyman, inventor and Fellow of the Royal Society. He supplied Aubrey with much information on alchemy and on the supernatural, as well as with accounts of his inventions.

Mr Francis Potter's father was one of the benefactors to the organ at the cathedral church at Worcester.

Francis Potter, BD, born at Mere, a little market town in Wiltshire, 'upon Trinity Sunday eve 1594, in the evening.' 'In 1625, at 10 o'clock on December 10, the mystery of the Beast was discovered'—these words I found written in his Greek Testament. He told me the notion came into his mind as he was going up stairs into his chamber at Trinity College, which was the senior fellow's chamber then (he lay with his brother Dr Hannibal Potter): this chamber is now united to the President's lodgings.

¶ Mr Francis Potter, BD, was born at the vicarage house at Mere in the county of Wilts.

His father was minister there, and also of Kilmanton in Somerset about three miles distant, and was also a prebendary of the cathedral church of Worcester. He had three sons, Hannibal, Francis, and (another). His wife's name was Horsey, of the ancient and worshipful family of the Horseys of Clifton in Dorset.

He was taught his grammar learnings by Mr Bright (the famous schoolmaster of those times) of the school at Worcester.

At 15, he went to Trinity College in Oxford, where his father (who was an Oxfordshire man born) had been a fellow. His brother Hannibal was his tutor. Here he was a commoner twenty-seven years, and was senior to all the house but Dr Kettell and his brother.

His genius lay most of all to the mechanics; he had an admirable mechanical invention, but in that dark time wanted encouragement, and when his father died (which was about 1637) he succeeded him in the parsonage of Kilmanton, worth, per annum, about £140. He was from a boy given to drawing and painting. The founder's (Sir Thomas Pope's) picture in Trinity College hall is of his copying. He had excellent notions for the raising of water; I have heard him say, that he could raise the water at Worcester with less trouble, i.e. fewer [pumps?], than there are; and that he had never seen a water-house engine, but that he could invent a better. Kilmanton is on a high hill, and the parsonage well is extraordinarily deep. There is the most ingenious and useful bucket well, that ever I saw. Now whereas some deep wells have wheels for men or dogs to go within them, here is a wheel with steps like stairs to walk on (outside the wheel) as if you were going up stairs, and an ordinary body's weight draws up a great bucket, which holds a barrel, and the two buckets are contrived so that their ropes always are perpendicular and consequently parallel, and so never interfere with one another. Now, this vast bucket would be too cumbersome to overturn, to pour out the water; and therefore he contrived a board with lifts about the sides, like a trough, to slide under the bucket when 'tis drawn up, and at the bottom of the bucket is a plug, the weight of the water jogging upon the sliding trough, the water pours out into the trough, and from thence runs into your pail, or other vessel. 'Tis extremely worth the seeing. I have taken heretofore a draught of it. I have heard him say that he would have undertaken to have brought up the water from the springs at the bottom of the hill to the town of Shaftesbury, which is on a waterless hill.

In 1625, going into his chamber, the notion of 25, the root of 666, for the root of the number of the Beast in the (Book of Revelation), came into his head; so he opposed 25 to 12, the root of 144.

When he took his degree of Bachelor of Divinity his question was *Whether the Pope was Anti-Christ.* He answered in the affirmative. In his younger years he was very apt to fall into a swoon, and so he did when he was disputing in the Divinity School upon that question.—I remember he told me that one time reading Aristotle, *On the Nature of Animals,* where he describes how that the lionesses, when great with young, and near their time of parturition, do go between two trees that grow near together, and squeeze out their young ones out of their bellies; he had such a strong idea of this, and of the pain that the lioness was in, that he fell into a swoon.

He was of a very tender constitution, and sickly most of his younger years. His manner was, when he was beginning to be sick, to *breath strongly* a good while together, which he said did emit the noxious vapours.

He was always much contemplative, and had an excellent philosophical head. He was no greatly read man; he had a competent knowledge in the Latin, Greek and Hebrew tongues, but not a critical. Greek he learned by Montanus' Interlineary Testament, after he was a man, without a grammar, and then he read Homer. He understood only common arithmetic, and never went farther in geometry than the first six books of Euclid; but he had such an inventive head, that with this foundation he was able to do great matters in the mechanics, and to solve phenomena in natural philosophy. He had but few books, which when he died were sold for fifty-six shillings, and surely no great bargain. He published nothing but his *Interpretation of the number 666*, printed at Oxford in 1642, which has been twice translated into Latin, into French, and other languages. He made that fine sun-dial with its furniture, on the north wall of the quadrangle at Trinity College, which he did by Samminitatus's book of sun-dialling (it has been gone since about 1670, and another is there put). He lived and died a bachelor. He was very hospitable, virtuous and temperate; and as I said before, very contemplative. He looked the most like a monk, or one of the pastors of the old time, that I ever saw one. He was pretty long visaged and pale clear skin, grey eye. His discourse was admirable, and all new and unvulgar. His house was as undecked as a monk's cell; yet he had there so many ingenious inventions that it was very delightful. He had a pretty contrived garden there, where are the finest box hedges that ever I saw. The garden is a good large square; the middle is a good high mount, all fortified (as you may say) and adorned with these hedges, which at the interstices have a high pillar (square cut) of box that shows very stately both summer and winter.

On the buttery-door in his parlour he drew his father's picture at length, with his book (foreshortened), and on the spectacles in his hand is the reflection of the Gothic south window. I mention this picture the rather, because in process of time it may be mistaken by translation for his son Francis's picture, author of the book aforesaid.

I never have enjoyed so much pleasure, nor ever so much pleased with such philosophical and hearty entertainment as from him. His book was in the press at Oxford, and he there, when I was admitted of the College, but I had not the honour and happiness to be acquainted with him till 1649 (Epiphany), since which time I had close friendship with him to his death, and correspond frequently with him. I have all his letters by me, which are very good, and I believe near 200, and most of them philosophical.

I have many excellent good notes from him as to mechanics, etc., and I never was with him but I learned, and always took notes; but now indeed the Royal Society has outdone most of his things, as having a better apparatus, and more spare money. I have a curious design of his to draw a landscape or perspective (1656), but Sir Christopher Wren has fallen on the same principle, and the device is better worked. He was smith and carpenter enough to serve his turn, but he did not pretend to skill in each. He gave me a quadrant in copper, and made me another in silver, of his own projection, which serves for all latitudes. He showed me, 1649, the best way of making an arch was a parabola with a chain; so he took off his girdle from his cassock, and applied it to the wall to demonstrate.

He invented and made with his own hands a pair of beam compasses, which will divide an inch into a hundred or a thousand parts. At one end of the beam is a roundel, which is divided into a hundred parts, with a centre bar to turn about it with a handle: this handle turns a screw of a very fine thread, and on the back of the sail or beam is a graduation. With these compasses he made the quadrants aforesaid. He gave me a pair of these compasses, which I showed to the Royal Society at their first institution, which they well liked, and I presented them as a rarity to my honoured friend, Edmund Wyld Esq. There are but two of them in the world.

Memorandum that at the Epiphany, 1649, when I was at his house, he then told me his notion of curing diseases, etc, by transfusion of blood* out of one man into another, and that the hint came into his head reflecting on Ovid's story of Medea and Jason,† and that this was a matter of ten years before that time. About a year after, he and I went to try the experiment, but 'twas on a hen, and the creature too little and our tools not good; I then sent him a surgeon's lancet. I received a letter from him concerning this subject, which many years since I showed, and was read and entered in the books of the Royal Society, for Dr Lower would have arrogated the invention to himself, and now one Griffith, doctor of physic, of Richmond, is publishing a book of the transfusion of the blood, and desires to insert Mr Potter's letter.

In 166– he was chosen fellow of the Royal Society, and was there admitted and received with much respect.

As he was never a strong man, so in his later times he had his health best, only about four or five years before his death his eyesight was bad, and before he died quite lost.

Memorandum: he played at chess as well as most men. Col. Bishop, his contemporary at Trinity College, is accounted the best of England. I have heard Mr Potter say that they two have played at Trinity College (I think two days together) and neither got the mastery. Memorandum: he would say that he looked upon the play at chess as very fit to be learned and practised by young men, because it would make them to have a foresight and be of use to them (by consequence) in their ordering of human affairs. Which N.B.

He has told me that he had oftentimes dreamt that he was at Rome, and being in fright that he should be seized on and brought before the pope, did wake with the fear.‡

'Twas pity that such a delicate inventive wit should be staked to a private preferment in an obscure corner (where he lacked ingenious conversation) from whence men rarely emerge to higher preferment, but contract a moss on them like an old fence in an orchard for want of ingenious conversation, which is a great want even to the deepest thinking men (as Mr Hobbes has often said to me).

The last time I saw this honoured friend of mine, October 1674. I had not seen him in three years before, and his shortsightedness then was come even to blindness, which did much grieve me to behold. He had let

* Memorandum: Mr Meredith Lloyd tells me that Libavius speaks of transfusion of blood, which I dare swear Mr F. Potter never saw in his life.

† In which Medea rejuvenates Jason's aged father Aeson by draining his blood and filling his veins with a magic potion (Metamorphoses, VII, 240 ff) Ed.

‡ Pope . . . (against whom Robert Grosseteste, bishop of Lincoln, wrote) dreamt that the bishop of Lincoln came to him, and gave him a great blow over the face with his staff.

his beard be uncut, which was wont to be but little. I asked him why he did not get some kinswoman or kinsman of his to live with him, and look to him now in his great age? He answered me that he had tried that way, and found it not so well; for they did begrudge what he spent that was too much and went from them, whereas his servants (strangers) were kind to him and took care of him.

In the troublesome times 'twas his happiness never to be sequestered. He was once maliciously informed against to the Committee at Wells (a thing very common in those times). When he came before them, one of them (I have forgotten his name) gave him a pint of wine, and gave him great praise, and bade him go home, and fear nothing.

William Prynne
1600–69

A militant puritan, Prynne's chief weapon was the political pamphlet, of which he wrote large numbers from 1627 onwards. His attack on stage plays as immoral was published in 1632, but passages in it were taken as referring to the queen, who had appeared in court masques, and he was savagely punished by a fine, the loss of both ears in the pillory, and life imprisonment. He continued to write from prison, and was released in 1642 by the House of Commons. After the execution of Archbishop Laud in 1645, Prynne turned his attacks to the extreme independent sects, who denied any state control of religion. He then attacked the army and was imprisoned again. His pamphleteering continued, with little effect, until the Restoration, when his writings and speeches favoured the return of the king. He did good work as keeper of the records at the Tower from 1661 to 1669. His total publications were about 200 in number: Anthony Wood reckoned that he wrote a page for every day of his adult life.

Memorandum: Sir John Birkenhead and Mr Prynne were always antagonists in the parliament house.

William Prynne, esquire, was born (as his nephew George Clarke assures me; enquire further about this) at Aust in Gloucestershire, where his father had an estate. I find by the heralds' books that he is descended of an ancient family. His father, and also he, lived at Swanswick, a pleasant seat in Somerset, about three miles from Bath, where his grandfather, Sherston, his mother's father, lived and had been mayor, and a very wise magistrate; here he learned his grammar-learning. He was of Oriel College in Oxford, where I think he took the degree of MA. From hence, was admitted of Lincoln's Inn. He was always temperate and a very hard student, and he had a prodigious memory.

In 1637 he was stigmatised* in the pillory, and then banished to Mount Orgueil in Jersey, where he was very civilly treated by the governor, Carteret, a very ancient family in that island. In 1640 he was with Burton and Bastwyck, called home by the parliament, and hundreds met him and them, out of London, some miles. He was a learned man, of immense reading, but is much blamed for his unfaithful quotations. His manner of study was thus: he wore a long quilt cap, which came two or rather three at least inches, over his eyes, which served him as an umbrella to defend his eyes from the light. About every three hours his man was to bring him a roll and a pot of ale to rekindle his wasted spirits. So he studied and drank, and munched some bread; and this maintained him till night; and then he made a good supper. Now he did well not to dine, which breaks off one's fancy, which will not presently [at once] be regained; and 'tis with invention as a flux—when once it is flowing, it runs strongly; if it is checked, flows but drop by drop: and the like for perspiration—check it, and 'tis spoiled.

> Thou that with ale or viler liquors,
> Didst inspire Wythers, Prynne, and vicars†
> And teach, though it were in despite
> Of nature and the stars, to write . . . etc.
> *Hudibras*; part 1st.

He was burgess of the city of Bath, before and since the king's restoration. He was also Keeper of the Records in the Tower of London.

He endured several imprisonments for the king's cause, and was (really) very instrumental in his restoration.

Upon the opening of the parliament, viz letting in the secluded members, he girt on his old long rusty sword (longer than ordinary). Sir William Waller marching behind him (as he went to the House), W. Prynne's long sword ran between Sir William's short legs, and threw him down, which caused laughter.

He was of a strange saturnine complexion. Sir C.W. said once, that he had the countenance of a witch.

---

* His ears were not quite cut off, only the upper part, his tips were visible. Bishop William Laud, Archbishop of Canterbury, was much blamed for being a spectator, when he was his judge.

† He was one of the assembly of divines and triers.

Robert Pugh
1609–79

Roman Catholic writer and pamphleteer.

Captain Pugh, my acquaintance, a writer and a poet. Bred as a Jesuit; but turned out because he was a captain, viz in the late wars.

He has a Latin poem, printed, which will be augmented; and printed a book against Dr Bates' *Review of recent motions*.

¶ He was born of a good family in Penrhyn in North Wales. He was educated at St Omer. When his study was searched, his orders were there found, and also a letter from the queen-mother, whose confessor he had sometimes been, to the king, that, if he should fall into any danger of the law, upon sight of that letter he should obtain his majesty's pardon.

¶ My honoured friend, captain Robert Pugh, died in Newgate on January 22, 1679, Wednesday night, 12 o'clock.

He wrote a book, which is almost finished, 'Of the several states and governments which have been here since the troubles', in the earl of Castlemaine's hands.

All his books were seized on; amongst others his almanac, wherein he entered all the vices of Charles II, which was carried to the council board (the King's council of state): but, as I have said, the earl of Castlemaine has got the former-mentioned treatise.

William Radford
1623–73

(From a letter to Anthony Wood) William Radford, my good friend and old acquaintance and fellow colleger, ended his days at Richmond, where he taught school, fourteen days since. I was with him when he first took [to] his bed.

And when I was sick of the smallpox at Trinity College, Oxford, he was so kind as to come to me every day and spend several hours, or I think melancholy would have spoiled a scurvy antiquary. He was recounting not many days before he died your brother Ned's voyage and Mr Mariett's to London on foot.

Sir Walter Raleigh

?1552–1618

Raleigh's rapid rise to favour, followed by his exploits as a privateer and attempts to colonise America, made him a legend in his own lifetime; and this legendary aspect was enhanced by his sacrifice to political ends on a trumped-up charge of treason when James I wished to make peace with Spain. Aubrey's stories reflect his heroic qualities embellished in some of the details, especially in the stories of his sexual prowess. His fall from Elizabeth's favour was certainly occasioned by his seduction of one of her maids-of-honour, and nothing he could do could regain him his former place. His pride and unscrupulousness had earned him many enemies, and he was known to be an enemy of James I. He was convicted of treason in 1603, but released in 1615; on the failure of his expedition to South America, he was executed (on the sentence passed in 1603) in 1618.

He was a tall, handsome, and bold man; but his blemish was that he was damnably proud. Old Sir Robert Harley of Brampton-Brian castle, who knew him, would say 'twas a great question who was the proudest, Sir Walter, or Sir Thomas Overbury, but the difference that there was, was judged on Sir Thomas's side.

He had two wives. His first was Elizabeth Throckmorton; second, mother of Carew Raleigh, second son.

Sir Carew Raleigh, of Downton in Wiltshire, was his eldest* brother who was gentleman of the horse to Sir John Thynne of Longleat, and after his death married his lady; by whom he had children as in the pedigree.

I have heard my grandfather say that Sir Carew had a delicate clear voice, and played singularly well on the olpharion† (which was the instrument in fashion in these days), to which he did sing.

His grandchildren, Walter and Tom (with whom I went to school at Blandford in Dorset 4 years) had also excellent tuneable voices, and played their parts well on the viol; ingenious, but all proud and quarrelsome.

Sir Walter Raleigh was of Oxford; see Anthony Wood's *Antiquities* on this.

Sir Walter Raleigh was of Oriel College. Mr Child's father of Worcestershire was his chamber-fellow, and lent him a gown, which he could never get, nor satisfaction for it—from Mr Child.

---

* They (Walter and Tom, his grandchildren) say that Sir Carew was the *elder knight*.
† 'Tis as big as a lute, but flat-bellied, with wire strings [a type of guitar?].

He went into Ireland, where he served in the wars, and showed much courage and conduct, but‡ he would be perpetually differing with (I think, Gray) then lord deputy, so that at last the hearing to be at council table before the queen, which was that he desired; where he told his tale so well and with so good a grace and presence that the queen took especial notice of him and at once preferred him. So that it must be before this that he served in the French wars.

He was a second to the Earl of Oxford in a duel. He was acquainted and accepted with all the heroes of our nation in his time.

Sir Walter Long, of Draycot (grandfather to this old Sir James Long) married a daughter of Sir John Thynne, by which means, and their consimility of disposition, there was a very conjunct friendship between the two brothers (Sir Carew and Sir Walter) and him; and old John Long, who then waited on Sir W. Long, being one time in the Privy Garden with his master, saw the Earl of Nottingham wipe the dust from Sir Walter R.'s shoes with his cloak, in compliment.

In the great parlour at Downton, at Mr Raleigh's is a good piece (an original) of Sir W. in a white satin doublet, all embroidered with rich pearls, and a mighty rich chain of great pearls about his neck, and the old servants have told me that the pearls were near as big as the painted ones. He had a most remarkable aspect, an exceeding high forehead, long faced, and sour eye-lidded, a kind of pig-eye.

N.B. At an obscure tavern, in Drury Lane (a bailiff's) is a good picture of this worthy, and also of others of his time; taken upon some execution [of a writ for distraint] (I suppose) formerly.

I have heard my grandmother say that when she was young, they were wont to talk of this rebus [word puzzle], viz

> The enemy to the stomach, and the word of disgrace
> Is the name of the gentleman with the bold face.*

His beard turned up naturally.

He was the first that brought tobacco into England.—In our part of North Wilts, e.g. Malmesbury hundred, it came first into fashion by Sir Walter Long.

I have heard my grandfather Lyte say that one pipe was handed from man to man round about the table. They had first silver pipes; the ordinary sort made use of a walnutshell and a straw.

It was sold then for its weight in silver. I have heard some of our old yeomen neighbours (Josias Taylor) say that when they went to Malmesbury or Chippenham market, they culled out their biggest shillings to lay in the scales against tobacco.

---

‡ Ask, for more details, Mr Justice Ball.
* Raw + lye (lie) = Rawlye (Raleigh). *Ed.*

Sir Walter Raleigh, standing in a stand† at Sir Robert Poyntz's park at Acton, made the ladies quit it till he had done.

Within these 35 years 'twas scandalous for a divine to take tobacco. Now the customs of it are the greatest his majesty hath.

Rider's Almanac (1682, that is)—'since tobacco brought into England by Sir Walter Raleigh, 99 years, the custom whereof is now the greatest of all others and amounts to yearly . . .'

¶ Mr Michael Weekes, registrar of the Royal Society and an officer of the custom house, does assure me, out of the custom house books, that the custom of tobacco over all England is £400,000 per annum.

Sir Walter Raleigh was a great chemist; and amongst some manuscript formulae, I have seen some secrets from him. He studied most in his sea voyages, where he carried always a trunk of books along with him, and had nothing to divert him.

Memorandum: he made an excellent cordial, good in fevers etc; Mr Robert Boyle has the recipe, and makes it and does great cures by it.

A person so much immersed in action all along and in fabrication of his own fortunes (till his confinement in the Tower), could have but little time to study, but what he could spare in the morning. He was no slug; without doubt he had a wonderful waking spirit, and great judgement to guide it.

Durham House was a noble palace; after he came to his greatness he lived there, or in some apartment of it. I well remember his study, which was a little turret that looked into and over the Thames, and had the prospect which is pleasant perhaps as any in the world, and which not only refreshes the eye-sight but cheers the spirits, and (to speak my mind) I believe enlarges an ingenious man's thoughts.

Sherborne Castle, park, manor, etc did belong (and still ought to belong) to the Church of Salisbury. 'Twas alienated; then Sir W.R. begged it as a boon from Queen Elizabeth; where he built a delicate lodge in the park, of brick, not big, but very convenient for the bigness, a place to retire from the Court in summertime, and to contemplate etc. Upon his attainder, 'twas begged by the favourite, Carr, Earl of Somerset, who forfeited it (I think) about the poisoning of Sir Thomas Overbury. Then John, Earl of Bristol, had it given him for his good service in the embassy in Spain, and added two wings to Sir Walter Raleigh's lodge. In short and indeed 'tis a most sweet and pleasant place and site as any in the west, perhaps none like it.

In his youth his companions were boisterous blades, but gradually those that had wit; except otherwise upon design to get them engaged for him—e.g. Sir Charles Snell, of Kington Saint Michael in North Wilts, my good neighbour, an honest young gentleman, but kept a

† Perhaps an arbour or summer-house? *Ed.*

perpetual sot, he engaged him to build a ship (the *Angel Gabriel*) for the design for Guiana, which cost him the manor of Yatton Keynell, the farm at Easton Piers, Thornhill and the church-lease of Bishops Cannings; which ship, upon Sir Walter Raleigh's attainder, was forfeited. No question he had other such young gentlemen.

From Dr John Pell: In his youthful time, was one Charles Chester, that often kept company with his acquaintance; he was a bold impertinent fellow, and they could never be at quiet because of him; a perpetual talker, and made a noise like a drum in a room. So one time at a tavern Sir W.R. beats him and seals up his mouth (i.e. his upper and nether beard) with hard wax. From him Ben Jonson takes his Carlo Buffono (i.e. 'jester') in *Every Man out of his Humour*.

I have now forgotten (see *History*) whether Sir Walter was not for the putting of Mary Queen of Scots, to death; I think, yes. But besides that, at a consultation at Whitehall, after Queen Elizabeth's death, how matters were to be ordered and what ought to be done, Sir Walter Raleigh declared his opinion, 'twas the wisest way to keep the government in their own hands, and set up a commonwealth, and not be subject to a needy beggarly nation. It seems that there were some of this plot who kept not this so secret but that it came to King James's ear; who where the English nobility met and received him, being told upon their presentment to his majesty their names, when Sir Walter Raleigh's name was told, 'Raleigh', said the king, 'On my soul, mon, I have heard *rawly** of thee.' He was such a person (every way) that (as King Charles I says of the Lord Strafford) a prince would rather be afraid of than ashamed of. He had that awfulness and ascendancy in his aspect over other mortals, that the king . . .

It was a most stately sight, the glory of that reception of his majesty, where the nobility and gentry were in exceeding rich equipage, having enjoyed a long peace under the most excellent of queens; and the company was so exceeding numerous that their respect carried a secret dread with it. King James did not inwardly like it, and with an inward envy said that, though so and so (as before),† he doubted not but he should have been able on his own strength (should the English have kept him out) been able to have dealt with them, and get his right.‡ Said Sir Walter Raleigh to him 'Would to God that had been put to trial.' 'Why do you wish that?' said the king.—'Because,' said Sir Walter, 'that then you would have known your friends from your foes.' But that reason of Sir Walter was never forgotten nor forgiven.

Old Major§ Stansby of Hampshire, a most intimate friend and neigh-

---

* Rarely, i.e. special things about you. *Ed.*
† Despite the riches of the English . . . *Ed.*
‡ From Dr Whistler.
§ Ask Sir R. Henley, if not colonel.

bour and contemporary of the late Earl of Southampton (lord treasurer), told me from his friend, the earl, that as to the plot and business about the Lord Cotham, etc he being then governor of Jersey, would not fully, or etc, do things unless they would go to his island and there advise and resolve about it; and that really and indeed Sir Walter's purpose was when he had them there, to have betrayed them and the plot, and to have then delivered them up to the king‖ and made his peace.

As for his noble design in Guiana, see the printed books. See a Latin voyage which John, Lord Vaughan, showed me, where is mention of Captain North (brother to the Lord North) who went with Sir Walter, where is a large account of these matters. Mr Edmund Wyld knew him¶ and says he was a learned and sober gentleman and good mathematician, but if you happened to speak of Guiana he would be strangely passionate, and say 'twas 'the blessedst country under the sun' etc, reflecting on the spoiling of that brave design.

Queen Elizabeth loved to have all the servants of her Court proper men, and (as beforesaid Sir W.R.'s graceful presence was no mean recommendation to him), I think his first preferment at Court was captain of her majesty's guard. There came a country gentleman (or sufficient yeoman) up to town, who had several sons, but one an extraordinary proper handsome fellow, whom he did hope to have preferred to be a yeoman of the guard. The father (a goodly man himself) comes to Sir Walter Raleigh a stranger to him, and told him that he had brought up a boy that he would desire (having many children) should be one of her majesty's guard. Quoth Sir Walter Raleigh, 'Had you spoken for yourself, I should readily have granted your desire, for your person deserves it, but I put in no boys.' Said the father, 'Boy, come in.' The son enters, about 18 or 19, but such a goodly proper young fellow, as Sir Walter Raleigh had not seen the like—he was the tallest of all the guard. Sir Walter swears him immediately; and ordered him to carry up the first dish at dinner, where the queen beheld him with admiration,* as if a beautiful young giant had stalked with the service.

In his youth for several years (ask Anthony Wood how long) he was under straits for want of money. I remember that Mr Thomas Child of Worcestershire told me that Sir Walter borrowed a gown of him when he was at Oxford (they were both of the same college), which he never restored, nor money for it.

He loved a wench well; and one time getting up one of the maids of honour up against a tree in a wood ('twas his first lady) who seemed at

‖ Sir Walter was governor of Jersey in 1601: hence, correctly, queen. *Ed.*
¶ Captain North. *Ed.*
* Like Saul, taller by the head and shoulders than other men.

first boarding to be something fearful of her honour, and modest, she cried, 'Sweet Sir Walter, what do you ask me? Will you undo me? Nay sweet Sir Walter! Sweet Sir Walter! Sir Walter!' At last as the danger and the pleasure at the same time grew higher, she cried in the ecstasy 'Swisser Swatter Swisser Swatter.' She proved with child, and I doubt not but this hero took care of them both, as also that the product was more than an ordinary mortal.

When he was arrested by the officer about the business which cost him his head, he was carried in a wherry, I think only with two men. King James was wont to say that he was a coward to be so taken and conveyed, for else he might easily have made his escape from so slight a guard.

He was prisoner in the Tower (how many?) years; ask where his lodgings were? He there (besides his compiling his *History of the World*) studied chemistry. The Earl of Northumberland was prisoner at the same time, who was the patron to Mr Harriot and Mr Warner, two of the best mathematicians then in the world, as also Mr Hughes author of *On Globes*. Serjeant Hoskins (the poet) was a prisoner there too.

I heard my cousin Whitney say that he saw him in the Tower. He had a velvet cap laced, and a rich gown, and trunk hose.

At the end of *History of the World*, he laments the death of the most noble and most hopeful Prince Henry, whose great favourite he was, and who, had he survived his father, would quickly have enlarged him, with rewards of honour. So upon the prince's death ends his first part of his *History of the World*, with a gallant eulogy of him, and concludes *My harp also is turned to mourning, and my organ into the voice of them that weep*.* He had an outline for the second part, which he, in discontent, burnt, and said, 'If I am not worthy of the world, the world is not worthy of my works.'

He was sometimes a poet, not often. Before Spenser's *Faery Queene* is a good set of verses, which begins thus:

Methinks I see the grave where Laura lay;

at the bottom W.R.: which, 36 years since, I was told were his.

His intimate acquaintances and friends were: Edward de Vere Earl of Oxford, Sir Francis Vere. Sir Horatio Vere. Sir Francis Drake. Nicholas Hill, Thomas Cavendish. Mr Thomas Harriot. Sir Walter Long, of Draycot in Wiltshire. Cavaliero Surff, etc. Ben Jonson. When Serjeant Hoskyns was a prisoner in the Tower, he was Sir Walter's critic and editor.

See Lord Bacon's sayings and letters. As the queen Elizabeth was

* *Job* xxx, 31.

playing on the virginals, someone made this observation, that 'when *Jack*'s went up, *keys* went down,' reflecting on Raleigh.

Old Sir Thomas Malet, one of the Justices of the King's Bench in the time of Charles I and II, knew Sir Walter; and I have heard him say that, notwithstanding his so great mastership in style and his conversation with the learnedst and politest persons, yet he spoke broad Devonshire to his dying day. His voice was small, as likewise were my schoolfellows', his grandnephews.

He was scandalously accused with atheism; but he was a bold man, and would venture at discourse which was unpleasant to the churchmen. I remember the first Lord Scudamore said "'twas basely said of Sir W.R., to talk of *the anagram of Dog*'. In his speech on the scaffold, I heard my cousin Whitney say (and I think 'tis printed) that he spoke not one word of Christ, but of the great and incomprehensible God, with much zeal and adoration, so that he concluded he was an a-Christ [agnostic] not an atheist. He took* a pipe of tobacco a little before he went to the scaffold, which some formal persons were scandalised at, but I think 'twas well and properly done, to settle his spirits.

I remember I heard old father Symonds (of the Jesuits) says, that a father was at his execution, and that to his knowledge he died with a lie in his mouth: I have now forgotten what it was. The time of his execution was contrived to be on my Lord Mayor's day (viz the day after St Simon and St Jude) 1618, that the pageants and fine shows might draw away the people from beholding the tragedy of one of the gallantest worthies that ever England bred.

Mr Elias Ashmole told me that his son Carew Raleigh told him he had his father's skull; that some years since, upon digging up the grave, his skull and neckbone being viewed, they found the bone of his neck lapped over so, that he could not have been hanged. Ask Sir John Elowys for the skull, who married Mr Carew Raleigh's daughter and heir.

'Twas Sir Walter Raleigh's epigram on Robert Cecil, Earl of Salisbury, who died in a ditch three or four miles west from Marlborough, returning from Bath to London, which was printed in an octavo book about 1656 (perhaps one of Mr Osborne's):

> Here lies Robert, our shepherd whilere,
> Who once in a quarter our fleeces did sheer:
> For his oblation to Pan his manner was thus,
> He first gave a trifle, then offered up us
> . . . .
> In spite of the tarbox he dyed of the shabbo†

---

* [From] J. Stone, I think.

† This continues the shepherding metaphor—shabbo or scab is a skin disease of sheep, cured by the application of tar. *Ed.*

This I had from old Sir Thomas Malett, one of the Judges of the King's Bench, who knew Sir Walter Raleigh, and did remember these passages.

He was governor of Jersey (Caesaria).

> *On Sir Walter Raleigh*
> Here lieth, hidden in this pit,
> The wonder of the world for wit.
> It to small purpose him did serve;
> His wit could not his life preserve.
> He living, was beloved of none;
> Yet in his death all did him moan.
> Heaven hath his soul, the world his fame,
> The grave his corpse, Stukley his shame.

This I found among the papers of my honoured friend and neighbour Thomas Tyndale, esquire, who died in 167– aged 85. This Stukley was . . .*

His book sold very slowly at first, and the bookseller complained of it, and told him that he should be a loser by it, which put Sir W. into a passion; and said that since the world did not understand it, they should not have his second part, which he took and threw into the fire, and burnt before his face.†

Mr Elias Ashmole says that Diggory Wheare in his *Winter Lectures* gives him an admirable encomium, and prefers him before all other historians.

¶ I have heard old Major Cosh say that Sir W. Raleigh did not care to go on the Thames on a wherry boat: he would rather go round about over London Bridge.

¶ My old friend James Harrington, esquire (Oceana) was well acquainted with Sir Benjamin Ruddyer, who was an acquaintance of Sir Walter Raleigh's. He told Mr J.H. that Sir Walter Raleigh being invited to dinner to some great person where his son was to go with him, he said to his son 'Thou art expected today at dinner to go along with me, but thou art such a quarrelsome, affronting . . . that I am ashamed to have such a bear in my company.' Mr Walter humbled himself to his father, and promised he would behave himself mighty mannerly. So away they went (and Sir Benjamin, I think, with them). He sat next to his father and was very demure at least half dinner time. Then said he, 'I, this morning, not having the fear of God before my eyes but by the instigation of the devil, went to a whore. I was very eager of her, kissed and embraced her, and went to enjoy her, but she thrust me from her, and vowed I should not, "For your father lay with

---

* Enquire who this Stukley was.
† From his grand nephews, my school-fellows.

me but an hour ago".' Sir Walt, being so strangely surprised and put out of his countenance at so great a table, gives his son a damned blow over the face. His son, as rude as he was, would not strike his father, but strikes over the face the gentleman that sat next to him and said 'Box about: 'twill come to my father anon.' 'Tis now a common-used proverb.

¶ A copy* of Sir W. Raleigh's letter, sent to Mr Duke, in Devon, written with his own hand.

Mr Duke

I wrote to Mr Prideaux to move you for the purchase of Hayes,† a farm sometime in my father's possession. I will most willingly give whatsoever in your conscience you shall deem it worth, and if at any time you shall have occasion to use me, you shall find me a thankful friend to you and yours. I am resolved, if I cannot persuade you, to build at Colliton; but for the natural disposition I have to that place, being born in that house, I had rather seat myself there than anywhere else; I take my leave, ready to reciprocate all your courtesies to the uttermost of my power.

Your very willing friend, in all I shall be able

Walter Raleigh

Court, the xxvi of July, 1584

¶ Sir John Elowys married the daughter and heir of Sir Walter Raleigh, who was the son of Carew Raleigh of Surrey, who was the son of Sir Walter Raleigh, the hero. Ask Sir John Elowys for his skull for Oxford or the Royal Society.

> ¶ Even such is time, which takes in trust
> Our youth, our joys, and all we have,
> And pays us but with age and dust.
> Within the dark and silent grave,
> When we have wandered all our ways,
> Shuts up the story of our days.
> But from which grave and earth and dust
> The Lord will raise me up I trust.

These lines Sir Walter Raleigh wrote in his Bible, the night before he was beheaded, and desired his relations with these words, viz 'Beg my dead body, which living is denied you; and bury it either in Sherborne or Exeter church.'‡

¶ I am promised the *very original* examination of Sir Walter Raleigh, in the Tower, by Lord Chancellor Bacon, George Abbot (Archbishop of

* I think I sent the original to Anthony Wood.
† Hayes is in the parish of East Budleigh. His father had 80 years this farm of Hayes, and wrote 'esquire'.
‡ Aubrey finally found his grave in St Margaret's Westminster. *Ed.*

Canterbury), and Sir Edward Coke, under their own hands, to insert in my book.

An attorney's father (that did my business in Herefordshire before I sold it [my estate there]) married Dr Burhill's widow. She said that he [Burhill] was a great favourite of Sir Walter Raleigh's (and, I think, had been his chaplain), but all or the greatest part of the drudgery of his books, for criticisms, chronology, and reading of Greek and Hebrew authors, was performed by him for Sir Walter Raleigh, whose picture my friend has as part of the doctor's goods.

¶ Sir Walter Raleigh's eldest son, Walter, by his first wife, was killed in America, as you may find in the *History of the World*.

My cousin Whitney was coetanean (contemporary) with this Walter Raleigh at Oxford. I have now forgotten of what house he was of: but I remember he told me that he was a handsome lusty stout fellow, very bold, and apt to affront. Spoke Latin very fluently; and was a notable disputant and courser, and would never be out of countenance or baffled; fought lustily; and, one time of coursing, put a turd in the box, and besmeared it about his antagonist's face.

Walter Raleigh, Carew Raleigh's son, Sir Walter's grandson was knighted by King Charles II at the same time when Sir Thomas Overbury was, and some wished that they might both have better fortunes than the other Sir Walter Raleigh and the other Sir Thomas Overbury.

Thomas Randolph
1605–35

Poet and dramatist, protégé of Ben Jonson.

Thomas Randolph, the poet, Cambridge:—I have sent to A. a Wood his nativity etc which I had from his brother John, an attorney, viz Thomas Randolph was the eldest son of William Randolph by his wife Elizabeth Smyth; he was born at Newnham near Daventry in Northamptonshire, June 15, 1605.

At the age of nine years, he wrote the history of our Saviour's incarnation in English verse, which his brother John has to show under his own handwriting—never printed, kept as a rarity.

From Mr Needler: his hair was of a very light flaxen (colour), almost white (like J. Scroope's). It was flaggy, as by his picture before his book appears. He was of a pale ill complexion and pock-pitten—from Mr

Thomas Fludd, his schoolfellow at Westminster, who says he was of about my stature or scarce so tall.

His father was steward to Sir George Goring in Sussex. He had been very wild in his youth; and his father (i.e. grandfather to Thomas Randolph) left him but a groat or threepence in his will, which when he received he nailed to the post of the door. His father was a surveyor of land, i.e. a land measurer.

In 1623 he was elected to Trinity College in Cambridge.

He (once) encountered captain Stafford (an ingenious gentleman and the chief of his family, and out of which the great Duke of Buckingham branched [was descended], on the road. He gave him a pension of I think £100 per annum, and he was tutor to his son and heir.

He was very precocious, and had he lived but a little longer would have outlived his fame.

He died in the twenty-eighth year of his age at Mr Stafford's, Blatherwycke, aforesaid.

Eleanor Radcliffe
Countess of Sussex, ?–1666

Countess of Sussex: a great and sad example of the power of lust and slavery of it. She was as great a beauty as any in England and had a good wit. After her lord's death (he was jealous) she sends for one formerly her footman, and makes him groom of the chamber. He had the pox and she knew it; a damnable sot. He was not very handsome, but his body of an exquisite shape [hence the arrows of love]. His nostrils were stuffed and borne out with corks in which were quills to breath through. About 1666 this countess died of the pox.

Edmund Rich
?1170–1240

Edmund Rich was a teacher at Oxford and a preacher before becoming archbishop of Canterbury in 1234. His time as archbishop was troubled, and he died in exile in France. He was canonised in 1248, largely at the insistence of Louis IX of France.

271

Seth Ward, lord bishop of Salisbury, tells me that he finds Saint Edmund was born at Abingdon. He was archbishop of Canterbury. He built the college at Salisbury, by St Edmund's church; it is now Judge Wyndham's son's house. He resigned his archbishopric and came and retired hither. In St Edmund's church here were windows of great value. Gondomar (the Spanish ambassador) offered a good sum for them; I have forgotten what. In one of them was the picture of God the Father, like an old man (as the fashion was) which much offended Mr Shervill, the recorder, who in zeal (but without knowledge) clambered up on the pews to break the window, and fell down and broke his leg (about 1629); but that did not excuse him for being questioned in the Star Chamber for it. Mr Attorney Noy was his great friend, and showed his friendship there. But what Mr Shervill left undone, the soldiers since have gone through with, that there is not a piece of glass-painting left.

Sir John Rocklington

Concerning furzecutters: Bryanston by Blandford in Dorset was, in Henry VIII's time, belonging to (Sir John, I think) Rocklington. He had a fair estate, and no child, and there was a poor cottager whose name was Rogers that had a pretty wife whom this knight did visit and had a mind to have a child by her. As he did suppose, he afterwards had; and in consideration of affection, etc, settled his whole estate on this young Rogers. William, lord marquis Hartford (duke of Somerset), was son of the granddaughter of this Rogers.

This present lord Roberts of Truro (now earl of Radnor) his grand-father (or great-grandfather) was a furze cutter in Cornwall—which I have heard old parson Wodenote of Linkinhorne in Cornwall say many times.

Henry Rolle
?1589–1656

Lord chief justice under the commonwealth from 1649–56.

I remember about 1646 (or 1647) that Mr John Maynard (now Sir John, and serjeant) came into the Middle Temple hall, from Westminster Hall, weary with business, and hungry, when we had newly dined. He sat down by Mr Bennet Hoskyns (the only son of serjeant Hoskyns the poet), since baronet, and some others; who having made an end of their commons, fell into various discourse, and what was the meaning of the text (Romans 5.7) 'For a just man one would dare to die; but for a good man one would willingly die.' They asked Mr Maynard what was the difference between a just man and a good man. He was beginning to eat, and cried: 'Hoh! you have eaten your dinners and now have leisure to discourse; I have not.' He had eaten but a bite or two when he replied: 'I'll tell you the difference at once: serjeant Rolle is a *just man*, and Matthew Hale is a *good man*'; and so fell to make an end of his dinner. And there could not be a better interpretation of this text. For Serjeant Rolle was just, but by nature penurious; and his wife made him worse: Matthew Hale was not only just, but wonderfully charitable and open-handed, and did not sound a trumpet neither, as the hypocrites do.

Laurence Rooke
1622 62

Founder-member of the Royal Society; professor of astronomy at Gresham College, London.

Laurence Rooke, born in Kent, was of (King's) College in Cambridge, a good mathematician and a very good man, an intimate friend of Dr Seth Ward (now lord bishop of Salisbury).

I have heard him read at Gresham College on the sixth chapter of Oughtred's *Key to Mathematics*, an excellent lecture: ask for his papers which the bishop of Salisbury.

He was a temperate man and of strong constitution, but took his sickness of which he died by sitting up often for astronomical observations. He lies buried in the church of St Benet Finke in London, near the Old Exchange.

His dear friend the bishop (then of Exeter) gave to the Royal Society a very fair pendulum clock, dedicated to Mr Rooke's memory.

Walter Rumsey
1584–1660

*A successful barrister and later judge on the Welsh circuit until 1647, when he
was dismissed by parliament. He was reappointed in 1660, but died the same
year.*

Walter Rumsey, of Lanover in Monmouthshire, esquire (born there) was
of Oxford; afterwards of the society of Gray's Inn, where he was a
bencher.

He was one of the judges in South Wales, viz Caermarthen, Pembrokeshire, and Cardigan circuit. He was so excellent a lawyer, that he
was called 'the picklock of the law'.

He was an ingenious man, and had a philosophical head; he was most
curious for grafting, inoculating, and planting, and ponds. If he had any
old dead plum tree, or apple-tree, he let them stand, and planted vines at
the bottom, and let them climb up, and they would bear very well.

He was one of my counsel in my law-suits in Breconshire about the
entail. He had a kindness for me and invited me to his house, and told me
a great many fine things, both natural and antiquarian.

He was very polished, and a good musician, played on the organ and
lute. He could compose.

He was much troubled with phlegm, and being so one winter at the
court at Ludlow, (where he was one of the counsel), sitting by the fire,
spitting and spawling, he took a fine tender sprig, and tied a rag at the
end, and imagined he might put it down his throat, and fetch up the
phlegm, and he did so. Afterwards he made this instrument of whale-
bone. I have oftentimes seen him use it. I could never make it go down
my throat, but for those that can 'tis a most incomparable engine. If
troubled with the wind it cures you immediately. It makes you vomit
without any pain, and besides, the vomits of apothecaries have some
poison in them. He wrote a little octavo book, of this way of medicine,
called *The Compendium of Health*. I had a young fellow (Mark Collins),
that was my servant, that used it incomparably, more easily than the
judge; he made the instruments. In Wiltshire, among my things, are
some of his making still. The judge said he never saw anyone use it so
dexterously in his life. It is no pain, when down your throat; he would
touch the bottom of his stomach with it.

John Rushworth

?1612–90

Rushworth's Collections, *a history of parliamentary proceedings and the general events of the political history of England from the early seventeenth century until 1648, are a valuable if erratic source for the history of the Civil War. Rushworth was clerk-assistant to the House of Commons, and was closely associated with Sir Thomas Fairfax, but played little part in politics after the rise of Cromwell.*

'I was born in Northumberland, but my parents were both born in the county of York. The title of the books I wrote went by the name of *Historical Collections;* except *The Earl of Strafford's trial,* which I took with my own pen in characters at the time of his trial, which I have impartially published in folio. And I gave the first precedent of my method in writing and declaring only matter of fact in order of time, without observation or reflection: but Dr Nalson, a learned man, finds fault with me, but I leave it to posterity to judge.

I being near of kin to Sir Thomas Fairfax, the parliament's general, he made choice of me to be his secretary in the wars, by which means I am better enabled to give account of military affairs, both in the first wars and in the second which happened in the year 1648 all which I am now upon the perfecting the same, but the time favours not the coming forth of it.

There is another thing which enables me the better to proceed with the work I am now upon, my intimacy with all the debates and passages in the house of Commons: for that house made choice of me to be assistant at the table to Mr Ellsing, clerk of that parliament to the house of Commons, by which means I was privy to all circumstances in their proceedings.

I might particularly demonstrate more concernments of my own, as being with the king Charles the First at the camp at Berwick, at the great council at York, at Newbourne near Newcastle upon the Scots invading of England, et cetera.

Both the houses of parliament had the confidence in me that they sent by me their addresses to the king after he left the parliament and went to York. And so it fell out that I rode several times, with that expedition between London and York (being 150 miles) in 24 hours at a time.

Sir, pardon my boy's ignorance in writing.

Jo. Rushworth

Southwark,
July 21, 1687.

Mr Rushworth tells me he is superannuated [out of date, i.e. out of touch with current affairs]. He has forgotten to put down the name of the place where [he was] born: as also that he was secretary to Sir Orlando Bridgeman, when Lord Keeper of the great seal, which was a considerable place.

¶ (From a letter to Anthony Wood) Yesterday I saw Mr Rushworth: which was a great mortification. He has quite lost his memory with drinking brandy. Remembered nothing of you etc. His landlady wiped his nose like a child.

¶ John Rushworth, of Lincoln's Inn, esq, historian died in the Rules Court Alley in Southwark, at the widow Bayley's house, a good woman and who was very careful and tendful of him, on Monday the twelfth day of May 1690. He was about 83, onwards to 84. He had no son, but three or four daughters, virtuous women: one is married to Sir Francis Vane in the north. He had forgotten his children before he died.

Richard Sackville
Third Earl of Dorset, 1589–1624

Richard, earl of Dorset (eldest son and heir to the Lord Treasurer): he lived in the greatest grandeur of any nobleman of his time in England. He had thirty gentlemen, and gave to each £50 per annum, besides keeping his horse. George Villiers (after, duke of Buckingham) was a petitioner to have had a gentleman's place under him, and missed it, and within a twelvemonth was a greater man himself; but the duke ever after bore a grudge to the earl of Dorset—From the countess of Thanet.

Richard Sackville
Fifth Earl of Dorset, 1622–77

Richard Sackville earl of Dorset, father of the present earl (Richard)—'twas he that translated *The Cid*, a French comedy, into English, about 1640. It was Sam Butler told me that my lord of Dorset translated it.

Sam Butler (Hudibras) one time at the tavern said that 'twas *this* earl of Dorset's father that translated the comedy called *The Cid*, written by Corneille. Methinks he should not be mistaken; but the world is mighty apt to it, you see.

He died in 1677. He was a fellow of the Royal Society. He married

Frances Cranfield, daughter of the earl of Middlesex, by whom he had several sons and daughters.

His eldest son is Richard, earl of Dorset and Middlesex, a most noble lord and my most kind friend.

Thomas Sackville
First Earl of Dorset, 1536–1608

As Lord Buckhurst, Thomas Sackville played an important part at Elizabeth's court, largely as a diplomat, though it was he who announced the sentence of death to Mary Queen of Scots at Fotheringhay. In 1598 he was appointed lord treasurer, and held this office until his death, dealing with matters efficiently and impartially. His early travels had given him cultivated tastes, and he was a great patron of the arts. He rebuilt Knole, in Kent, between 1603 and 1605.

Epigram on the Earl of Dorset, who died suddenly at the council board.

> Uncivil death! that would'st not once confer,
> Dispute, or parley with our treasurer,
> Had He been thee, or of thy fatal Tribe,
> He would have spared thy life, and ta'en a Bribe.
>
> He that so often had, with gold and wit,
> Injured strong lawe, and almost conquered it,
> At length, for want of evidence to shew,
> Was forced himself to take a deadly blow.

These verses I transcribed out of the collection of my honoured friend and neighbour, Thomas Tyndale esquire.

Memorandum: the trial was with this [the present] Sir Richard Temple's great grandfather. The lord treasurer had in his bosom some writings, which as he was pulling out to give in evidence, said 'Here is that will strike you dead!' and as soon as he had spoken these words, fell down stark dead in the place.—from Sir Richard Temple. (Memorandum:—an extraordinary perturbation of mind will bring an apoplexy: I know several instances of it.)

'Twas this lord that got Salisbury House with its grounds, next to St Bride's, in exchange for a piece of land, near Cricklade in Wiltshire, I think called Marston, but the title was not good, nor did the value answer his promise.—From Seth, Bishop of Salisbury, who says that all the parish of St Bride's belonged to the Bishop of Salisbury, as also all Shoe Lane.

Robert Sanderson
1587–1663

Bishop of Lincoln and Regius Professor of Divinity at Oxford 1642–8 and 1660–3.

Dr Robert Sanderson, lord bishop of Lincoln, would confess to his intimate friends, that 'he studied and mastered only Tully's Offices,* Thomas Aquinas's *Secunda Secundie*, and Aristotle's Rhetoric, and that all other books he read but cursorily': but he had forgotten, by his favour, to speak of Aristotle's Organon etc. [logic books], else he could never have compiled his own excellent *Logic*.—From Seth Ward, bishop of Salisbury, and Pierson, bishop of Chester. And bishop Ward said that he would do the like were he to begin the world again.

He was a lover of music, and was wont to play on his bass viol, and also to sing to it. He was a lover of heraldry, and gave it in charge in his articles of enquiry; but the clergymen made him such a lamentable imperfect return that it signified nothing. The very parliamentarians reverenced him for his learning and his virtue, so that he always kept his living, which N.B.

He had no great memory, I am certain not a sure one; when I was a freshman and heard him read his first lecture, he made a mistake in the Lord's Prayer. He always read his sermons and lectures. Had his memory been greater, his judgement had been less: they are like two well-buckets.

In his *Logic*, he recommends disputation to young men, as the best exercise for young wits.

Sir William Saunderson
?1586–1676

Sir W. Saunderson:—he did read and write to his dying day. Sir Christopher Wren said that as he wrote not well, so he wrote not ill. He died at Whitehall (I was then there): went out like a spent candle—died before Dr Holder could come to him with the sacrament.

---

* Harsenet, archbishop of York, always carried it in his bosom.

Sir Henry Savile
1549–1622

Scholar, warden of Merton College, Oxford, and later provost of Eton College. He endowed two professorships at Oxford, one for geometry, one for astronomy, and helped to found the Bodleian Library there. He edited a number of Latin texts, the most important being the Works *of Chrysostom published in eight folio volumes in 1610–1613.*

Sir Henry Savile, knight, was born in Yorkshire. He was a younger, or son of a younger, brother, not born to a foot of land. He came to Merton College, Oxford; he was made warden there.

He was a learned gentleman, as most of his time. He would fain have been thought (I have heard Mr Hobbes say) to have been as great a scholar as Joseph Scaliger. But as for mathematics, I have heard Dr Wallis say that he looked on him to be as able a mathematician as any of his time. He was an extraordinarily handsome and beautiful man; no lady had a finer complexion. Queen Elizabeth favoured him much; (he read (I think) Greek and politics to her): he was also preferred to be provost of Eton College.

He was a very severe governor, the scholars hated him for his austerity. He could not abide wits: when a young scholar was recommended to him for a good wit, 'Out upon him, I'll have nothing to do with him; give me the plodding student. If I would look for wits I would go to Newgate, there be the wits';* and John Earles (afterwards Bishop of Salisbury) was the only scholar that ever he took as recommended for a wit, which was from Dr Goodwyn, of Christ Church.

He was not only a severe governor, but old Mr Yates (who was fellow in his time) would make lamentable complaints of him to his dying day, that he did oppress the fellows grievously, and he was so great and a favourite to the queen that there was no dealing with him; his fault was that he was too much inflated with his learning and riches.

He was very munificent, as appears by the two chairs he had endowed of Astronomy and Geometry. Bishop Ward, of Salisbury, has told me that he first sent for Mr Gunter, from London, (being of Oxford University) to have been his professor of Geometry: so he came and brought with him his sector and quadrant, and fell to resolving of triangles and doing a great many fine things. Said the grave knight, 'Do you call this reading of Geometry? This is showing of tricks, man!' and so dismissed him with scorn, and sent for Briggs from Cambridge.

* This I was told by Robert Skinner, Bishop of Oxford, 1646.

I have heard Dr Wallis say, that Sir H. Savile has sufficiently confuted Joseph Scaliger *On the squaring of the circle*, on the very margins of the book: and that sometimes when J. Scaliger says 'AB = CD by construction', Sir H. Savile writes sometimes in the margin, 'And your rule is an ass by construction'.

He left only one daughter, mother to this present Sir Charles Sedley, who well resembles his grandfather Savile in the face, but is not so proper a man.

He had travelled very well, and had a general acquaintance with the learned men abroad; by which means he obtained from beyond sea, out of their libraries, several rare Greek MSS., which he had copied by an excellent amanuensis for the Greek character.

Someone put a trick upon him, for he got a friend to send him weekly over to Flanders (I think), the sheets of the curious Chrysostom that were printed at Eton, and translated them into Latin, and printed them in Greek and Latin together, which quite spoiled the sale of Sir Henry's.

Memorandum: he gave his collection of mathematical books to a peculiar little library belonging to the Savilian professors.

Sylvanus Scory
c. 1540–1617

Sylvanus Scory (enquire if he was not knighted?) was the son and heir of Scory, bishop of Hereford.

His father, John Scory, in the reign of Edward the Sixth, was bishop of Rochester, and translated from thence to Chichester, and afterwards to Hereford.

He was a very handsome gentleman, and had an excellent wit, and his father gave him the best education, both at home and beyond the seas, that that age would afford, and loved him so dearly that he fleeced the church of Hereford to leave him a good estate, and he did let such long, and so many leases, that, as Mrs Masters (daughter of Herbert Westphaling esq, eldest son and heir to bishop Westphaling, of Hereford) told me, they were not out till about these 60 years. To my remembrance, she told me the estate left him was £1500 per annum, which he reduced to nothing (allowing himself the liberty to enjoy all the pleasures of this world), and left his son so poor, that when he came among gentlemen, they would fancy a crown or ten shilling for him.

I have heard Sir John Denham say (at Chalks, 1652) that he had been well informed that he was the most accomplished gentleman of his time.

'Tis a good testimonial of his worth, that Mr Benjamin Jonson (who ever scorned an unworthy patron) dedicated his . . . to him. I have heard Sir John Denham also say that he was the greatest confidant and intimate favourite of Monsieur of France (brother to the French king), who was a suitor to queen Elizabeth, and whom her majesty entirely loved (and as a signal of it one time at St Paul's Church, London, openly kissed him in time of divine service) and would have had him for her husband, but only for reasons of state. When her majesty dismissed him, 'twas done with all passion and respect imaginable. She gave him royal presents; he was attended to Dover by the flower of the courtiers; among others, by this spark of whom I now write. When Monsieur took his leave of him he told him that though 'twas so that her majesty could not marry him (as aforesaid), yet he knew that she so much loved him that she would not deny him any request, whereby he might honour and benefit a friend; and accordingly writes his love-letter to his mistress, the queen of England, and in it only begs that single boon, to look upon Mr Scory (the bearer), with a particular and extraordinary grace, for his sake; delivered him the letter (and as I take it, gave him a jewel). As Sylvanus returned to London, through Canterbury, the mayor there (a shoemaker), a pragmatical fellow, examined him, who and whence, etc and what his business was, and if he had a pass? 'Yes,' quoth he, 'I have a pass.' and produces Monsieur's letter, superscribed to her Majesty, which, one would have thought, had been enough to have shown. The mayor very fairly breaks open the love-letter, and reads it. I know not how, this action happened to take wind, and 'twas brought to court, and became so ridiculous that Sylvanus Scory was so laughed at and jeered that he never delivered the letter to the queen, which had been the easiest and most honourable step to preferment that mortal man could have desired.

John Selden
1584–1654

Although Selden qualified as a barrister he was never an active lawyer, but spent most of his time in antiquarian and historical research on legal and other matters. He edited a number of early legal works, but his own contributions were more important, particularly his attack on the justification for paying tithes (1617). This made the clergy, whose income was largely derived from tithes, his implacable enemies. He entered parliament in 1621, and consistently opposed Charles I's attempts to move towards an absolute monarchy, affirming the 'ancient liberties'. He remained in favour with the

parliamentary side during the Civil War, although he did not actively
support them. His most important work, on the law of the sea, appeared in
1636: his Table Talk *appeared posthumously in 1689.*

John Selden, esquire, was born (as appears by his epitaph, which he
himself made, as I well remember Archbishop Usher, Lord Primate,
who did preach his funeral sermon, did then mention, that is as to 'in
hope of certain resurrection') at Salvington, a hamlet belonging to West
Tarring in the county of Sussex.

His father was a yeomanly man, of about forty pounds per annum,
and played well on the violin, in which he took delight, and at
Christmas time, to please himself and his neighbours, he would play to
them as they danced. My old Lady Cotton★ (wife to Sir Robert Cotton,
grandmother to this Sir John Cotton) was one time at Sir Thomas
Alford's, in Sussex, at dinner in Christmas time, and Mr John Selden
(then a young student) sat at the lower end of the table, who was looked
upon then to be of parts extraordinary, and somebody asking who he
was, 'twas replied his son that is playing on the violin in the hall. (This
from Sir William Dugdale, from the Lady Cotton.) I have heard
Michael Malet (Judge Malet's son) say, that he had heard that Mr John
Selden's father taught on the lute. He had a pretty good estate by his
wife. He was of Hart Hall in Oxford, and Sir Giles Mompesson told me
that he was then of that house, and that he was a long scabby-polled
boy, but a good student.

Thence he came to the Inner Temple. His chamber was in the Paper
Buildings which look towards the gardens, uppermost story, where he
had a little gallery to walk in. He was quickly taken notice of for his
learning, and was solicitor and steward to the Earl of Kent, whose
countess being an ingenious woman and loving men, would let him lie
with her, and her husband knew it. After the earl's death he married
her. He did lie with Mrs Williamson (one of my lady's women) a lusty
bouncing woman, who robbed him on his death-bed. I remember in
1646, or 1647, they did talk also of my lady's she-blackamoor.

His great friend heretofore was Mr Hayward, to whom he dedicates
his *Titles of Honour*; also Ben Jonson. His treatise, that tithes were not
in accordance with divine law, drew a great deal of envy upon him from
the clergy. W. Laud, Archbishop of Canterbury, made him make his
recantation before the High Commission court, of which you may have
an account in Dr Peter Heylen's history: after, he would never forgive
the bishops, but did still in his writings level them with the presbytery.
He was also severe and bitter in his speeches against ship-money, which
speeches see.

★ She was living in 1646, or 1647, an old woman, eighty or more. (This from Sir
William Dugdale, from the Lady Cotton.)

He was one of the assembly of divines, and Whitlock, in his memoirs, says he was wont to mock the assembly men about their little gilt Bibles, and would baffle them sadly: said he, 'I do consider the original.'

Montagu, Bishop of Norwich, was his great antagonist; see the books written against each other. He never owned the marriage with the Countess of Kent till after her death, upon some law account. He never kept any servant in his own service, but my lady's were all at his command; he lived with her in White Friars, which was, before the conflagration, a noble dwelling. He kept a plentiful table, and was never without learned company. He was temperate in eating and drinking. He had a slight stuff, or silk, kind of false carpet, to cast over the table where he read and his papers lay, when a stranger came in, so that he needed not to displace his books or papers.

He died of a dropsy; he had his funeral escutcheons all ready months before he died.

When he was near death, the minister (Mr Johnson) was coming to him to absolve him: Mr Hobbes happened then to be there: said he, 'What, will you that have written like a man, now die like a woman?' So the minister was not let in.

He died in White Friars (aforesaid) the last day of November, 1654; and on Thursday, the 14th day of December, was magnificently buried in the Temple Church. His executors were Matthew Hale (since Lord Chief Justice of the King's Bench), John Vaughan (since Lord Chief Justice of the Common Pleas), and Rowland Jewkes, esquire; enquire as to the fourth executor. They invited all the parliament men, all the benchers, and great officers. All the judges had mourning, as also an abundance of persons of quality. The Lord Primate of Ireland, Usher, preached his funeral sermon.

He would tell his intimate friends, Sir Bennet Hoskyns, etc, that he had nobody to make his heir, except it were a milkmaid, and that such people did not know what to do with a great estate. Memorandum:— Bishop Grosseteste, of Lincoln, told his brother, who asked him to make him a great man; 'Brother,' said he, 'if your plough is broken, I'll pay the mending of it; or if an ox is dead, I'll pay for another: but a ploughman I found you, and a ploughman I'll leave you.'

He never used any artificial help to strengthen his memory; 'twas purely natural.

He was very tall, I guess about six foot high; sharp oval face; head not very big; long nose inclining to one side; full popping eye (gray). He was a poet*, and Sir John Suckling brings him in the 'Session of the Poets'.

* He has a learned set of verses before Hopton's *Concordance of Years*; before Ben Jonson's Works etc.

The poets met, the other day,
And Apollo was at the meeting, they say,
....
'Twas strange to see how they flocked together:
There was Selden, and he stood next to the chair,
And Wenman not far off, which was very fair,
etc.

He was one of the assembly of divines in those days (as was also his highness the Prince Elector Palatine), and was like a thorn in their sides; for he did baffle and vex them; for he was able to run them all down with his Greek and antiquities. Sir Robert Cotton (the great antiquary, that collected the library) was his great friend, whose son, Sir Thomas Cotton, was obnoxious to the parliament, and skulked in the country: Mr Selden had the key and command of the library, and preserved it, being then a parliament man. He intended to have given his own library to the University of Oxford, but received disobligation from them, for that they would not lend him some MSS; wherefore by his will he left it to the disposal of his executors, who gave it to the Bodleian Library, at Oxford.

He understood many languages:—Latin, Greek, Hebrew, Arabic, besides the learned modern.

In his writing he used his learned friend, Mr Henry Jacob, of Merton College, who did transcribe etc, for him, and as he was writing, would many times put in things of his own head, which Mr Selden did let stand, as he does, in his preface, acknowledge.

In his younger years he affected obscurity of style, which, after, he quite left off, and wrote perspicuously. 'Twill be granted that he was one of the greatest critics of his time.

I remember my saddler who wrought many years to that family* told me that Mr Selden had got more by his prick than he had done by his practice. He was no eminent practiser at bar; not but that he was or might have been able enough; but after he had got a sweet ease he chiefly addicted himself to his more ingenious studies and records.

I have heard some divines say (I know not if maliciously) that 'twas true he was a man of great reading, but gave not his own sentiment.

He was wont to say 'I'll keep myself warm and moist as long as I live, for I shall be cold and dry when I am dead.'

¶ John Selden esquire would write sometimes, when notions came into his head, to preserve them, under his barber's hands. When he died his barber said he had a great mind to know his will, 'For,' said he, 'I never knew a wise man make a wise will.' He bequeathed his estate

* The Earl of Kent's.

(£40,000 value) to four executors, viz, Lord Chief Justice Hales, Lord Chief Justice Vaughan, Roland Jukes and . . . (his flatterer)—from Fabian Philips.

¶ Mr Johnson, minister of the Temple, buried him, according to the usage of the Directory of Public worship [1644], where amongst other things, he quoted 'the saying of a learned man' (he did not name him) 'that when a learned man dies, there dies a great deal of learning with him,' and that 'if learning could have kept a man alive our brother had not died.'

William Shakespeare
1564–1616

Aubrey's informant about Shakespeare was Mr Beeston 'whom Mr Dryden calls "the chronicle of the stage"'. Beeston's father had been master of one of the playhouses, and Aubrey says that he 'knew all the old English poets'. The comment about his comedies and those of the Restoration period is shrewd; but the tragedies were rarely given until the mid-eighteenth century. The John Combe referred to in the rhyme was Shakespeare's partner in an attempt to enclose some common land at Stratford in 1614–1615.

Mr William Shakespeare was born at Stratford upon Avon in the county of Warwick. His father was a butcher, and I have been told heretofore by some of the neighbours, that when he was a boy he exercised his father's trade, but when he killed a calf he would do it in a high style, and make a speech. There was at that time another butcher's son in this town that was held not at all inferior to him for a natural wit, his acquaintance and contemporary, but died young.

This William being inclined naturally to poetry and acting, came to London, I guess, about 18; and was an actor at one of the playhouses, and did act exceedingly well (now B. Jonson was never a good actor, but an excellent instructor).

He began early to make essays at dramatic poetry, which at that time was very low; and his plays took well.

He was a handsome, well-shaped man: very good company, and of a very ready and pleasant smooth wit.

The humour of the constable in *Midsummer Night's Dream*,* he

* Perhaps Dogberry in *Much Ado About Nothing*. Ed.

happened to take at Grendon in Bucks—I think it was midsummer night that he happened to lie there—which is the road from London to Stratford, and there was living that constable about 1642, when I first came to Oxford: Mr Josias Howe is of that parish, and knew him. Ben Jonson and he did gather humours of men daily wherever they came. One time as he was at the tavern at Stratford on Avon, one Combes, an old rich usurer, was to be buried, he makes there this extemporary epitaph,

> Ten in the hundred the Devil allows,
> But Combes will have twelve, he swears and vows:
> If any one asks who lies in the tomb,
> 'Hoh!' quoth the Devil, ''Tis my John o Combe.'

He was wont to go to his native country once a year. I think I have been told that he left £2 or 300 per annum there and thereabout to a sister.

I have heard Sir William Davenant and Mr Thomas Shadwell (who is counted the best writer of comedies we have now) say that he had a most prodigious wit, and did admire his natural parts beyond all other dramatical writers. He was wont to say (B. Jonson's *Underwoods*) that he 'never blotted out a line in his life'; said Ben Jonson, 'I wish he had blotted out a thousand.'

His comedies will remain wit as long as the English tongue is understood, for that he handles the ways of men. Now our present writers reflect so much upon particular persons and coxcombies, that twenty years hence they will not be understood.

Though, as Ben Jonson says of him, that he had but little Latin and less Greek, he understood Latin pretty well, for he had been in his younger years a schoolmaster in the country—from Mr Beeston.

Sir Philip Sidney
1554–86

Soldier and poet. He was related to the Herberts of Wilton by his sister's marriage, and so Aubrey has a number of Wiltshire stories about him, as well as Tyndale's letter about the identity of the characters in the Arcadia. *Sidney went to Oxford, but he left before taking a degree, and his real education was travel abroad. He spent some time in France and Germany, and later travelled to Austria, Hungary, Italy and even Poland. On his return, he was active as a diplomat, but he disliked Court life and only spent time there in an attempt to gain an office which would give him an income. In 1585 he went with Leicester on his expedition against the Spanish in the Netherlands. The following year he was wounded at the siege of Zutphen, and died a month later.*

Sir Philip Sidney, knight, was the most accomplished cavalier of his time. He was the eldest son of the right honourable Sir Henry Sidney, knight of the noble order of the Garter, Lord President of Wales, and Lord Deputy of Ireland, 1570. I suppose he was born at Penshurst in Kent (near Tunbridge).

He had the best authors provided for him by his father that could then be had.

He travelled France, Italy, Germany; he was in the Poland wars, and at that time he had to his page* (and as an excellent accomplishment) Henry Danvers, (afterwards Earl of Danby), then second son of Sir John Danvers of Dauntscy in Wilts, who accounted himself happy that his son was so bestowed. He makes mention, in his *Art of Poesie*, of his being in Hungary (I remember).

He was not only of an excellent wit, but extremely beautiful; he much resembled his sister, but his hair was not red, but a little inclining, viz, a dark amber colour. If I were to find a fault in it, methinks 'tis not masculine enough; yet he was a person of great courage. He was much at Wilton with his sister, and at Ivychurch (which adjoins to the park pale of Clarendon Park), situated on a hill that overlooks all the country westwards, and north over Salisbury and the plains, and into that delicious park (which was accounted the best of England) eastwards. It was heretofore a monastery (the cloisters remain still); 'twas called the monastery of Edros. My great uncle, Mr Thomas Browne, remembered him; and said that he was often wont, as he was hunting on our pleasant plains, to take his table book out of his pocket, and write down his notions as they came into his head, when he was writing his *Arcadia* (which was never finished by him).

He was the reviver of poetry in those dark times, which was then at a very low ebb—e.g. *The Pleasant Comedy of Jacob and Esau*, acted before King Henry VIII's grace (where, I remember, is this expression, that 'the pottage was so good, that God almighty might have put his finger in't'; *Gammer Gurton's Needle*; and in these plays there is not three lines but there is 'by God' or 'by God's wounds'.

He was of a very munificent spirit, and liberal to all lovers of learning, and to those that pretended to any acquaintance with Parnassus; in so much that he was cloyed and surfeited with the poetasters of those

---

* This my cousin Elizabeth Danvers, now Viscountess Purbeck, his niece, has told.

days. Among others Mr Edmund Spenser made his address to him, and brought his *Faerie Queene*. Sir Philip was busy at his study, and his servant delivered Mr Spenser's book to his master, who laid it by, thinking it might be such kind of stuff as he was frequently troubled with. Mr Spenser stayed so long that his patience was wearied, and went his way discontented, and never intended to come again. When Sir Philip perused it, he was exceedingly delighted with it, that he was extremely sorry he was gone, and where to send for him he knew not. After much enquiry he learned his lodging, and sent for him, mightily caressed him, and ordered his servant to give him . . . pounds in gold. His servant said that that was too much; 'No', said Sir Philip, 'he is extraordinary,' and ordered an addition. From this time there was a great friendship between them, to his dying day.

(I have heard Dr Pell say that he has been told by ancient gentlemen of those days of Sir Philip, so famous for men at arms, that 'twas then held as a great disgrace for a young gentleman to be seen riding in the street in a coach, as it would now for such a one to be seen in the streets in a petticoat and waistcoat; so much is the fashion of the times now altered.)

He married the daughter of Sir Francis Walsingham, principal secretary of state (I think his only child—query), whom he loved very well insomuch that having received some shot or wound in the wars in the Low Countries, where he had command of (the Ranukins, I think), he would not contrary to the injunction of his physicians and surgeons, forbear his carnal knowledge of her, which cost him his life: upon which occasion there were some roguish verses made.

His body was put in a leaden coffin (which, after the firing of St Paul's [1666], I myself saw), and with wonderful great state was carried to St Paul's church, where he was buried in our Lady's chapel. There solemnised this funeral all the nobility and great officers of court; all the judges and sergeants at law; all the soldiers, and commanders, and gentry that were in London; the lord mayor, and aldermen, and livery-men*. His body was born on men's shoulders (perhaps 'twas a false coffin).

When I was a boy 9 years old, I was with my father at one Mr Singleton's, an alderman and woollen-draper in Gloucester, who had in his parlour, over the chimney, the whole description of the funeral, engraved and printed on papers pasted together,† which, at length, was, I believe, the length of the room at least; but he had contrived it to be turned upon two pins, that turning one of them made the figures

---

* Members of the city livery companies. *Ed.*
† Published by Thomas Laut, London 1587. *Ed.*

march all in order. It did make such a strong impression on my young fantasy, that I remember it as if it were but yesterday. I could never see it elsewhere. The house is in the great long street, over against the high steeple; and 'tis likely it remains there still. 'Tis pity it is not redone.

In St Mary's church at Warwick is a sumptuous monument of the Lord Brooke round a great altar of black marble is only this inscription:

'Here lies the body of Sir Fulke Greville, knight, servant to Queen Elizabeth, councellor to King James, and friend to Sir Philip Sidney.'

On a little tablet of wood:

England, Netherlands, the Heavens and the Arts
Of . . . Sydney hath made . . . parts
. . . for who could suppose
That one heap of stones could Sidney enclose.

Key of Pembroke's Arcadia (from a letter to Aubrey from D. Tyndale, 18 February 1687).

Sir,

All the good bodies thank you for your remembrance, which I ought to have told you sooner if a pain in my head had not hindered me. I wish I could give you *the key you desire*, but all I know of it is not worth anything; though conversant amongst his relations, could learn no more than Pamela being my Lady Northumberland, Philoclea my Lady Rich, two sisters, the last beloved by him, upon whose account he made his *Astrophel and Stella*; Miso, Lady Cox, Mopse, Lady Lucy, persons altogether unknown now; Musedorus and Pericles, the two ladies' husbands. Lord Rich being then his friend he persuaded her mother to the match, though he repented afterwards: she then very young and secretly in love with him but he no concern for her; her beauty augmenting, he says in his *Astrophel and Stella* he didn't think 'the morn would have proved so fair a day'. Their mother was beautiful and gallant (whether he meant Ginesis by her or no, I know not); but their father died, they being young. She remarried to Dudley (Leicester and Northumberland), and afterwards to her gentleman of the horse, Sir Christopher Blunt, which was beheaded with Lord Essex. It is thought that he meant himself by Amphialus and his lady, Sir Francis Walsingham's daughter and heir, the Queen of Corinth. If he did make his own character high, they said Philisides was himself too, but it was all a guess. He made it young, and dying deserved his follies might be burnt.

Some others I have guessed at but have forgotten. Therefore cannot satisfy the lady, which I would for your sake.

¶ In this tract is the Earl of Pembroke's noble seat at Wilton; but the *Arcadia* and the *Daphne* is about Ivychurch and Wilton; and these romancy plains and boscages did no doubt conduce to the heightening of

Sir Philip Sidney's fancy. He lived much in these parts, and his most masterly touches of his pastorals he wrote here upon the spot, where they were conceived. 'Twas about these purlieus that the muses were wont to appear to Sir Philip Sidney, and where he wrote down their dictates in his table book, though on horseback.* For those nimble fugitives, except they be at once registered, fly away, and perhaps can never be caught again. But they were never so kind as to appear to me, though I am the lessee of the land; it seems that they reserve that grace only for the proprietors, to whom they have continued a constant kindness for a succession of generations of the no less ingenious than honourable family of the Herberts.

Sir Henry Spelman
?1564–1641

Antiquarian and legal writer. He was of independent means, and was largely self-taught, having studied at Cambridge and Lincoln's Inn without taking a degree or becoming a barrister. His Glossary *on the origins of English law was a major work, which led him to study Anglo-Saxon and to found a Cambridge lectureship in the subject.*

From Justice Ball at Windsor:—when he was about 10 or 12 he went to school to a cursed schoolmaster, to whom he had an antipathy. His master would discountenance him, and was very severe to him, and to a dull boy he would say *as very a dunce as H. Spelman.* He was a boy of great spirit, and would not learn there. He was (upon his importunity) sent to another schoolmaster, and profited very well.

I have heard his grandson say, that the Spelmans' wits open late. He was much perplexed about lawsuits and worldly troubles, so that he was about 40 before he could settle himself to make any great progress in learning, which when he did, we find what great monuments of anti-quarian knowledge he has left to the world.

W. Laud, Archbishop of Canterbury, had a great esteem for him, and made him one of the members of the High Commission court; yet (he being one that was extremely rigid as to the licensing of books, and against any *nouvelle*) hindered the printing of the second part of his glossary, which began at M, where there were three M's that scandalised the Archbishop, viz—Magna Carta, Magnum Consilium Regis [The King's Council]; and . . .

* I remember some relations of mine and old men that have seen Sir Philip do thus.

From George Lee:—he was a handsome gentleman (as appears by his picture in the Cottonian Library), strong and valiant, and wore always his sword, till he was about 70 or more, when, finding his legs falter through feebleness as he was walking, 'Now,' said he, ''tis time to leave off my sword.'

When his daughter-in-law (Sir John's wife) returned home from visiting her neighbours, he would always ask her what of antiquity she had heard or observed, and if she brought home no such account, he would chide her (jestingly).

He lies buried in the south cross aisle of Westminster Abbey. I very well remember his pennant that hung up there, but it was either taken down or fell down when the scaffolds were put up at the coronation of his majesty King Charles II.

Sir William Dugdale knew Sir Henry Spelman, and says he was as tall as his grandson, Harry Spelman. He has been told that Sir Henry did not understand Latin perfectly till he was forty years old. He said to Sir William, 'We are indebted to Mr Speed and Stowe for *stitching up* for us our English History.' It seems they were both tailors (which N.B.).

Edmund Spenser
?1552–99

Son of a London clothier, Spenser's first poems appeared when he was 17 or 18. He took a Cambridge degree, and then became a member of the Earl of Leicester's household. Here he met Sir Philip Sidney. He lived from 1580 onwards in Ireland, but suffered in the 1598 rebellion, and died in London the following year. His allegorical epic The Faerie Queene *was published in 1590 and 1596, but remained incomplete at his death.*

Mr Edmund Spenser was of Pembroke Hall in Cambridge; he nursed the fellowship there which Bishop Andrewes got. He was an acquaintance and frequenter of Sir Erasmus Dryden. His mistress, Rosalind, was a kinswoman of Sir Erasmus' lady's. The chamber there at Sir Erasmus' is still called Mr Spenser's Chamber. Lately, at the college taking down the wainscot of his chamber, they found an abundance of cards with stanzas of the *Faerie Queene* written on them.—from John Dryden esquire, Poet Laureate.

Mr Beeston says he was a little man, wore short hair, little band and little cuffs.

¶ Mr Samuel Woodford (the poet, who paraphrased the psalms) lives in Hampshire near Alton, and he told me that Mr Spenser lived sometime in these parts, in this delicate sweet air; where he enjoyed his muse, and wrote a good part of his verses. I have said before that Sir Philip Sidney and Sir Walter Raleigh were his acquaintances. He had lived some time in Ireland, and wrote a description of it, which is printed with Morison's *History, or Description of Ireland.*

Sir John Denham told me, that Archbishop Usher, Lord Primate of Armagh, was acquainted with him, by this token: when Sir William Davenant's *Gondibert* came forth, Sir John asked the lord primate if he had seen it. Said the primate, 'Out upon him, with his vaunting preface, he writes against my old friend, Edmund Spenser.'

Richard Stokes
?–1681

Richard Stokes, MD—his father was fellow of Eton College (enquire if not prebend of Windsor, and if not schoolmaster of Eton? ask Christopher Wase about these things).

He was bred there and at King's College. Scholar to Mr W. Oughtred for mathematics (algebra). He made himself mad with it, but became sober again, but I fear like a cracked glass: see my Lives, and Surrey notes. He edited Mr Oughtred's Trigonometry. He became a Roman Catholic; married unhappily at Liège, dog and cat, etc. Became a sot. Died in Newgate, prisoner for debt, 1681.

Thomas Street
1621–89

Mr Thomas Street,* astronomer, was born in Ireland, his widow thinks, Castle Lyons, March the 5th, 1621.

He had the true motion of the moon by which he could [discover how to find true longitude]—(he hath finished the tables of the moon and also of Mercury, which was never made perfect before)—but two of his

---

* His astronomical tables are the best that ever were yet made.

familiar acquaintance tell me that he did not commit this discovery to paper: so it is dead with him. He made attempts to be introduced to king Charles II and also to king James II, but courtiers would not do it without a good gratuity.

He was of a rough and choleric humour. Discoursing with prince Rupert, his highness affirmed something that was not according to art; said Mr Street, 'Whoever affirms that is no mathematician.' So they would point at him afterwards at court and say, 'There's the man that huffed Prince Rupert.'

He was one of Mr Ashmole's clerks in the Excise Office, which was his chiefest livelihood.

He has left with his widow (who lives in Warwick Lane) an absolute piece of Trigonometry, plain and spherical, in manuscript, more perfect than ever was yet done, and more clear and demonstrated.

He died in Cannon Row (vulgarly Channel Row) at Westminster, the 17th of August 1689. He made this following epitaph himself:

> Here lies the earth of one that thought some good,
>   Although too few him rightly understood:
> Above the starres his heightned mind did flye,
> His hapier spirit into Eternity.

His acquaintance talk of subscribing towards an inscription. No man living has deserved so well of astronomy.

Sir John Suckling
1609–42

Courtier and poet. He travelled abroad in 1628–30, and joined the army of Gustavus Adolphus in 1631–2. His first play was produced in 1637, and attracted attention because of the lavish production. At the beginning of the Civil War, he set up a plot to give the king control of the army, but parliament came to hear of it, and he was forced to flee abroad. He died in Paris in 1642. Aubrey's account comes largely from Suckling's close friend Sir William Davenant.

Sir John Suckling, knight, was the eldest son of Sir John Suckling of the Green Cloth [Controller of the Royal Household], in the time (I think, of Charles I). He was born in February 1609.

I have heard Mrs Bond say, that Sir John's father was but a dull fellow (her husband, Mr Thomas Bond, knew him): the wit came by the mother. Ask Dr Busby if he was not of Westminster School? He might be about his time. I have heard Sir William Davenant say that he went to the University of Cambridge at eleven years of age, where he studied three or four years (I think, four). By 18 he had well travelled France and Italy, and part of Germany, and (I think also) of Spain.

He returned into England an extraordinarily accomplished gentleman, grew famous at Court for his ready sparkling wit which was envied, and he was (Sir William said) the bull that was baited. He was incomparably ready at reparteeing, and his wit most sparkling when most set upon and provoked. He was the greatest gallant of his time, and the greatest gamester, both for bowling* and cards, so that no shop-keeper would trust him for 6d., as today, for instance, he might, by winning, be worth £200, the next day he might not be worth half so much, or perhaps be sometimes less than nothing. Sir William (who was his intimate friend, and loved him entirely) would say that Sir John, when he was at his lowest ebb in gaming, I mean when unfortunate, then would make himself most glorious in apparel, and said that it exalted his spirits, and that he had then best luck when he was most gallant, and his spirits were highest.

Sir William would say that he did not much care for a lord's conversation, for they were in those days damnably proud and arrogant, and the French would say that 'My lord d'Angleterre looked comme un mastiff-dog', but now the age is more refined, and much by the example of his gracious majesty, who is the pattern of courtesy.

In 163– there happened, unluckily, a difference between Sir John Suckling and Sir John Digby (brother to Sir Kenelm) about a mistress or gaming, I have now forgotten. Sir John was but a slight-timbered man, and of middling stature; Sir John Digby a proper person of great strength, and courage answerable, and admitted to be the best swordsman of his time. Sir John, with two or three of his party assaults Sir John Digby going into a playhouse; Sir J.D. had only his lackey with him, but he flew on them like a tiger, and made them run. 'Twas pity that this accident brought the blemish of cowardice to such an ingenious young spark. Sir J.D. was such a hero that there were very few but he would have served in the same manner.

In 163– when the expedition was sent into Scotland, Sir John Suckling, at his own charge, raised a troop of a hundred very handsome young proper men, whom he clad in white doublets, and scarlet breeches, and scarlet coats, hats and feathers, well hosed and armed. They say 'twas one of the finest sights in those days. But Sir John

---

* He was one of the best bowlers of his time in England. He played at cards rarely well, and did use to practise by himself abed, and there studied how the best way of managing the cards could be. His sisters coming to the Piccadilly bowling-green crying for fear he should lose all their dowries.

Minnes made a lampoon of it:

> 'The ladies opened the windows to see
> So fine and goodly a sight-a' etc

I think the lampoon says he made an inglorious charge against the Scots.

Enquire in what army he was in the Civil Wars.

He went into France, where after some time being come to the bottom of his fund that was left, reflecting on the miserable and despicable condition he should be reduced to, having nothing left to maintain him, he (having a convenience for that purpose, lying at an apothecary's house, in Paris) took poison, which killed him miserably with vomiting. He was buried in the Protestants' churchyard. This was (to the best of my remembrance) 1646.

His picture, which is like him, before his *Poems*, says that he was but 28 years old when he died.

He was of middle stature and slight strength, brisk round eye, reddish-faced and red nose (ill liver), his head not very big, his hair a kind of sand colour; his beard turned up naturally, so that he had a brisk and graceful look. He died a bachelor.

Memorandum: he made a magnificent entertainment in London, for a great number of ladies of quality, all beauties and young, which cost him hundreds of pounds, where were all the rarities that this part of the world could afford, and the last service of all was silk stockings and garters, and I think also gloves.

In 1637 Sir John Suckling, William Davenant, poet laureate (not then knighted), and Jack Young came to the Bath. Sir John came like a young prince for all manner of equipage and convenience, and Sir W. Davenant told me that he had a cart-load of books carried down, and 'twas there, at Bath, that he wrote the little tract in his book about Socinianism. 'Twas as pleasant a journey as ever men had; in the height of a long peace and luxury, and in the venison season. The second night they lay at Marlborough, and walking on the delicate fine downs at the backside of the town, whilst supper was making ready, the maids were drying of clothes on the bushes. Jack Young had espied a very pretty young girl, and had got her consent for an assignation, which was about midnight, which they happened to hear on the other side of the hedge, and were resolved to frustrate his design. They were wont every night to play cards after supper a good while; but Jack Young pretended weariness, etc, and must needs go to bed, not to be persuaded by any means to the contrary. They had their landlady at supper with them; said they to her, 'Observe this poor gentleman how he yawns, now is his mad fit coming upon him. We beseech you that you make fast his doors, and get somebody to watch and look to him, for about midnight he will fall to be most outrageous: get the ostler, or some strong fellow, to stay up, and we will content him, for he is our worthy friend, and a very honest gentleman, only, perhaps, twice in a year he falls into these fits.' Jack Young slept not, but was ready to go out as the clock struck to the hour of appointment, and then going to open the door he was disappointed, knocks, bounces, stamps, calls, 'Tapster! Chamberlain! Ostler!' swears and curses dreadfully; nobody would come to him. Sir John and W. Davenant were expectant all this time and ready to die with laughter. I know not how, he happened to get open the door, and was coming down stairs. The ostler, a huge lusty fellow, fell upon him, and held him, and cried, 'Good sir, take God in your mind, you shall not go out to destroy yourself.' J. Young struggled and strived, insomuch that at last he was quite spent and dispirited, and fain to go to bed to rest himself. In the morning the landlady of the house came to see how he did, and brought him a medicine. 'Oh sir', said she, 'you had a heavy fit last night, pray, sir, be pleased to take some of this to comfort your heart.' Jack Young thought the woman had been mad, and being exceedingly vexed, flirted the porringer of caudle in her face. The next day his comrades told him all the plot, how they cross-bit him. That night they went to Bronham House, Sir Edward Baynton's (then a noble seat, since burnt in the Civil Wars), where they were nobly entertained several days. From thence, they went to West Kington, to Parson Davenant's, Sir William's eldest brother, where they stayed a week—mirth, wit, and good cheer flowing. From thence to Bath, six or seven miles.

Memorandum: Parson Robert Davenant has told me that that tract about Socinianism was written on the table in the parlour of the parsonage at West Kington.

¶ My Lady Southcot, whose husband hanged himself, was Sir John Suckling's sister, to whom he writes a consolatory letter, viz the first. She afterwards married Dr Corbet, DD, of Merton College, Oxford. At her house in Bishopsgate Street, London, is an original of her brother, Sir John, by Sir Anthony van Dyck, all at length, leaning against a rock, with a play-book, contemplating. It is a piece of great value. There is also another rare picture, viz of that pretty creature Mrs Jane Shore, an original.

When his *Aglaura* was acted he brought all the clothes himself, which were very rich; no tinsel, all the lace pure gold and silver, which cost him . . . I have now forgotten. He had some scenes to it, which in those days were only used at masques.

Memorandum: Mr Snowdon tells me, that after Sir John's unlucky encounter, or quarrel, with Sir John Digby, wherein he was baffled: 'twas strange to see the envy and ill-nature of people to trample, and scoff at, and deject one in disgrace; inhumane as well as un-christian.

The Lady Moray (query) had made an entertainment for several persons of quality at Ashley (in Surrey, near Chertsey), whereat Mr Snowdon then was. There was the Countess of Middlesex, whom Sir John had highly courted, and had spent on her, and in treating her, some thousand of pounds. At this entertainment she could not forbear, but was so severe and ungrateful as to upbraid Sir John of his late received baffle; and some other ladies had their flirts. The Lady Moray (who invited them) seeing Sir John out of countenance, for whose worth she always had a respect: 'Well,' said she, 'I am a merry wench, and will never forsake an old friend in disgrace, so come sit down by me, Sir John' (said she), and seated him on her right hand, and encouraged him. This raised Sir John's dejected spirits that he threw his repartees about the table with so much sparklingness and gentleness of wit, to the admiration of them all.

¶ Sir John Suckling—from Mr William Beeston—invented the game of cribbage. He sent his cards to all gaming places in the country, which were marked with private marks of his; he got £20,000 by this way. Sir Francis Cornwallis made *Aglaura*, except the end.

Thomas Sutton
1532–1611

Sutton's career began as a soldier, but his money came largely from his shrewd exploiting of the Durham coalfields, on which he took leases and then shipped the coal to London. He settled in London in 1580, and was said to be the richest commoner in England. The first notice of his intention to found a hospital or school dates from 1594. The actual foundation at Charterhouse was made in 1610, but Sutton, who had intended to be first master himself, was too ill to do so, and died the following year.

Thomas Sutton, founder of the Charterhouse Hospital—from old Thomas Tyndale, esquire, (the father)—was first a garrison soldier at Berwick. He was a lusty healthy handsome fellow, and there was a very rich brewer who brewed to the navy, etc, who was ancient and he had married a young buxom wife who enjoyed the embraces of this more able performer as to that point. The old brewer doted on his desirable wife and dies and left her all his estate which was great. Sutton married this widow and was a man of good understanding, and improved it well, but the particular ways by which he did it I have now forgotten it; but he was much upon mortgages, and fed several with hopes of being his heir. 'Twas from him that B. Jonson took his hint of the fox, and by Signor Volpone is meant Sutton.

The later end of his days he lived in Fleet Street at a woollen-draper's shop opposite to Fetter Lane, where he had so many great chests full of money that his chamber was ready to groan under it; and Mr Tyndale, who knew him and I think had money of him on mortgage during his law-suit (see the Lord Stafford's case in Coke's *Reports*), was afraid the room would fall. He lived to establish his hospital, and was governor there himself.

The Earl of Dorset (I think, Richard) mightily courted him and gave presents to him, hoping to have been his heir; and so did several other great persons.

John Taylor
1580–1653

Taylor was a 'drop-out' from the grammar-school at Gloucester, who could not master Latin and became apprentice to a London waterman. He was press-ganged and served at the Siege of Cadiz in 1596 and on the Azores voyage in 1597. His descriptive tours in verse still make excellent reading, and he made his living from verse after about 1630 until 1645. He kept a pub in Long Acre from 1645 until his death.

John Taylor, the water-poet: his works are a fair folio, printed, London, 1630.

He was born in the city of Gloucester:— . . . Taylor, a painter, was his brother, who told me thus 23 years since (he lives yet at Oxford): and his picture hung in the Schools (Bodleian) gallery.

He came to London and bound (apprenticed) himself to a water-man, in which capacity he wrote his poems. I have heard Josias Howe, MA, say that he will choose out six verses (ask which) there as good as you will find in any other.

He was very facetious and diverting company; and for stories and lively telling them, few could outdo him.

In 1643, at the Act time, I saw him at Oxford. I guess he was then near 50. I remember he was of middle stature, had a good quick look, a black velvet, a plush-gippe [tunic] and silver shoulder-belt; was much made of by the scholars, and was often with Josias Howe at Trinity College.

He had heretofore in the long peace several vagaries [voyages] e.g. he came from London to Salisbury in his sculler. He went so to Calais. He went to Scotland (I think round Great Britain) hugging the shore in his sculler.

Ever since the beginning of the civil wars he lived in Turnstile Alley in Long Acre, about the middle on the east side over against the Goat (as it is now), where he sold ale. His conversation was incomparable for three or four mornings' draughts. But afterwards you were entertained with old stories warmed over. His sign was his own head, and very like him, which about 22 years since was removed to the alehouse, the corner house opposite to Clarendon House. Under his picture are these verses; on one side:—

> There's many a head stands for a signe.
> Then, gentle reader, why not mine?

On the other:—

> Though I deserve not, I desire
> The laurel wreath, the poet's hire.

This picture is now almost worn out.

Silas Taylor
1624–78

Antiquary and musician. Pepys, who was MP for Harwich, knew him, and said he was 'a good scholar and a great antiquary', but had mixed feelings about his musical talent, saying on one occasion that he 'composed bravely', but elsewhere that an anthem of his was dull and old-fashioned: 'the Duke of York, when he came out, told me that he was a better store-keeper than anthem-maker, and that was bad enough too.'

He was a captain in the Parliament army, under Col. Massey. He was a sequestrator, in Herefordshire, and had, in those times, great power, which power he used civilly and obligingly, that he was beloved by all the King's party.

He was very musical, and has composed many things, and I have heard anthems of his sung before his majesty, in his chapel, and the king told him he liked them. He had a very fine chamber organ in those unmusical days. There was a great friendship between Matthew Locke, since organist of the Queen's chapel, and him.*

His father left him a pretty good estate, but he bought church lands (during the Commonwealth) and had half of the bishop's palace at Hereford, where he laid out much money in building and altering. Col. John Burch had the other half.

* Mr Lock married Mr Garnon's daughter in Herefordshire.

The times turning, he was fain to disgorge all he had got, and was ruined, but Sir Paul Neile got for him the keeper of the King's stores at Harwich, worth about £100 per annum.

He was a great lover of antiquities, and ransacked the MSS. of the church of Hereford (there were a great many that lay uncouth and unkiss [in disorder]).

He also ransacked the library of the church of Worcester, and evidences, where he had the original grant of King Edgar (ruler of the sea), whence the Kings of England derive the right to the sovereignty of the sea. 'Tis printed in Mr Selden's *Mare Clausum*. I have seen it many times and it is as legible as but lately written (Roman character). He offered it to the King for £120, but his majesty would not give so much. Since his death, I acquainted the Secretary of State that he died in debt, and his creditors seized on his goods and papers. He told me that it did of right belong to Worcester Church. I told one of their prebends, and they cared not for such things. I believe it has wrapped herrings by this time.

He had several MSS by him of great antiquity: one thin quarto of the Philosopher's Stone, in hieroglyphics, with some few Latin verses underneath; the most curiously drawn that ever I saw. His majesty offered him £100 for it, and he would not accept it. Tell Dr Crowder (one of the Worcester prebendaries) of the deed of King Edgar.

Memorandum: Captain Taylor searched the records in the Tower etc., and retrieved some privileges that the borough [of Harwich] had lost, for which the borough ought ever to have his remembrance in esteem: and though he died above £100 in their debt, yet the town lost not by him, for the reason aforesaid.

The history or collection of this ancient borough he pawned a little before his death to Mr Baker, the printseller by the old Exchange, for £4 15s. I acquainted Sir Philip Parker, whom the borough usually chooses for their burgess [M.P.], to buy it for his borough. He would not lay out so much money, which would do them more service than all his roast beef, wine and ale at an election.

The finger of God.* All that family came to unfortunate ends. His eldest son, wife and children, were all burnt in their beds, near Lothbury; another son (a dragoon), a churchyard wall fell on him and killed him.

He surveyed very ingeniously and carefully the antiquities of Herefordshire, that is about three-quarters of the county, before the restoration of his majesty. He then left the country, and went to his friend, Sir Edward Harley, then governor of Dunkirk, who gave him some command. These papers are in the hands of Sir Edward Harley at Brampton Brian castle.

* Because Taylor had bought church lands. *Ed.*

300

John Tombes
?1603–76

One of the first Baptist clergy.

Mr John Tombes, BD was born at Bewdley in Worcestershire.

In (1618) he was admitted at Magdalen Hall in Oxford. He read to pupils and was tutor there to John Wilkins, afterwards bishop of Chester. He was a great master of the Greek tongue, and the Hebrew he understood well. He always carried a little Greek Testament about with him; he had it almost by heart. He was an admirable disputant, 'tis requisite for one to be a good grammarian, as well as logician. I have forgotten if he was pupil to the learned Mr Pemble; but his favourite he was. He was soon taken notice of for his curious searching, piercing wit: he preached somewhere eastwards from Oxford, and had a company following him; and 'twas predicted he would do a great deal of mischief to the Church of England, that the greatest wits have done the most mischief to the church, introducing new opinions, etc. He was vicar of a market-town in Herefordshire, where he was very well beloved by his parish, and Sir . . . Croftes, eldest brother to the now bishop of Hereford, built a house in Leominster, to live there, to hear him preach. In 1645, 1646, he was master of the Temple at London, i.e. minister. In 1647 he was supplanted there by parson Johnson. Then he went into his own country, to Bewdley (a market-town), at which time Mr Baxter (his antagonist) preached at Kidderminster, the next market town, two miles distant. They preached against one another's doctrines, and printed against each other. Mr Tombes was the chorus-leader of the Anabaptists: both had great audience; they went several miles on foot to each doctor. Once (I think oftener) they disputed face to face, and the followers were like two armies, about 1500 of a party; and truly, at last they fell by the ears, hurt was done, and the civil magistrate had much ado to quiet them. About 1664 he came to the Act at Oxford (query), and did there at evening service set up a challenge to maintain against all comers the Anabaptistical doctrine; but not a man would grapple with him. Now though *prima facie* this might seem very bold to challenge a whole University, 'twas not so very strange neither, for he came thoroughly prepared, after thirty years' study and thoughts, and most of them surprised.

Dr Sanderson, lord bishop of Lincoln, and he, had a great esteem for each other, so also had Dr Barlow (now bishop there). Putting aside his Anabaptistical positions, he was conformable enough to the Church of England. About 1658 or 9, he married the widow of Wolston Abbott, of

Salisbury, and was wont to hear the Common Prayer there, and received the sacraments; and sometimes waited on bishop Ward, who respected him for his learning. He was thought to be as great a divine as most we had after bishop Sanderson died. I remember he never, or seldom, was wont to say 'our saviour Christ', but 'My lord Christ'. He seemed to be a very pious and zealous Christian. I have heard him say (though he was much opposite to the Romish religion) that truly, for his part, should he see a poor zealous friar going to preach, he should pay him respect. He was but a little man, neat limbed, a little quick searching eye, sad, grey.

Ezreel Tong
1621–80

Notorious for his involvement with Titus Oates in the fabrication of the 'Popish Plot' of 1680.

Ezreel Tong, DD, was born at Tickell, in Yorkshire, between Bawtry and Doncaster.

He was buried on 23 December (1680) in the vault of the churchyard of St Mary Stayning, London; where, before the conflagration (1666), was a church, of which he was the parson; but I have heard his brother, captain Tong (of the King's Guards) say 'twas worth but £18 per annum, for he had gathered it.

Mr Jones (who preached his funeral sermon: printed) says that he has left two tomes in folio of alchemy. His excellency lay *there*.

About 1658 or 1659, the then power (Cromwell) made an academy of the Bishop's Palace at Durham, for the benefit of the north. Dr Tong was the governor, or one of the professors. Ned Bagshawe was proposed to have been another. This Dr had an excellent school there, and followed precisely the Jesuits' method of teaching; and boys did profit wonderfully, as needs they must, by that method.

He afterwards taught at Islington, at Sir Thomas Fisher's house, where was a long gallery, and he had several printed heads of Caesars, etc.; verbs under such a head, governed a dative case; under another, an ablative. The boys had it as ready as could be. I have been there.

¶ Ezreel Tong, DD, invented, among other things, the way of teaching children to write a good hand in twenty days' time, by writing over, with black ink, copies printed from copper-plate in red ink:— viz, the children (that is, aged about 8 or 9) were to do it four hours in the day: i.e. two hours or two half-hours in the morning at a time (as the boy's

302

temper could endure it, without tiring him); and then to play as long; and then to it again, to keep up the idea in the child fresh. Since his death, Mr Robert Moray (projector of the Penny Post) has engraved several plates printed off in red letters, by which means boys learn (to admiration) as aforesaid—which N.B.

His funeral sermon was preached in the church of St Michael, Wood Street; the church of St Mary Staining being burned, and never to be re-edified, but both parishes put together.

Thomas Triplett
1603–70

He went to school to Dr Gill, as appears by his ballad, which will last longer than any sermon, that ever he made.

After his sequestration* he kept a school at Dublin (when the king was beheaded); afterwards at Hayes, Surrey, twelve miles from London. 'Twas here our common friend George Ent went to school to him, who told me that he had forgotten the smart of his old master, Gill; he was very severe.

I'll tell you a story of our old friend (i.e. George Ent). His master Triplett was a great lover of honey, and one of his schoolfellow's mother having sent a pot of honey to the doctor, G. Ent put his schoolfellow to beg a little of his master, and he had got a small loaf and so they would have a feast. The doctor was in his study; and the boy takes the confidence to approach, with his, 'Quaeso, preceptor, da mihi mel (Please, teacher, give me some honey).' G. Ent was sneaking behind. Said the disturbed doctor, 'You audacious rascal,' and gave him a good cuff on the ear, 'how dare you be thus impudent? Sirrah, who put you on?' The boy answered (whiningly) 'G. Ent.' The enraged doctor flies out of his study (he was a very strong man), gives poor George a kick in the breech, and made him fly down a flight of seven or eight stairs to the landing place, where his head first came to. He was stunned, but 'twas well his neck was not broken. 'Twas a most cruel and inhumane act to use a poor child so. It so happened that a day or two before G.E. had lost a tooth. He writes a letter to his father (now Sir George Ent) and encloses the tooth in it; relates the story and that he lost the tooth by that means. The next the grave and learned Dr. Ent comes to Hayes (the fame of whose learning and testimony did give great credit and reputation to this

* Dismissed from his living by the Puritans. *Ed.*

303

school); expostulates with the doctor about his son. To be short, took him away, and placed him with Mr William Radford at Richmond (an honest sequestered fellow of Trinity College, Oxford, and an excellent schoolmaster, having been bred at Thames under Dr Birt, and afterwards sent to Winchester). This accident well-nigh did break Dr Triplett's school. But shortly after this time, happened the restoration of his majesty, and then he was also restored to his former preferments.

William Twisse
?1578–1646

Twisse, after his conversion as a boy, described by Aubrey, became a famous Puritan writer, though he was never as aggressive as some of his fellow-thinkers. He supported a moderate policy in the early years of the Civil War, and was speaker of the assembly of divines at Westminster in 1643. He died in 1646 and was buried in state in Westminster Abbey.

William Twisse, DD, of Newbury:—his son Dr Twisse, minister of the new church near Tothill Street, Westminster, told me that he had heard his father say that when he was a schoolboy at Winchester College that he was a rake-hell, and that one of his schoolfellows and comrades (as wild as himself) died there; and that his father going in the night to the house of office, the phantom or ghost of his dead schoolfellow appeared to him and told him, 'I am damned'; and that this was the beginning of his conversion.

Memorandum: the Dr had a melancholic and hypochondriac temperament.

Thomas Tyndale
1588–1672

These notes were collected by Aubrey when he was working on his comedy The Country Revel; *Tyndale, who was a Wiltshire neighbour of Aubrey's, was the model for an old gentleman, 'an old courtier of the Queen's'.*

In those days (Queen Elizabeth) the great men prospered, and when a senator went to the Parliament House a-foot, or a-horseback with his footcloth, he had at his heels half a dozen or ten tall fellows with blue coats and badges and long basket-hilt swords. Now forsooth only a lackey and a little spit-pig [short sword].

T.T.—The advantage that king Charles I had: gentlemen then kept good horses, and many horses for a man-at-arms, and men that could ride them; hunting horses. Now we are come all to our coaches forsooth! (Sir Philip Sidney). Now young men are so far from managing good horses, they know not how to ride a hunting hag nor handle their weapons. So God help the king if, etc.

In Sir Philip Sidney's time 'twas as much disgrace for a cavalier to be seen in London riding in a coach in the street as now 'twould be to be seen in a petticoat and waistcoat. They rode in the streets then with their rich footclothes (horse-clothes), and servants waiting on them blue coats and badge, six, eight, twelve or more.

T.T., an old gentleman that remembers Queen Elizabeth's reign and court, one of true gravity and prudence, not one that depends upon the grave cut of his beard to be thought so. He has seen much in his time both at home and abroad; and with much choler inveighs against things now:—'Alas! O'God's will! Nowadays everyone, forsooth! must have coaches, forsooth! In those days gentlemen kept horses for a man at arms, besides their hackney and hunting horses. This made the gentry robust and hardy and fit for service; were able to be their own guides in case of a rout or so, when occasion should so require.* Our gentry forsooth in these days are so effeminated that they know not how to ride on horseback.—Then when the gentry met, it was not at a poor blind sordid alehouse, to drink up a barrel of drink and lie drunk there two or three days together; fall together by the ears. They met then in the fields, well-appointed, with their hounds or their hawks; kept up good hospitality; and kept a good retinue, that would venture that blood and spirit that filled their veins which their masters' tables nourished; kept their tenants in due respect of them. We had no depopulation in those days.'

'You see in me the ruins of time. The day is almost at end with me, and truly I am glad of it: I desire not to live in this corrupt age. I foresaw and foretold the late changes, and now easily foresee what will follow after. Alas! O'God's will! It was not so in Queen Elizabeth's time: then youth had respect to old age.'

'Revels—then the elders and better sort of the parish sat and beheld the pastimes of the young men, as wrestling, shooting at butts, bowling and dancing. All this is now lost; and pride, whoring, wantonnesses, and drunkennesses. Then the charity of the feast, St Peter's box, maintained the old impotent poor.'

* See Macchiavelli's *Prince*.

James Ussher
1581–1656

Archbishop of Armagh 1625–56; 'learned to a miracle' according to Selden, his published works run to 27 books.

Memorandum: Ussher, Lord Primate (of Ireland) was at Llantrithed* for several months, and directed himself much to talk with the poor people to understand Welsh, for that 'it had,' he said, 'a great affinity with the Irish.' He said the Old Testament was translated by the Universities, but the New Testament was translated by the bishops; but the Old is much better done.†

Henry Vaughan
1622–95

Vaughan's poems, published between 1647 and 1650 under the title Silex Scintillans *were only recognised as masterpieces in the nineteenth century.*

[From a letter to Anthony Wood] There are two Vaughans, twins, both very ingenious and writers. One wrote a poem called *Olor Iscanus (The Swan of Usk)* (Henry Vaughan, the first-born), and another book of divine meditations. His brother wrote several treatises, whose names I have now forgotten, but names himself *Eugenius Philalethes*.

They were born at Llansanfraid in Brecknockshire by the river Usk (Isca). Their grandmother was an Aubrey: their father, a coxcomb and no honester than he should be—he cosened me of 50s once.

'Eugenius Philalethes' was of Jesus College. Whither Henry was I have forgotten; but he was a clerk sometime to Judge Sir Marmaduke Lloyd.

Henry Vaughan, 'Silurist':—you know Silures [the ancient British tribe] contained Brecknockshire, Herefordshire, etc.

¶ (A letter from Henry Vaughan to Aubrey) 'My brother and I were born at Nauton, in Brecknockshire, in the parish of St Bridget's, in the year 1621.

I stayed not at Oxford to take my degree, but was sent to London,

---

* Home of Sir John Aubrey, Aubrey's cousin. *Ed.*
† i.e. in the 'King James' Bible of 1611, the Authorised Version. *Ed.*

being then designed by my father for the study of the law, which the sudden eruption of our late civil wars wholly frustrated.

My brother continued there for ten to twelve years, and I think he could be no less than Master of Arts. He died upon an employment for his majesty, within five or six miles of Oxford, in the year that the last great plague visited London (1665). He was buried by Sir Robert Moray, his great friend (and then secretary of state for the kingdom of Scotland); to whom he gave his books and MSS.

My profession also is physic, which I have practised now for many years with good success (I thank God) and a repute big enough for a person of greater parts than myself.'

Edward de Vere
Seventeenth Earl of Oxford, 1550–1604

Courtier. He was renowned for his extravagance and eccentric temper, and was as often out of favour as in favour with Elizabeth. He is chiefly remembered for his small number of lyric poems. His travels in fact lasted under two years, from 1575–6.

Mr Thomas Henshawe, FRS, tells me that Nicholas Hill was secretary to Edward de Vere, the great Earl of Oxford, who spent £40,000 pounds per annum in seven years' travel. He lived at Florence in more grandeur than the Duke of Tuscany.

This Earl of Oxford, making of his low obeisance to Queen Elizabeth, happened to fart, at which he was so abashed that he went to travel for seven years. On his return the queen welcomed him home and said, 'My lord, I had forgotten the fart.'

A poor man asked of Mr Hill one time to give him 6d. (or 1s, or such an alms). Said Mr Hill, 'What do you say, if I give you ten pounds?' 'Oh,' said he, 'ten pounds would make me a man.' And he did put it down in the account. 'Item, £10 for making a man—' which his lordship allowed and was well pleased at it.

Francis Villiers
1629–48

Posthumous son of Charles I's favourite, George Villiers, duke of Buckingham.

In this parish (Kingston) in the lane between Kingston and Sathbyton Common, was slain the beautiful Francis Villiers, at an elm in the hedge in the east side of the lane, where, his horse being killed under him, he turned his back to the elm and fought most valiantly with half a dozen. This elm was cut down, 1680. The enemy coming on the other side of the hedge, pushed off his helmet and killed him, July 7 1648, about six or seven o'clock in the afternoon. On this elm was cut an ill-shaped V for Villiers, in memory of him.

William de Vischer
1595–1668

From Mr Bovey:— William de Visscher, merchant in London, born at Emden in East Friesland in Germany, a Hanse town—now under the Dutch. At two years old, was brought into England by his father, an eminent merchant; lived 55 years in one house at St Mary Hill, and died in the 74th year of his age. He lived there till the fire of London; he died about three years after—he did not enjoy himself afterwards.

In the last great dearth of corn in England,* when there was a great complaint and cry of the poor, he bade them be of good comfort for they should not starve, for he would give them his labour and the use of his estate for that year. He being a man of vast credit, gave his factors order that what corn they could buy at such and such rates beyond sea, to hire fly-boats and send them over to the port of London, of which he bought in one year two thousand five hundred sail. The corn that cost him 12s per bushel beyond sea, he sold here for 14s.; and some of the places from whence he had corn (they selling it by reason of the greatness of the price) afterwards wanted it themselves and were fain to be supplied from hence,

* About thirty years since. I believe it was 1647, or 1648—enquire.

i.e. in some places, for which they were fain to pay half value more than the first cost, or else must have starved.

Many disasters happened to many of the ships that were bound for London (some that never arrived were destroyed by foul weather; some wind-bound so long till their corn fired for want of airing, and was fain to be thrown overboard) that in the whole matter, after all the adventures run, he did not gain five and twenty hundred pounds. The fly-boats carried 800 tons, and some more.

He left two sons and a daughter behind him, named Isabella (who was married to Mr James Bovey, by which he has one son and one daughter).

He was a very eminent merchant, as most was of his time; and was valued by common reputation (when he married his daughter) to be worth £120,000.

He stayed in London during the whole time of the plague, and had not all that time one sick in his family. He was a temperate man, and had his house very cleanly kept.

Sir Isaac Wake
?1580–1632

Diplomat and writer.

Sir Isaac Wake: he had a fine seat at Hampstead in Middlesex, which looks over London and Surrey, where he made those delicate walks of pines and firs, also corme-trees [sorb-apple trees] etc.—The Lord Chief Baron Wild had it afterwards. His study was mighty pleasant.

The lord de la Ware, who married the daughter and heir of the chief baron, sold this seat about 1683 to a citizen of London, who pulled it down to build a house (1686).

The chief baron told his cousin Edmund Wyld Esq that Sir Isaac Wake was the first that planted pines and firs in England. E. W. might have had the study for £8 per annum.

Edmund Waller
1606–87

Poet and royalist politician. He was a moderate, member of parliament (from the early age of sixteen) but favoured the king, and was involved in a plot to seize London for the latter, as a result of which he narrowly escaped execution. He was imprisoned from 1643 to 1644, and in exile in France until 1652. He returned to parliament in 1661, and attended regularly until his death in 1687. His poems were widely admired as 'occasional' pieces, and he was a favourite with Charles II.

Edmund Waller, esquire, son and heir of Robert Waller by Anne Hamden. He was cousin-german to Oliver Cromwell, Protector, whose mother was his mother's sister.

He was born at Beaconsfield, in Bucks, in the fair brick house, the farthest on the left hand, as you go to Wycombe.

He had grammar learning from the information of Mr Dobson, minister of High Wycombe, who taught a private school there, and was (he told me) a good schoolmaster, and had been bred at Eton College school. I have heard Mr Thomas Bigge, of Wycombe, say (who was his schoolfellow, and of the same form), that he little thought then he would have been so rare a poet; he was wont to make his exercise for him.

His paternal estate, and by his first wife, was £3000 per annum. His second wife was Mary Bracey; a woman beautiful and very prudent, by whom he has several children (I think 10 or 12).

About 23, or between that and thirty, he grew (upon I know not what occasion) mad; but 'twas (I think) not long ere he was cured:—this from Mr Thomas Bigg.

The human heart does not receive its disturbance from the heavens (Ovid)

Memorandum:—he was proud: to such, a check often gives distemper.

He was passionately in love with Dorothea, the eldest daughter of the Earl of Leicester, whom he has eternised in his poems: and the earl loved him, and would have been contented that he should have had one of the younger daughters; perhaps *this* might be the check.*

Waller (I think, Walter) was his tutor at King's College, Cambridge, who was a very learned man, and was afterwards vicar of Broad Chalke, Wilts.

He has been a member in parliament, for Beaconsfield, in King

---

* Mr Thomas Bigg of Wycombe has been dead these twenty years, who could have told me the cause. I believe that I am right. You see how things become antiquated.

James's time, and has been of all the parliaments since the restoration of Charles II (1680, aged 74 or more).

One of the first refiners of our English language and poetry. When he was a brisk young spark, and first studied poetry, 'Methought', said he, 'I never saw a good set of English verses; they want smoothness; then I began to essay.' I have several times heard him say, that he cannot versify when he will; but when the fit comes upon him, he does it easily, i.e. in plain terms, when his Mercury and Venus are well aspected.

He told me he was not acquainted with Ben Jonson (who died about 1638), but familiarly with Lucius, Lord Falkland; Sydney Godolphin, Mr Hobbes, etc.

He was very much admired at Court before the late Civil Wars. 1643, he being then a member of the House of Commons, he was committed prisoner to the Tower, for the plot, with Tomkins (his cousin-german) and Chaloner, for firing the City of London, and delivering the parliament, etc, to the king's party. He had much ado then to save his life, and in order to it, sold his estate in Bedfordshire, about £1300 per annum, to Dr Wright, MD, for £10,000 (much under value) which was procured in 24 hours' time, or else he had been hanged (ask E. Wyld, esquire). With which money he bribed the whole House, which was the first time a House of Commons was ever bribed. His excellent rhetorical speech to the House (see his speech to save his life), as also his panegyric to Oliver, Lord Protector, he would not suffer to be inserted in the edition of his poems since the restoration of King Charles II.

After he had obtained his pardon of the parliament, he went to France, where he stayed some years, and was there very kindly received, and esteemed.

When King Charles II returned, he received Mr Waller very kindly, and no man's conversation is more esteemed at Court now than his. The Duchess of York (daughter to the Duke of Modena) very much delights in his company, and has laid her commands on him to write, which he has dedicated to her highness.

His intellectuals are very good yet (1680), and makes verses; but he grows feeble. He wrote verses of the Bermudas fifty years since, upon the information of one that had been there; walking in his fine woods, the poetic spirit came upon him.

He is of somewhat above a middle stature, thin body, not at all robust; fine thin skin, his face somewhat of an olive complexion; his hair frizzed, of a brownish colour; full eye, popping out and working; oval faced, his forehead high and full of wrinkles. His head but small, brain very hot, and apt to be choleric—*the more learned, the more ready to anger*—Cicero. He is somewhat magisterial, and has a great mastership of the English language. He is of admirable and graceful elocution, and exceeding ready.

He has spent most of his time in London, especially in winter; but oftentimes in the summer he enjoys his muse at Beaconsfield, which is incomparable air, and where are delicious walks in the woods. Now I speak of woods, I remember he told us there, that he cut down and grubbed up a beech wood of his, at Beaconsfield in Bucks, and without sowing, but naturally, there grew up a wood all of birch.

He was admitted a fellow of the Royal Society.

He has but a weak tender body, but was always very temperate. Someone (ask Samuel Butler) made him damnable drunk at Somerset House, where, at the water-stairs, he fell down, and had a cruel fall. 'Twas pity to use such a sweet swan so inhumanely.

He has a great memory, and remembers a history, etc, etc, best when read to him; he used to make his daughters read to him. Yet, notwithstanding his great wit and mastership in rhetoric, etc, he will oftentimes be guilty of misspelling in English. He writes a lamentably bad hand, as bad as the scratching of a hen.

I have heard him say that he so much admired Mr Thomas Hobbes' book *De Cive*, when it came forth, that he was very desirous to have it done into English, and Mr Hobbes was most willing it should be done by Mr Waller's hand, for that he was so great a master of our English language. Mr Waller freely promised him to do it, but first he would desire Mr Hobbes to make an essay; he (T.H.) did the first book, and did it so extremely well, that Mr Waller would not meddle with it, for that nobody else could do it so well. Had he thought he could have better performed it, he would have himself been the translator.

Memorandum: his speech against ship-money which is in his book of poems: his panegyric to Oliver the Protector I have: and also to King Charles II.

He says that he was bred under several ill, dull, ignorant schoolmasters, till he went to Mr Dobson, at Wycombe, who was a good schoolmaster, and had been an Eton scholar.

Memorandum: later end of August 1680, he wrote verses, called *Divine Love*, at the instance and request of the lady Viscountess Ranelagh.

He missed the provostship of Eton College, 1681.

¶ He lies buried in the church-yard (south east of the church), where has grandfather and father were buried. This burying place is railed about like a pound, and about that bigness. There is a walnut tree planted, that is, perhaps, 50 years old: (the walnut tree is their crest). There are nine graves or cippi, no gravestone or inscription.

From Capt. Edmund Hamden, his cousin-german, 1690: Edmund Waller, esquire, was born in the parish of Amersham, in Buckinghamshire, at a place called Winchmore Hill, which was sold by his father, and which he had a very great desire to have bought again, not long before his death, but the owner would not sell it: part of the house has been new-built, but the room wherein he was born is yet standing: said he, to his cousin Hamden, 'A stag, when he is hunted, and near spent, always returns home'. He died at 83, and his wit was as florid then as any time in his life. He derived his poetic wit from the Hamdens; several of them have been poets.

Whereas Rutt, that kept the inn (the Crown, I think) at Beaconsfield, told me, many years since, that he had been mad; Captain Hamden affirms it is false; but his brother [? cousin] was a fool, as to discourse or business, but was very learned. And whereas Dr Birch told me that he had a prodigious memory; his sons affirm that he had no good memory, and was never good to learn a thing by heart, but some things that pleased him he did strongly retain.

Captain Hamden told me that the soldiers came to Beaconsfield to search for money: his mother told them if they would go along with her, she would show them where she had buried £5000, and had them to the house of office.

¶ Mr Christopher Wase repeating to him the bitter satirical verses made on Sir Carre Scroop, viz—

> Thy brother murdered, and thy sister whored,
> Thy mother too—and yet thy pen's thy sword;

Mr Waller replied *sur le champ* 'that men write ill things well and good things ill; that satirical writing was downhill, most easy and natural; that at Billingsgate one might hear great heights of such wit; that the cursed earth naturally produces briars and thorns and weeds, but roses and fine flowers require cultivation.' All his writings are free from offence.

His poems are reprinted now (1682) by his own orders and his pictures (young and old) before it, and underneath

> *But his songs are a greater image*
> Ovid, *Tristia*, I vii. 11

He made some verses of his own dying but a fortnight, or little more, before his decease.

¶ Edmund Waller esquire (poet) said that poetry was abused when 'twas turned to any other subject than the praise of the Creator. The principal service of God is neglected, and petitions and thanksgivings for ourselves, used in its stead.

John Wallis
1616–1703

Mathematician and founder-member of the Royal Society.

John Wallis, DD, was born at Ashford, in the county of Kent, in (1616). His father was minister there. He went to school there.

He was admitted at Emmanuel College in Cambridge; 'where he was a pupil, then a fellow of King's College at the same place' (Mr Oughtred's preface to his *Key to Mathematics*). He was a good student, but fell not to the study of mathematics until he was above twenty.

A remarkable passage of his life was, that he was a witness of W. Laud's (archbishop of Canterbury) trial, for his introducing popish innovations into the University of Cambridge. The first remarkable passage of his life was his deciphering the letters of King Charles I taken at Naseby, which book is called the *King's Cabinet Opened*. He was scholar to Mr W. Oughtred.

In 1649 after the visitation by the parliament,* he came to Oxford, and was made Savillian Professor of Geometry. He was a Fellow of the Royal Society. Great contests between him and Mr Thomas Hobbes, of Malmesbury: sure their Mercuries are in square or opposition. In 1657, he got himself to be chosen by unjust means to be keeper of the archives of the University of Oxford, at which time Dr Zouch had the majority of voices, but because Dr Zouch was a malignant (as Dr Wallis openly protested, and that he had talked against Oliver), he was put aside. Now for the Savillian Professor to hold another place besides, is so downright against Sir Henry Savile's statutes, that nothing can be imagined more; and if he does, he is downright perjured. Yet the Dr is allowed to keep the other place still.

In (1654) he took his degree of Doctor, at the Act, at Oxford, and went out grand compounder† (which costs £200), only that he might take precedence over Dr Seth Ward, who was about a year his senior. In 1661 Dr Ward was made dean of Exeter, and the next year bishop of the same place; and so Dr Wallis's £200 was merely cast away. The bishop protested he was troubled for the loss of his brother Wallis's two hundred pounds.

He has written several treatises, and well; and to give him his due

---

* Commissioners were sent to remove royalist or high church sympathisers from the Universities. *Ed.*

† Candidates for degrees with estates of over £300 p.a. paid this extra fee, and took precedence over ordinary degree-holders. *Ed.*

praise, has exceedingly well deserved of the commonwealth of learning, perhaps no mathematical writer so much.

'Tis certain that he is a person of real worth, and may stand with much glory upon his own basis, needing not (to) be beholding to any man for fame, of which he is so extremely greedy, that he steals flowers from others to adorn his own cap,—e.g. he lies at watch, at Sir Christopher Wren's discourse, Mr Robert Hooke's, Dr William Holder, etc; puts down their notions in his note book, and then prints it, without owning the authors. This frequently, of which they complain.

But though he does an injury to the inventors, he does good to learning, in publishing such curious notions, which the author (especially Sir Christopher Wren) might never have the leisure to publish himself.

When Mr Oughtred's *Key to Mathematics* was printed at Oxford (third edition, with additions) Mr W.O. in his preface, gives worthy characters of several young mathematicians that he informed, and, amongst others, of John Wallis, who would be so kind to Mr Oughtred, as to take the pains to correct the press (proofs), which the old gentleman does with respect there acknowledge, after he has enumerated his titles and preferments: 'an ingenious, pious, industrious man, deeply versed in all recondite literature, most perspicacious in things mathematical, and in the unravelling and explanation of ciphered writings most intricately concealed (which is an argument of very subtle ingenuity) miraculously successful.' This last, on the cyphers, was added by Dr Wallis himself; which when, the book being printed, the old gentleman saw, he was much vexed at it; and said, he had thought he had given him sufficient praise, with which he might have rested content.

He has a good temporal estate in Kent. He has only two daughters, handsome young gentlewomen; one married to Mr Blencowe of Middleton Cheyney.

He lives at a well-built house, near New College in Oxford; is a Justice of the Peace there, and has been 167–, 1679, 1680.

Seth Ward
1617–89

A close friend and informant of Aubrey. Ward was both a popular clergy-man and one of the leading mathematicians of his day. He was a founder member of the Royal Society, and was Savile Professor of Astronomy from 1649 to 1660, after which he became first Dean, then Bishop of Exeter. He was translated to Salisbury in 1667. Bishop Burnet said of him that 'he was a profound statesman, but a very indifferent clergyman'; his popularity was due to his hospitality and generosity rather than his spiritual merits.

Seth Ward, Lord Bishop of Salisbury, was born at Buntingford, a small market-town in Hertfordshire, in 1618, December (when the great blazing star appeared). His father was an attorney there, and of a very honest repute.

At sixteen years old he went to Sidney Sussex College in Cambridge; he was servitor* to Dr Ward (Master of the College, and Professor of Divinity), who, being much taken with his ingenuity and industry, as also with his suavity of nature, quickly made him scholar of the house, and after Fellow. Though he was of his name, he was not at all akin to him (which most men imagined because of the great kindness to him); but the consimility of their dispositions was a greater tie of friendship than that of blood, which signifies but little, as to that point.

His father taught him common arithmetic, and his genius lay much to the mathematics, which being natural to him, he quickly and easily attained. Sir Charles Scarborough, MD (then an ingenious student, and fellow—query—of Caius College in Cambridge), was his great acquaintance; both students in mathematics; which the better to perfect, they went to Mr William Oughtred, at Albury in Surrey, to be instructed by him in his *Key to Mathematics*, which was then a book of riddles. Mr Oughtred treated them with exceeding humanity, being pleased at his heart when an ingenious young man came to him that would ply his algebra hard. When they returned to Cambridge, they read the *Key to Mathematics* to their pupils, which was the first time that book was ever read in a university. Mr Laurence Rooke, a good mathematician and algebrist, (and I think had also been Mr Oughtred's disciple) was his great acquaintance. Mr Rooke (I remember) did read (and that admirably well) on the sixth chapter of the *Key to Mathematics* in Gresham College.

In 1644, at the breaking out of the Civil Wars, he was a prisoner, together with Dr Ward, Dr Collins, Sir Thomas Hatton, etc, for the king's cause, in St John's College in Cambridge, and was put out of his fellowship at Sidney College. Being got out of prison, he was very civilly and kindly received by his friend and neighbour, Ralph Freeman, of Apsten, esquire, a virtuous and hospitable gentleman, where he continued some time.

In (1648) the visitation of the parliament was at Oxford, and turned out a great many professors and fellows. The astronomy reader (Greaves) being sure to be ejected, Seth Ward, MA (living then with my Lord Wenman, in Oxfordshire, and Greaves being unwilling to be

---

* Aubrey notes elsewhere 'expunge servitor, so that it sounds better.' *Ed.*

turned out of his place, but desired to resign it rather to some worthy person, whereupon Dr Charles Scarborough and William Holder, DD, recommended to Greaves, their common friend, Mr Seth Ward) was invited to succeed him, and came from Mr Freeman's [correctly, Lord Wenman's] to Oxford, had the astronomy professor's place, and lived at Wadham College, where he conversed with the warden, Dr John Wilkins.

In 1656 he had from Brownrigg, Bishop of Exeter, the grant of the chantor's place of Exeter (which then signified nothing).

In 1659, William Hawes, then president of Trinity College in Oxford, having broken in his lungs a vein (which was not curable), Mr Ward being very well acquainted and beloved in that college; by the consent of all the fellows, William Hawes resigned up his presidentship to him and died some few days after. In 1660, upon the restoration of King Charles II, Dr Hannibal Potter (the president sequestered by the parliamentary visitors) re-enjoyed the presidentship again.

¶ Dr Seth Ward, now Bishop of Salisbury, when he was president of Trinity College, Oxford, did draw his geometrical schemes with black, red, yellow, green and blue ink to avoid the perplexity of A, B, C, etc.

I should have said that, in 1654, he took his degree of doctor in divinity, at the Act, at Oxford, at the same time with Dr John Wallis.

He then enjoyed his chantor's place at Exeter, and, I think, was certainly minister of St Lawrence Jewry church in London.

In 1661, the Dean of Exeter died, and then it was his right to step in next to the deanery.

In 1663, the Bishop of Exeter died: Dr Ward, the dean, was in Devonshire at that time at (I think 'twas Tavistock), at a visitation, where were a great number of the gentry of the county. Dean Ward was very well known to the gentry, and his learning, prudence and courtesy had won them all to be his friends. The news of the death of the bishop being brought to them, who were all very merry and rejoicing with good entertainment, with great alacrity the gentlemen all cried, with one voice, 'We will have Mr Dean to be our bishop'. This was at that critical time when the House of Commons were the king's darlings. The dean told them that for his part he had no interest or acquaintance at Court; but intimated to them how much the king esteemed the members of parliament (and a great many parliament men were then there), and that his majesty would deny them nothing. 'If 'tis so, gentlemen,' (said Mr Dean), 'that you will needs have me to be your bishop, if some of you make your address to his majesty, 'twill be done.' With that, they drank the other glass, a health to the king, and another to their wished-for bishop; had their horses at once made ready, put foot in stirrup, and away they rode merrily to London; went to the king, and he immediately granted them their request. This is the first time that ever a bishop was made by the House of Commons. Now, though envy cannot deny, that this worthy person was very well worthy any preferment that could be conferred on him, yet the old bishops (e.g. Humphrey Henchman, Bishop of London; John Cosins, Bishop of Durham; etc) were exceedingly disgruntled at it, to see a brisk young bishop that could see through all their formal gravity, but only forty years old, not come in the right door but leap over the pale. It went to their very hearts. Well, Bishop of Exeter he was, to the great joy of all the diocese. Being bishop he had then free access to his majesty, who is a lover of ingenuity and a discerner of ingenious men, and quickly took a liking to him. In 1667, Alexander Hyde, the Bishop of Salisbury, died, and then he was made Bishop of Salisbury.

He is (without all manner of flattery) so prudent, learned, and good a man, that he honours his preferment as much as the preferment does him; and is such a one that cannot be advanced too high. My Lord (Lucius) Falkland was wont to say that he never knew anyone that a pair of lawn sleeves* had not altered from himself, but only Bishop Juxon; had he known this excellent prelate, he would have said he had known one more. As he is the pattern of humility and courtesy, so he knows when to be severe and austere; and he is not one to be trampled or worked upon. He is a bachelor, and of a most magnificent and munificent mind. He has been a benefactor to the Royal Society, (of which he was one of the first members and institutors†). He also gave a noble pendulum clock to the Royal Society to perpetuate the memory of his dear and learned friend, Laurence Rooke.

Enquire, was the bishop ever professor at Gresham College?

He gave, in 167–, a sum of money towards the making of the river at Salisbury navigable to Christ Church. In 1679 he gave to Sidney Sussex College £1000.

He has perused all the records of the church of Salisbury, which, with long lying, had been stuck together; read them all over, and taken abridgments of them, which had not been done by any of his predecessors I believe for some hundreds of years.

He had an admirable habit of body (athletic, which was a fault), a handsome man, pleasant and sanguine; he did not desire to have his wisdom judged by the gravity of his beard, but his prudence and ratiocination. This, methinks, is strange to consider in him, that being a great student (and that of mathematics and difficult knotty points, which does use to make men unfit for business), he is so clear and ready, as no solicitor is more adroit for looking after affairs.

* i.e. a bishop's vestments. *Ed.*
† The beginning of scientific experiments was at Oxford, 1649, by Dr Wilkins, Seth Ward, Ralph Bathurst, etc.

¶ I searched all Seth, Bishop of Salisbury's, papers that were at his house at Knightsbridge where he died: of which I will give and bring to you an account when I come to Oxford about the latter end of this month. I have taken care with his nephew and heir to look over his papers in his study at Salisbury. He tells me the custom is, when the Bishop of Salisbury dies that 'the dean and chapter lock up his study and put a seal on it'. It was not opened lately, but when it is he will give me an account for you.

Seth Ward, Lord Bishop of Salisbury, studied the common law, and I find this paper, which is his own handwriting, amongst his scattered papers which I rescued from being used by the cook since his death, which was destinated with other good papers and letters to be put under pies.

He wrote a reply to Bullialdus, which might be about the bigness of his *Astronomia Geometrica*, which he lent to somebody (forgot), and is lost. In the bishop's study are several letters between Bullialdus and him, and between Hevelius and him.

The bishop's will not observed: the people there* say so: cousin Freeman said so.

¶ Whereas I put down in my memorandums, from Ward's own mouth, viz that he said, occasionally, that 'he was born when the great comet appeared'; that, I am sure, was in 1618. But his nephew, Seth Ward, treasurer of the church of Salisbury and his executor, told me that the last summer he searched in the register at Buntingford where he was born and finds thus:

'Seth Ward christened April 5, 1617.'

¶ The black malice of the dean of Salisbury—he printed sarcastical pamphlets against him—was the cause of his disturbed spirit, whereby at length he quite lost his memory.

For about a month before he died he took very little sustenance, but lived on the stock and died a skeleton.

He deceased at his house at Knightsbridge near London, on Sunday morning, January the sixth, 1689.

The gazettes and newsletters were severally mistaken as to the day of his death.—This from Mr Seth Ward, BD.

* At Buntingford, where he had endowed a hospital. *Ed.*

Walter Warner

?–1640

Mathematician.

From Dr John Pell:— Mr Walter Warner:— his youngest brother was High Sheriff of Leicestershire, about 1642. He and his brother died both bachelors. Dr Pell has seen him that was sheriff; but was well acquainted with Walter. The estate came to a middle brother, a lame man.

Walter had but one hand (born so), he thinks a right hand; his mother was frightened, which caused this deformity, so that instead of a left hand, he had only a stump with five warts upon it, instead of a hand and fingers. He wore a cuff on it like a pocket. The Doctor never saw his stump, but Mr Warner's man has told him so.

This Walter Warner was both mathematician and philosopher, and 'twas he that put out Thomas Hariot's Algebra, though he mentions it not.

Mr Warner did tell Dr Pell, that when Dr Harvey came out with his circulation of the blood, he did wonder whence Dr Harvey had it; but coming one day to the earl of Leicester, he found Dr Harvey in the hall, talking very familiarly with Mr Prothero (in Welsh, ap Roderic), to whom Mr Warner had discoursed concerning the exercitation of his *On the Circulation of the Blood*, and made no question but Dr Harvey had his *hint* from Prothero. Memorandum: Dr Pell says that Mr Warner reasoned demonstratively by beats of the pulses that there must be a circulation of the blood.

When Mr Hariot died, he made Sir Thomas Alesbury and Mr Prothero his executors, by which means his papers came to be divided into two hands. Those which fell to Sir Thomas Alesbury, fell, after his death, to his son-in-law, Edward, earl of Clarendon, Lord Chancellor, and in his son's hands (this present, 1680, earl of Clarendon) 'tis believed are these that are yet left; none of them were printed, save that *The Practice of the art of analysis*, which was printed by Mr Warner upon this occasion, viz Sir Thomas Alesbury obtained of Algernon, earl of Northumberland (son to that earl, prisoner in the Tower), a continuation of the annuity, during Warner's life, upon condition that he should, out of Mr Hariot's papers, draw out some piece fit to be published, which he did, under the title aforesaid: but did not set his name to it, and accordingly Warner had his money as long as he lived. The other part of Mr Hariot's papers, which were in Mr Prothero's keeping, came to the hands of the lord John Vaughan, eldest son to the earl of Carbery, lately governor of Jamaica.

Mr Warner's younger brother was a good husband and an industrious man, and would say that he had so much money, he could improve it to very great advantage; whereupon his eldest brother (Walter) did let him sell his land, by which means he did so improve his estate by grazing, etc that he became High Sheriff as aforesaid (ask of the attorneys when). Dr Pell has seen him, and spoke with him.

Mr Walter Warner made an inverted logarithmical table, i.e. whereas Brigg's table fills his margin with numbers increasing by units, and over against them sets their logarithms, which because of incommensurability must needs be either too great or deficient, Mr Warner (like a dictionary of the Latin before the English) fills the margin with logarithms increasing by units and sets to every one of them so many continual proportions between 1 and 10, and they for the same reason must also have the last figure incomplete. These, after the death of Mr Warner, came to the hands of Mr Herbert Thorndike, prebendary of Westminster, and by him left the hands of Dr Richard Busby, schoolmaster and prebendary of Westminster, which, before Mr John Pell grew acquainted with Mr Warner, were ten thousand, and at Mr Warner's request were by Mr Pell's hands, or direction, made a hundred thousand. The difference of the hands will show the workman's in the originals which Dr Busby has.

Mr Tovey, of Leicestershire, was his kinsman: he could tell when and where he died:—from Seth, bishop of Salisbury.

The bishop thinks he was of Cambridge University, but is not certain. Dr Pell believes that he was of no university.

Ask Dr Pell, what is the use of those inverted logarithms? For W. Warner would not do such a thing in vain. Mr Tovey was fellow of Christ's College in Cambridge; was beneficed in Leicestershire; and married a niece of Mr Warner's; and from Mr Tovey they (the tables) came to Mr Thorndike.

George Webb
1581–1642

Protestant bishop of Limerick 1634–42.

Dr Webb, one of king Charles I's chaplains, afterwards bishop of Limerick in Ireland, has some sermons, or divinity, in print; and a translation of Terence, English and Latin.

He died and was buried in Limerick, about two or three days before the town was taken by the Irish, who dug up the body again—it was about 1642.

He was of Corpus Christi College, Oxford: born at Brumhum in Wiltshire.

I confess I do not like that super-zeal in the Canon Law, not to let alone there the bodies of heretics. It is too inhumane.—This, as to the bishop's body being dug up again, which I fear was so: for his nephew who was his archdeacon, was with him when he died and the town taken, and I remember, being then a freshman. I heard him tell the story. He was minister in the next parish to Mr Hine.

James Whitney
1593–166?

[From letters to Anthony Wood] Parson Whitney was a great remember-berer of names of Oxford men, being an old fellow there; and were he alive now he would be 81.

¶ My old cousin, parson Whitney, told me that in the Visitation of Oxford in Edward VI's time they burned mathematical books for conjuring books, and if the Greek professor had not accidentally come along, the Greek testament had been thrown in the fire for a conjuring book, too.

John Whitson
1557–1629

Whitson was Aubrey's step-grandfather. He was a merchant-venturer, twice Mayor of Bristol and four times MP for the city, and was a great founder of local charities.

John Whitson, alderman of the city of Bristol: John Whitson was born at Cover in the Forest of Dean in the county of Gloucester. He went to school at Bristol, where he made a good proficiency in the Latin tongue. He was bound apprentice to Alderman Vawe, a Spanish merchant of this city. He was a handsome young fellow; and his old master the alderman being dead, his mistress one day called him into the wine cellar and bade him broach the best butt in the cellar for her; and truly he broached his mistress, who after married him. This story will last perhaps as long as Bristol is a city. He had a good natural wit, and gained by the Spanish trade a fair estate. His second wife was the daughter of Hine, alderman of London, a very beautiful dame, as by her picture, at length, in the dining room, does appear. By her he had a daughter, his only child, who was counted the flower of Bristol, who was married to Sir Thomas Trenchard of Dorsetshire, who dying (together with her child), the alderman gave him compensation for the manor of Dunderhill (his daughter's dowry) and had it again.

His third wife was . . . by whom he had no issue. His fourth and last wife was Rachel, daughter of Richard Danvers of Tockenham, Wilts, esquire, widow of John Aubrey of Burleton in the county of Hereford, esquire, (my father Richard Aubrey being then eleven years of age). He had no issue by her. The alderman made Richard a good falconer, but did cut down his woods and never made him any satisfaction; but let his good works be set in balance against it.

He lived nobly; kept a plentiful table; and was the most popular magistrate in the city, always chosen a member of parliament. He kept a noble house, and did entertain and treat the peers and great persons that came to the city. He kept his hawks. I remember five that had been bred up under him, but not one of them came to good, they lived so luxuriously, just as the servants of Sir John Robinson, governor of the Tower. He had a very good healthy constitution, and was an early riser; wrote all his letters and despatched his business betime in the morning.

He was charitable in his life in breeding up of poor scholars; particularly I remember William Haywood, DD, whom he preferred to St John's College in Oxford, where are certain Bristol fellowships. His father was a cooper in Ballance Street, his mother, whom I well remember, was a midwife in the city.

He had a fair house in St Nicholas Street, where is the stateliest dining room in the city.

He had been thrice mayor of this city, as is to be seen in the table of mayors in St Nicholas Street in golden letters.

His beloved and only daughter dying, and so being childless, Richard Wheeler, his nephew, who was bred a merchant under him with others, was his heir; but he proving a sot and capricious coxcomb, he settled all his estate upon the city of Bristol for pious uses, and was, I do believe, the greatest benefactor that ever the city had. He gave the manor of Durdery and the manor of Burnet and divers houses in Bristol.

He died about the seventy-sixth year of his age by a fall from his horse, his head pitching on a nail that stood on its head by a smith's shop. He was buried very honourably; besides all his relations in mourning, he had as many poor old men (or men and women) as he was

323

years old, in mourning gowns and hoods, the mayor and aldermen in mourning; all the trained band (he was their colonel) attended the funeral and their pikes had black ribbons and drums were covered with black cloth.

John Wilkins
1614–72

Like his friend Seth Ward, Wilkins was a scientist first and a theologian second. He was one of the most active founding members of the Royal Society (of which he was the first secretary), and wrote on astronomy, mathematics, and ciphers, as well as compiling an English dictionary. He was warden of Wadham College, Oxford from 1652–9, but showed himself very tolerant, and many royalists sent their sons there. He was a friend of Evelyn and Pepys, both of whom often refer to him.

John Wilkins, Lord Bishop of Chester: his father was a goldsmith in Oxford. Mr Francis Potter knew him very well, and was wont to say that he was a very ingenious man and had a very mechanical head. He was much for the trying of experiments, and his head ran much upon the *perpetual motion*. He married a daughter of Mr John Dod (who wrote on the commandments), at whose house, in Northamptonshire, she lay in with her son John, of whom we are now to speak. He had a brother (Timothy), esquire-beadle in Oxford, and a uterine brother, Walter Pope, MD.

He had his grammar learning in Oxford (I think from Mr Sylvester). He was admitted of Magdalen Hall in Oxford. His tutor there was the learned Mr John Tombs (chorus-leader of the Anabaptists). He read to pupils here (among others, Walter Charlton, MD, was his pupil).

He has said oftentimes that the first rise, or hint of his rising, was from going accidentally a-coursing of a hare: where an ingenious gentleman of good quality falling into discourse with him, and finding him to have a very good wit, told him that he would never get any considerable preferment by continuing in the university; and that his best way was to betake himself to some lord's or great person's house, that had good benefices to confer. Said Mr J. Wilkins, 'I am not known in the world: I know not to whom to address myself upon such a design.' The gentleman replied, 'I will recommend you myself,' and did so, to (as I think) lord Viscount Say and Sele (query), where he stayed with very good liking till the late Civil Wars, and then he was chaplain to his highness the Prince Elector Palatine of the Rhine, with whom he went (after the peace concluded in Germany was made*), and was well preferred there by his highness.

After the visitation at Oxford by the parliament, he got to be Warden of Wadham College. He married the widow of Dr French, canon of Christchurch, Oxford, and sister to Oliver, [then] Lord Protector, who made him in 1659 Master of Trinity College in Cambridge, (in which place he revived learning by strict examinations at elections of fellows: he was much honoured there, and heartily loved by all:) where he continued till 1660, (the restoration of his majesty). Then he was minister of Saint Laurence Jewry church in London; and was Dean of Ripon in Yorkshire. His friend, Seth Ward, DD, being made Bishop of Exeter, he was made there dean, and in 1668 by the favour of George, Duke of Buckingham, was made Bishop of Chester; and was extremely well beloved in his diocese. In 1672 he died of the stone. He left a legacy of £400 (query) to the Royal Society, and had he been able would have given more. He was no greatly read man; but one of much and deep thinking, and of a working head; and a prudent man as well as ingenious. He was one of Seth, Lord Bishop of Salisbury's most intimate friends. He was a lusty, strong grown, well set, broad shouldered person, cheerful, and hospitable.

He was the principal reviver of experimental philosophy (in the spirit of Lord Bacon) at Oxford, where he had weekly an experimental philosophical [scientific] club, which began 1649, and was the cradle of the Royal Society. When he came to London, they met at the Bull-head tavern in Cheapside (e.g. 1658, 1659, and after), till it grew too big for a club, and so they came to Gresham College parlour.

Bishop J. Wilkins: the little picture in octavo is most like him.

John Wilmot
Second Earl of Rochester, 1647–80

Rochester's poems are among the most bawdy in the English language, and reflect the most dissolute side of Charles II's Court. Although never a favourite of Charles's, and often banished from the Court, he was one of Charles's boon-companions, particularly in his love-affairs. His escapades were numerous, the most notable being the abduction of the heiress Elizabeth Malet, for which he was sent to the Tower. However, he later married her.

---

* At the end of the Thirty Years' War (1648). *Ed.*

He died in 1680, with Bishop Burnet in attendance, who had spent the previous month with him, and whose account of his deathbed repentance was later printed.

John, Earl of Rochester:—he went to school at Burford; was of Wadham College, Oxford: I suppose, had been in France.

About 18, he stole his lady, Elizabeth Malet, a daughter and heir; a great fortune, for which I remember I saw him a prisoner in the Tower about 1662. His youthly spirit and opulent fortune did sometimes make him do extravagant actions, but in the country he was generally civil enough. He was wont to say that when he came to Brentford the devil entered into him and never left him till he came into the country again to Alderbury or Woodstock.

He was ranger of Woodstock park and lived often at the lodge at the west end, a very delightful place and noble prospect westwards. Here his lordship had several lascivious pictures drawn.

His lordship read all manner of books. Mr Andrew Marvell, who was a good judge of wit, was wont to say that he was the best English satirist and had the right vein. 'Twas pity death took him off so soon.

In his last sickness he was exceedingly penitent and wrote a letter of his repentance to Dr Burnet, which is printed. He sent for all his servants, even the pigherd boy, to come and hear his palinode. He died at Woodstock Park, 26 July 1680.

His immature death puts me in mind of these verses of Propertius:

> *In the flower of your youth, and in your first new spring,*
> *Like a rose plucked by a young girl's hand, you lie.*

Thomas Willis
1622–75

A Wiltshire doctor and neighbour of Aubrey's.

Thomas Willis, MD—from himself—born at Great Bedwyn in the county of Wilts., January 27th, 1621. His father was steward to Sir Walter Smyth there, and had been sometime a scholar at St John's College in Oxford.

¶ 1647 and 1648 (enquire, if not longer) frequented Abingdon market (in the hope of finding patients), and Dr Lydall and he had a horse between them: this was before he was a doctor. He grew more and more into good practice. He studied chemistry in Peckwater Inn chamber. He was in those days very mathematical, and I have heard him say his genius lay more to mathematics than chemistry. His father was steward to Sir John (I think) Smyth, and had a little estate at Hinksey, where my lady Smyth (widow) died.

He went to school to Mr Sylvester in Oxford, over the meadows, where he aired his muse, and made good exercise:— from William Hawes, his schoolfellow. In about 1657 (enquire there) riding towards Brackley to a patient, his way led him through Astrop, where he observed the stones in the little rill (stream) were discoloured and of a kind of saffron colour; thought he, this may be an indication of iron; he gets galls, and puts some of the powder into the water, and immediately it turned blackish; then said he, 'I'll not send my patients now so far as Tunbridge', and so he in a short time brought these waters into vogue, and has enriched a poor obscure village. He was middle statured: dark red hair (like a red pig): stammered much.

He was first servitor to Dr Iles, one of the canons of Christ Church, whose wife was a knowing woman in physic and surgery, and did many cures. Tom Willis then wore a blue livery-cloak, and studied at the lower end of the hall, by the hall-door; was pretty handy, and his mistress would oftentimes have him to assist her in the making of medicines. This did him no hurt, and allured him on.

George Withers
1588–1677

A minor poet and writer of Puritan pamphlets.

Mr George Withers was born at Bentworth, near Alton, in Hampshire, on the eleventh of June, 1588.

He married Elizabeth, eldest daughter of H. Emerson, of South Lambeth, in the county of Surrey, esqre, whose ancestors he entombed in the choir of St Saviour's, Southwark, near the monument of bishop Andrews, with a statue of white marble. She was a great wit, and would write in verse too.

He was of Oxford. He would make verses as fast as he could write them. And though he was an easy rhymer, and no good poet, he was a good prophet. He had a strange sagacity and foresight into mundane affairs.

He was an early observer of *Quicquid agunt homines* (whatever men do); his wit was satirical. I think the first thing he wrote was 'Abuses whipped and stripped', for which he was committed prisoner to, I believe, Newgate. I believe 'twas in king James's time. He was a captain in the Parliamentary army, and the Parliament gave him for his service Mr John Denham's estate at Egham, in Surrey. The motto of his colours was, *For king, law and company*.

After the restoration of his majesty he was imprisoned in the Tower about three quarters of a year. He died the second of May, 1667. He was pupil to bishop Warner of Rochester.

Thomas Wolsey
?1475–1530

The most lively account of Wolsey's meteoric career from humble priest to cardinal and lord chancellor is that written by his usher, George Cavendish. Aubrey's notes consist of a piece of gossip from one of his relations based on Cavendish's account, and details of his buildings, in which Aubrey, as an antiquary, was much interested—indeed, the bulk of Aubrey's manuscripts are antiquarian, and considerably less entertaining than his biographical collections.

Thomas Wolsey, cardinal, was a butcher's son, of Ipswich, in Suffolk.

He was a fellow of Magdalen College in Oxford, where he was tutor to a young gentleman of Limington, near Ilchester, in Somerset, in whose gift the presentation of that church is, worth the better part of £200 per annum, which he gave to his tutor, Wolsey. He had committed hereabout some debauchery (I think, drunk: no doubt he was of a high rough spirit) and spoke derogatorily of Sir Amias Paulet (a Justice of Peace in the neighbourhood) who put him into the stocks,* which when he came to be cardinal, he did not forget; he laid a fine upon Sir Amias to build the gate of the Middle Temple; the arms of Paulet, with the quarterings, are in glass there to this day (1680). The cardinal's arms, were, as the story says, on the outside in stone, but time has long since

---

* From my cousin Lyte, of Lytes Cary, about a mile from Limington, thirty years since. The tradition was very fresh; I have forgotten his pupil's name.

defaced that, only you may still discern the place; it was carved in a very mouldering stone. Remains of him show that he was a great master of the Latin tongue. Dr John Pell tells me, that he finds in a preface to a grammar of Haynes, schoolmaster, of Christ Church, London, that 'twas he that made the accedence before W. Lilly's Grammar.

His rise was, his quick and prudent despatch of a message to Paris for Henry VIII.

He had a most magnificent spirit. Concerning his grandeur, see Stowe's *Chronicle* etc. He was a great builder, as appears by Whitehall, Hampton Court.—Esher, in Surrey, a noble house, built of the best burnt brick (perhaps) that ever I saw; stately gate-house and hall.† This stately house (a fit palace for a prince) was bought about 1666 by a vintner, of London, who is since broke, and the house is sold, and pulled down to the ground, about 1678. I have the sketch of the house among my Surrey papers. He had a very stately cellar, for his wines, about Fish Street, called Cardinal Wolsey's cellar.—He built the stately tower at Magdalen College in Oxford, and that stately palace at Winchester (where he was bishop), called Wolsey House; I remember it pretty well, standing, 1647. Now, I think, it is mostly pulled down. His noble foundation of his College of Christ Church in Oxford, where the stately hall was the only part completed by him. There were designed (as yet may appear by the building) most magnificent cloisters (the brave design whereof Dr John Pell has deteriorated with his new device) to an extraordinary spacious quadrangle, to the entrance whereof was carrying up a tower (a gate-house) of extraordinary rich and noble Gothic building. See J. Owen's *Epigrammata*:

> The house may be unfinished, and like a ruin,
> And a broad space lies open in your honour.

When the present Great-Duke of Tuscany was at Oxford, he was more taken with that, than all the rest of the buildings he saw there, and took a second view of it.

It should not be forgotten what a noble wall there was for the chapel, which did run from the college along the street as far as the Blue Boar inn: which was about seven foot or more high, and adorned with a very rich Gothic plinth-top. It was pulled down by Dr John Fell (the dean) about 1670, to use the stones about the college.

Memorandum:—about the buildings of the college are frequent the pillars, and axes, and cardinal's caps.

Concerning this great cardinal's fall, see the histories of that time. Returning to London from York, he died at Leicester, where he lies buried (to the shame of Christ Church men) still without any monument.

† See my Surrey notes if William Wainfleet did not build it; both their scutcheons are there.

329

'And though, from his own store, Wolsey might have
A palace or a college for his grave
Yet here he lies interred, as if that all
Of him to be remembered were his fall.
Nothing but earth to earth, nor pompous weight
Upon him but a pebble or a quayte [quoit or weight]
If thou art thus neglected, what shall we
Hope after death that are but shreds of thee?'

See Dr Corbet's Poems: his *Iter Boreale* [*Northern Journey*].

See his life by Thomas Fuller, BD, in his *Holy State*, where is a picture of his which resembles those in glass in Christ Church. He was a lusty man, thick neck, not much unlike Martin Luther. I believe he had Taurus ascending with Pleiades, which makes the native to be of a rough disposition.

He was bachelor of arts so young, that he was called the boy-bachelor. From Dr John Pell (out of the aforesaid preface).

¶ One of Oseney bells at Winslow in Bucks, which is the great bell there, but was the third at Oseney; but they have not long since cut it something less, one Derby deceiving them £60 of their metal. Cardinal Wolsey, being Abbot of St Alban's (to which Winslow did belong), at the pulling down of Oseney Abbey, gave this bell to Winslow. Mr Stephens was born at Winslow.

Sir Christopher Wren
1631–1723

Aubrey evidently intended to write a full biography of Sir Christopher Wren, particularly as he would have been included in the projected Lives of the Mathematicians, *and he would have met him frequently at the Royal Society; but only these details survive, saying nothing of his achievements in science or architecture, and nothing of the rebuilding of London which Aubrey witnessed.*

Sir Christopher Wren, surveyor of his majesty's buildings, born at East Knoyle (in the parsonage house) in the county of Wilts near Shaftesbury, Thursday, 20 October 1631, 8 p.m.—the bell rang VIII as his mother fell in labour with him (from himself).

He was knighted at Whitehall on Friday, 14 November 1673, at

5 a.m. (from Mr Robert Hooke, the next day).

¶ In 1669, Dr Christopher Wren was invited by the Bishop of Salisbury [Seth Ward] where he made a particular survey of the cathedral church. He was at least a week about it, and a curious discourse it was: it was not above two sheets. Upon my writing the *Natural History of Wilts*, I had occasion to insert it there, and they told me that it was lent to somebody—they could not tell to whom. But in February last Mr Cole thinks it not unlikely that Mr Nash (the surveyor of the fabric) of Salisbury may have that paper. I desired him to enquire but have not yet received any answer.*

¶ Dr Christopher Wren has put a trick on us, as it seems; for he has made himself a year younger than indeed he is, though he need not be ashamed of his age, he has made such admirable use of his time. I met the other day accidentally with the parson of Knoyle, who justifies the register, and not only so but proves it by his neighbour that was his nurse and her son that suckled with him—evidence notorious.

¶ It ought never to be forgotten, what our ingenious countryman Sir Christopher Wren proposed to the silk stocking weavers of London, viz a way to weave seven pair or nine pair of stockings at once (it must be an odd number). He demanded four hundred pounds for his invention; but the weavers refused it, because they were poor, and besides, they said it would spoil their trade; perhaps they did not consider the proverb that light gains, with quick returns, make heavy purses. Sir Christopher was so noble, seeing they would not adventure so much money, that he breaks the model of the engine all to pieces, before their faces.

Edward Wright
?1558–1615

Mathematician and expert on navigation; he redrew existing charts on the basis discovered by Mercator (and still in use today), which Mercator had not been able to develop to the full.

Amongst Mr Laurence Rooke's papers (left with Seth, lord bishop of Salisbury) I found: *A hypothesis of fixed stars* by Edward Wright, three sheets, of his own handwriting. I deposited it in the Royal Society, but Mr R. Hooke says that it is printed in a book by itself.

It appears by his preface that his worth was attended by a great deal of envy.

* Aubrey later found the paper, as a copy in among his manuscripts. *Ed.*

He was in the voyage of the right honourable the earl of Cumberland in the year 1589.

John Collins says that he happened upon the logarithms and did not know it, as may be seen in his *Errors:* and Mr Robert Norwood says to the reader in his Trigonometry 'neither is Mr Edward Wright to be forgotten though his endeavours were soonest prevented,' speaking of the logarithms.

¶ Mr Edmund Wright was of Caius College, in Cambridge. He was one of the best mathematicians of his time; and the *then* new way of sailing, which yet goes by the name of 'sailing by Mr Mercator's chart', was purely his invention, as plainly Mr Mercator brought this invention in fashion beyond seas.

He did read mathematics to Prince Henry, and caused to be made, for his Highness' more easy understanding of astronomy, a sphere of wood, about three-quarters of a yard diameter, which lay neglected and out of order in the Tower in London, and Sir Jonas Moore begged it of his present majesty who showed it to me.

Sir Edward Zouche

Knight-marshal of the household in 1618.

Mr Philips also tells me that Robson was the first that brought into England the art of making Venice glasses, but Sir Edward Zouche (a courtier and drolling favourite of King James) appressed this poor man Robson, and forced it from him, by these four verses to King James, which made his majesty laugh so that he was ready to beshit his breeches. The verses are these:

> Severn, Humber, Trent and Thames,
> And thy great Ocean and her streames
> Must putt down Robson and his fires
> Or downe goes Zouche and his desires.

The king granted this ingenious manufacture to Zouche, being tickled as aforesaid with these rhymes; and so poor Robson was oppressed and utterly undone, and came to that low degree of poverty that Mr Philips told me that he swept the yard at Whitehall and that he himself saw him do it.

Sir Robert Mansell had the glassworks afterwards, and employed Mr James Howell (author of *The Vocal Forest*) at Venice as a factor to furnish him with materials for his work.